Futures Markets: Their Economic Role

Anne E. Peck, editor

Philip McBride Johnson
Anne E. Peck
William L. Silber
Jerome L. Stein
Hans R. Stoll
Robert E. Whaley

American Enterprise Institute for Public Policy Research
Washington, D.C.

ISBN 0-8447-3592-2
AEI Studies 434
1 3 5 7 9 10 8 6 4 2

Contents

Foreword

Futures markets, like most markets, usually perform their essential economic roles without drawing much public attention. Major new developments in patterns of usage or in prices, however, sometimes attract the attention of the public and of government.

Pronounced changes in futures market trading have occurred in recent years. In the more volatile and inflationary economic climate of the 1970s, the number of contracts traded in agricultural commodities and metals increased dramatically. Even more significant, however, was the introduction of trading in financial futures contracts and their phenomenal growth. Between 1970 and 1984 futures trading volume increased more than tenfold, and by the end of 1984 financial futures accounted for 50 percent of total trading.

The framework for futures market regulation also changed, first with the establishment of the Commodity Futures Trading Commission in 1974 and subsequently with the Futures Trading Acts of 1978 and 1982. The four-year sunset provision in the 1974 legislation, together with the government studies mandated by the 1982 act, ensured that several important issues would be on the national policy agenda for the next round of reauthorization.

The remarkable expansion of trading in financial futures has meant a more important and pervasive economy-wide role for futures markets. This expanded role has raised new issues, issues that deserve careful analysis by recognized scholars in the private sector as well as by experts in government. The studies in this volume are intended to contribute to a better understanding of the economic role of futures markets and of the role of regulation.

In view of the new opportunities and the new issues that emerged with the growth of futures market activities and AEI's continuing program of research and dissemination of regulatory policy analyses, we received encouragement from several sources in industry and government to examine futures markets and their regulation. Futures markets, the context in which they developed, and relations with other markets were analyzed in an earlier AEI publication, *A Treatise on Markets: Spot, Futures, and Options*, by Joseph M. Burns.

The studies in this volume were commissioned as part of AEI's project on the Economics and Regulation of Futures Markets. A companion volume, *Futures Markets: Regulatory Issues*, also edited by Anne E. Peck who served as project director, contains a series of related studies. In a third publication, *Futures Markets: An Overview*, Philip McBride Johnson draws upon these studies and upon his experience as a legal practitioner and former chairman of the Commodity Futures Trading Commission to highlight the major implications for policy.

These studies make a new and timely contribution to public policy formation for these important markets. The entire project of which these published studies are a part was carried out under the auspices of AEI's Center for the Study of Government Regulation directed by Marvin H. Kosters. The government regulation studies program at AEI has addressed a wide range of issues concerning the appropriate role of government. These studies by leading scholars and practitioners in their fields analyze the contribution that efficiently functioning futures markets make to achieving broader economic goals. They are particularly relevant in the current climate of public concern about meeting capital investment needs and about appropriate regulatory structures for financial services markets as a whole.

WILLIAM J. BAROODY, JR.
President
American Enterprise Institute

Preface

These studies analyze the economic role of futures markets by carefully examining markets for different commodities and futures instruments. The implications for policy making are discussed in the context of how futures markets function and how they contribute to economic performance. The primary purpose of the studies is to foster better understanding of these markets and their economic contribution to promote more informed policy choices.

The project on the economics and regulation of futures markets under which these studies were carried out was stimulated by the remarkable expansion of financial futures trading and the issues that arose in connection with developments such as the emergence of trading in stock index futures and options on futures contracts. Questions were raised in the congressional hearings prior to reauthorization of the Commodity Futures Trading Commission (CFTC) about the growing array of derivative financial instruments trading on futures markets, the economic purposes they served, the extent to which they might be competitive with the well-established securities markets, and possible conflicts or overlap in the regulatory systems administered by different federal government agencies. Congressional concerns about these issues led to requests in the Futures Trading Act of 1982 for studies to be conducted by federal government agencies.

The Federal Reserve Board (FRB), the Securities and Exchange Commission (SEC), and the CFTC were directed by the act to carry out a joint study of the economic purposes of futures and options markets, to consider their effects on capital formation, and to evaluate the adequacy of their regulation. The CFTC was directed to examine the implications of trading on futures markets by individuals possessing material, nonpublic information. Finally, the FRB announced a study to review federal margin regulation policy. These three federal studies were underway by the spring of 1983.

In view of this concentration of government interest, the American Enterprise Institute proposed a project that would contribute additional research by leading scholars outside government to develop better understanding in the Washington policy community of futures markets, their economic roles, and the related regulatory issues. The studies developed in this research effort are published in two volumes: *Futures Markets: Their Economic Role* and *Futures Markets: Regulatory Issues*. A list of the studies in the companion volume and a list of all the contributors are at the end of the book.

The studies in this volume assess the economic contributions of futures and options markets by drawing upon evidence from the long history of futures trading in largely agricultural products, by examining the contributions of newer financial futures and options markets, and by analyzing the specific implications for capital formation. The studies analyze how trading in financial futures instruments facilitates the management of interest rate and security price risks, thereby reducing the cost of capital and increasing incentives to invest in productive assets. Finally, the studies discuss the key underlying economic differences between futures and securities markets that provide the basis for the different forms and methods of regulation that have been developed in these markets and their adequacy for ensuring efficient market performance.

Studies in the companion volume, *Futures Markets: Regulatory Issues*, address specific market practices, institutions, or participants and associated regulatory concerns. Each of the current congressional concerns has a historical context. Some concerns, like the regulation of futures margins, have long histories of congressional debate. Other issues, like trading floor practices, arise in a new context because different, but related, financial instruments are traded under separate regulatory systems. The specific issue areas discussed in the companion volume are trading floor practices, the role of margins, characteristics of small public traders, cash settlements, and livestock futures.

Taken together, the AEI studies show that careful analysis of various futures markets and instruments and of industry practices is essential for understanding their economic contribution. They indicate that a complex set of institutional arrangements, commercial and financial practices, privately administered rules, and federal regulations have evolved in a highly competitive market environment to foster efficient and financially secure trading. As a final theme, the studies demonstrate that sound public policy toward futures markets must be based on a thorough understanding of how they function, and not on superficial similarities to features of other related markets.

In developing this project on the Economics and Regulation of Futures Markets, the Center for the Study of Government Regulation at AEI consulted extensively with government officials, private sector representatives, and academic scholars. These consultations contributed importantly to shaping the character of the studies and reviewing them as they were written. To provide for systematic advice and review while the project was underway, an advisory committee, chaired by Gary L. Seevers, was established. Representatives from the major futures exchanges, users of futures services, and research professionals from universities and business firms made up the committee. A research advisory committee was also established to identify issues for examination and to survey research under way by leading scholars. This committee was cochaired by Philip McBride Johnson and William L. Silber. The members of these advisory committees are listed in the back of the book.

The general advisory committee met in Washington at the outset of the project to assist in identifying the policy issues that should receive priority, and members or their representatives met jointly with the authors when their studies were planned and drafted. Subsequent meetings were held in New York and Chicago. These committees made invaluable contributions to the research, both for the advice and criticism that they provided and for the access to knowledgeable people in the industry that they made possible.

Although these studies were carried out entirely separately from the government studies, the project benefited from frequent consultation with government agency officials and staff. In particular, Susan M. Phillips, chairperson of the CFTC; members of the CFTC's economics staff; Frederick Struble, associate director of the FRB; and members of the FRB staff provided information to authors and helpful suggestions in response to draft papers.

Authors of the individual essays acknowledge the assistance they received in preparing their papers. Here I want to acknowledge the several additional people who provided formal review of some or all of the studies. They include: Robert M. Bear, Robert M. Bor, Galen Burghardt, Thomas Coleman, Read P. Dunn, Jr., Kenneth R. French, Marvin L. Hayenga, Marvin H. Kosters, Raymond M. Leuthold, Terrence F. Martell, Gary Perlin, Todd E. Petzel, Mark J. Powers, Donald J. Puglisi, Gordon C. Rausser, Charles E. Robinson, Gary L. Seevers, Sarahelen Thompson, and Terrance J. Wear. I want to acknowledge their assistance, as well as that of the advisory committees and members of their staff, and thank them for their contributions.

ANNE E. PECK
Project Director

xiii

Futures Markets: Their Economic Role

1

The Economic Role of Traditional Commodity Futures Markets

Anne E. Peck

The concepts and techniques of futures trading have recently been introduced to markets for commodities vastly different from the agricultural markets in which the system of trading first developed and to which it was largely constrained for nearly 100 years. In fact, metals futures markets were the only exceptions to the agricultural bounds of futures trading until 1972 and the introduction of currency futures markets. The de facto bounds arose in part from a regulatory vacuum. Before 1974 futures trading was regulated by the Commodity Exchange Authority (CEA), a bureau in the U.S. Department of Agriculture. The CEA did not regulate the introduction of new futures markets, nor did it regulate futures markets other than those for domestic agricultural products (and it regulated those only after the initiation of trading had been shown to be a success).

The absence of an explicit regulatory authority for all futures trading meant that innovative proposals in new products had to be approved by the regulators, if any, of the underlying markets. The original proposal of the Chicago Board of Trade (CBT) in the late 1960s and early 1970s to begin a futures market in securities issues is illustrative. The CEA had no interest in the proposal; but, since the proposal involved securities, the Securities and Exchange Commission (SEC) was interested. Indeed, the SEC asserted regulatory authority over the proposal and rejected it. A revised submission from the CBT proposed an organized options market for individual securities. The proposal could not be rejected on the grounds that options markets were themselves new, and a pilot program was finally approved. The Chicago Board Options Exchange (CBOE) began

I would like to acknowledge the many thoughtful comments and suggestions I received on an earlier version of this paper from Thomas Coleman, Read Dunn, Michael Gorham, Raymond Leuthold, Todd Petzel, Charles Robinson, Frank Rose, Gary Seevers, and Sarahelen Thompson. The omissions and errors are entirely my own doing.

1

trading in 1973, several years after the initial CBT proposal to trade futures on securities.

Similarly, many of the new futures markets in financial instruments would not have been feasible before the Commodity Futures Trading Commission (CFTC) was created and given exclusive regulatory jurisdiction over all futures trading. Proposals for new markets no longer needed the explicit approval of the agencies responsible for regulation in the underlying market, although the CFTC has been very receptive to their reviews of contract proposals. It is not surprising that each proposed new market has attracted substantial concern— a concern that goes beyond the perceived infringement of regulatory authority. The Federal Reserve and the Treasury, for example, were concerned over the effects futures markets in government issues might have on their ability to finance the federal debt and to conduct monetary policy. More recently Congress voiced concern over the possible effect of futures markets in the financial instruments, particularly in stock indexes, on the process of capital formation.

The perception underlying the concerns is not misplaced, even though the concerns are often attempts to constrain the exclusive regulatory jurisdiction of the CFTC as well. If a new market is successful, it will be so because firms within the market find it useful. Commercial firms' use of the new futures market will affect their businesses and may thus have profound effects on the process of price discovery or risk management within the industry. Many of the same concerns have been expressed virtually every time a new market has been introduced. With more than 100 years of experience, the agricultural markets have provided extensive evidence on the economic effects of futures markets, and a summary of that experience is a useful beginning to understanding present concerns.

A second reason for this assessment of the role of the more traditional futures is simply their continuing importance. In 1970 a mere 12.6 million futures contracts were traded on the principal commodity exchanges. Grains and oilseeds accounted for more than 60 percent of the total and livestock and food products for virtually all the rest. In 1983 some 137.2 million contracts were traded, a more than tenfold increase. Although much of the growth in trading is accounted for by the new markets for financial products, the traditional markets also contributed impressively to the total industry growth. Trading in grains and oilseeds, for example, increased more than fivefold in the fourteen-year period, livestock futures trading increased fourfold, and trading in food products more than doubled. Major growth and innovation occurred in trading in industrial commodities, with new and increasingly successful contracts in petroleum products and sustained growth in copper futures trading. Finally, trading in precious metals, primarily silver and gold, contributed substantially to total market growth. Taken together, these commodities accounted for 88 million of the 137.2 million contracts traded in 1983, approximately 64 percent of the total.

The purpose of this chapter is to summarize the evidence and experience from traditional markets on the effects of futures trading on commodity markets and pricing. The assessment begins with a discussion of the evolution of futures markets and their role in the marketing of agricultural products. The principal participants— commercial firms and speculators—and their characteristic uses are then introduced. From these descriptions an assessment of the economic effects of futures markets begins. A consideration of their effect on storage decisions and hence on intertemporal commodity prices is followed by an assessment of their effect on basic commodity production and consumption decisions. Finally, the specific effects of speculation are considered.

The chapter is not a review of the literature, although its debts to that literature will be made clear. Many important lines of investigation, especially much of the fairly recent theoretical modeling of alternative market structures and assumptions, are not mentioned because they do not bear directly on the questions at hand. Similarly, not all studies bearing on the specific issues discussed here are mentioned. The references are meant to be illustrative, not exhaustive.[1] This chapter seeks to explain the important purposes for which futures markets have come to be used in agricultural markets and then to consider the effects of those uses on pricing more generally.

Evolutionary Development of Futures Markets and Their Role in the Marketing of Traditional Commodities

The pace of product innovation by futures exchanges in recent years has been truly phenomenal. Not more than twenty years ago, futures markets were limited to agricultural and metals products. Among agricultural products conventional wisdom dictated that only storable commodities were adaptable to futures trading. Given the pace and diversity of current innovation, one might assume that the initial development and adaptation of futures markets were as rapid. In fact, futures markets required some fifty years to develop into forms recognizable today. A brief description of this development—the emergence of futures markets—is a useful point with which to begin the assessment of their unique economic contributions.

The Evolution of Commodity Futures Markets. Because their development was evolutionary, no specific date can be attached to the beginning of organized futures markets. They emerged as organized forward markets for grains—first in corn and then in wheat—in Chicago in the second half of the nineteenth century. Forward contracting was itself not revolutionary. Examples of futurity in commercial contracts can be traced as far back as seventeenth-century Japan. The first continuing record of the use of forward contracts in Chicago dates to 1851.[2] Incorporated in 1833, Chicago grew rapidly into the major terminal market of the Midwest because of its central location and the successive completion of major water and rail links with eastern markets and expanding production areas in the West. In 1848 the Michigan-Illinois Canal opened, providing river access to Chicago (and hence cheap transportation) from the interior fertile lands along the Illinois River. Farmers quickly responded to the new market opportunities along the river and canals. Irwin estimated, for example, that trade in corn to Chicago for subsequent eastern shipment grew from 67,000 bushels in 1847 to over 3 million bushels in 1851.

Although the canals greatly expanded the agricultural area that could economically ship to Chicago and hence Chicago's role as a terminal market, such transportation was usable only seasonally. Canal and lake transportation was closed in winter, which was the most reliable time for shipment of grain by road to the river or canal market. Thus corncribs and grain elevators spread quickly along the canal system. Farmers delivered most of their corn in winter and dealers held it until late spring or early summer for shipment to Chicago. According to Irwin, about 80 percent of corn received in Chicago from 1854 to 1858 arrived there between May and September.

Financing requirements grew apace with the increasing trade in corn and to a lesser extent wheat, both to finance the ever-increasing size of crops in storage and to expand storage space. Under such circumstances it is not surprising that merchants along the canal system went to Chicago to find buyers for their grain on a forward basis. In the *Chicago Journal* Irwin found a continuing series of reports of forward contracts beginning in 1851, with isolated references to such contracts even earlier. The early contracts were informal, specifying only quantity, price, and time of delivery. Irwin also reported that some contracts included a provision that a proportion of the final price be paid at the contracting date, although "the contracts were personal and each party relied principally upon the integrity of the other for fulfillment."[3] Forward contracting grew in volume

4

as the Chicago markets developed and greatly increased with the provisioning required by the Crimean War in Europe and the Civil War.

Over the same period grain trading became more regularized. The Chicago Board of Trade was organized in 1848 as a merchants' association to centralize trading in grain and provisions. In 1859 it was chartered by the state of Illinois and authorized to establish and enforce grain standards. The acceptance of grading standards promoted homogeneity among contracts and permitted the development of the warehouse receipt as conveying title to grain and as collateral in financing grain transactions.The merchants' association was slow to recognize formally the emerging practice of trading in forward contracts. The first rule of the CBT explicitly referring to these contracts did not appear until 1865. In 1863 rules had been adopted according to which members could be suspended if they did not meet their contractual obligations. Evidently this proved insufficient to enforce forward contracts, and in 1865 a margin provision was adopted.

> On all time contracts made between members of this association satisfactory margins may be demanded by either party, not to exceed 10 per cent on the value of the article bought or sold on the day such margin is demanded, said margin to be deposited at such place or with such person as may be mutually agreed upon. Such margin may be demanded on or after the date of contract, and from time to time, as may be deemed necessary to fully protect the party calling for same. Should the party called upon for margin, as herein provided, fail to respond within 24 hours thereafter, it shall be optional with the party making such call to consider the contract filled at the market value of the article on the day said call is made, and all differences between said market value and the contract price shall be settled the same as though the contract had fully expired.[4]

Margin deposits were not to be required on all trades but could be requested by either buyer or seller. In addition, an adjustment in margin could be required—the first so-called variation margin requirement. Forward contracting was firmly established, and trading of those contracts was developing. Contracts included accepted grade standards, were of common sizes (1,000 or 5,000 bushels) and delivery times (for example, May and the opening of the canal), and were enforceable among members of the association. The margin rules, though optional, provided additional contract security. Because these contracts were fairly uniform, they could be exchanged, and the CBT became the primary site of such trading.

5

The final element in the creation of true futures markets, as distinct from physical or forward markets, was the development of the principle of offset, whereby an individual could easily reverse a contractual obligation. Formal clearinghouse offset was not established until 1891, at the Minneapolis Grain Exchange. The principle of offset developed earlier, however, in the ring settlement procedures at the CBT.

Suppose merchant A purchased 5,000 bushels of corn for May delivery in Chicago from an elevator on the Illinois River. Several weeks later, the merchant found this grain would not be needed and sold the contract to merchant B on the exchange. In some sense, merchant A would no longer be involved in this 5,000-bushel contract if the delivery and financial responsibilites could be sorted out. If A paid (or was paid) the difference in price between the purchase and sale contracts, A would have no further financial obligations. Suppose the original contract for forward delivery was priced at $1.00 per bushel and was sold to merchant B for $0.90. If the loss of $0.10 per bushel were paid to the original seller, the elevator, A would have no further obligation. The elevator would have $0.10 and a forward contract for sale of the grain to B at $0.90. If both parties fulfilled their obligations, merchant A would in fact have had no further obligation either. With a default by either party, however, A could become involved in the resulting dispute.

These basic procedures—though simplified in the discussion above—became formalized as the ring settlement method. It entailed the settlement of price differences on contract purchases and sales and permitted traders to enter and leave the market without having to wait until delivery to settle their accounts. Ring settlement methods were formalized in 1883 at the CBT with the formation of a clearinghouse. The sole purpose of this first clearinghouse was "facilitating the offsetting of trades between houses without waiting for customers to close them."[5] Firms with customers' accounts were required to maintain the bookkeeping for those accounts internally. Each day the firm settled its net position with all other firms through the payment of price differences to the clearinghouse. The ring settlement system remained in effect in Chicago until the 1920s.

In 1891 the Minneapolis Grain Exchange organized the first complete clearinghouse system. The clearinghouse, in addition to its daily accounting responsibility, became the third party to all transactions on the exchange, thereby creating true clearinghouse offset as it is known today and completing the evolution of forward contract trading to futures trading. Every potential buyer or seller must still find his opposite in the trading on the exchange floor. After the trade

6

is recorded with the clearinghouse, however, and both the buyer and seller agree to its terms, the clearinghouse becomes the third party to the transaction. At this point the buyer has a contractual obligation to accept delivery from the clearinghouse, and the seller has a contractual obligation to deliver to the clearinghouse. Contracts are completely impersonal, and the seller no longer must rely to any extent on the integrity of the buyer (and vice versa) to ensure contract performance. The integrity of each contract depends on the integrity of the clearinghouse.

The operations of the clearinghouse were designed to maximize contract integrity. Buyers and sellers alike are required to post margins with the clearinghouse directly (technically, clearing member firms are required to post the necessary margins for their own accounts and for those of firms and individuals clearing through them). The clearinghouse insists on daily settlement of all open positions, the so-called mark-to-market system. Losses on open positions are not paper losses: they are paid each day through the clearinghouse. The settlement price at the close of trading is used to value all open positions. The losses from positions adversely affected by the price change are then paid out to firms with open positions that show profits. Since the clearinghouse has no market position of its own (every buyer must have found a seller, and vice versa), the daily profits of traders always equal the daily losses of other traders. In addition, the margin each trader has deposited ensures that payment of losses can be made daily. If an initial margin is depleted, the trader is required to deposit additional funds, so-called variation margin. If the requested variation margin is not deposited promptly, the clearinghouse can close the outstanding positions of the trader. In principle, therefore, funds are always available to the clearinghouse to make the daily transfers, and default risk is very small.

With the development of clearinghouse offset, organized trading in forward contracts had evolved into futures markets. Forward contracts remain valuable to grain merchants, as will be seen, because each is unique in size, quality, timing, and location of actual delivery. Performance on a forward contract, however, continues to rely on the integrity of each party to the contract. In contrast, futures contracts are uniform and impersonal, their integrity established by the clearinghouse and margin system. Each market has come to have a unique role in facilitating the merchandising of grain. Although the distinctions between and the ultimate complementarity of futures and forward markets are evident today, no such distinctions were apparent during their development. Separate wheat futures markets emerged at nearly all major terminal markets, for example, including not only Chicago,

7

Kansas City, and Minneapolis but also New York, Duluth, Milwaukee, St. Louis, and Omaha. In each case futures markets emerged from organized trading in forward contracts that were themselves uniquely valuable to local merchants because of their specific location and variety.

That the resultant futures markets at each location remained active for some years is testimony to the evolutionary nature of their development. More recent experience suggests that multiple futures for the same commodity are unlikely to coexist successfully. One market usually dominates trading very quickly, and the other markets inevitably expire. Wheat is not, of course, the perfect example of a homogeneous commodity, and high transportation and especially communication costs and delays in the middle to late nineteenth century surely account for some of the sustained trading in essentially regional futures markets. Nevertheless, some portion of the sustained proliferation of early futures markets is a direct result of their evolutionary character.

Merchants of the time appear not to have realized the precise value of the evolution. Rothstein's recent analysis of the adoption of hedging practices during this period clearly shows the suspiciousness with which even grain merchants viewed the emerging markets. Rothstein documents the remarkable change in attitude toward the new markets of a prominent Milwaukee grain merchant. In 1858 the merchant opposed the new markets: "I hope anybody will lose who ever enters into those kind of gambling operations of selling ahead. . . . there is no speculation so dangerous, not even betting on a faro table."[6] Some twenty-five years later, in 1873, the same merchant wrote:

> In order that there be no speculation about buying wheat here, I mean to sell a seller Feby [against the shipment] and when you use this wheat, then buy it in here. If wheat goes up here, it will with you and this mode covers all speculation. . . . I do not know that you will understand this, but it is an excellent thing, if we do not want to speculate.[7]

Recognizing the fundamental usefulness of a futures market took the merchant more than two decades. It is thus no surprise that centralization of trading took much longer.

Finally, although the discussion here has focused on the grain trade and developments primarily in Chicago in the second half of the nineteenth century, the independent development of futures markets was not limited to either Chicago or grains. The Minneapolis Grain Exchange in fact completed the evolution with the introduction of clearinghouse offset. Active futures markets also emerged at many other midwestern grain markets. Irwin documents the nearly parallel and apparently unrelated development of a cotton futures market at the New York Cotton Exchange.[8] The present Chicago Mercantile Exchange can be traced to 1874 and the formation of the Chicago Produce Exchange (later the Butter and Egg Board), on which the trading of forward contracts in eggs and butter developed in much the same way as the grain exchanges. Similarly, the New York Mercantile Exchange originated from forward contract trading on the New York Butter and Cheese Exchange, organized in 1872. The New York Produce Exchange emerged as a futures market in this period. The Coffee, Sugar, and Cocoa Exchange began in 1882 as the Coffee Exchange. Sugar was added in 1916, but cocoa trading (on the originally separate Cocoa Exchange) was not begun until 1925. The Commodity Exchange dates to the 1920s with trading in metals—copper, silver, zinc, lead—and hides, albeit on separate exchanges.

Unfortunately, few analyses exist of the history of these exchanges and the evolution of organized futures trading on them. Irwin's account of the experiences of the Chicago Mercantile Exchange, the Chicago Board of Trade, and the New York Cotton Exchange are suggestive. Futures trading appeared on each exchange largely independently and was traceable to commercial practices within the specific commodity's market. In each case growing storage requirements led to the use of forward contracts, and trading in forward contracts led to organized futures markets. The case for independence and reliance on commercial practice within the industry is made stronger by noting that trading in butter and egg futures emerged some thirty to forty years after that in grains and cotton. The Chicago Mercantile Exchange, when formally organized as a futures market, did borrow the trading rules and arrangements of the well-established markets. Irwin's account shows clearly, however, that it was developments in the egg business that led to the emergence of a futures market.[9]

Evolution notwithstanding, futures markets have not replaced either cash or forward markets for agricultural and metals products. Each market remains uniquely valuable in the marketing, processing, and distribution of these commodities. Cash markets are immediate delivery markets in which transactions simultaneously price and convey ownership of commodities. Forward markets permit an individual buyer and seller to agree on a future transfer of commodity on terms, including price, that are mutually convenient. Futures are centralized forward-pricing markets, all contract terms are standardized, and only price is negotiated.

9

Complementary Roles of Cash, Forward, and Futures Markets. The most common cash (also called physical or spot) market transaction is at the point of first marketing of the commodity by the producer to a merchant or processor. A farmer deciding to sell grain, for example, delivers it to a local elevator, has it weighed and graded immediately, and receives a check on the same day. The price is a cash market price. Before actually delivering the grain, the farmer does not know exactly what the price will be, although quotations can be obtained from the elevator of prices paid for standard grades that day. Surveys by Paul et al. and by Helmuth show that most grain moves from the farm through cash market transactions.[10] Although cash transactions are very common in grain marketing, centralized cash grain markets no longer play an important role in the movement of grain except perhaps for the organized trading in St. Louis of corn being barged to New Orleans (so-called CIFNOLA trading). In livestock marketing, however, centralized markets in Omaha, St. Louis, and throughout the major producing regions continue to be important both as sources of current price information and as sales channels.

Cash prices refer to specific locations and qualities. A published cash price quotation will normally be for the most common grade of the commodity (for example, number 2 yellow corn, number 1 yellow soybeans, or 900–1,000-pound choice steers). Individual cash buyers also maintain discount and premium schedules for commodities that do not meet standard grade specifications. Premiums and discounts may vary during a marketing season and do vary substantially between seasons or years. For example, in a year with a very wet corn harvest and associated high average levels of moisture in newly harvested corn, discounts for moisture higher than the standard 14 percent will be large. If the harvest occurs in much drier conditions, so that most of the crop does not require drying before storage, corn that is above the standard moisture level will probably be discounted much less.

Forward markets add a time dimension to cash markets. Like a cash contract, a forward contract is specific as to location, quality, and amount. Commodity ownership is not transferred, however, on the date the contract is entered into; rather, a forward contract sets the transfer sometime in the future, although the price is established on the contracting date. (Forward contracts may also be basis priced, with price levels established later through futures transactions.) With a forward contract, buyer and seller agree at the outset on what price will be paid for the commodity when it is delivered under the terms of the contract.

A farmer who has decided to plant 75 acres of corn, for example, knows what the basic costs of production are. Further, the farmer may expect a yield of 115 bushels to the acre but, to be conservative, may be planning on the basis of 100 bushels to the acre. A local elevator will quote a forward price for corn to be delivered in the fall (October–November), at harvest. If the price covers the costs of production, the farmer may decide at once, while planting the corn, to sell it to the elevator for delivery in the fall. This forward contract usually includes provisions for delivery either earlier or later than agreed upon and for delivery of corn that does not meet other agreed upon specifications.

Forward contracts are used extensively in the export and import of commodities. In fact, virtually all such contracts are forward contracts—contracts made today for delivery sometime in the future—if only because the physical movement of commodities takes time. In addition, they are widely used by processors of agricultural commodities, such as flour millers and corn processors, to ensure a continuous supply of the commodity for their processing facilities, facilities that typically do not have large on-site storage capacity. Forward contracts are also common in livestock marketing and assure packers of a continuous supply of animals to their plants.

Forward contracts are not commonly accompanied by payment of a performance bond by either buyer or seller. That is, neither buyer nor seller is required to advance money to ensure contract performance. As market prices change over the period of the contract, the contract will assume a value to either the buyer or the seller, and one will have an incentive to default on the contract. Fulfillment of the terms of the contract depends on the integrity of the two contracting parties. Defaults are not common, in part because either the buyer or the seller will normally hedge the contractual obligation with a futures position, a common commercial use of futures markets discussed in the next section.

Finally, forward contracts for agricultural products are illiquid. A particular forward contract is specific as to quantity, quality, and location. These conditions make it attractive to the original buyer and seller but are unlikely to be attractive to any other potential buyer or seller. It is therefore relatively difficult to trade a forward commitment if market conditions change and the buyer, for example, no longer needs the commodity.

Futures contracts are standardized forward contracts, and futures markets are the organized trading of those contracts. All corn futures contracts, for example, are identical in that they are obligations to make or take delivery of a fixed amount and quality of corn in a specified location at some point in the future. Potential delivery months are prespecified, as is the time within the delivery month when delivery may be made. The only item to be negotiated when buying or selling a futures contract is price. Standardization of contract terms facilitates centralization of trading, and, although production and cash transactions remain regionally dispersed, futures trading is not. Futures contracts are traded on exchanges according to the rules of the exchanges, with regulatory oversight by the CFTC. All trades are by open outcry at the exchange—buyers and sellers offering the desired number of contracts and price to all assembled traders.

Unlike cash or forward contracts, futures contracts are rarely used to transfer actual ownership of commodities. The standardization of contract terms that facilitates market liquidity and price discovery discourages users of the physical commodity from accepting delivery. The standardized terms of futures contracts rarely coincide with the precise needs of a commercial user in timing, location, or quantity. Thus futures contracts are rarely held until delivery; instead, they are either replaced with contracts of more distant maturities (rolled over) or they are closed (offset) as the actual physical commodity is acquired at times and locations matching specific needs. Actual delivery occurs in less than 1 percent of the futures contracts traded.

Two additional institutional features—margins and the clearinghouse—distinguish futures from forward contracts. Margins are performance bonds that both buyer and seller must deposit before trading. The funds ensure, on a daily basis, that neither party has an incentive to default on the contract. The bond is renewed each day as open positions are marked to the market, margin accounts adjusted, and additional funds deposited if required. Once a futures transaction has been checked to ensure that both buyer and seller agree to the recorded transaction, the clearinghouse becomes the third party to the contract.

The third-party role of the clearinghouse enhances market liquidity by facilitating exit from the market and by depersonalizing contract performance. To fulfill contractual obligations, a buyer must either accept delivery of the commodity in the designated month or sell a like amount before the expiration of the contract. The latter transaction is an offset trade that makes the individual net even in the records of the exchange (having bought from and sold to the clearinghouse, in equal amounts).

Margins combined with daily marking of positions to the market reduce the risk of contract default virtually to zero. The clearinghouse, as a third party to all transactions, establishes the principle of offset as a means of reversing a previous decision. Standardization of all contracts implies that only price is being determined. Taken together, these features reduce the costs of entering and exiting from the market, permit centralization of trading, and thereby greatly increase market liquidity.

Futures markets in agricultural and metals products have become the primary markets determining underlying values, and all other transactions, spot and forward, are priced in relation to these prices with due allowance for time, place, and quality differences. Both spot and forward market transactions remain important since they are the primary means by which commodity ownership is actually transferred. These transactions are not made independently of market prices, however, and futures positions are often necessary components of the total transaction.

Commercial Firms' Use of Futures Markets

Firms engaged in the production, processing, and distribution of agricultural and metals products use futures markets extensively in their commercial transactions. These firms are known as hedgers; they include farmers, feedlot operators, mine owners, merchants, farmers' cooperatives, import and export firms, wheat millers, corn processors, meatpackers, metal fabricators, sugar refiners, and coffee roasters. This list of users, though not exhaustive, is indicative of the diversity of firms that find futures markets useful in the course of their normal business operations. Given the diversity of firms and their needs, there is little likelihood that a single definition of hedging will encompass all legitimate potential business uses of futures markets.

Working's summary definition is perhaps as all-encompassing as is possible:

> Hedging in futures consists of making a *contract to buy or sell on standard terms, established and supervised by a commodity exchange, as temporary substitute for an intended later contract to buy or sell on other terms.* Then the hedger seeks to make the second purchase or sale, perhaps several months later, on terms that suit him better than those of the standard (futures) contract.[11]

Futures markets are used by commercial firms to price a transaction temporarily. The definition does not directly address motives, although it implies both the greater liquidity of a futures market and management of the price risks inherent in commodity ownership. How and why commercial firms use futures markets is the subject of this section. Understanding such use is fundamental to assessing the role

13

of futures markets in the economy since these are the firms engaged in the allocation of the economy's resources in production, consumption, and marketing of these products.

The Arbitrage Use of Futures Markets. The most common example of a hedging transaction focuses on seasonal storage of an agricultural commodity and the use of futures markets to secure a return to storage through a predictable change in the relation between cash and futures prices. Consider an elevator in Chicago that is in a deliverable location for the CBT corn futures contract. Assume that it is early October and that new crop corn is in plentiful supply and is trading at $2.53¼ per bushel in Chicago. At the same time the closing price of the December corn futures contract is $2.85¼. In this circumstance the elevator might purchase 5,000 bushels of corn and simultaneously sell one contract of December corn futures with the intention of storing corn until December. In this idealized example, the elevator has assured itself of a $0.32 per bushel gross return to corn storage from October until mid-December.

The hedged return is invariant to changes in prices. If cash prices in Chicago decline to $2.00 by December, the December future will also be priced at $2.00, since it is in delivery and delivery is in Chicago. If the elevator sells the stored corn in December and simultaneously lifts (buys back or offsets) the futures positions, the cash purchase and sale lose $0.53¼ per bushel ($2.00 − $2.53¼) while the futures positions gain $0.85¼ ($2.85¼ − $2.00) for a gross return of $0.32 per bushel. If prices rise to $3.50 by December, the cash side of the transaction earns $0.96¾ per bushel ($3.50 − $2.53¼) while the futures side earns −$0.64¾ ($2.85¼ − $3.50), for the same gross return of $0.32 per bushel. The difference between the cash and the futures price at the time the corn was bought and stored is variously called the basis, the spot premium or discount, and the carrying charge or, if negative, the inverse carrying charge (although the last terms are usually reserved for futures price differences, not differences between cash and futures prices). In the example cash (spot) corn was $0.32 under the December future in October, the spot discount was $0.32, or the basis was 32 under the December future. The basis in December was zero, and the returns to storage are simply the change in basis from October, when the hedge was placed, to December, when the hedge was lifted.

In the example the basis prevailing when the arbitrage hedge was placed is a perfect forecast of the returns to storage and is an ideal situation. The hedger is in the delivery location and can rely on the convergence of cash and futures prices in the delivery month.

Working examined evidence of the reliability of this relation for a similar "ideal" situation in wheat—an elevator located in Kansas City hedging in Kansas City wheat futures.[12] He found that the currently observed basis predicted as much as 95 percent of the subsequent change in basis.

More generally, the essence of an arbitrage hedge is the predictability of the basis over time. In the delivery location predictability is nearly absolute. Clearly, not all (indeed, very few) grain elevators operate in this ideal environment. The operational question, then, is the predictability of the basis in relation to the cash price over the relevant storage period. The former determines the returns to hedged storage, and the latter determines those to unhedged storage. Figure 1–1 provides a graphic display of a typical basis relation for a series of years.Cash prices that are averages of quotations from elevators in the upper Illinois River basin are plotted in relation to the price of the May corn future on the Chicago Board of Trade. Corn prices, even measured relatively, are not identical every year, but the seasonal change in the basis relation is similar each year. Corn held until May averaged about $0.12 per bushel under the May future, with a range of almost $0.08. Since the basis is known at the time the corn is bought and put into storage, returns from hedged storage are clearly very predictable.

Arbitrage hedging is done to profit from the reliably predictable difference in prices in the two markets. For agricultural commodities such arbitrage requires storage space and is largely done, therefore, by commercial elevator firms. In contrast, nearly anyone could engage in such arbitrage in the precious metals market since specialized storage facilities are not required. The difference, however, is that grain elevators' primary business is merchandising grain—providing time and space utility in grain marketing. To the extent that the basis is both more stable and more predictable than absolute price levels over relevant storage periods, arbitrage hedging reduces the business risks inherent in commodity storage. For seasonally produced, continuously consumed, storable commodities, storage serves an important market function. That futures markets permit such firms to reduce the risks of storage implies a reduction in their storage margins. Empirical evidence on the reduction in storage margins is considered in the section "The Role and Effects of Futures Markets in Forward Pricing" in the form of the effects on seasonal price stability. Seasonal price changes are shown to have been significantly reduced when futures markets were present.

Arbitrage hedging links local prices to central prices directly. Thus, one might expect improved integration among regional market

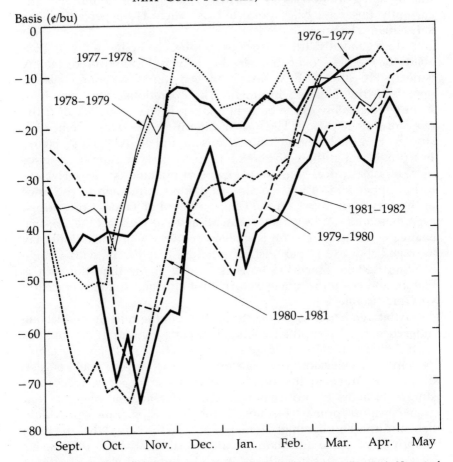

FIGURE 1–1
THE CORN BASIS IN THE UPPER ILLINOIS RIVER BASIN,
MAY CORN FUTURES, 1976–1982

SOURCE: Chicago Board of Trade, *Commodity Markets: Development, Economic Uses, and Trading in Futures* (Chicago: Chicago Board of Trade, 1983), p. 21.

prices. Direct evidence from agricultural markets has not, to my knowledge, been analyzed.[13] Indirect evidence might compare an elevator's bid and asked prices when futures markets are open with those prices when futures are closed. Or average elevator margins for commodities like corn and wheat might be compared with those for nonfutures commodities the same elevators handle, such as barley and durum wheat.

In the absence of direct or indirect evidence, anecdotal evidence at least suggests the price transmission efficiencies caused by the availability of hedging on futures markets. When, for example, the grain futures markets closed after the presidential announcement of a grain embargo in January 1980, sales of grain in country locations were reported to be light and at prices significantly below those prevailing on previous days and below those that might have been anticipated if the futures market were open. Buyers of grain, having no hedging alternative, were forced to lower their bids dramatically to reflect the greatly increased risks of buying grain. When the markets reopened, local prices resumed their normal relations with futures prices. Prices were, to be sure, below those prevailing before the announcement, but they were significantly above those found during the two days the markets were closed.

Operational Hedging. A second reason for commercial use of futures markets derives from the much greater liquidity characteristic of those markets than of the underlying spot markets. Large commercial transactions can be priced very quickly with minimal effect on prices, leaving firms time to search for the specific grades or qualities in suitable locations to fulfill the terms of the contract. Working called this use of futures markets operational hedging; in essence, it is the use of futures as a substitute for an actual purchase or sale of a commodity, normally for a very short period to give a firm the time required to assemble the desired commodity on terms suitable for the contract.[14]

The classic example of operational hedging is a flour mill's use of wheat futures. Characteristically, flour mills do not have large, on-site storage capacities and are therefore unlikely to have in store the specific grades and qualities of wheat required to fill an order when it is being negotiated with a baker. A baker may call to order two to three months' flour requirements for delivery beginning in a month or so and wants a fixed price commitment from the miller for the entire order. Futures markets serve two related functions for the miller. First, the prices provide the miller with precise estimates of standard wheat values. To this standard a premium or discount will be added or subtracted to reflect the relative value of the specific wheats required to fill the order. The total calculation provides the miller with a firm price to bid on the baker's contract, and futures have established the basis for the bid.

If the bid is accepted, the miller immediately purchases wheat futures as a temporary substitute for the required wheat. The large quantities of the specific grades and quality of wheat needed to fill the order are unlikely to be immediately available in the local cash market precisely because of their specificity. Even if a local elevator happened to have wheat matching the miller's need, such large purchases would have a significant price effect. The same quantity of futures purchases, however, will affect the price by no more than a quarter or a half of a cent. With the hedge in place, the miller has the opportunity to accumulate the wheat as it becomes available and to shop for the most favorable terms. Although the futures positions may serve as only a very temporary substitute, their relative liquidity makes them a very attractive substitute.

The use of futures in agricultural commodities for operational convenience has received by far the least attention by economists. In part, the explanation is the overwhelming dominance of arbitrage hedging in the historical statistics of market use. In this context, however, it is worth noting that before 1960 flour mill hedging alone accounted for more than 50 percent of all long hedging on the three major wheat markets.[15] The average has declined substantially in more recent periods because of the tremendous growth of commodity exports and sympathetic growth in long hedging by exporters. Despite this relative decline in the importance of mill hedging, operational convenience remains an important reason for commercial use of futures markets because the typical export firm's use of futures combines both arbitrage and operational motives. The more distant the export commitment, the more important are arbitrage relations. The more distant the commitment, the less likely it is that the firm owns the grain it is committed to deliver, and the more important is the firm's estimation of cash values specific to future locations and times in relation to futures prices. That is, the export firm has sold forward at prices derived from basis expectations, much as an elevator purchases grain in response to basis expectations.

Whatever the time horizon of the export commitment, futures will almost invariably be the purchase that immediately covers the transaction. Cash markets are not liquid enough to accommodate the size of most export orders immediately without substantial (albeit short-term) effect on price, but the liquidity of an active futures market can accommodate all but the largest orders without substantial effect on price. The futures purchases occur whether or not the firm actually owns the grain that is to be exported. If the grain is owned, it has very likely been hedged by sales of futures, and the purchase of futures lifts the hedge as well as having priced the transaction. If the grain committed to export is not owned, futures purchases price the transaction and provide time to shop for the specific lots required by the transaction. Finally, to the extent that the shopping time involved in export transactions is months rather than days or weeks, arbitrage relations assume a substantially greater importance than in pure operational hedging.

Finally, the use of futures markets for operational convenience significantly reduces the firm's exposure to price risks. Without futures the miller's processing margin would be as variable as cash wheat prices between the time the flour contract was accepted and the time the actual wheat was purchased. More important, without futures the miller's original bid would have had to include a sizable premium reflecting the potential risks of price change between the contract date and the date the desired wheat could actually be found in the market. With futures the miller's margin can be very nearly determined at the time of the sale, although the actual margin will depend on whether the miller is able to purchase wheat of appropriate quality at the anticipated premium or discount. The availability of futures markets and their use for operational convenience significantly reduce risks and hence margins in the marketing process.

Anticipatory Hedging. A third reason for the business use of futures is to price today an anticipated purchase or sale of the commodity that cannot be carried out today in the cash market. Most producers' hedging, some processors' hedging, and most end users' hedging illustrate this motive. By the nature of their businesses, these firms must buy or sell the physical commodity. If their marketing decisions are restricted to the cash market, factors other than price are likely to dominate their decisions. Farmers, for example, could not sell their crops until they were harvested. Processors who did not have extensive storage facilities could buy only as their processing operations required the physical commodity. With a futures market these firms can buy or sell as their market judgment dictates and not as required by the physical operation of their businesses. Such hedging is termed "anticipatory hedging" because the futures purchases or sales are made in anticipation of actual need or availability.

Some of the most detailed analyses of anticipatory hedging opportunities have focused on the cattle-feeding industry and have examined the effects on producers' returns of various futures marketing strategies. As the foundation for these studies, a typical cattle-feeding operation is simulated. Feeder cattle, for example, are purchased at about 600 pounds, fed for five or six months, and marketed at about 1,100 pounds. All inputs—primarily corn and protein supplement—are purchased at the beginning of the feeding period. Finally, the feedlot is generally assumed to be continuously filled to capacity, and possible losses from death are not a factor.

In the simplest of these evaluations, cash market sales of finished

19

cattle are compared with results of futures sales of the cattle when they were put on feed. A second strategy includes futures sales at placement, but only when the futures price covers at least the costs of production. Otherwise the cattle are marketed when finished. In another variant the restriction on timing is removed, and futures sales are permitted at any time after the cattle have been put on feed. Various price-forecasting schemes have been used as well to guide the timing of futures sales.

Leuthold and Tomek, in surveying the results of these analyses, conclude that routine anticipatory hedging—for example, always selling futures when the cattle are placed on feed—does significantly reduce the variability of feeding returns but also results in very low average returns.[16] Anticipatory hedges using some price forecasting or break-even decision criteria generally provide higher and less variable returns than the alternative of cash market sales. Even with relatively simple, common-sense trading strategies, analyses have shown that feedlot operators can effectively use futures markets to time sales decisions to their advantage.

Like all anticipatory hedges, cattle feeders' use of futures markets requires the exercise of judgment concerning price; that is, it is fundamentally a price-fixing decision. Prices look "good" today for the commodity that must eventually be bought or sold. There is an important difference, however, between the cash market decision and a futures decision. Once a cash market decision is made, subsequent changes in prices do not appear in the accounting of the firm's profits or losses. Futures decisions, however, involve margin funds, and market losses or gains are subtracted from or added to the margin account daily. The losses or gains in the futures position are real; during the period for which the futures position is a temporary substitute for the eventual cash market transaction, the losses or gains are daily measures of the judiciousness of the marketing decision.

Finally, anticipatory hedges can involve more than the sale or purchase of the single output or input. Cattle feeding is again a useful example, and a study by Leuthold and Mokler is illustrative.[17] As before, the basic cattle-feeding operation is simulated. The operator's planning horizon is expanded, however, to include three months before the feeder cattle and other inputs are purchased. During this period the price relations among fat cattle, feeder cattle, and corn futures are examined daily; if a profitable feeding margin can be secured, feeder cattle and corn futures are purchased and fat cattle futures sold. When the feeders and corn are actually bought, the hedges in futures are lifted. Meanwhile, the hedge of the finished cattle remains in place until the cattle are fattened and sold. If a profitable three-way hedge is not found during the planning period, production continues as planned, and the search continues for a profitable feeding margin, as in the earlier examples.

One of the most interesting aspects of Leuthold and Mokler's results is that a profitable feeding margin was available in every eight- to nine-month planning and feeding period. But, as the authors note, "each feeder must decide whether to take market positions and establish a profit level when a positive margin first appears, or to wait for larger margins, knowing that some lots of animals will never be forward priced."[18] The judgmental nature of anticipatory hedges remains, even with the assurance (in this study) of a profitable opportunity.

Commercial Use and Levels of Activity on Futures Markets. Some of the first evidence that futures markets are primarily commercial and not speculative markets was the observation that hedging was largely of the storage or arbitrage kind and showed a pronounced seasonal pattern, which was mirrored by the total activity on a number of grain markets. In particular, reported hedging was almost always net short, as it would be if storage hedging dominated and thus varied seasonally with the accumulation and decumulation of stocks of grain. The basic pattern, first noted by Hoffman and Irwin in the corn and wheat markets, persisted until the early 1970s.[19] It is shown in figures 1–2, 1–3, and 1–4 for data from the corn, wheat, and soybean markets.

In figure 1–2 visible supplies of each commodity are presented. These show the expected postharvest peaks and subsequent declines characteristic of commodities that are produced once a year, are storable, and are consumed year round. Figure 1–3 shows the average seasonal net hedging in each of these markets. Hedgers' use of these futures markets was net short most of the time during the year and followed a seasonal tendency closely related to the stocks pattern. That is, short hedging increased quickly after harvests (shown as an increasingly more negative net hedging in the month or months immediately after harvest) and thereafter declined as stocks of the commodities also declined. Figure 1–4 shows a sympathetic seasonal pattern in total open positions in each market, evidence that overall activity (the open interest) responds directly to hedgers' needs and not to speculative interests. Grain prospects are characteristically most uncertain in the months immediately before harvest. If speculative interests dominated, one would expect trading to peak during periods of the greatest speculative interest. Instead, trading was at

FIGURE 1–2
MONTHLY AVERAGE VISIBLE SUPPLY OF WHEAT, CORN, AND SOYBEANS, 1947–1948 TO 1971–1972

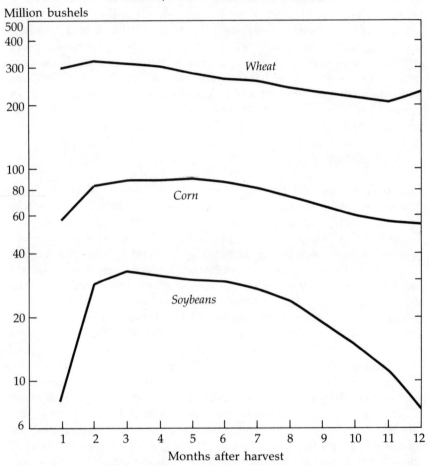

Million bushels

Months after harvest

SOURCE: Anne E. Peck, "Reflections of Hedging on Futures Market Activity," *Food Research Institute Studies*, vol. 17, no. 3 (1979).

its lowest before harvest, rising and peaking with the increases in commercial use.

Since the 1971–1972 crop year, the patterns in market use have changed significantly and sympathetically with the dramatic changes in commercial flows of these commodities. Beginning with the 1972–1973 crop year, government-held stocks of corn and wheat were depleted, and export demand was unprecedented. Futures markets

FIGURE 1–3
Average Monthly Net Hedging in Wheat, Corn, and Soybean Futures Markets, 1947–1948 to 1971–1972

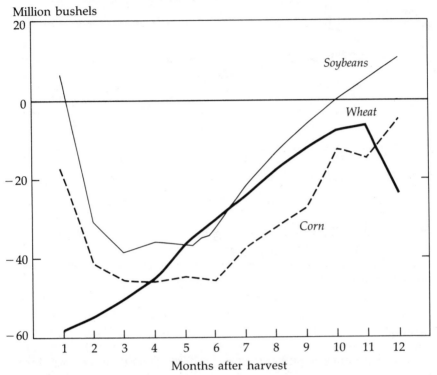

Million bushels

Months after harvest

Source: Peck, "Reflections of Hedging on Futures Market Activity."

activity grew apace with commercial activity. In 1971 month-end open interest of futures contracts averaged 149.5 million bushels of wheat, 261.8 million bushels of corn, and 290.8 million bushels of soybeans. By 1977 these figures were 335.4, 590.2, and 498.3 million bushels, respectively. Commercial use of futures markets grew more than proportionately. Short hedging of corn, which was averaging 46.6 percent of total open interest in the pre-1972 period, averaged 61.9 percent of the open interest from 1972 to 1977. Simultaneously, long hedging grew from 23.9 to 61.9 percent of the open interest. In the soybean market long hedging grew from 20.7 to 42.2 percent of the open interest and short hedging from 29.9 to 42.0 percent. Long hedging in the wheat market grew from 22.9 to 61.1 percent of the open interest and short hedging from 44.7 to 64.6 percent.

As these figures suggest, hedging became much more balanced

23

FIGURE 1-4

MONTHLY AVERAGE TOTAL OPEN INTEREST IN WHEAT, CORN, AND
SOYBEAN FUTURES MARKETS, 1947–1948 TO 1971–1972

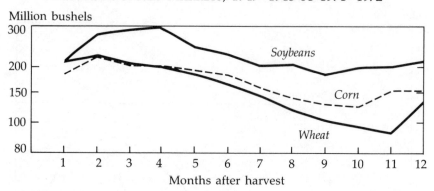

SOURCE: Peck, "Reflections of Hedging on Futures Market Activity."

in the 1972–1977 period, with long hedging nearly always as large
as short hedging. Net hedging averaged near zero and showed no
significant seasonal tendency. Similarly, the total open interest showed
no seasonal pattern.

The emerging balance in hedgers' positions in these markets is
due primarily to the much greater than proportional growth in long
hedging. Most of this growth is a direct reflection of export growth
and the concomitant increases in hedging by export firms, which are
at least partially operational. Some growth in both long and short
hedging is no doubt increased anticipatory hedging as well: the
returns to successful timing of market decisions increased significantly with more volatile markets. Nevertheless, the major market
change has been in the needs of firms in the export trade, and these
changes are clearly reflected in the data on market use.

The relative composition of commercial users of other agricultural and metals markets is not as clearly reflected in the aggregate
data on market positions, nor are the relations between commercial
use and total activity as revealing. Comparable data do not exist from
the metals or imported agricultural commodity markets. Data from
the live cattle, pork belly, and old Maine potato markets indicate
that overall activity on these futures markets is related to total
commercial use. Except for pork bellies, however, which are storable,
there is little evidence of a relation between levels of commercial use
and any measure of activity in the underlying physical market. Leuthold, for example, finds no significant relation between variables

24

such as placements on feed, slaughter, and marketings and futures market commitments in the live cattle, live hog, and feeder cattle markets.[20]

Summary. Although the motives for hedging vary, the diversity of commercial firms that find futures markets useful is testimony to their economic contributions. Futures markets provide a reliable basis for predicting storage returns, a liquid market to price and permit time-consuming acquisition of actual commodity needs, and a continuous market alternative for firms with marketing constraints. In each case firms use futures markets to manage the price risks inherent in their underlying businesses. The direct benefits are in the reduced margins that firms require when they use futures to reduce some of the price risks. As has been intimated in the preceding discussion, the more general economic effects of futures markets flow directly from the ways in which they are regularly used by those involved in the production, marketing, and processing of commodities. Before considering these, however, I turn to the role of speculators on futures markets.

The Role of Speculative Participation in Commodity Futures Markets

Speculation is an essential element in the formation of market prices—be they cash prices or futures prices. In the absence of a futures market, speculation on commodity prices usually requires a sizable investment in storage or transportation facilities to maintain ownership. Similarly, the production, processing, marketing, and ultimate use of agricultural products are time consuming, and at each stage the commodity is owned by someone. Ownership, either actual or prospective, is speculative.

With a futures market firms involved in the production or marketing of the commodity can use futures positions as temporary substitutes for intended purchases or sales of the commodity or its products, thereby separating physical ownership from price change speculation. Conceptually, a futures market could exist with trading restricted to commercial firms; if all firms in the production, marketing, processing, and consumption chain participated, price risks associated with commodity ownership at many of the stages in the chain could be largely internalized. Just as the underlying physical processes are themselves not coincident in timing, however, firms' individual purchase or sale decisions are rarely coincident. Thus one

25

firm's futures sale or purchase would probably be coincident with another firm's futures purchase or sale only infrequently. Like cash markets, such a market would often be extremely illiquid.

The noncommercial participants in futures markets—speculators—absorb the frequently unbalanced demands of commercial buyers and sellers. Imbalances may occur between total numbers of buyers and of sellers, between the degree of futurity desired by buyers and that desired by sellers, or between the timing of buying and selling within a day. Reflecting the three dimensions of possible imbalance in commercials' desired transactions, three forms of speculative participation in futures markets are commonly identified: position trading, spreading, and market making. Each of these is described below.

The view that speculators absorb temporary imbalances in market timing suggests that the imbalances have price effects and that speculative returns ought to be connected to the commercial participants' positions. Thus the discussion of each kind of trader also considers the possible links between positions and profits and summarizes the empirical evidence. Finally, the distinction between commercial users and speculative participants is unique to futures markets. Such a distinction is not made, for example, in physical markets. The rest of the section takes up the more general links between speculative concentration on markets, market performance issues, and the related need for the regulatory distinction between commercial and speculative participants in futures markets.

A Typology of Speculative Traders. Position trading is the most frequently identified form of speculation. Position trading absorbs the imbalance between aggregate commercial buyers and sellers of futures contracts in the market on any given day. This form of trading is done in the expectation of making a profit from price changes over time, where the relevant time period may be as short as a day or two or as long as several weeks. Position traders use both fundamental analyses of data on market supplies and demand and technical analyses of past price data (and sometimes other indicators of market information) to determine their trading strategies. In recent years position traders have accounted for an average of 20–30 percent of futures contracts open at the end of the day in the principal grain markets. Their ranks include professional traders, most of the so-called amateur traders, professionally managed accounts, and commodity mutual funds or pools.

Although it is convenient to think of position traders as absorbing the imbalances in commercial positions in a futures market, it is not an easy matter to link the profits of these traders to returns to speculators for assuming this net position. Nevertheless, a number of economists have proposed such links. Keynes was the first to propose a direct link.[21] At the time, commercial users were most often net sellers of futures contracts; therefore, futures speculators (position traders) had to be net buyers since buying and selling must match on a futures market. To induce speculators to buy futures contracts and absorb commercials' net selling, Keynes argued that futures prices would have to be biased downward, rising on average over the life of each contract so as to ensure a return to the speculative buyers. Cootner, noting the seasonal nature of commercial use of most grain futures markets, modified the theory to require upwardly biased prices and hence a regular return to speculators, if they are net short in response to net long hedging.[22]

The basic connections between net hedging, biased prices, and speculative profits theorized by Keynes and Cootner have been formalized in numerous economic models of futures markets and clearly have a great deal of intuitive appeal. Extensive empirical analysis in search of the hypothesized connection has, however, yielded no consistent verification. The exchange between Telser and Cootner in 1960 occasioned by Telser's assumption in an earlier article that futures prices were unbiased is illustrative of the debate and the difficulties of empirical resolution.[23] At the same time, Gray's analyses led him to conclude that bias was not a universal characteristic of futures prices and, when found, was attributable to the unique structural characteristics of a market rather than to futures trading per se.[24]

In a recent test for persistent bias induced by unbalanced commercial positions, Gray examined data from the corn and soybean markets from 1960 to 1977.[25] In each year his trading rule consisted of buying futures on the date that short hedging reached its maximum, holding that position until hedging first became net long, and then selling futures on the date net hedging reached its peak and holding the position until hedging became net short again. The test was designed to permit hedging pressure its maximum effect, initiating buying and selling decisions only at the times hedging was most unbalanced. A speculator following this strategy over the eighteen-year period would have lost an average of nearly four cents per bushel per trade in corn and twenty-two cents per bushel per trade in soybeans. Whatever the intuitive appeal of the link between speculative net positions and average price changes, it was certainly not the source of speculative profits over a fairly long recent period in two of the largest agricultural markets.

27

Additional, though now dated, insight is gained from Rockwell's examination of the amounts and source of profits that can be imputed to speculators. Using a technique developed by Houthakker, Rockwell combines data on traders' positions with market prices to measure actual speculative returns in the twenty-five agricultural futures markets more or less active over the period 1947–1965.[26] The results of these calculations varied among markets, especially between the three largest and the twenty-two smaller markets. Speculators as a group did earn substantial trading profits, but only the profits of large speculators were consistent and significant. Small, amateur speculators appeared to break about even on average across all markets. Rockwell's most interesting finding, however, is that speculative profits were attributable to price-forecasting skills, either short term or long term, and that little could be attributed to price biases related to hedgers' net positions.

More recent explorations of the link between hedging imbalance and speculative profits have cast the relation into a more formal framework of portfolio analysis and market models based on the capital asset pricing model. The results are again mixed. Dusak finds no evidence of price bias in wheat, corn, and soybean futures. Carter, Rausser, and Schmitz find evidence of a connection between systematic returns and net speculative positions, although their results have been seriously compromised by Marcus's criticism of their technique.[27] The argument continues. It is likely that economists will continue to search for direct links between imbalances in hedging needs, speculative positions, and speculative returns. The intuitive appeal of the connection is almost inviolate even though the empirical evidence is at best mixed. Position traders do earn profits as a group; nevertheless, the profits do not appear to be a predictable return from absorbing the changing requirements of commercial users.

A second form of speculation is spread trading. A spread trader can be seen to absorb imbalances in the degree of futurity required by commercial buyers and sellers. If, for example, a buyer was looking to the nearby future and a seller required a more distant future, a spread trader might match those positions. Spread traders seek to profit from predicting changes in relative prices rather than prices per se, holding simultaneous positions to buy and sell different futures. Spreads may be established within one market or between two or more markets.

An example of an intramarket spread is buying December corn and selling March corn, where both transactions are entered simultaneously—for example, in September. The trader expects that the December price will gain on the March price before December. Such a trader will often have no opinion about which direction underlying values will go. Common (and most frequently watched) intramarket spreads are old crop–new crop spreads, such as September/December corn prices or May/July wheat prices. The economic importance of these spreads is discussed in the next section.

Intermarket spreads include those between two markets for the same commodity as well as between markets for different commodities. For example, there are three active wheat futures markets— Chicago, Kansas City, and Minneapolis. One intermarket spread trade consists of buying Chicago July wheat and selling Kansas City July wheat. Such a trade is made if Chicago wheat prices are expected to increase in relation to Kansas City prices. Again, increases or decreases in prices per se are immaterial.

Perhaps the most common spread among markets for different commodities is between soybean futures and soybean product futures. Buying soybean futures and selling soybean meal and soybean oil futures is called "putting on the crush" and is done when the processing margin is expected to narrow. The "reverse crush," selling beans and buying products, is done when the margin is expected to widen. Other intermarket spread trades can be derived from production considerations. For example, the relation between new crop corn and soybean prices (December corn and November beans) is frequently analyzed with a view to the relative incentives it reflects to plant corn and soybeans.

The third form of speculation on futures markets is market making, also known as scalping. Market makers trade in large volumes during the daily trading session but rarely carry open positions overnight. That is, only occasionally will a market maker speculate on price changes over even so short a period as overnight. Their trading has been described as standing "ready either to buy at ⅛ cent below the last price or to sell at ⅛ cent above it."[28] Today, the ⅛ cent would be ¼ cent, reflecting the change in the minimum permitted price change on grain futures. Working goes on to note that the definition must be qualified. A scalper will under some conditions trade only on price changes, is not always equally willing either to buy or to sell, and is not always unwilling to buy except at a price below the last one. The description does, however, capture the essential nature of market making. Scalpers' profits are derived from skillfully accommodating the flow of orders as they come to the market. Unlike specialists on the stock market, scalpers are not assigned to any one market, nor do they hold an "inventory" of public orders. Their income is derived solely from their trading.

The activity of scalpers is not measurable in the day's end open positions since they do not generally have open positions. Rather, their activity is included in the volume of trading during the day, which also reflects the changes in positions of all other traders during the day. The daily volume figures contain almost no information on the composition of trading. Rutledge's survey of the scanty evidence suggested that 90–95 percent of the volume is speculative and most of that is likely to be market making.[29] On active markets like those for the grains, the volume of trading during the day averages one-quarter to one-third of the open interest. Thus, if position trading constitutes only one-quarter of the open interest, market making activity is nearly as large. Put another way, the largest class of speculation on a futures market will frequently be that of the market makers.

In spite of the market makers' comparative importance, only two direct studies have been made of the returns to market making. Examining two months of a "representative" cotton trader's record, Working estimated a gross return of \$4.64 per contract to his market making. More recently Silber analyzed the one and one-half month trading record of a "representative" market maker on the New York Futures Exchange (NYFE), finding gross returns of \$10.56 per contract.[30] In both cases the returns per contract were less than the minimum permitted unit price change—\$5 per contract in cotton and \$25 per contract for the stock index—a result consistent with Working's definition of the market-making trader. It should also be remembered that these are gross returns and do not account for the costs of clearing the trades or the costs of membership on the exchange.

Market makers may be seen as absorbing the temporary imbalances in timing of orders to buy and sell within a trading day. The direct association with imbalances in commercial users' demands breaks down, however, since market makers buy from and sell to other speculators as well. They do not distinguish among orders coming to the floor of an exchange. Their trading serves to match orders from buyers and sellers desiring to hold positions for longer periods of time who are not in the market at the same instant.

Distinguishing speculators as position traders, spread traders, and market makers emphasizes the importance of differences in perspectives and timing. It also fits conveniently into a market balance framework, which serves to underline the importance of speculation as responding to temporary imbalances among buyers and sellers in the marketplace. As noted earlier, however, the connection between their profits and specific imbalances is tenuous at best, particularly among position traders. Further, the assessment of the economic effects of speculation is a much broader topic than the assessment of its role in absorbing commercial demands on a market; it is considered in the section on price discovery below. Nevertheless, the market balance concept is useful in describing the comparative speculative composition of markets and in assessing instances of speculative inadequacy.

Comparative Levels of Speculation and Their Price Effects. To compare the composition of various markets, a single measure reflecting the level of speculation in relation to hedging is useful. Two such indexes have been used, both derived from the concept of market balance. At any time the total purchases of futures contracts must equal the total sales (for every buyer there must be a seller), and the total open interest in a contract is the sum of all sales or all purchases. If positions are categorized by whether they are held by hedgers or by speculators (either position traders or spreaders), the open interest may be subdivided on both the buying and the selling sides. Long speculation, SL, is the buying of both position traders and spreaders; when added to the buying of hedgers, HL, it must equal the total open interest and must also equal short speculation, SS, plus short hedging, HS. That is:

$$HL + SL \equiv HS + SS$$

Suppose, for example, that the total open interest in a market is 10 million contracts. If long hedgers hold 6 million of these, long speculators must be holding 4 million. Similarly, if short hedgers hold 5 million of the total, short speculators must hold the remaining 5 million. In the identity above, the open interest is not explicitly included. A market with the same amounts of hedging as above might have twice as much long speculation (that is, 8 million contracts). If so, short speculation would have to be 9 million contracts, and the total open interest would be 14 million. Differing amounts of speculation can accommodate the same amounts of hedging, although the open interest would vary as well.

The given amounts of long and short hedging also define the minimum amount of speculation that must be in this market. Conceptually at least, the 5 million sale contracts could be the purchase of 5 of the 6 million contracts held by long hedgers. Thus a minimum of 1 million contracts of short speculation are required by the unbalanced positions of commercial users.

The concept of minimum speculative requirements of a market is shown graphically in figure 1–5. The hedging ratio is defined as long hedging divided by short hedging when short hedging exceeds long hedging (and vice versa otherwise). In the example above, the

31

FIGURE 1–5

RELATION BETWEEN HEDGING AND SPECULATIVE RATIOS FOR WHEAT, CORN, AND SOYBEANS, 1964–1977

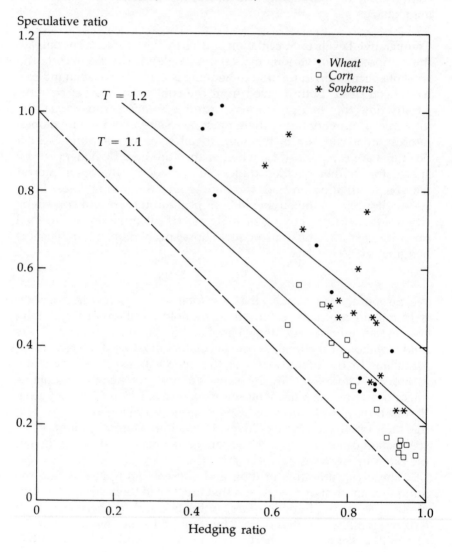

SOURCE: Anne E. Peck, "The Adequacy of Speculation on the Wheat, Corn, and Soybean Futures Markets," in Ray A. Goldberg, ed., *Research in Domestic and International Agribusiness Management* (Greenwich, Conn.: JAI Press, 1981), vol. 2, p. 23.

hedging ratio is 5/6, or 0.83. The hedging ratio is always less than one since the denominator always contains the larger of the two amounts of hedging (in this case 6 million contracts of long hedging). When short hedging is greater, the speculative ratio is long speculation (by definition, the greater of the two measures of speculation) divided by short hedging. When long hedging is greater, the ratio is short speculation divided by long hedging. In the original example with 10 million open interest, the speculative ratio is 5/6 (0.83), 5 million contracts of short speculation divided by 6 million long hedging. The speculative ratio can take any positive value.

The dotted line in the figure connects all points of minimally required speculation on markets with varying levels of unbalanced hedging (that is, with varying hedging ratios). Mathematically, the dotted line is

$$SR = 1 - HR$$

where SR = speculative ratio, and HR = hedging ratio. More generally, a series of lines parallel to the dotted line are defined as

$$SR = M - HR$$

Each such line represents market compositions that are equally speculative, although the degree of imbalance varies significantly for market compositions on the line. M, the intercept term, is strictly greater than one and is one measure of the degree of speculation, given data on market composition. In the earlier example, $M = SR + HR = 0.83 + 0.83 = 1.66$. In other words, speculation in the example was 66 percent greater than that minimally required to absorb the unbalanced hedging. M is an upper-bound estimate of the amount of speculation that might be considered "excess." By construction, the measure assumes that only net hedging must be absorbed by speculation; commercial buying and selling directly offset each other to the maximum extent possible.

A second measure recognizes that not all hedging on opposite sides of the market can be offsetting. Working observed that markets with very unbalanced hedging demands tend to require less relative speculation than those with more balanced hedging.[31] The solid lines in figure 1–5 show varying market compositions that are equally speculative in this view. Mathematically, the lines are defined by the relation

$$SR = (1 + \alpha) - (1 - \alpha)HR$$

and Working's index is $T = 1 + \alpha$, the intercept. Manipulation of the relation gives

$$T = 1 + \frac{SS}{HL + HS} \text{ when } HS \geq HL$$

$$= 1 + \frac{SL}{HS + HL} \text{ when } HL \geq HS$$

In the earlier example, $T = 1.36$; that is, in this view, speculation was only 36 percent greater than that required to absorb both the long and the short hedging. The Working index is probably a lower-bound estimate of the amount of speculation above that needed to absorb the commercial positions.

The data in table 1–1 are evidence of the extent to which speculation varies both over time in a given market and between markets. Estimates of the degree to which speculation is greater than minimally required by commercial use (M) range from 1.35 for wheat futures in the 1972–1977 period to 12.3 for pork bellies. The lower-bound estimates (T) range from 1.18 to 8.99. Thus speculation on wheat futures over the 1972–1977 period was 18 percent to 35 percent greater than required, depending on the definition. Speculation in pork belly futures, on the other extreme, was 800 to 1,100 percent greater than the minimum. By either measure, the contrast is striking.

The commodities for which speculative indexes are reported in table 1–1 appear to form two groups in the most recent period reported there. The wheat, corn, and soybean markets have generally low levels of speculation while Maine potatoes, live cattle, and pork bellies have substantially greater levels. Indeed, levels of speculation in pork belly futures may be so much greater than the others as to warrant putting them into a third group. Among the grains, wheat and corn appear less speculative than soybeans. Note, however, that the live cattle market is no more speculative than the soybean market was on average in the 1947–1971 period, and by current standards that was not a highly volatile period.

Perhaps the most interesting comparison in these data is the change in degree of speculation in the grain and oilseed markets before and after 1971–1972. The popular view would allege that all three of these markets became a great deal more speculative after the 1971–1972 crop year; indeed, speculation on these three futures markets was frequently alleged to be the source of both excessive price volatility and absolute price levels that were either "too high" or "too low." Absolute levels of speculation on these futures markets did in fact increase; but, the increase was dwarfed by increases in commercial use of the markets, and speculation declined dramatically

TABLE 1–1
MEASURES OF THE DEGREE OF SPECULATION ON SELECTED
COMMODITY FUTURES MARKETS, 1947–1977

	Index of Average Degree of Speculation	
	Lower bound (T)	Upper bound (M)
All wheat		
1947–1971	1.59	1.89
1972–1977	1.18	1.35
Corn		
1947–1971	1.61	1.92
1972–1977	1.20	1.40
Soybeans		
1947–1971	1.95	2.60
1972–1977	1.31	1.62
Maine potatoes		
1952–1974	2.92	3.37
Live cattle		
1971–1977	2.17	2.41
Pork bellies		
1970–1977	8.99	12.3

SOURCE: Adapted from Anne E. Peck, "The Role of Economic Analysis in Futures Market Regulation," *American Journal of Agricultural Economics*, vol. 62, no. 5, (1980), table 1, p. 1039. Calculations here assume that all unreported, small positions are speculative.

in relation to the demands placed on the market by commercial users. On each of the three principal markets, speculation was significantly below that experienced in the relatively calm, "nonspeculative" decades of the 1950s and 1960s.

The data plotted in figure 1–5 show the decline in speculation in much more detail than the averages in the table. For each commodity, crop-year annual average speculative indexes are plotted for the period 1964–1977. For all three commodities, the time-ordered observations show increasing balance in commercial uses. That is, ordering the observations from left to right along the horizontal axis is not a bad proxy for identifying them by years. With that identification, the data there clearly reveal the relative decline in speculation, with the observations from the more balanced and more recent markets lying closest to the dashed line defining minimal speculation.

These comparisons serve to emphasize the need to consider a

market's composition and balance in determining its degree of speculation. Having done this, one wants to draw conclusions about market performance from the comparative indicators. In the present context two aspects of the possible linkage beg for attention. First, are there measurable differences in pricing performance between markets like those for grains and livestock with their disparate levels of speculation? Second, are the declines in speculation on the grain and oilseeds markets related to any aspect of pricing performance? Unfortunately, very little research has attempted to examine the possible relations between market performance and composition.

The observed decreases in speculation in the grain and oilseeds markets have been associated statistically with increased price variability during the day, with other measures of price volatility and trading activity held constant. Given that these three markets evidenced relatively low levels of speculation and significant declines in speculation in recent years, the results were taken to suggest that speculation had become inadequate, unable to absorb commercial demands without significant, albeit short-run, price effects.

It is important to place these results in perspective. Causality was not established, merely statistical association. Further, no studies have been made of the relation between price volatility and the degree of speculation. It seems likely that there would be wide ranges of speculative accommodation of commercial positions that have no price effects. If the association reported here is evidence of a relation between inadequate speculation and price volatility, it is also likely that excessive speculation may be associated with increased volatility. The data from these markets are simply not from markets with excessive speculation. The absence of research notwithstanding, the concept of excessive speculation has a long history in the regulation of futures markets.

Excessive Speculation and the Role of Speculative Position Limits. Congressional concern about commodity futures markets dates to the late 1880s and arose from the widely held perception that futures markets were speculative markets. In fact, the first futures bills to be seriously debated in Congress—the Hatch and Washburn bills in the House and Senate—were bills to tax speculative purchases and sales of grain and cotton futures contracts discriminatorily. Cowing reports that the bills passed their respective houses of Congress by substantial majorities—80 percent of Congress favored them—but ultimately failed because the vote to suspend the rules at the end of the Fifty-second Congress to give the House time to consider differences in the two bills fell short of the required two-thirds majority.[32]

The Grain Futures Act of 1922 was the first legislation authorizing federal regulation of futures markets. The constitutional authority for such regulation came from commerce clauses in section 3 of the act: futures transactions are

> affected with a national public interest; . . . that the transactions and prices of grain on such boards of trade are susceptible to speculation, manipulation, and control, and sudden or unreasonable fluctuations in the prices thereof frequently occur as a result of such speculation, manipulation, or control . . . and that such fluctuations in prices are an obstruction to and burden upon interstate commerce in grain.[33]

Section 3 of the present legislation, the Futures Trading Act of 1982, is virtually identical, although specific references to grains have been deleted in favor of more general terminology. The Grain Futures Administration, though largely an oversight agency, was empowered to collect reports of individuals' trading activity as needed for market oversight and to require exchanges to maintain records.

Major review and revisions of the legislation, the Commodity Exchange Act of 1936, added more specific antispeculative clauses, empowering regulators to establish limits on the amount of futures contracts in a single commodity an individual speculator could own at the end of the day or could trade during the day. Bona fide hedgers were exempted from the so-called position limits, and, since the distinction required a definition of hedging, the section went on to define hedging.

Whether by design or not, the 1936 act thus isolates a concern separate from manipulation, which is itself dealt with at length in later sections of the act. Bona fide hedgers are, for example, not exempted from the prohibitions against manipulation, and Johnson notes that at least half the alleged manipulation cases brought under the act have been cases against hedgers.[34] Such allegations almost always focus on delivery situations and concern substantial positions held in the underlying physical market as well as the futures market.

The perceived need for the new section arose largely from the results of a detailed analysis of two "unusual" price episodes in the 1925 and 1926 wheat markets. The analysis, summarized by Hoffman, indicated a substantial positive relation between changes in positions of large traders (those owning 500,000 bushels or more) and daily price changes and an even greater degree of association with position changes of very large (2 million bushels) traders.[35] In addition, the net positions of large traders were compared to price changes over time. Petzel's recent analysis of the data from the 1925 episode confirms a significant degree of same-day correlation between position changes of the twenty largest speculators and price changes. He found no evidence, however, of significant lead or lag cross-correlations; hence, causality between the positions and prices cannot in fact be deduced from the data.[36]

Nevertheless, these two episodes created significant concern about the effects on markets of very large speculative positions, whether or not such positions were established with the intent or even the result of manipulating prices. Perhaps the clearest example of the distinction drawn by this section of the act is in its best-known violation. In 1976 the Hunt family was found to be in violation of the speculative position limits in soybeans, holding an aggregate position of 22.7 million bushels, which is substantially above the limit of 3 million bushels. Even though the aggregate position was large, price manipulation was never alleged.

Speculative position limits were originally established at 2 million bushels on the major markets. The level reflected the high correlation found between prices and positions of the largest speculators in the two earlier (1925 and 1926) episodes in the wheat market. The initial limits have been revised only in the past decade to 3 million bushels, and limits were established only for commodities regulated by the Commodity Exchange Authority. More recently the CFTC has required that position limits be established for virtually all futures markets, directing the exchanges to establish limits for all commodities for which there are no federal limits. In addition, the restriction on the amount of trading during a trading session has been removed. Only positions open at the end of the session are limited.

Limits on the positions of individual speculators as distinct from other traders required, perforce, a definition of bona fide hedging. The remainder of section 4a in the act defined legitimate commercial uses that would be exempt from speculative limits. The early definition of hedgers was quite restrictive, including only those who actually owned the underlying commodity, who had fixed sales commitments, or who produced the commodity. Subsequent revisions broadened the definition somewhat by including those who might use futures to cover prospective needs of the commodity, as for example, in processing. Such positions were limited to twelve months' normal requirements. In 1974 specific legislative definitions were removed, and the new CFTC was directed to promulgate regulations defining bona fide hedging transactions and positions. The new regulations significantly broadened the definition of hedging, including for the first time cross-hedging as a legitimate commercial use.

The difficulties with this approach are clear. Almost any definition of bona fide hedging will be restrictive—some legitimate commercial uses will be excluded. The closer the identification of futures positions with either actual or prospective cash market positions, the more restrictive will be the definition. Second, the historical record shows that changes in the established limits are very infrequent and generally not responsive to changing levels of market use. When established in 1936, the 2-million-bushel limits constituted some 1.5 percent of the average open contracts in the Chicago wheat market and 3.0 percent of those in corn. In 1977–1978 the new 3-million-bushel limits were still only 1.4 percent of the average open interest in wheat and 0.5 percent in corn. Even a 3-million-bushel position today is not nearly so large as a 2-million-bushel position was in 1936. A related problem is whether "large" should be defined in relation to the futures market alone or whether some reference to the physical market is appropriate. The potential price effects of a large speculative position must surely differ according to whether the underlying commodity is in short supply or is ample.

Definitional difficulties aside, a concern over excessive speculation is in fact a concern about large speculative positions and their disruptive potential in a market. Regulation of excessive speculation is regulation of large traders. In this view, the pork belly market is not excessively speculative, nor are waves of public speculation in specific markets matters for concern. More generally, there is no direct connection in this regulatory view between hedging demands in a market and levels of speculation. In at least one respect this separation is justified. There are no examples of futures markets that continue to exist only as speculative markets. If substantial commercial use does not develop on a new market or commercial use declines on an existing market, the market declines. Nevertheless, studies of the relation between pricing performance and the levels and composition of overall speculation would surely be useful in establishing the need for and appropriate design of controls on speculative excesses.

Conclusions. Speculation on commodity prices occurs with or without futures markets. There can be no doubt that a futures market increases such speculation since a potential futures speculator need not invest in facilities to produce, store, market, process, or otherwise use the commodity. It remains to consider the effects of futures markets on the process of commodity price formation. Narrowly conceived, the issue is whether futures markets and the accompanying increase in speculation stabilize or destabilize commodity prices. "Narrowly" is used advisedly—speculation on futures markets affects the stability of commodity prices only through its effects on the allocative decisions of commercial users. As Gray notes, price variation over time will change only insofar as hedgers change their buying and selling decisions to reflect changes in their rates of production or consumption of the underlying commodity.[37]

The Role and Effects of Futures Markets in Commodity Storage

A futures market provides simultaneous quotations of value for a commodity deliverable at successively distant dates. This proposition, though so basic as not to need statement, indicates that important economic effects of futures markets derive from their role in facilitating storage decisions in markets for storable commodities. This section begins by describing the relations among futures prices, first for perfectly storable commodities like gold and silver and then for storable agricultural products. Pricing characteristics with and without futures markets are considered, and the particular effects of futures markets on storage decisions and hence on prices are derived. Finally, the empirical evidence of these effects is summarized.

The focus in this section is on holders of stocks, their willingness to carry inventory over time, and the role of futures markets in their decisions. To the extent that futures affect storage decisions, prices of the commodity over time will also be affected. In empirically assessing the effects of futures markets in this regard, however, it is not possible to isolate their storage effects from the concurrent influences of improved information, a centralized marketplace, and more efficient speculation. For example, the analysis of storage decisions suggests that futures markets reduce seasonal price fluctuations for storable commodities. Much the same conclusion is reached, however, in arguing that futures markets improve the information content of market prices by reducing transaction costs. Thus, although the focus here is on commercial uses of futures and their implications, the more general context of the empirical assessments cannot be ignored.

The Theory of the Price of Storage. The difference between two simultaneously quoted prices for successive delivery dates for a storable commodity must relate to the costs of storing that commodity between the two dates, as long as supplies of the commodity are ample. Consider, for example, the prices of silver deliverable in June and September, both quoted in June. Silver is perfectly storable, is continuously produced, and is virtually always available in ample quantity. (The only recent exception to the assumption of ample supply was the extraordinary accumulation of silver by the Hunt family in 1979–1980.) In this circumstance arbitrage can be relied on to ensure that the difference in price between two futures contracts is no more or less than the costs of storage. If the difference widens beyond costs, it is a simple matter to buy the nearby future (June), sell the more distant (September), accept and finance delivery of silver in June, and redeliver in September. If the difference is less than storage costs, it clearly pays to defer actual purchases, buying instead the more distant (but underpriced) future. As long as supplies are ample, anyone who desires to own silver will buy it through futures purchases until the full storage costs are reflected in the price differences.

The costs of storage that determine the spread are physical storage costs (warehousing and insurance) plus financial costs. Physical costs are constant for silver, but financial costs are not. Even with a constant interest rate, changes in the price of silver imply changes in financing costs and hence in the full costs of storage. With changing interest rates as well as changing silver prices, the spreads between delivery months will vary substantially, although the variation is directly related to interest rates. In examining futures price differences in the gold market, for example, Gray and Rutledge found that 85 percent of the weekly variation was explained by variation in short-term interest rates.[38]

The relation between futures prices for a storable agricultural commodity was first investigated by Holbrook Working.[39] His analysis showed that the difference between two simultaneously quoted prices for wheat with different delivery times was directly related to the level of private or free stocks of wheat available at the nearby delivery date. The price difference is thus a market-determined price of storage. If supplies are large, the market's price of storage approximates the total costs of storage, as in the silver market. In these circumstances hedging of stored wheat ensures a return to storage that covers costs and merchants are encouraged to store wheat that is currently in surplus. If, however, current supplies are relatively small, the market's price of storage is less than the full costs of storage and can be negative. In these circumstances an owner of hedged wheat earns a return on storage less than that required to cover the full costs. The market-determined disincentive for continued storage is the amount by which the market's price for storage falls below the full costs of storage. This amount is determined by current supplies.

41

As in the silver market, arbitrage can be relied on to prevent the difference from exceeding the full costs of storage. Unlike silver stocks, however, wheat stocks vary significantly during the crop year, and with increasing scarcity arbitrage cannot prevent the difference from declining to less than full costs. As scarcity increases, the owners of the remaining stock place more and more value on the flexibility their ownership provides. New orders can be more readily accommodated and processing operations more nearly planned if, in growing scarcity, the merchant actually has the requisite stocks. Ownership yields convenience in these circumstances, and the degree of benefit increases with decreases in available market stocks.

For seasonal commodities, then, a third element in the cost of storage is the so-called convenience yield. In periods of ample supply the convenience derived from actual ownership is zero. With decreasing supplies convenience increases, and the net marginal costs of storage decline. Because scarcity is relative, there is no upper bound on the potential value to a merchant of ownership. Hence there is no lower bound on the possible negative difference between futures prices for a seasonal, storable agricultural product. Negative prices of storage, sometimes called inverse carrying charges, occur regularly in grain markets—reflecting seasonal, temporary shortages of grain. In his analysis of the wheat market, Working found that the degree of inverse in price between a nearby and a more distant future reflects the extent and significance of current storage.

Working summarized the relation between futures price differences and stocks of a commodity in the so-called supply-of-storage curve shown in figure 1–6. The relation shifted during the thirty-year period of his analysis, but its implications are clear. Stocks levels and price differences are closely related in a very nonlinear fashion. Large stocks will be carried between crop years when the market's price of storage covers the full costs of storage. For example, the large wheat carryouts of 1892 and 1893 in Working's figure constituted more than one-half of the average annual wheat production for that period.

Since Working's analysis, supply-of-storage curves have been estimated for a number of commodities. The empirical relation is almost always estimated by using year-end stocks of the commodity and the price difference between the last old crop future and the first new crop future. Even in a year of relatively small production, stocks immediately after the harvest are normally plentiful, and the markets nearly always reflect full carrying costs during this period. Significant variation in year-end stocks is common, however, and permits a clear view of the underlying relations. Examples of more

FIGURE 1–6

RELATION OF WHEAT STOCKS TO CARRYING CHARGE
IN CHICAGO WHEAT FUTURES, 1892–1932

Price difference between July and September wheat futures
(September over or under July, in cents per bushel)

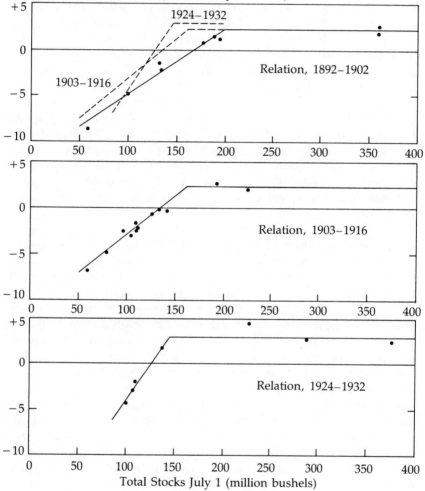

Total Stocks July 1 (million bushels)

SOURCE: Holbrook Working, "Hedging Reconsidered."

recent estimates of supply-of-storage relations are available for wheat, cocoa, coffee, and cotton.[40] The analyses are not identical; each commodity and time period introduces its own complications. In more recent analyses adjustments in the observed price differences must be made for interest rate variation and its effect on the financial

43

component of storage costs. In many markets government agencies have become significant owners of commodity stocks, and total stocks must be adjusted by the percentage of government ownership each year.

In addition, Weymar demonstrated the logical necessity of including expectations in explaining observed price spreads.[41] For example, an analysis of the September quotations of the May/July wheat spread requires estimates, in September, of stocks expected in May. Similarly, if the price difference covers a fairly substantial period, for instance a December/July spread in wheat, events anticipated between December and July must have an influence. These effects are particularly important in the imported commodity markets, where the level of stocks on a particular date in the future depends heavily on shipments anticipated before that date. In such circumstances it is also true that the surplus or shortage reflected in a specific level of stocks will depend to a significant extent on the shipments expected after that date. With these caveats, the main point is that the observed price differences are reliable reflections of current surplus or shortage.

The Role of the Price of Storage in Facilitating Storage Decisions. The remaining question is how futures markets affect merchants' storage decisions. Stocks of a seasonally produced, storable commodity will vary during the year and between crop years with or without a futures market. In the absence of a futures market, the price difference important in storage decisions is that between today's cash price and an expected price. Simply stated, if prices are expected to increase, merchants are willing to carry more stocks than if they are not. Brennan provided empirical evidence of such storage relations in estimates of the relation between monthly expected price changes and levels of stocks for cheese, butter, and eggs—markets that did not have active futures markets.[42] The estimated relations (not reproduced here) are very similar to the supply-of-storage curves described earlier. Thus futures markets do not determine whether storage will occur but affect the decision to store and the predictability of storage returns.

In the absence of a futures market, the storage return is speculative and depends entirely on events that occur after the decision to store or not is made. With a futures market, storage returns can largely be determined at the time the decision to store is made if that decision is hedged with a classic, arbitrage hedge. The evidence presented earlier was clear: returns from hedged storage were substantially more predictable and stable than returns from unhedged storage.

A futures market facilitates storage decisions through the substantial guidance it provides about prospective returns and through its substantial reduction of risks. It is the combination of these effects that is important. The price-of-storage relations show that futures prices reflect current surplus and shortage well. They thus guide inventory decisions in a rational way. In periods of surplus the market reflects full carrying charges and thus induces storage. In periods of shortage less than full costs are available, inducing merchants to sell unneeded stocks. The more severe the current shortage, the stronger the market-reflected inducement to bring stocks to the market. That the storage decision can be hedged implies that risks are reduced and more storage is likely at all prices. The analysis suggests that effects of a futures market on prices for a storable commodity are both seasonal and annual. Prices within crop years are stabilized, as are those between crop years.

Analyses of Seasonal Price Variation. It is logical to look first at within-season price variability to assess the effects of futures markets. Since most of the major accumulation and decumulation of stocks of a commodity occurs within the crop year, the strongest effects might be expected within the crop year. Prices of storable commodities as diverse as wheat, onions, and pork bellies have been examined. In each analysis seasonal variation in prices during a period before futures trading was introduced was compared with that from a period after trading began. Interpreting the results of these analyses requires a number of caveats, which are addressed after the evidence is summarized.

Although onions are a relatively obscure commodity, legislative concern over futures trading and its eventual ban occasioned several analyses of their seasonal price volatility. In the first, Working demonstrated that the period of futures trading was associated with much reduced average seasonal price changes in the onion market.[43] Gray's analysis of data from a period of years after the futures market had been closed established that the onion market returned to its earlier pattern of volatility.[44] Their combined results are shown in figure 1–7. The period 1949–1958, during which the onion futures market was active, was the period of the least seasonal variation in prices. Variation both before and after was significantly higher.

Most of the commodities for which these tests are applicable are commodities in which futures trading originated and for which price

FIGURE 1–7
Index Numbers of Marketing Season Prices Received by Farmers for Onions, Selected Periods, 1922–1962

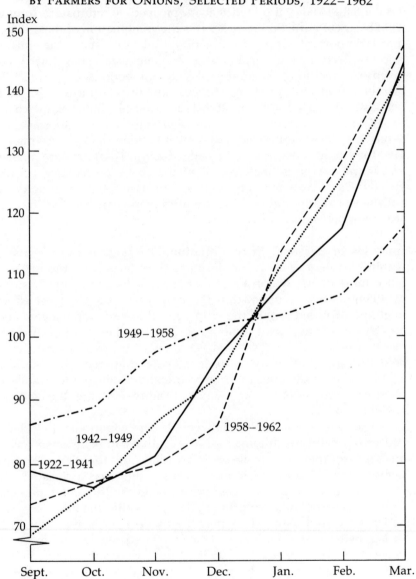

NOTE: The periods of no futures markets are 1922–1941 and 1958–1962; 1942–1949 was a transition period with little trading, and 1949–1958 was the period of active futures trading in onions.
SOURCE: Gray, "Onions Revisited."

data are difficult to assemble. Tomek, however, examined an eighty-one-year record of monthly wheat prices from 1841 to 1921, a period that spanned the development of the wheat futures market, and found a significant reduction in seasonal price variation after futures markets became active.[45]

In addition to assessing the effect of futures markets on seasonal price change, research has also examined their related effects on short-run price volatility. Working, for example, found that a significant decline in within-month price volatility was also associated with the period of active futures trading in onions. Powers found significant declines in monthly volatility in pork belly prices after the introduction of futures markets. Taylor and Leuthold examined monthly and weekly price variation in the live cattle market from periods before and after the introduction of futures trading.[46] Both series showed significant declines in short-run volatility in relation to annual average price levels. Live cattle, though not storable in the usual sense, can be fed for varying periods, and current prices in relation to very near-term futures can guide the pace of marketing finished animals in a way analogous to storage decisions. As the authors all note, however, the effects on volatility measured by weekly and monthly data cannot be separated from the effects of improved information per se.

As the analyses demonstrate, futures markets are significantly associated with both reduced seasonal variation and short-term volatility of commodity prices, as predicted by the supply-of-storage and arbitrage arguments. The term "significantly associated with" is used advisedly here, since before-and-after comparisons cannot establish causality directly. Tomek's analysis of the wheat market is the most extreme case in point, of which Tomek himself was very aware. He notes that "observed changes in price behavior cannot be attributed solely to the advent of futures trading" and goes on to discuss changes in transportation and especially communications that also occurred over his data period and would be expected to have similar effects on prices.[47] Similar caveats, though perhaps not so extreme, apply to the other analyses as well. Although causality cannot be inferred in each case, the consistency of the evidence among commodities is reassuring and does suggest causality. The results are as predicted, and, to my knowledge, no contradictory results have been found for any storable commodity.

Analyses of Annual Price Variation. It is not so straightforward to evaluate the effects of futures markets on price variation between years. Futures markets provide forward prices as well as indications

TABLE 1–2

COMPARATIVE RESPONSIVENESS OF EXPORTS AND YEAR-END STOCKS
TO INCREASES AND DECREASES IN DOMESTIC PRODUCTION OF WHEAT,
FOUR MAJOR EXPORTING COUNTRIES, 1970–1971 TO 1980–1981
(millions of metric tons)

	Average Deviation from Trend Values		Average Change in Year-End Stocks
	Production	Exports	
United States			
Increased production	3.1	−2.6	5.1
Decreased production	−3.0	1.8	−5.7
Canada			
Increased production	1.7	0.2	−0.3
Decreased production	−2.9	−0.3	−4.1
Argentina			
Increased production	1.3	1.0	0.0
Decreased production	−1.0	−1.0	0.0
Australia			
Increased production	2.1	0.5	1.1
Decreased production	−1.7	−0.4	−2.0

SOURCE: Adapted from Anne E. Peck, "Futures Markets, Food Imports, and Food Security," Agriculture and Rural Development Division Working Paper no. 43, World Bank.

of storage returns and, as between crop years, also influence prospective production and consumption decisions. Their effects on year-end storage levels are thus not separable from simultaneous supply-and-demand adjustments, and any effect on annual price stability is a joint effect. The difficulty in directly evaluating the between-year storage effects of futures markets seems even more perverse given that the supply-of-storage curve is usually estimated by using year-end stocks data and thus specifically depicts the stocks and stabilization possibilities of interest.

The clear responsiveness of U.S. stocks to prices of storage led Working to analyze the price responsiveness of storage in relation to that in other countries where there were no futures markets.[48] He concluded that nearly one-half of the year-to-year changes in U.S. production of wheat were absorbed in changes in year-end stocks. In contrast, the other major wheat-exporting countries exported most of their production variability, and adjustments in stocks were of

TABLE 1–3

COMPARATIVE RESPONSIVENESS OF EXPORTS AND YEAR-END STOCKS
TO INCREASES AND DECREASES IN DOMESTIC PRODUCTION OF CORN,
TWO MAJOR EXPORTING COUNTRIES, 1970–1971 TO 1980–1981
(millions of metric tons)

	Average Deviation from Trend Values		Average Change in Year-End Stocks
	Production	Exports	
United States			
Increased production	10.8	0.9	3.4
Decreased production	−9.4	−1.0	−6.4
Argentina			
Increased production	1.2	1.0	0.1
Decreased production	−1.5	−1.2	−0.1

SOURCE: Adapted from Peck, "Futures Markets, Food Imports, and Food Security."

only minor importance. Comparable analyses of more recent data from both the corn and wheat markets are shown in tables 1–2 and 1–3, although their interpretation is admittedly less straightforward. The basic data on production, exports, and stocks change for each country are adjusted to deviations from a linear trend. For each country, the eleven-year period (1970–1971 to 1980–1981 crop years) is divided into years of production increases (more than trend) and those of production decreases. For each group of years export deviations (from their trends) and stock changes were recorded, and all three series were averaged by group to obtain the numbers in the tables.

For U.S. wheat years of increased production averaged 3.1 million metric tons (mmt) greater than trend values. Exports in these years actually declined by 2.6 mmt, and stocks necessarily increased an average of 5.1 mmt from the previous year. Similarly, in years of decreased U.S. production, exports increased, and again stocks absorbed both changes. This responsiveness on the part of U.S. stocks holders contrasts sharply with stocks behavior among the other major exporters. Argentina shows the sharpest difference. Virtually all the changes in production were absorbed by exports, and none appear in stock changes. Storage in both Canada and Australia was somewhat more responsive, but neither country absorbed nearly as much of its own instability as the United States did. International comparisons in the corn market are more difficult because the United States is by far the largest exporter. Comparisons between the United States and Argentina are shown in table 1–3. Though perhaps less meaningful, the contrast is striking. Stock changes absorb almost none of the production variability in Argentina but account for about half the variation in the United States.

The differences in the role of storage among the major grain exporters are striking. The United States is the least destabilizing major exporter in the world market and is the only exporter with active grain futures markets. Not all of this contrast, of course, can be attributed to the greater responsiveness of stocks in the United States induced by futures markets. Some of it must be attributed to government policies, especially to the marketing boards prevalent in the other major exporters. Combined, however, with Working's evidence from the earlier period—a period during which such interventions were not significant—the evidence is very suggestive. If permitted to do so, storage responds to prices in a way that will stabilize international commodity markets and is particularly impressive in the presence of futures markets.

The Role and Effects of Futures Markets in Forward Pricing

The preceding section focused on storable commodities, the meaning of futures price relations for those commodities, and the effects of futures markets on storage decisions and hence on price stability over time. By rationalizing storage decisions, futures markets led to more stable seasonal price variation. Most storable commodities are annually (rather than continuously) produced, are stored for consumption during the crop year, and are carried in significant but variable quantities between crop years.

Examining the role of storage between crop years is only a partial analysis of the effects of futures markets. In addition to the stocks response, the additional crop year brings new production and the prospect of substantially revised consumption needs. A complete analysis must thus consider the effects of futures markets not only on stocks carried between crop years but also on the amounts of new production and prospective consumption. This section considers these issues. With a focus on production and consumption adjustments facilitated by futures markets, it is no longer necessary (or desirable) to restrict the discussion to storable commodities. In fact, the economic analysis is considerably simplified if interseasonal storage is not a factor. Therefore, this section begins with an analysis of the effects of futures markets for nonstorable commodities and then considers the additional effects of storability. The simple models lend themselves to a welfare analysis as well, and tests of market performance are summarized in that framework.

Nonstorable Commodities. Conceptually, the role of futures markets for nonstorable commodities is simple—they reflect in prices anticipated supply and demand. A necessary complexity when dealing with agricultural products, however, is to include the requisite lags between the planning and realization of production. With annual, nonstorable crops, the lags connect crop years—production realized in the current crop year was planned in the preceding crop year. For livestock commodities the lags are more complex; they can include feeding periods, farrowing decisions, and even decisions to expand or contract the breeding stock. The analysis here presents the simplest case; modifications required for the more complex relations are then considered.

In the absence of a futures market, producers must form an independent expectation of what prices will be at harvest at the time they make their production decisions. As D. Gale Johnson noted nearly forty years ago, resources will be misallocated to the extent that producers' forecasts are retrospective and not prospective.[49] Resource misallocation implies significant social losses. The situation is illustrated in figure 1–8 with linear supply and demand curves. The supply curve is an expected supply relation in the sense that actual supplies will depend on a number of unpredictable events after planting and before harvest. Market demand is also an expectation. In any particular year it could shift up or down depending on consumer incomes, prices of other goods, or the level of export or import demand. Confronted with these prospective relations, the rational producer would conclude that the expected price is $\overline{P}$ and would gauge planned production accordingly to $\overline{Q}$. Any other expected price would be self-defeating. A higher one would induce more production, which would cause lower realized prices at harvest. Similarly, a lower expected price would create higher prices. Thus, if all producers were rational in the sense that they anticipated the effects of their collective production decisions, they would plan to produce an amount $\overline{Q}$ of the commodity.

In contrast with the model, numerous studies of producers' supply response in this situation have found that producers form their expectations of next year's price on the basis of current and past prices. Perhaps the most widely (and successfully) used model of the decision is Nerlove's adaptive model, which assumes that

FIGURE 1–8
INTERTEMPORAL PRICING OF A NONSTORABLE COMMODITY

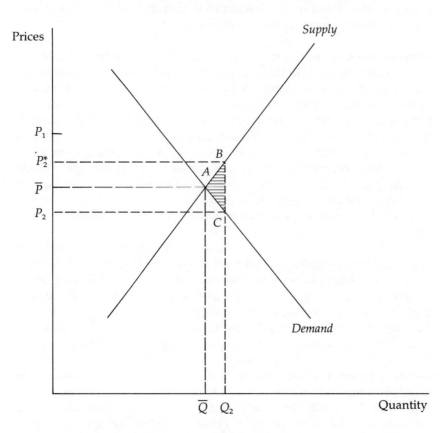

producers change their view of expected price from year to year by a proportion of the error they made in the preceding year.[50] The assumption implies that producers' expected price is a weighted average of past prices, where increasingly distant prices have decreasing effect. A number of other approaches have also been employed to extrapolate expected prices from past prices, but the Nerlovian model has remained one of the most popular.[51] It is particularly convenient for present purposes, although similar results could be derived with any of the extrapolative models. The essential point is that all such models assume that current and past prices are used to formulate expected prices.

Suppose that current prices in the figure are P_1, perhaps because of an unfavorable growing season and a consequent relative shortage. If producers had expected a price of $\bar{P}$, the adaptive expectation model implies that some portion of the forecast error $(P_1 - \bar{P})$ will affect their forecasts for next year, for example, to a price P_2^*. This expected price calls forth too much production given an unchanged demand relation, and actual prices in the next period will be P_2. The forecast, P_2^*, was self-defeating, eliciting a supply that could not be sold at that price. As is well known, such a response causes social losses and unnecessary price instability, which could be eliminated with a rational forward price, that is, one that reflected the joint actions of producers and consumers. If the expected price for the second period was $\bar{P}$, there would be no ex ante misallocation of resources or social loss, whereas the losses associated with P_2^* are the shaded area on the figure.[52] After the fact losses may still occur if demand shifts or if yields are not as expected, but such losses cannot be reduced by planting-time adjustments of producers.

The question then is to what extent a futures market influences these relations. A particularly interesting example derives from the potato market and Maine potato futures trading. In the 1940s a futures market in Maine potatoes began on the New York Mercantile Exchange, becoming an active market in the early 1950s. Delivery months began with the harvest in November and extended until the end of the storage season in May. Although no fall potatoes are stored from May until the new crop is available in November, the futures contracts for that crop traded well in advance of the producers' production decisions in the spring and continued trading over the growing period. The first new crop future, the November contract, began trading in the preceding November or December, well in advance of the April planting decision. Thus the market provided a continuously available forward price by which producers could gauge their production and which was not linked to current conditions by interyear storage.

Before planting decisions, the market had to reflect both the prospective supply relation and the response of consumers once that supply was available. Tomek and Gray analyzed the preplanting quotations of the November futures and compared them with the eventual harvest prices. The results are shown graphically in figure 1–9.[53] The preplanting (February 28) quotation of the November future is plotted against the final closing price, both deflated by an appropriate index. The data, taken from the 1953–1971 crop years, form a nearly vertical line: the preplanting futures price was a virtual constant from year to year. Every year the preplanting quotation was

FIGURE 1–9

FEBRUARY 28 AND FINAL CLOSING PRICES OF NOVEMBER POTATO
FUTURES, DEFLATED BY ANNUAL INDEX OF PRICES RECEIVED FOR ALL
FARM PRODUCTS, 1953–1971

(dollars per hundredweight)

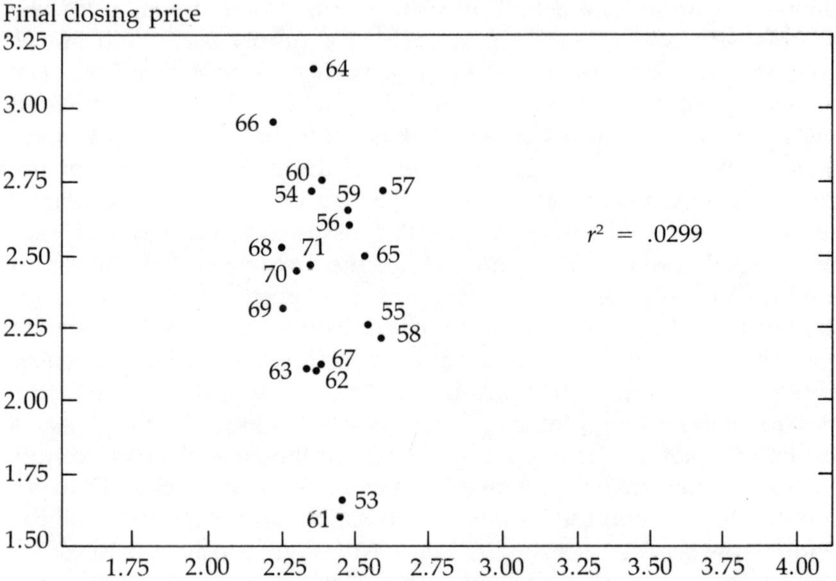

Final closing price

$r^2 = .0299$

February 28 closing price

SOURCE: Roger W. Gray, "The Futures Market for Maine Potatoes: An Appraisal,"
Food Research Institute Studies, vol. 11, no. 3 (1972), p. 324.

approximately the mean price, $\bar{P}$. Actual prices at harvest varied
from year to year, causing the vertical scatter of observations in the
figure.

The effects of this market-determined forward price on Maine
potato producers' decisions were dramatic. Before futures markets,
a Nerlove adjustment model explained some 75 percent of the annual
acreage planted, and both past prices and acreage were significant
explanatory variables.[54] Gray's reestimates of the supply relation with
data from the period of an active futures market found that neither
lagged price nor lagged acreage coefficients of the same Nerlovian
model were significant explanatory variables and that the regression
explained only 7 percent of Maine producers' decisions.[55] Maine
acreage planted to potatoes had virtually stabilized during the period
of an active futures market. The rational, if constant, futures prices

had completely eliminated the retrospective responses of Maine growers. In this circumstance the ex ante social loss was eliminated because, every year, the futures price was the mean price, $\overline{P}$.

The rational anticipation of Maine potato prices and the consequent stabilization of production are even more interesting when they are set against the continued retrospective responses of potato producers in other major producing areas. Other production was not deliverable on the Maine contract, and producers, especially in the West, did not respond to the futures prices. Gray's estimates show that they continued using current and past prices to form an expectation and hence their production continued a cobweb-like, feast or famine cycle. Consequently, harvest-time potato prices continued in a cobweb-like pattern. The price pattern was so pronounced that the last year's price could predict some 53 percent of the variation in the current year's price, whereas the predictive accuracy of the preplanting futures prices was nil. Not only was the market providing a rational forward price, but it was doing so at the same time that reasonably reliable predictions of the eventual outcomes were available. Cash prices in the current year were a good, if perverse, forecast of prices in the following year. Futures prices, however, remained responsive to both demand and potential supply adjustments and therefore remained at equilibrium prices at least until actual production decisions had been made. Such prices, though not useful as predictions in this circumstance, dramatically affected production decisions.

The Maine potato market is not the only example of a nonstorable commodity in which a futures market was introduced. Fresh eggs, live hogs, and live cattle are other examples, but these systems differ significantly as well. They are nonstorable commodities in the sense that, once delivered on a futures contract, none can be redelivered on a subsequent contract. Unlike potatoes, however, they are continuously produced through production processes that can be significantly altered at several stages. For live animals, decision points include breeding, putting on feed, the rate of gain while on feed, and variable marketing weights. As a consequence, there is substantial short-run price responsiveness in actual marketings of the finished animals.[56] For fresh eggs, the key decisions are about the size of the laying flock, and they are price responsive nearly continuously.

Because of the relatively complicated production processes, models of the potential allocative effects of futures prices are much more complex analytically. There have, however, been a number of evaluations of the "forecasting" performance of futures prices on these markets—to what extent they anticipate eventual cash prices—and comparisons of futures price performance with that of other potential forecasts. Such comparisons are clearly relevant to the question at hand, although their interpretation is not always straightforward.

In the simplest system futures prices were useless "forecasts," and better forecasts were easily constructed; nevertheless, the futures prices were rational and optimal in a welfare sense. Martin and Garcia provide comparative analyses of the forecasting performances of the cattle and hog markets.[57] In both markets and over almost all forecast horizons (one to eight months before maturity of each future), futures prices were found to be unbiased estimates of the eventual cash prices. Futures prices more than two or three months from their expiration date, however, were not good predictors—they explained eventual prices very poorly. In fact, lagged values of the actual cash prices did nearly as well and in some cases were even better.

The relatively poor forecasting performance of futures prices for hogs is further developed in the work of Leuthold and Hartmann.[58] They compared futures prices with forecasts from a purposely simple recursive model of supply and demand for hogs and found that their simple model predicted subsequent prices consistently better than futures prices did. They report 125 percent and 141 percent rates of return from trading futures based on the forecasts of their naive model. The evidence leads them to conclude that the live hog market is inefficient in an information sense since it does not reflect publicly available information well.

The interesting aspects of the evidence are the parallels with the evidence from the potato market. Potato futures prices were unbiased but useless predictors—results not very dissimilar from Martin and Garcia's results. Better predictions were available, as for the Leuthold and Hartmann results. In both cases the better forecasts were based on models tht precluded any response by producers to the predicted price. These similarities to the potato market results certainly suggest that the live animal markets are also rational pricing markets. Rational forward prices allocate productive resources optimally, and thus a major effect of futures markets for nonstorable commodities is in rationalizing production decisions. The evidence also shows that rational prices may not be informationally efficient; as Stein has shown, however, efficiency is irrelevant to the welfare effect of futures markets, which is the present concern.[59]

Storable Commodities. The possibility of storing the commodity between production periods fundamentally alters the preceding analysis. For a storable commodity, relations among futures prices of differing maturities reflect the market value of continued storage and provide a reliable guide to the returns that can be expected from that storage. Evidence adduced in the preceding section showed that storage decisions within crop years were affected and resulted in less extreme seasonal price changes. The focus here is on the additional effects of a futures market on consumption and production decisions, that is, on the expectational character of futures prices.

The simplest storable commodity is one like corn or wheat that is produced once a year, is consumed continuously, and can be stored between seasons. The possibility of interyear storage requires consideration of the supply and demand expected in the following year; indeed, in the extreme, all future years must be considered.[60] For present purposes the level of stocks carried out of the second year is assumed to be known, fixed at average levels. The assumption is a strong one, but it simplifies the discussion immeasurably without significantly changing the conclusions. With the assumption, there are still seven important relations: supply and demand in the present period; supply and demand in the next period; market-clearing equations for each period; and a cost-of-storage relation.

The basic model is shown in figure 1–10. To focus on the interyear adjustments and the role of futures markets, supply in the current year (Q_1) is assumed known. In other words, this year's harvest is in, and current period prices must be determined. These prices depend on the consumption this period but also on expected prices next year, since some of the crop may be carried forward into the following crop year. D_1 and D_2 are the anticipated demand relations in each year, and Q_2 is the expected supply relation in the second period. The lower panel shows the cost-of-storage relation SS with stock levels shown as deviations from equilibrium levels. In equilibrum production is $\overline{Q}$ in each period, prices are $\overline{P}$, and stocks do not change between periods. That is, since there is incentive to store neither more nor less than average, the stocks relation is shown in this form.

To consider the effect of storage on commodity pricing, suppose first that the present crop is larger than normal, Q_1^+. If storage were not possible, prices in the present period would decline to A, all the excess would be consumed in the present period, and there would be no residual effects on expectations in the coming crop year. With the possibility of storage, some of the present surplus can be transferred to the next period. As prices in the present period decline toward A, owners of storage space will begin to have an incentive to store. How much they will store depends on the marginal costs of storage and the realization that the amount stored from the present period will add to surplus in the next period and have significant

FIGURE 1–10

INTERTEMPORAL PRICING OF A STORABLE COMMODITY

Two-Period Pricing Relation

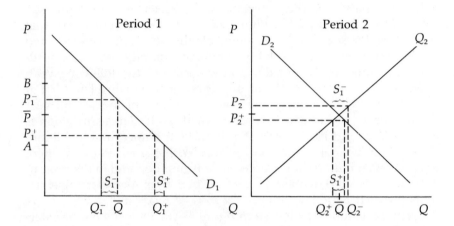

Storage Market Equilibrium

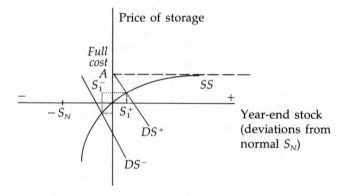

price effects then. If marginal storage costs were as much as $\bar{P} - A$, there would be no incentive to store any of the present surplus. If storage were costless, nearly all the present period surplus could be carried forward.

The net demand for the commodity to put into storage this period is the difference between excess supplies in the present period and excess demand for those supplies in the next period. The net demand for storage, assuming that the current surplus production is Q_1^+, is shown as DS^+. At a cost of storage A, there will be no increase in the normal levels of stocks carried forward. The slope of the storage demand relation is a function of the slopes of the demand and supply relations in the two periods. The storage supply relation, SS, is nonlinear, a direct reflection of the relation between futures prices and stocks. The supply-of-storage curve becomes nearly horizontal at the full costs of storage and, conversely, becomes nearly vertical as stocks are drawn down to zero. Stocks are exhausted at $-S_N$, since the diagram is drawn in deviations from long-run equilibrium stock levels (S_N). The shape underlines a fundamental asymmetry in the pricing of storable commodities—there is a defined limit on how much can be used from storage in a current shortage but no limit on how much can go into storage in a current surplus.

Given excess production in the current period, equilibrium in the storage market occurs at a level of storage S_1^+, an increase over normal levels. This amount is shown as a reduction in the amount consumed in the first period, resulting in a current price of P_1^+. Simultaneously S_1^+ must be added to the expected supply-and-demand equilibrium in the second period, since the market is assumed to return to equilibrium at the end of that period. Clearly prices in the next period will be below equilibrium as well, so that less is produced and the excess supply from storage into the period (S_1^+) can be consumed. The net effects are shown as P_2^+, the price expected to prevail in period 2. Total consumption in the second period will be Q_2^+ plus S_1^+, the excess will be entirely consumed in the second period, and the market will be in equilibrium again. The fundamental point is that current period surpluses affect prices both in the current period and in subsequent periods.

Similar arguments link the two periods in situations of current shortage as well, exemplified by the effects of current production Q_1^-. The full effects of the shortage (a price of B) are not felt in the current period. Rather, normal stocks are drawn down by an amount S_1^-, and prices increase only to P_1^-. Prices in the second period are also increased by an amount sufficient to replenish stocks to their normal levels and satisfy demand, to P_2^-. The demand for storage in this case is shown as DS^-. As before, the current situation affects events in the next period. With a current shortage, current stocks can be drawn down with the knowledge that increased production can replenish them in the next period. Since replenishment requires price incentive, prices in the subsequent period will be expected to be higher as well.

The ability to draw on current stocks in times of shortage is rather like being able to borrow production from the next period to supplement current consumption. Because the next period's production can be expected to replenish stocks, given an appropriate price incentive, current stocks can be depleted. Obviously present stocks limit how much can be borrowed. If, for example, the shortage were more severe than that shown as Q_1^-, current prices would be affected proportionately more than the next period's expected prices. The limits on the extent to which stocks may be depleted thus distinguish the price effects of shortage from those of surplus crop years.

The fundamental asymmetry is neatly illustrated with data from two crop years in the soybean market, 1972–1973 and 1975–1976. At the end of the 1972–1973 crop year, stocks of soybeans were exceptionally low, whereas those at the end of the 1975–1976 crop year were exceptionally high. The carryout of 59.6 million bushels from the 1972–1973 crop year was in fact the smallest during the decade, and the carryout of 244.9 million bushels from 1975–1976 was the largest. Futures prices in May of each year reflected these extremes as well. In early May 1973 the price of the nearby July future was $6.93¼ per bushel, and the first new crop future, the November future, traded at $4.69. The difference, $2.24¼, was a clear signal of the extent of the current shortage and of stocks being drawn down from normal levels. In early May 1976, on the other extreme, July soybean futures traded at $4.89¼ while November futures were priced at $5.06½. The carrying charge of $0.17¼ was a clear reflection of the present surplus.

In both years new information came into the market in May that raised overall prices. In 1973 the July future rose from $6.93¼ to $10.58 by the end of the month. In 1976, the July future rose from $4.89¼ to $5.79. In both years the November future rose as well— but in varying amounts. In May 1973 the new crop November future increased in price from $4.69 to $6.31, an increase of only $1.62 as compared with the $3.64¾ increase in the July future. In May 1976 the November future rose from $5.06½ to $5.91½, an increase of $0.85, which was nearly equal to the $0.89¾ increase in the July future. Because stocks were ample in 1975–1976, the link between the present crop year and the next year was very close indeed. In 1972–1973, however, the current shortage was already severe, and new information affected prices in the current crop year much more strongly than in the next since there was little more that could be borrowed from the next crop year.

In spite of the asymmetry in storage effects, the analysis clearly shows the relatively greater importance of rational forward prices in markets for storable commodities. In their absence misallocation occurs in both production and storage decisions, thereby compounding welfare losses in relation to the nonstorable case. The empirical question is thus the extent to which futures prices for storable commodities are rational. Two sorts of evidence are available on rationality— bias and predictability. The extensive literature on the question of bias in futures prices was discussed above, since the question has traditionally been considered in the context of speculative profits. It is sufficient to note here that the evidence shows that bias is not characteristic of futures prices. Biases have been found, but they appear to reflect particular market circumstances or time periods and not general tendencies. Thus futures prices generally guide production and storage decisions in appropriate ways, and there are no ex ante social losses.

The remaining question is the degree of predictability of futures prices. Tomek and Gray provide evidence for two storable commodities, corn and soybeans.[61] Because their concern is with production decisions and related interyear storage amounts, they compare the pricing of the new crop futures contracts before planting dates with their subsequent harvest prices. For corn the first new crop future is the December contract; for soybeans it is November. Prices of each contract on the preceding April 30 predate planting decisions for both crops. Expiration prices of each future (in December or November) are taken to represent harvest values for each of the crops. Their evidence shows no significant difference between the preplanting and expiration quotations of the futures. Whereas the earlier bias evidence included all futures, Tomek and Gray's evidence shows that the new crop futures in particular are unbiased.

In addition, the preplanting prices are shown to be both as variable from year to year and good predictors of the postharvest prices. In fact, Just and Rausser provide more general evidence that futures prices predict subsequent prices as well as the forecasts of several of the well-known forecast firms.[62] These results are in sharp contrast to the results from the potato market discussed earlier. The contrast in comparative variability and predictability is a reflection of the contrasting nature of rational forward prices in the two markets. With nonstorable commodities there is no link between production periods—what happens in this period will have no effect on decisions or prices in the next period (except insofar as a current change is a permanent change in a demand or supply relation). In contrast, current market events do influence next period prices and vice versa when the commodity is storable precisely because it is storable. Rational

61

forward prices for storable commodities must be nearly as variable from year to year as the subsequent, realized market prices because of the inventory links.

With inventories linking crop years, futures prices for these commodities also turn out to be good predictors of subsequent market prices. Tomek and Gray found that the preplanting quotations of new crop corn and soybean prices explained 65 or more percent of the subsequent harvest values. In addition, the coefficients of a linear regression showed that the relation was not significantly different from a 45-degree line, in contrast to the nearly vertical line apparent in figure 1-9 for prices from the nonstorable commodity. As the model suggests, there is predictable variation in prices from year to year, and the evidence shows that futures prices reflect much of that variation.[63]

Tomek and Gray also note that inventories facilitate adjustment to new information entering the market between the planting and harvest dates. If, for example, late spring rains significantly damage the emerging crop, prospects for realizing all the intended production diminish, and futures prices for the new crop year will immediately increase. Because of the inventory link, prices in the current crop year will also rise, and the degree of similarity in their increase depends only on the extent of current surplus or shortage. The concurrent rise in present prices will reduce current consumption and increase the amount of stocks that were previously intended to be carried into the next year, thereby ameliorating to some extent the full effects of the new information. In Tomek and Gray's terminology, the presence of inventory adds a "self-fulfilling" dimension to the preplanting "forecast" of new crop prices. Inventory adjustments to new information will help ameliorate the effects of the information, thereby improving the predictive quality of futures prices.[64]

In spite of their comparatively good performance, futures markets for storable commodities should not be viewed as independent forecasts. Futures prices for storable commodities are themselves directly linked to current cash prices according to the supply-of-storage relation. As a general rule, therefore, there is no more expectational information in futures prices than in current prices. For example, a futures price for a storable commodity can never "forecast" an increase in current prices more than the full costs of storage because futures prices can never exceed current prices by more than the costs of storage. Thus information implying that prices should increase raises both the current cash price and the futures price, more or less maintaining the cost-of-storage difference. Differential effects can occur, as evidenced by the earlier example from the soybean market, but these are generally small in relation to the effects on prices reflected in both the cash and the futures prices. Put another way, expectations are reflected nearly equally in current and in futures prices. In this sense cash prices will be nearly as good predictions of subsequent cash prices as futures prices.

Although the performance of futures prices for storable commodities differs substantively from that for nonstorable commodities, prices for both appear to be rational, thereby facilitating optimal production, consumption, and storage decisions. An interesting consequence of rationality in futures markets for nonstorable commodities was the suggestion that rational prices may not at the same time be informationally efficient. In a number of cases substantially better forecasts of subsequent prices could be found. Gray found a similar circumstance in the pricing performance of the wheat market during the period of the government price support program in the 1950s and early 1960s.[65]

During that period government support prices for wheat were set consistently above market-clearing prices. Producers had approximately six months after harvest to decide whether to put their wheat "under loan," thereby removing it from the market. Prices were relied upon to induce farmers to commit wheat to the loan program; although not all producers elected to participate in the program, participation was sufficient to ensure that the support price could be reached. Immediately after harvest, cash market prices reflected total available supplies because producers had six months in which to decide whether to put their wheat under loan. It was well known that market prices would be at or near loan levels within six months, since the wheat was removed from the market and placed in the loan program. That is, by December wheat prices would be at or above the loan price.

With the government program "forecasting" prices, what price did the futures market reflect? Gray found evidence that prices of the December future rose consistently and significantly from July to December.[66] In July the December future could be priced at no more than the full costs of storage above cash prices in July, prices that had to remain "low" so as to induce farmers to move wheat into the loan program. If the July quotation of the December future had been at loan price levels, July cash wheat prices could have been no less than the cost of storage below the futures price, and there would have been no incentive for farmers to move their wheat under loan. In December, with no wheat removed from the market, cash prices would have had to fall to their original market-clearing levels. In other words, for the futures market to have "forecasted" the known price effects of wheat moving under loan would have been self-defeating. Such prices would not have reflected participants' response to them.

Summary. The most important economic effects of futures markets are those that can be adduced from the behavior of producers, storers, and consumers. While it is true that a futures market facilitates increased speculation on the prices of the underlying commodity, fundamental effects on prices occur only if producers, consumers, and storers change their economic decisions in response to the prices reflected on these markets. Futures speculators do not store excess supplies of a commodity today for later use. Elevator owners, merchants, and farmers store the commodity. Thus fundamental changes in the seasonal variation of a commodity's price or in stocks held between years must be traced to the indirect effects of the market's prices on the incentives for elevators and others to store the commodity. For both storable and nonstorable commodities, the most important effect of a futures market is in providing rational forward prices. Such prices eliminate ex ante social costs associated with economic responses based on retrospective expectations and the evidence confirms that futures prices for both storable and non-storable commodities have performed this fundamental economic function well.

The Price Discovery Role of Futures Markets

The preceding section analyzed the effects futures markets have on the production, consumption, and storage of commodities. Little has been said about the price discovery process per se, except to note that the results of the empirical measures of these effects cannot be attributed to commercial decisions alone. Even though these are clearly the decisions that actually alter the allocation of commodities over space, time, and form and of the productive resources devoted to them, the decisions are based on prices, and speculation is a central element of the price discovery process. Futures markets lower transactions costs and thereby facilitate speculation. Uniform contract terms, clearinghouse offset and third-party guarantee, and low margins all contribute to lowering the costs of participation and thereby increase market liquidity and price efficiency.

Speculation and Market Liquidity. Estimates presented earlier suggested that approximately 50 percent of the speculation on an active futures market is market making by individuals who provide immediate market entry or exit for commercial and other speculative traders. In an active futures market, orders entering the trading ring can be executed at prices very close or identical to the price of the most recent transaction. Unlike specialists in securities markets, market makers in futures markets are not assigned to specific commodities, and there is no formal quotation of a bid-ask spread. Thus the level of activity in a market is an important determinant of the amount of market making it attracts and will support. Hence the level of activity directly affects the costs of entering or exiting from the market.

In an active market scalpers stand ready to buy or sell at a price no more than the minimum permitted change (a "tick") below or above the last quoted price. Such trading is not information trading—a pure unit-change scalper hopes that no new information will emerge while a position is open. Consider an active market with numerous competitive scalpers. Suppose that the last transaction is an outside order to sell, executed by a floor broker and taken by a market maker. In an active market numerous market makers would have been willing to accept the order at the bid price, and it is likely that if the next order were also a sell order, it would be taken at the same price. If the next order were one to buy, it would be accepted at the market maker's asked price. Roll diagrammed the sequence of possible prices as in figure 1–11.[67]

In reality, of course, a scalper's trading is more complex. Market value changes continuously during the day, and indications of changing value may be reflected in the sequence of orders as they appear

FIGURE 1–11

IDEALIZED SEQUENCES OF TRANSACTIONS PRICES IN A
LIQUID MARKET

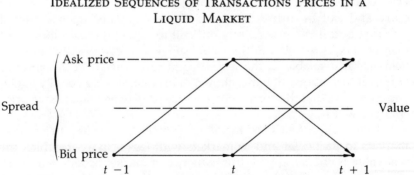

SOURCE: Roll, "Effective Bid-Ask Spread."

in the trading pit. Thus scalpers must also be aware of emerging price trends, even those of short duration, and must adjust their trading accordingly to be successful. Direct empirical evidence of scalpers' trading activity is limited, but Working and more recently Silber have analyzed the trading records of "representative" scalpers.[68]

Although the records are from very different markets (cotton and a stock index) and time periods (the 1950s and the 1980s), the similarity in their conclusions is remarkable. Both found that the average return per contract traded was less than the value of the permitted unit price change. In addition, Working concluded that a trader's returns were due solely to his success in pure scalping, with the net gains thus derived offset to a certain degree by net losses resulting from intraday price trends. Judging the emergence of such price trends is indeed important; they were the source of great variation in the trader's daily returns and of net losses. Silber's evidence from the "representative" index trader is even clearer on this point. The average profit on trades held open longer than three minutes was negative. Trades of shorter duration were consistently profitable. Recognizing trends is important to a scalper; they are the source of consistent losses. Such evidence suggests that scalpers specialize in skillfully accommodating the very short-term imbalances in orders coming into the market. The longer a position is open, the greater the chance of a change in real price, and the greater the likelihood of loss.

Active market making clearly creates liquidity, and hence the costs of market entry and exit are low. In the comparatively active markets from which the records of representative traders were taken, these costs clearly approached the minimum—the smallest permitted price change. There is little additional direct evidence of the costs of entry and exit in futures markets. Bid-ask spreads are not quoted publicly, and it is consequently difficult to assess the contribution of market makers directly. Roll's model suggests, however, that indirect evidence is available in the record of price changes. In the absence of new information, all paths shown in his diagram are equally likely, and he shows that the correlation coefficient between successive price changes will be $-\frac{1}{2}$.[69]

Thompson extends the model considerably, applying it to futures markets in particular and to markets with less activity in which the real value is changing with the sequence of market orders.[70] In these cases she shows that the correlation between successive price changes will still be negative, although its magnitude will decline markedly. Thus the correlation coefficients between price changes from the

TABLE 1–4

COMPARATIVE STATISTICAL DEPENDENCY IN PRICE CHANGES FROM ACTIVE AND INACTIVE FUTURES MARKETS, 1974

Commodity	Contract	Number of Observations	Serial Correlation Coefficient	F-Test
Wheat	July 1974	30,198	−0.30	2994
	September 1974	27,670	−0.24	1734
Corn	July 1974	29,508	−0.33	3573
	September 1974	20,902	−0.19	807
Oats	July 1974	7,145	−0.12	112
	September 1974	6,166	−0.09	51
Soybeans	July 1974	28,358	−0.30	2769
	September 1974	8,498	−0.00	0
Soybean meal	July 1974	8,996	−0.38	1535
	September 1974	6,392	−0.24	390
Soybean oil	July 1974	22,597	−0.29	2005
	September 1974	11,953	−0.10	126
Broilers	July 1974	5,224	−0.21	247
	September 1974	4,945	−0.13	81

SOURCE: Adapted from tables 1–3 in Martell and Helms, "Reexamination of Price Changes."

record of transactions during the trading day can be expected to be negative in a trading market. They will be more negative the more actively the market is traded, and therefore such analyses may indirectly reveal the effects of active market making.

Four sets of transactions-based price data have been analyzed.[71] Although the specific purpose of each of these analyses was not necessarily investigating market making, their results provide remarkably consistent insights into the effects of market making on price formation. The specific results of two of the studies are considered below.

In table 1–4 Martell and Helms's results for seven commodities and two contracts are summarized. For the July 1974 contracts the data are all price change transactions recorded from February 19, 1974, through June 28, 1974. For the September contract the period was February 19 through August 20, 1974. In all cases there were more transactions in the July than in the September contracts, even though data for the latter contract include two more months of prices. The contrast is particularly sharp between the soybean contracts,

TABLE 1-5

RELATION BETWEEN MEASURES OF DEPENDENCY AND AVERAGE BID-ASK SPREADS IN THE COCOA AND COFFEE FUTURES MARKETS, 1981–1983

Period	Contract		Number of Transactions		Serial Correlation Coefficients		Average Price Change	
	Near	Distant	Near	Distant	Near	Distant	Near	Distant
Coffee							(cents/pound)	
January 12–16, 1981	March	September	1,023	193	−0.16	−0.06	0.081	0.199
June 8–12, 1981	July	December	882	447	−0.02	−0.09	0.149	0.182
January 11–15, 1982	March	September	1,281	35	−0.21	−0.05	0.065	0.272
June 7–11, 1982	July	December	1,360	258	−0.07	−0.02	0.095	0.206
January 10–14, 1983	March	September	1,192	98	−0.15	−0.11	0.059	0.152
June 6–10, 1983	July	December	1,222	352	−0.12	−0.03	0.064	0.096
Average			1,160	231	−0.12	−0.06	0.086	0.186
Cocoa							(dollars/metric ton)	
January 12–16, 1981	March	September	1,019	151	−0.09	−0.01	1.16	2.38
June 9–12, 1981	July	December	598	476	−0.09	0.00	1.69	1.46
January 11–15, 1982	March	September	1,359	53	−0.13	0.04	1.08	2.48
June 7–11, 1982	July	December	831	200	−0.04	0.10	1.27	2.02
January 10–14, 1983	March	September	1,992	114	−0.11	0.14	0.97	2.85
June 6–10, 1983	July	December	1,840	856	−0.07	−0.01	1.41	1.89
Average			1,273	308	−0.09	0.04	1.26	2.18

SOURCE: Adapted from tables 1–3 in Thompson, "Price Changes from Transaction to Transaction."

where the July contract was more than three times as active as the September.

The serial correlation coefficients clearly reflect these comparative levels of activity. In all cases they are negative, and in all but one they are very significant. More important, serial correlations between price changes in the more active July contracts are always greater than those for the less active September contracts. In each case the serial correlation is less significant in the less active contract. The extreme contrast is again soybeans, where price changes in the markedly inactive September contract show no significant market-making pattern. An active market is supported by scalping, and such speculation ensures that prices fluctuate in a very narrow bid-ask difference around equilibrium prices. Less active markets have significantly less scalping, and market entry costs are commensurately higher.

Thompson's empirical analysis of coffee and cocoa data completes the connection between market liquidity, serial correlation measures, and bid-ask spreads. Her data consisted of six sets of transactions prices from the coffee and cocoa futures markets, where each set contained observations from both a nearby, actively traded contract and a more distant, inactive contract (see table 1–5). As the averages indicate, the nearby contracts were four to five times as active as the more distant contracts. Thompson also examined serial correlations between the price changes. The results are consistent with the previous analyses; in the more active contracts price changes show a much stronger degree of dependency as they fluctuate between bid-ask bounds. An interesting aspect of these correlations is that they are comparatively much smaller than those reported in any of the other liquidity studies. The transaction record from the Coffee, Sugar and Cocoa Exchange, however, records all transactions, whereas that from the Chicago Board of Trade includes only transactions for which there was a change in price. Thus the correlations here can be expected to be lower.

The contrast in performance between active and inactive months is similar to that noted earlier. For coffee transactions-based correlations are nearly twice as large for the nearby, active months as for the distant, inactive ones. For cocoa the contrast is even greater, with negative correlations consistent only in the active contracts. Finally, Thompson provides several direct measures of the average bid-ask spread in each market and thereby connects the observed patterns in dependency with entry and exit costs. One measure, the average of the absolute values of price change, is shown in the table. In both markets, the average price change between transactions is

69

markedly smaller in the more active contracts, averaging 50 percent less than changes in the much less active markets.

Taken together, the studies of individual traders' records and of statistical relations among prices confirm the important contribution of market making to the formation of continuously available and reliable prices. Active speculative trading in markets results in prices that fluctuate within very narrow bands, reducing market entry and exit costs to a minimum. In markets with much less speculation, prices fluctuate more widely and irregularly around equilibrium values, resulting in much larger market entry costs.

Price Efficiency. Speculation, particularly position trading and spreading, influences the process of price discovery as well. The two preceding sections have focused on seasonal price formation and storage adjustments to futures prices and on effects between crop years to incorporate both prospective production and consumption decisions and storage decisions. In both sections speculation was incidental to the analyses, which concentrated on adjustments by firms within the industry. There is no doubt, however, that the seasonal and annual price-stabilizing effects derived in each case are directly or indirectly related to the increased price speculation facilitated by a futures market as well as to commercial firms' adjustments.

Fundamentally, futures markets are expected to increase the information content of market prices. They can do so in at least three ways. First, transactions costs (that is, market entry costs) are typically lower in an active futures market than in a spot market, and the incentive for all participants to search for more and better information is consequently greater. Second, futures markets attract additional speculation, of which some is responsible for the marked decrease in transaction costs but some is willing to assume longer-term (at least overnight) price risks as well. Since speculative returns depend solely on trading expertise, the incentive to search for information is greater than for a commercial firm whose profits are relatively less dependent on trading returns. Thus the added speculation is expected to improve the amount of information reflected in the current price. Finally, in processing information, speculators must take into account the responses of all participants to the prices implied by any single piece of information, thus improving the rationality of market prices.

All of this suggests that market prices ought to become more informationally efficient with the introduction of futures markets. Fundamental models of supply-and-demand relations, when they are linked by storage possibilities, will continue to show a theoretical dependency between current and some past prices, but the number of significant past prices should decline, as should the degree of importance of specific lagged prices. Cox tested this proposition directly with weekly cash price data from six markets—onions, potatoes, pork bellies, hogs, cattle, and frozen concentrated orange juice—for which there were periods before and during futures trading (and, for onions, a period afterward).[72] Initial regressions from periods before futures trading examined the dependency of current prices on past prices for five through ten previous weeks. The model that best explained current price from past prices in the period before futures was then applied to data from the period after futures trading.

In all cases comparisons of the estimated coefficients showed that current prices became less dependent on past information with the introduction of futures trading. In fact, the entire set of coefficients on prices lagged more than one week were found not to contribute significantly to explaining current prices during the futures trading period. Not all dependencies were eliminated within the period of Cox's analysis. Most of the commodities, however, are nonstorable or semiperishable, and a model of weekly market supply-and-demand relations is likely to contain some production-in-process or storage links that will be reflected in price links. These results thus confirm a consistent and remarkable degree of improvement in the amount of information contained in current prices when futures trading is introduced in a commodity market.

A different approach to measuring the effects of futures trading on the degree of information contained in price focuses on the comparative amounts of unexplainable variation in price before and after futures trading. In tests using weekly data, Powers found that the advent of futures trading reduced the random (or residual, unexplained) variation in live beef prices by nearly one-third, from twenty to thirty cents per hundredweight.[73] The reduction in variation in pork belly prices was nearly one-fourth, from $1.00 to $0.78 per hundredweight. That is, with futures trading there was significantly less unsystematic variation in weekly cash prices.

Finally, the question whether futures prices are themselves fully efficient has been the focus of a great deal of research. In a process first described by Working and later modeled by Samuelson, futures prices ought to fluctuate randomly over time.[74] Since new information bearing on price emerges unpredictably, prices ought to change unpredictably. Fama distinguished three degrees of pricing efficiency: efficiency with respect to past prices; efficiency with respect to publicly available information; and efficiency with respect to all information.[75] They are weak-form, semistrong-form, and strong-

71

form efficiency, respectively. Most analyses of the pricing efficiency of futures prices have been weak-form tests, examining statistical characteristics of observed (usually daily closing) price changes for deviations from randomness.

Irwin and Uhrig's recent analysis of dependency relations among futures price changes provides a useful summary of the results of standard tests, and their tests of specific trading rules well illustrates the variability in results among commodities and over changing time periods.[76]

The results are more mixed with tests of semistrong-form efficiency, where the behavior of futures prices is examined in relation to a specific information series or to forecasts derived from several fundamental series. Conklin, for example, examined changes in grain futures prices in relation to the weekly release of export sales information and concluded that market prices were efficient with respect to this information.[77] Leuthold and Hartmann's comparison of hog futures prices with forecasts derived from a simple price prediction model showed that substantial profits could be made by trading on the model's predictions and led them to conclude that the hog market was inefficient with respect to fundamental supply-and-demand information.[78] In an analysis of pricing in the soybean complex, Rausser and Carter developed a model based on fundamental information that consistently outperformed futures prices.[79] The authors thus concluded that futures markets in the soy complex did not completely reflect all available information.

Information is, of course, costly to acquire and process in these models, and speculation on futures prices is itself not costless, even though the costs are much reduced with futures markets. Nevertheless, costs do not explain all the documented inefficiencies, and additional studies will no doubt find other information-specific inefficiencies. These additional studies are required, however, to permit more general conclusions. Are the inefficiencies documented so far transitory in the same sense that deviations from random behavior in price changes appear to be largely transitory? Or are these systematic patterns in informational inefficiencies in markets that relate either to commodity characteristics or to observable changes in the important variables influencing prices? Although firm conclusions are not possible on the degree of information efficiency in futures prices, it is clear that these inefficiencies are small in comparison to the overall improvements in pricing efficiency coincident with futures markets.

Conclusions. Taken together, these studies show that futures speculation measurably improves pricing efficiency in commodity markets.

The resulting futures price series may not be altogether informationally efficient, but speculation in futures clearly improves both market
liquidity and the information content of prices. Transactions costs
are reduced—the more active the futures market, the lower market
entry or exit costs are likely to be. These reductions increase the
number of participants and provide greater incentive to search for
relevant information. As a consequence the information content of
market prices is improved.

Conclusions

Futures markets evolved in the mid-nineteenth century with the
expansion of trading in major food and feed grains associated with
the development of the Midwest as a region of surplus agricultural
production. Two critical elements in their evolution were the development of recognized grading standards, which led to standardized
contract terms, and the solution to contract default problems through
the establishment of a clearinghouse arrangement. Futures contracts
are homogeneous, specifying uniform grade, location, quality, and
times of delivery. The system of initial and maintenance margins
created with the clearinghouse substantially reduces the incentive
for either buyers or sellers to default on their contractual obligations.
The emerging system of trading thus lowered transaction costs,
promoting a centralized market in place of otherwise fragmented and
illiquid regional markets. Futures markets have thus become the
primary price discovery markets for most of the storable agricultural
products. The futures markets in industrial products, metals, and
livestock products, though later in developing, have assumed a similarly important role in the pricing and marketing systems for those
products.

Although futures markets have become the primary pricing
markets for many commodities, they have not replaced either spot
or forward markets. Both remain important in the marketing of
commodities and are the primary means by which ownership is
actually transferred from producers to processors and consumers.
More important, futures markets are widely used to complement the
fundamental purchase and sales decisions. Futures prices are the
referent prices in all transactions, whether they are for immediate or
delayed delivery, because they provide a standardized, competitively
determined reflection of underlying current and future value.

They do more than provide a referent value, however. Because
futures markets exist, transactions with almost any time horizon can
be agreed to nearly instantaneously. Farmers can, on a moment's
notice, receive a quotation for and sell to their local elevator a crop

that has not even been planted or has not yet been harvested. An importer can purchase an entire year's requirements from an exporter, fixing delivery terms, quality, and prices today even though deliveries are not to begin for six months. All such transactions are facilitated by an actively trading, liquid futures market. Buyers and sellers are both aware of current, standardized values and are willing to commit themselves to transactions quickly because their commitments can be instantaneously hedged in futures with a minimal effect on price.

Futures markets have economic effects both directly on the prices of commodities and indirectly on production, consumption, and storage decisions responsive to those prices. Futures trading measurably improves the process of price discovery. Transaction costs are generally low; consequently the incentive to search for and evaluate market information is high. Analyses have shown that market prices reflect the improved price discovery process in at least two ways. First, current prices have been shown to be more informationally efficient, depending less on prices from more than a period or two before the present observations. Some dependency remains, of course, since fundamental relations require price links between periods. Second, the unexplained component of market price variation is markedly reduced as more systematic, fundamental information is incorporated into current prices. Futures markets facilitate speculation on commodity prices. Nevertheless, it is the increased speculation that improves the informational content of prices and provides the nearly instant liquidity characteristic of actively trading markets.

The indirect effects of futures markets arise because the markets are widely used by firms engaged in the production, marketing, and processing of commodities. Though indirect, these effects are perhaps their most important contributions to the economy. First, futures markets rationalize storage decisions. Futures prices are simultaneous quotations of value for today and for successive dates in the future, given current information. The difference in prices among contracts is itself a price, the market price of storing the commodity over time. Evidence shows a strong positive, though nonlinear, relation between the price of storage and stock levels. The price difference between two futures maturities is an accurate reflection of the present degree of shortage and thus an indicator of the market's need for continued storage. In addition, the availability of a futures market permits individual storage decisions to be hedged and thereby provides a reliably predictable return to storage. Storage decisions are thus more responsive to price, and as a consequence commodity prices have been shown to be more stable seasonally.

Finally, futures prices are themselves anticipatory prices that reliably guide the optimal allocation of resources to the production and consumption of commodities. The effects are most clearly seen in annually produced commodities. Trading in futures contracts that price new crop production is continuous over the production period. Such prices must be rational since they reflect not only anticipated production relations but also anticipated consumption relations. They are not forecasts in the sense that the weather may be forecast; that is, forecasts of the weather have no influence on what the weather will in fact be. Futures prices must reflect the responses they create; they are rational forward prices. To the extent that production decisions in the absence of a futures market rely on price expectations that extrapolate past prices, resources are misallocated, and ex ante social losses occur. A futures market with rational forward prices eliminates those losses, stabilizes annual production and consumption decisions, and thus stabilizes annual prices.

Obviously, not all commodities are affected to the same extent, either directly or indirectly, when a futures market is introduced. The relative contributions depend on the physical characteristics of the commodity. If trading is already centralized and relatively active, there will be little gain from centralization with the institution of a futures market. Even then, however, the characteristically low margins and clearinghouse performance assurances will reduce market participation costs and increase speculative interest. Much of the increased speculation will add liquidity to the market, and transaction costs for all participants will be lower. The effects of futures will also differ for commodities that are storable and those that are not. For storable commodities futures markets serve both an allocative and a forward-pricing function. For nonstorable commodities they can function only as a forward-pricing market. In spite of the basic differences between storable and nonstorable markets, futures markets have stabilized prices to an impressive degree in both.

The effects of a futures market in a commodity marketing system derive largely from the way it is used by the commercial firms in the industry. There is no question that futures markets support a greater amount of speculation than physical markets; nevertheless, it is also true that futures markets depend on commercial use for their continued existence. The total activity in futures markets clearly depends on hedging, not speculative, patterns of use. As the underlying physical market changes, so also must contract terms in the futures market. If they do not change commensurately, the contract's value to firms will decrease, and ultimately the market will close. Often those same commercial interests have been vocal in their opposition to a new market. One is reminded of Rothstein's grain merchant who in 1858 thought the "new" system of trading was merely a "kind of gambling operations of selling ahead" and twenty-five years later wrote to convince others of its usefulness "if we do not want to speculate."[80]

Opposition to futures has continued, seemingly unabated—the introduction of each new market seems inevitably to be accompanied by often very vocal opposition from important segments of the underlying physical markets. Although the organized efforts of the onion growers and shippers are the only instance where such opposition actually closed a market, the countless hearings on the effects of the Maine potato and live cattle futures markets are symptomatic. Commercial interests do not always welcome the new system of trading. The more concentrated the market, the more vocal the opposition. Nevertheless, in most instances firms come to find futures markets very useful and adjust their buying and selling in accordance with the opportunities for increased risk management and more flexible decision making. These adjustments have brought increased price stability to markets where fluctuation has been associated with large social losses in the misallocation of productive resources.

Notes

1. Three very useful literature surveys are: B. A. Goss and B. S. Yamey, *The Economics of Futures Trading* (New York: John Wiley and Sons, 1976); Roger W. Gray and David J. S. Rutledge, "The Economics of Commodity Futures Markets: A Survey," *Review of Marketing and Agricultural Economics*, vol. 39, no. 4 (1971); and Avi Kamara, "Issues in Futures Markets: A Survey," *Journal of Futures Markets*, vol. 2, no. 3 (1982).

2. See Harold S. Irwin, *Evolution of Futures Trading* (Madison, Wis.: Mimir Publishers, 1954).

3. Ibid., p. 79.

4. U.S. Federal Trade Commission, *Report of the Federal Trade Commission on the Grain Trade*, vol. 5, *Futures Trading Operations in Grain* (Washington, D. C., 1920), pp. 27–28.

5. Ibid., p. 28. An excellent description of early ring settlement procedures is in G. Wright Hoffman, *Future Trading upon Organized Commodity Markets in the United States* (Philadelphia: University of Pennsylvania Press, 1932), chaps. 11 and 12.

6. Morton Rothstein, "The Rejection and Acceptance of a Marketing Innovation: Hedging in the Late Nineteenth Century," *Review of Research in Futures Markets*, vol. 2, no. 2 (1983), p. 208.

7. Ibid., p. 209.

8. Irwin, *Evolution of Futures Trading*.

9. Ibid.

10. Allen B. Paul, Richard G. Heifner, and John W. Helmuth, *Farmers' Use of Forward and Futures Markets*, Agricultural Economic Report no. 320 (Washington, D.C.: U.S. Department of Agriculture, Economic Research Service, 1976); and John W. Helmuth, "Grain Pricing," *Economic Bulletin*, no. 1, Commodity Futures Trading Commission (September 1977).

11. Holbrook Working, "Hedging Reconsidered," *Journal of Farm Economics*, vol. 35, no. 4 (1953).

12. Ibid.

13. Examining regional diversity in mortgage rates, Culbertson found a significant decline in regional differences was associated with the introduction of futures trading in mortgages, the GNMA futures contract. See William P. Culbertson, Jr., "GNMA Futures Trading: Its Impact on the Residential Mortgage Market," *International Futures Trading Seminar Proceedings* (Chicago: Chicago Board of Trade, 1978).

14. Working, "Hedging Reconsidered."

15. See Antoinette Nahmias, "Analysis of Operational Hedging: The Case of Flour Milling " (unpublished Ph.D. diss., Stanford University, 1985).

16. Raymond M. Leuthold and William G. Tomek, "Developments in the Livestock Futures Literature," in Raymond M. Leuthold and Parry Dixon, eds., *Livestock Futures Research Symposium Proceedings* (Chicago: Chicago Mercantile Exchange, 1979).

17. Raymond M. Leuthold and Scott Mokler, "Feeding-Margin Hedging in the Cattle Industry," *International Futures Trading Seminar Proceedings* (Chicago: Chicago Board of Trade, 1979), vol. 6, pp. 56–68.

18. Ibid., p. 66

19. See Hoffman, *Future Trading*, Chapters 19 and 20 for early evidence from the corn market. Irwin analyzes evidence from the wheat market. See Harold S. Irwin, "Seasonal Cycles in Aggregates of Wheat Futures Contracts," *Journal of Political Economy*, vol. 43, no. 1 (1935).

20. Raymond M. Leuthold, "Commercial Use and Speculative Measures of the Livestock Commodity Futures Markets," *Journal of Futures Markets*, vol. 3, no. 2 (1983).

21. John Maynard Keynes, "Some Aspects of Commodity Markets," *Manchester Guardian Commercial: European Reconstruction Series*, March 29, 1923.

22. Paul Cootner, "Return to Speculators: Telser versus Keynes," and "Rejoinder," *Journal of Political Economy*, vol. 68, no. 4 (1960).

23. Ibid.; Lester G. Telser, "Futures Trading and the Storage of Cotton and Wheat," *Journal of Political Economy*, vol. 66, no. 3 (1958); and idem, "Returns to Speculators: Telser versus Keynes—Reply," *Journal of Political Economy*, vol. 68, no. 4 (1960).

24. Roger W. Gray, "Characteristic Bias in Some Thin Futures Markets," *Food Research Institute Studies*, vol. 1, no. 3 (1960); and idem, "The Search for a Risk Premium," *Journal of Political Economy*, vol. 69, no. 3 (1961).

25. Roger W. Gray, "The Emergence of Short Speculation," *International Futures Trading Seminar Proceedings* (Chicago: Chicago Board of Trade, 1979), vol. 6.

26. Charles S. Rockwell, "Normal Backwardation, Forecasting, and the Returns to Commodity Futures Traders," *Food Research Institute Studies*, vol. 7, supplement (1967). See also Hendrik S. Houthakker, "Can Speculators Forecast Prices?" *Review of Economics and Statistics*, vol. 39, no. 2 (1957).

27. Katherine Dusak, "Futures Trading and Investor Returns: An Investigation of Commodity Market Risk Premiums," *Journal of Political Economy*, vol. 87, no. 6 (1973); Colin A. Carter, Gordon C. Rausser, and Andrew Schmitz, "Efficient Asset Portfolios and the Theory of Normal Backwardation," *Journal of Political Economy*, vol. 91, no. 2 (1983); and Alan J. Marcus, "Efficient Asset Portfolios and the Theory of Normal Backwardation," *Journal of Political Economy*, vol. 92, no. 3 (1984).

28. Holbrook Working, "A Theory of Anticipatory Prices," *American Economic Review*, vol. 48, no. 2 (1958), p. 186.

29. David J. S. Rutledge, "Trading Volume and Price Variability: New Evidence on the Price Effects of Speculation," *International Research Seminar Proceedings* (Chicago: Chicago Board of Trade, 1978), vol. 5.

30. Holbrook Working, "Tests of a Theory Concerning Floor Trading on Commodity Exchanges," *Food Research Institute Studies*, vol. 7, supplement (1967); and William Silber, "Marketmaker Behavior in an Auction Market: An Analysis of Scalpers in Futures Markets," *Journal of Finance*, vol. 39, no. 4 (1984).

31. Holbrook Working, "Speculation on Hedging Markets," *Food Research Institute Studies*, vol. 1, no. 2 (1960).

32. See Cedric B. Cowing, *Populists, Plungers, and Progressives* (Princeton, N.J.: Princeton University Press, 1965) for an interesting history of regulatory reform in this early period.

33. G. G. Udell, compiler, *Cotton and Grain Futures Acts, Commodity Exchange and Warehouse Acts, and Other Laws Relating Thereto*, U.S. House of Representatives, 1968, p. 32.

34. Phillip McBride Johnson, *Commodities Regulation*, 2 vols. (Boston: Little, Brown, 1982).

35. Hoffman, *Organized Commodity Markets*, chap. 17.

36. Todd E. Petzel, "A New Look at Some Old Evidence: The Wheat Market Scandal of 1925," *Food Research Institute Studies*, vol. 18, no. 1 (1981).

37. Roger W. Gray, "Price Effects of a Lack of Speculation," *Food Research Institute Studies*, vol. 7, supplement (1967).

38. Roger W. Gray and David J. S. Rutledge, "The Commodity Leverage Contract: An Economic Anaysis," unpublished manuscript, Food Research Institute, Stanford University, June 1978.

39. The original analyses are contained in Holbrook Working, "Price Relations between July and September Wheat Futures at Chicago since 1885," *Wheat Studies of the Food Research Institute*, vol. 9 (1933) and idem, "Price Relations between May and New-Crop Wheat Futures at Chicago since 1885," *Wheat Studies of the Food Research Institute*, vol. 10 (1934). Working summarized the results of these detailed analyses in "The Theory of the Price of Storage," *American Economic Review*, vol. 39, no. 6 (1953) and "Theory

of the Inverse Carrying Charge in Futures Markets," *Journal of Farm Economics*, vol. 30, no. 1 (1948).

40. Michael J. Brennan, "The Supply of Storage," *American Economic Review*, vol. 48, no. 1 (1958); Roger W. Gray and Anne E. Peck, "The Chicago Wheat Futures Market: Recent Problems in Historical Perspective," *Food Research Institute Studies*, vol. 18, no. 1 (1981); Telser, "Futures Trading and Storage"; Sarahelen Thompson, "Price Performance in Thin Markets" (Ph.D. dissertation, Stanford University, 1983); and Helmut Weymar, *The Dynamics of the World Cocoa Market* (Cambridge, Mass.: MIT Press, 1968).

41. Weymar, *Dynamics of the Cocoa Market*.

42. Brennan, "Supply of Storage."

43. Holbrook Working, "Price Effects of Futures Trading," *Food Research Institute Studies*, vol. 1, no. 1 (1960).

44. Roger W. Gray, "Onions Revisited," *Journal of Farm Economics*, vol. 45, no. 2 (1963).

45. William G. Tomek, "A Note on Historical Wheat Prices and Futures Trading," *Food Research Institute Studies*, vol. 10, no. 1 (1971).

46. Working, "Price Effects"; Mark J. Powers, "Does Futures Trading Reduce Price Fluctuations in the Cash Markets?" *American Economic Review*, vol. 60, no. 3 (1970); and Gregory S. Taylor and Raymond M. Leuthold, "The Influence of Futures Trading on Cash Cattle Price Variations," *Food Research Institute Studies*, vol. 13, no. 1 (1974).

47. Tomek, "Wheat Prices and Futures Trading," p. 110.

48. Holbrook Working, "Disposition of American Wheat since 1896, with Special Reference to Changes in Year-End Stocks," *Wheat Studies of the Food Research Institute*, vol. 4, no. 4 (1928).

49. D. Gale Johnson, *Forward Prices for Agriculture* (Chicago: University of Chicago Press, 1947).

50. Marc Nerlove, "Adaptive Expectations and Cobweb Phenomena," *Quarterly Journal of Economics*, vol. 72, no. 2 (1958).

51. Arnold B. Larson, "The Quiddity of the Cobweb Theorem," *Food Research Institute Studies*, vol. 7, no. 2 (1967); and B. E. P. Box and G. M. Jenkins, *Time Series Analysis: Forecasting and Control* (San Francisco: Holden-Day, 1970).

52. Jerome L. Stein, "Speculative Price: Economic Welfare and the Idiot of Chance," *Review of Economics and Statistics*, vol. 63, no. 2 (1981).

53. William G. Tomek and Roger W. Gray, "Temporal Relationships among Prices on Commodity Futures Markets: Their Allocative and Stabilizing Roles," *American Journal of Agricultural Economics*, vol. 52, no. 3 (1970).

54. William M. Simmons, *An Economic Study of the U.S. Potato Industry*, Agricultural Economic Report no. 6 (Washington, D.C.: U.S. Department of Agriculture, Economic Research Service, 1962).

55. Roger W. Gray, "The Futures Market for Maine Potatoes: An Appraisal," *Food Research Institute Studies*, vol. 11, no. 3 (1972).

56. Raymond M. Leuthold, "An Analysis of Daily Fluctuations in the Hog Economy," *American Journal of Agricultural Economics*, vol. 51, no. 4 (1969);

and Lester H. Myers, Joseph P. Havlicek, Jr., and P. L. Henderson, "Short-Term Price Structure of the Hog-Pork Sector of the United States," Purdue University Agricultural Experiment State Research Bulletin no. 855 (1970).

57. Larry Martin and Phillip Garcia, "The Price-forecasting Performance of Futures Markets for Live Cattle and Hogs: A Disaggregated Analysis," *American Journal of Agricultural Economics*, vol. 63, no. 2 (1981).

58. Raymond M. Leuthold and Peter A. Hartmann, "A Semi-strong Form Evaluation of the Hog Futures Market," *American Journal of Agricultural Economics*, vol. 61, no. 3 (1979) and "Reply," vol. 62, no. 3 (1980).

59. Stein, "Speculative Price."

60. The economic literature on the role and importance of stocks in commodity price models is extensive. A very early study is John Burr Williams, "Speculation and the Carryover," *Quarterly Journal of Economics*, vol. 5, no. 3 (1936). Examples of studies of the importance of stocks in stabilizing prices are Robert L. Gustafson, *Carryover Levels for Grain: A Method for Determining Amounts That Are Optimal under Specified Conditions*, U.S. Department of Agriculture Technical Bulletin 1178 (1958) and Brian D. Wright and Jeffrey C. Williams, "The Economic Role of Commodity Storage," *Economic Journal*, vol. 92, no. 5 (1982).

61. Tomek and Gray, "Temporal Relationships among Prices."

62. Richard E. Just and Gordon C. Rausser, "Commodity Price Forecasting with Large-Scale Econometric Models and the Futures Market," *American Journal of Agricultural Economics*, vol. 63, no. 2 (1981).

63. Tomek and Gray, "Temporal Relationships among Prices."

64. Ibid.

65. Roger W. Gray, "The Seasonal Pattern of Wheat Futures Prices under the Loan Program," *Food Research Institute Studies*, vol. 3, no. 1 (1962).

66. Ibid.

67. Richard Roll, "A Simple Implicit Measure of the Effective Bid-Ask Spread in an Efficient Market," *Journal of Finance*, vol. 39, no. 4 (1984).

68. Working, "Tests of a Theory"; and Silber, "Marketmaker Behavior."

69. Roll, "Effective Bid-Ask Spread."

70. Sarahelen Thompson, "Price Changes from Transaction to Transaction: A Measure of Liquidity in Futures Markets," University of Illinois, Department of Agricultural Economics Working Paper, 1984.

71. Terrence F. Martell and Billy P. Helms, "A Reexamination of Price Changes in the Commodity Futures Market," *International Research Seminar Proceedings* (Chicago: Chicago Board of Trade, 1978), vol. 5; Ruben C. Trevino and Terrence F. Martell, "The Intraday Behavior of Commodity Futures Prices," Columbia University Center for the Study of Futures Markets Working Paper no. 71, 1984; Sarkis J. Khoury and Gerald L. Jones, "Daily Price Limits on Futures Contracts: Nature, Impact, and Justification," *Review of Research in Futures Markets*, vol. 3, no. 1 (1984); and Thompson, "Price Changes from Transaction to Transaction."

72. Charles C. Cox, "Futures Trading and Market Information," *Journal of Political Economy*, vol. 84, no. 6 (1976).

73. Powers, "Does Futures Trading Reduce Price Fluctuations?"

74. Working, "Theory of Anticipatory Prices"; and Paul A. Samuelson, "Proof That Properly Anticipated Prices Fluctuate Randomly," *Industrial Management Review*, vol. 6 (1965).

75. Eugene Fama, "Efficient Capital Markets: A Review of Theory and Empirical Work," *Journal of Finance*, vol. 25, no. 1 (1970).

76. Scott H. Irwin and J. William Uhrig, "Statistical and Trading System Analysis of Weak Form Efficiency in U.S. Futures Markets," Purdue University, Department of Agricultural Economics, Station Bulletin no. 421 (1983).

77. Neilson C. Conklin, "Grain Exports, Futures Markets, and Pricing Efficiency," *Review of Research in Futures Markets*, vol. 2, no. 1 (1983).

78. Leuthold and Hartmann, "Evaluation of the Hog Futures Market."

79. Gordon C. Rausser and Colin Carter, "Futures Market Efficiency in the Soybean Complex," *Review of Economics and Statistics*, vol. 55, no. 3 (1983).

80. Rothstein, "Rejection and Acceptance of a Marketing Innovation."

2

The Economic Role of Financial Futures

William L. Silber

Background

Before 1972, futures trading was dominated by agricultural commodities. The introduction of foreign currency futures in 1972, interest rate contracts in 1975, and stock index futures in 1982 has shifted the industry from the almost exclusive province of agricultural interests to an integral component of the financial sector. The spectacular growth in trading of financial futures during the first decade of their existence—they now account for approximately 50 percent of all futures trading—has focused attention on the purposes and functions of this segment of the futures industry.

There is little doubt that futures markets for agricultural commodities provide important economic benefits. Trading standardized agricultural commodities for future delivery on organized exchanges permits an efficient mechanism for hedging and provides a forum for establishing and disseminating price information. These so-called risk-transfer and price-discovery functions of futures markets are now well documented in the academic and public policy literature.[1]

The main reason for special treatment of financial futures is that, in most cases, highly visible and well-functioning markets already existed for the underlying financial instruments, such as stocks, bonds, and foreign currencies, before the introduction of futures trading. Questions naturally arise under such circumstances: Are financial futures markets merely redundant or, worse, have they supplanted or will they supplant the "real" markets to the public's detriment? Although the spectacular growth of financial futures trading within a freely competitive market system should normally have been sufficient evidence of their economic contributions, the history of legis-

83

lative concern surrounding futures markets forces more careful consideration of the issues.

With this background, the discussion proceeds as follows. First there is a brief review of the risk-transfer and price-discovery functions of futures markets. Next these concepts are applied to financial futures, showing that their main contribution is a reduction in transactions costs and an improvement in market liquidity, the ultimate benefit being a reduction in the cost of capital to business firms. Practical evidence on the centrality of transactions economies to the success of financial futures is then presented, focusing primarily on how various institutions actually use financial futures. Additional evidence is offered within the framework of the success and failure of specific futures contracts. Finally some of the policy issues that have surrounded financial futures are discussed, including questions of contract proliferation, the consequences for the underlying cash markets, and the role of speculation and cash settlement in stock index contracts.

To anticipate the results somewhat, the discussion will show that although financial markets are highly liquid and visible institutions, futures markets on financial instruments are even more transactionally efficient than these underlying markets. Therefore, although price discovery and hedging could be accomplished in the cash markets, it is cheaper and more efficient for most participants to utilize financial futures for many of these objectives. Thus the main contribution of financial futures stems from a reduction in costs that permit transactions, such as hedging, and information transfer, such as price discovery, to occur more efficiently. To set the stage for these discussions, a brief review of the financial futures contracts currently in existence is offered along with a short sketch of market participants.

Contracts and Participants. Table 2–1 lists the major financial futures contracts in existence during 1984, including the year they were introduced and the exchange on which they are traded. For convenience, financial futures are divided into three groups: (1) foreign currencies; (2) interest rate contracts; and (3) stock index futures. Within each of these categories are various specific contracts that differ from each other with respect to the precise instrument used to settle contractual obligations. For example, under foreign currency futures are contracts on the German mark, Swiss franc, and the British pound. Within the interest-rate category are futures on long-term Treasury bonds, Treasury bills, and Eurodollar time deposits. Finally, the stock index group includes contracts on Standard and

TABLE 2–1
MAJOR FINANCIAL FUTURES CONTRACTS, 1972–1984

Contract	Exchange	Began Trading
Foreign currencies		
British pound	IMM	1972
Canadian dollar	IMM	1972
Japanese yen	IMM	1972
Swiss franc	IMM	1972
West German mark	IMM	1972
Interest rates		
Treasury bills	IMM	1976
Bank CDs	IMM	1981
Eurodollars	IMM	1981
GNMAs	CBT	1975
Treasury bonds	CBT	1977
Treasury notes	CBT	1982
Stock index		
Major Market index	CBT	1984
NYSE composite	NYFE	1982
S&P 500	CME	1982
Value Line	KCBT	1982

NOTES: CBT = Chicago Board of Trade; CME = Chicago Mercantile Exchange; IMM = International Monetary Market (Division of CME); KCBT = Kansas City Board of Trade; NYFE = New York Futures Exchange; and NYSE = New York Stock Exchange.
SOURCE: *Wall Street Journal* listing of futures contracts.

Poor's 500 index, the New York Stock Exchange Composite index, and the Value Line index.

As can be seen in the table, the first financial futures contracts on foreign currencies were introduced in 1972. They were soon followed by interest-rate futures in 1975, while stock index futures did not arrive on the scene until 1982. The late arrival of stock index contracts can be traced, in part, to their use of cash settlement to satisfy contractual obligations as opposed to traditional physical delivery. Extensive regulatory review was required to approve the cash settlement procedure primarily because of concern over the superficial similarity of the cash settlement process to gambling. The success of the stock index contracts and the Eurodollar contract has made the cash settlement procedure the likely source of continued innovation in financial futures.

The variety of specific contracts in table 2–1 reflects the innovative activity of the various futures exchanges combined with the natural selection process of the marketplace. In particular, contracts that attract significant hedging and speculative interests succeed, while those that do not fall by the wayside. That separate contracts on the German mark and the British pound should succeed appears sensible; however, no compelling a priori reasoning explains why contracts on long-term Treasury bonds (more than fifteen years to maturity) and Treasury notes (six to ten years to maturity) were both successful, while four-to-six-year Treasury notes and two-year Treasury notes failed. As is described below, the comparative advantage of specific contracts in providing transactionally efficient hedging services is an important part of the story and helps pinpoint the contribution of financial futures contracts to economic activity.

Describing the variety of financial futures contracts is far easier than identifying the specific participants in the marketplace. Economic agents participating in a futures market are often divided into hedgers, speculators, arbitragers, and market makers. Hedgers are usually members of the commercial trade who use futures contracts to offset risk exposure in the cash market; speculators consist of public participants who voluntarily assume risk when entering a futures contract in anticipation of potential gains; abritragers simultaneously operate in cash and futures markets to take advantage of pricing discrepancies; and the market makers in futures buy and sell continuously throughout a trading session to take advantage of temporary imbalances in order flow. Except for the last group, which consists primarily of individual floor traders on a futures exchange (sometimes referred to as scalpers), many of the larger financial institutions frequently act in all capacities. For example, commercial banks use Treasury-bond futures to hedge their portfolios of government securities, they may speculate on the course of monetary policy using the Treasury-bill contract, and they could act as arbitragers between the foreign exchange markets and foreign currency futures. In a similar vein, pension funds might hedge, speculate, and arbitrage in the stock index and Treasury-bond contracts; savings and loan associations and mortgage bankers have done the same in Government National Mortgage Association (GNMA) futures; while investment bankers have the flexibility to operate in all markets and in all capacities. Precise data on the extent of these activities are scarce,[2] but the incentive for these activities will become clearer below.

Purposes and Functions

The two most frequently cited economic contributions of futures markets are hedging and price discovery. Both are listed in "Guideline No. 1" of the Commodity Futures Trading Commission (CFTC) as required for newly proposed contracts,[3] and both appear in the academic literature on futures.[4] In fact, "Guideline No. 1" of the CFTC offers simple definitions of each of these concepts; it states that the price-discovery function of a futures market will be satisfied if "prices involved in transactions for future delivery in the contract . . . are . . . generally quoted and disseminated as a basis for determining prices to producers, merchants, or consumers of such commodity." The hedging use of a futures market is indicated when "transactions are utilized by producers, merchants, or consumers engaged in handling such commodity . . . as a means of hedging themselves against possible loss through fluctuations in price."

Price discovery is an information-based contribution of futures markets, whereas hedging implies a transactions role for futures contracts. In both cases the main contribution appears to lie in establishing prices for the future delivery of a commodity and for providing a forum for transacting at such prices. This is an obvious contribution to those dealing in the cash commodity who need prices to plan production and consumption decisions. Moreover, merchants and consumers who want to avoid the risk of future price fluctuations can eliminate that risk by buying or selling a futures contract today. Although these benefits of futures markets appear obvious, more careful consideration of the issues is required for all storable commodities and for financial futures in particular.

The Case of Perfectly Storable Commodities. For perfectly storable commodities such as precious metals and most financial instruments, a well-defined relationship exists between cash market prices and futures prices. More specificially, as long as the underlying commodity is in ample supply, so that spot market holdings can be carried forward into the future, the futures price equals the spot price plus carrying cost, where carrying costs are primarily the net interest cost of holding the cash commodity from the current date until the settlement date on the futures contract.[5]

This so-called arbitrage carry model holds because arbitragers will act to reap riskless profits when the model is violated and, in the process, will drive cash and futures prices back into line. If the futures price is above the spot price plus carrying cost, for example, arbitragers find it profitable to buy the cash commodity, sell the futures contract, and deliver the cash commodity on the settlement date of the contract. The arbitrager earns the difference between the (higher) futures price and the spot price plus carrying cost. Sales of the futures contract by arbitragers and their purchases of the cash commodity drive futures and spot prices together so that they do not differ by more than carrying costs. If the futures price were lower than the spot price plus carrying costs, arbitragers would buy the futures contract, sell the cash commodity, and stand for delivery. This procedure forces up the futures price and brings down the cash price until they differ by exactly the cost of carrying forward the cash market position.

The integration of the cash and futures market through the behavior of arbitragers is crucial for the hedging function of futures markets. Hedgers rarely buy or sell a futures contract and hold until the delivery date of the contract. Rather, hedgers use the futures contract as a temporary offset for a cash market position and rely on the comovement in cash and futures prices (guaranteed by the arbitragers) to validate the hedge. A pension fund that anticipates a cash inflow at the end of the month and must buy bonds at that time, for example, can hedge its anticipated needs by purchasing a Treasury-bond futures contract for one month and then selling it. If the cash price of bonds rises during the month, the long futures position generates a gain to offset the higher cash bond price the pension fund must pay at the end of the month. Similarly, if cash prices fall, the decline in futures prices generates a loss that offsets the lower cash bond prices the pension fund will pay. Thus comovement of cash and futures prices is essential for the hedging use of futures markets.

Although the integration of cash and futures markets is crucial to hedgers, the effectiveness of the process appears, at first glance, to erase the price-discovery and risk-transfer contributions of futures markets. As far as price discovery goes, if the futures price equals the cash price plus carrying costs, with the latter measured by an interest rate, then price discovery requires nothing more than a cash market and a credit market. Once the cash price is given by the spot market and the relevant interest rate is derived from the credit market, the futures market price seems redundant.

A similar argument appears to make the hedging function of the futures market redundant as well. Instead of the pension fund buying a futures contract in anticipation of buying bonds at the end of a month, the pension fund could borrow money now, buy bonds in the cash market, and repay the borrowed funds with the cash inflow one month hence.

Thus, although risk transfer and price discovery are important functions, they are not uniquely provided by futures markets. In particular, for perfectly storable commodities, the effective integration of cash and futures markets through arbitrage seems to render futures markets completely redundant economic institutions. Although this perspective seems plausible, it will become obvious shortly that it is much too narrow and simplistic to evaluate properly the economic contribution of futures markets.

Efficient Price Discovery and Hedging. For most storable commodities—like gold, silver, and most financial futures—the main contribution of futures markets is not that they provide unique opportunities for risk transfer and price discovery but that they offer risk-transfer facilities at lower cost and provide more reliable price information compared with the relevant cash markets. First the improved price discovery process is discussed and then the more efficient risk-transfer facilities are examined.

The cash markets for most commodities are fragmented among numerous commercial dealers and endless varieties of product. Forward markets for such commodities are similarly fragmented among alternative delivery dates and locations. Price information is not easily uncovered, especially by the nonprofessional public, in a market dominated by secretive dealers and confused by gradations of products. A futures contract specifies a homogeneous variety of product and designates a unique delivery date for settlement. This standardization is designed to permit third-party transfer of contracts and to reduce the search cost of locating potential buyers and sellers. By centralizing order flow to a unique location—the pit on the floor of a futures exchange—a single price emerges for the variety of the product specified in the futures contract. Thus a single price emerges for gold, silver, wheat, and corn (all highly storable commodities) as well as for Treasury bonds, Treasury notes, and certificates of deposit (CDs) to replace the multitude of cash market prices quoted for specific items by numerous dealers. Moreover, these prices are widely disseminated by the futures exchanges, so that price information is easily uncovered by the interested public.

A second component of the price-discovery role of futures markets emerges from the fact that futures prices combine the spot price with the cost of funds between the current date and the settlement date of the futures contract. The futures market quotes a combined price—for the spot commodity plus carrying cost—that reflects marginal carrying cost and the simultaneous execution of the spot market purchase or sale and related credit terms. This "bundling of price quotes" is a special contribution of futures markets (and forward markets) that cannot be directly inferred from spot markets as long as simultaneous execution in cash and credit markets is costly and requires skill.

Perhaps the most important outcome of the standardization of contract terms in futures markets is the liquidity that emerges as a result of the increased participation of hedgers and speculators in the marketplace. Although liquidity is defined in detail below, it can be identified for now with the ability to transact quickly without unduly influencing price. Most evidence shows that liquidity is positively related to the volume of trading.[6] Moreover, because of the large number of participants in liquid markets, transactions prices more accurately reflect the judgment of all potential traders, bringing transactions prices closer to true equilibrium prices compared with less liquid markets.[7]

The lower transactions costs of futures markets permits commercial hedgers a more efficient mechanism for transferring risk compared with cash markets. Selling out a cash market position on short notice might require substantial search efforts to locate buyers; entering a forward contract for delivery at some future date might be equally time consuming or impossible. Moreover, only a subset of potential transactors is usually uncovered through such efforts, leading to transactions prices that may not accurately reflect equilibrium prices. Under such circumstances, hedgers will have to sell at price discounts from the true equilibrium price, while long hedgers must pay excessive premiums. One of the main advantages of transacting in futures markets, therefore, stems from the greater volume of trading that generates transactions prices that more accurately reflect underlying supply and demand forces of the entire market.

Transferring risk by selling short in the futures market is often considered a special contribution of futures markets. In fact, this contribution requires more careful scrutiny than it is usually given. Selling short in the cash market usually requires that the seller borrow the commodity for the duration of the short sale (in order to deliver it). In executing a short sale in the cash market, one may have difficulty uncovering potential lenders of the commodity or be unable to borrow the specific grades needed to deliver to consummate the sale. Futures markets permit short sales without such complications because the underlying commodity does not have to be delivered as part of the sale.

The problem with such a simplistic view is that while short sales can occur in futures markets without borrowing the underlying asset, the price at which those sales take place will reflect transactions costs in the cash market. For example, if arbitragers cannot sell short easily and cheaply in the cash market, they will not turn around and prop up the futures price with their puchases. Futures prices will then be depressed relative to cash prices, with the discount reflecting the costs associated with selling short. Thus only if short selling is easily accomplished in the cash market will futures markets offer cost-effective short-selling facilities. But in that case where is the special benefit of short sales in futures markets?

The answer is that futures markets can effectively transfer the short-selling capabilities of some market participants (such as arbitragers) to other market participants. In particular, when an institution that does not have the credit arrangements to sell short in the cash market sells futures instead, those who can sell short easily in the cash market will arbitrage between the two markets and prevent futures prices from falling relative to cash prices. Thus these arbitragers allow the short sales in futures markets to occur without excessive price discounts (and the implicit costs they imply). This transfer of transactions services among market participants is a crucial aspect of the contribution of financial futures, and will be discussed more fully below.

Transactions Efficiency of Financial Futures

For all of the financial futures markets listed in table 2–1, well-organized and highly liquid cash markets existed prior to the introduction of futures trading. Commercial banks have always acted as dealers in foreign currencies, quoting bids and offers to each other and to corporate customers. Commercial banks and investment bankers form an active dealer network for trading Treasury securities, CDs, and other money market instruments; and, of course, the various stock exchanges provide a centralized market for equities trading. In comparison with agricultural and other commodity markets, the cash markets for financial instruments are well organized and highly liquid. At first glance, therefore, it appears difficult to argue that the dominant contribution of financial futures rests with the traditional price-discovery and liquidity advantages of futures markets compared with cash markets.

Nor does the answer seem to lie with the absence of forward contracting in financial markets. Foreign currencies, the first financial futures introduced, trade in an active forward market. The same holds for GNMAs, the first of the interest rate futures. Even for Treasury bills, the first short-term debt futures contract, transforming cash transactions into forward contracts by combined purchases and sales of different maturities is relatively easy.[8] Thus, while the "bundling of cash transactions with credit agreements for deferred delivery" might be important to the success of some financial futures, it cannot form the foundation for the success of the earliest contracts.

91

Even the provision of short-selling facilities cannot be cited as the cornerstone of the success of financial futures. While some cash markets do not provide any facilities for short selling (such as the markets for CD and Eurodollar time deposits), the most successful of all financial futures, Treasury bonds, has a cash market where selling short is easily accomplished. In fact, for some participants in the marketplace, selling short cash Treasury bonds is preferable to selling short Treasury-bond futures.[9]

One can argue that while none of these advantages holds for all financial futures, each financial futures contract succeeded for a somewhat different reason. For example, foreign currency futures and GNMA futures added liquidity to organized forward markets, and short-sale restrictions were overcome by the Eurodollar contract and stock index futures. In both of these cases, more effective risk-transfer and hedging facilities were added to the marketplace. Similarly, futures markets added a new dimension to price discovery in the cloistered dealer markets for Treasury securities and money market instruments by providing a single market price for a specific standardized security.

Each of these points accurately describes the contributions of specific financial futures contracts. But the common denominator permitting improved risk transfer and price discovery in each of these cases is the lower transactions costs of futures markets compared with cash markets. After all, each of these underlying cash markets permits risk transfer and price discovery, but futures markets improve substantially on these services, especially for nondealers. Futures markets bring the low cost of transacting faced by dealers to the rest of the financial community. As shown below, this "democratization of efficient transactions services" underlies much of the success of financial futures.

Improved Liquidity for All Participants. Transactions costs consist of two elements: (1) a commission paid to an agent executing a purchase or sale; and (2) the price discount or premium incurred to get the trade done. The latter is often measured by the spread between the best bid and offer in the market or by the spread quoted by a market-making dealer. The bid price represents what a public seller will get from an immediate sale while the higher offer price is what a public buyer must pay. The spread represents the costs of a *round turn*, an immediate purchase and sale.

Measuring liquidity costs seems fairly straightforward under these circumstances. Securities with narrow bid-asked spreads are more liquid than those with wider spreads, given that commissions for agent executions are fairly similar. If the quoted spread for a corporate bond is ½ point, it costs $5 per $1,000 to buy and sell immediately, while if the quoted spread on a government bond is ⅛ point, it costs $1.25 per $1,000 to buy and sell. Thus the government bond market would be more liquid than the corporate bond market.

An important dimension to liquidity that is often overlooked but is crucial to market traders is the size of trade that can be done at the prevailing spreads. If the bids and offers are good for $20 million of securities, the market is much more liquid than if the quotes are good for only $1 million. An attempt at selling $20 million in a market where the prevailing quote is good for only $1 million is likely to force the price lower than the prevailing bid to complete the trade. Similarly, the cost of buying $20 million will be higher than indicated by the offer in the market.

Although quoted spreads are usually good in specific markets for standard-sized trades, they can vary between different customers and with market conditions. Comparing the liquidity of futures markets with cash markets is, therefore, much more complicated than simply evaluating the respective bid-asked spreads. Care must be taken to identify precisely what is being measured. Thus the quoted spread on active long-term Treasury bonds is ⅛ per $100 (for example, a bid of 100–5/32 and an offer of 100–9/32) based on dealer quote sheets or *Wall Street Journal* listings, while the usual spread in the Treasury-bond futures market is 1/32. Even when commission costs are added to the latter, the nominal cost for a standard $1 million trade in bond futures would be substantially less than the comparable trade in the cash market.

Of course, preferred institutional customers of a government bond dealer can almost always expect a narrower spread than ⅛. Many actively traded bonds are quoted to customers on a 1/16 spread. Even with this narrower spread, however, the cash market for governments is at a disadvantage to futures because a customer is never certain that a dealer's quote is the best available at a particular time. In the futures market, the highest bid and lowest offer are automatically uncovered because of centralized order flow to the futures pit. In the cash market, however, the customer must search among several dealers to get the best bid and offer.

Medium-sized financial institutions that are not preferred dealer customers must be especially diligent in searching for the lowest offer and the highest bid when executing in decentralized dealer markets. Kenneth Garbade and William Silber showed that price dispersion among government securities dealers leads to higher execution costs for public traders in Treasuries.[10] Thus, nondealer financial institutions have multidimensional cost incentives to execute in the bond futures market rather than in the cash markets.

The only reason for trading in the cash market is that futures contracts are standardized instruments, implying there is basis risk (see note 9) when futures are used to hedge any particular cash instrument. For example, the price of a newly issued twenty-year government bond may not move that closely with the Treasury-bond contract because the latter prices off the cheapest deliverable long-term Treasury security (which may be a 7 ½ percent coupon bond with seventeen years to maturity). Thus, if an institution owns a recently issued Treasury issue, a better hedge may be simply to sell the bonds, especially since the cash market for recently issued Treasury bonds is quite liquid. For most other bonds, however, the liquidity advantage of futures markets dominates all other considerations.

For professional dealers in Treasuries, the advantage of futures markets is less clear. The cash markets in certain active issues can frequently dominate the futures market. Interdealer quotation screens offered by brokers in Treasury securities permit dealers to execute on much better terms than are available to the public. Moreover, in the cash markets one has no mark-to-market settlement and associated cash flows to worry about.[11] Thus dealers sometimes find the cash markets more cost effective than futures. The other side of the coin is that dealers frequently use the futures market to hedge inventory over short time intervals. The ability to execute quickly and in substantial size, without searching for the other side of the trade, is crucial to a market-making dealer. In contrast with the cash market, the futures market in bonds always has bids and offers of at least 1,000 contracts on either side of the market (implying that about $100 million can be traded without influencing market price).

One can see that, although professional dealers are sometimes ambiguous about their preference for cash versus futures markets, nondealer institutions and the public are not. Savings and loan associations, pension funds, nondealer commercial banks, and individuals can transact at costs approaching the interdealer market only by using financial futures. The best example of this democratization of transactions costs can be illustrated with short selling. Nondealer institutions usually do not have the credit lines for directly borrowing securities as part of a short sale. Thus they would have to execute such a transaction through a dealer, with the associated middleman's markup. The ability to sell short in futures markets without delivering securities is a clear reduction in costs to nondealers. These short sales do not depress futures prices relative to cash prices (which would be an implicit cost to short sellers) because dealers arbitrage between cash and futures markets and because *they* can sell short cheaply. Thus the futures market transfers the low-cost short-selling facilities of dealers to the nondealer public.

An extreme example of this transfer occurs in markets in which short selling is impossible (costs are infinite) because securities are not negotiable and hence they cannot be borrowed. Eurodollar time deposits are the best example of such an instrument. The only institutions that can sell Eurodollar time deposits are banks. A nonfinancial corporation with borrowing rates tied to the Eurodollar time deposit rate might like to sell short Eurodollar time deposits so that if rates go up (prices go down) the firm's higher borrowing cost will be offset by its short sale. The corporation can sell Eurodollars short in the futures markets, thereby hedging its future borrowing cost. The short sale will not depress futures prices relative to the spot market because banks would buy the relatively cheap futures contracts and offset the purchase by issuing (selling) Eurodollar time deposits (and investing the proceeds). Thus, even though short selling is impossible, issuers can always issue securities, and that has the same effect on price. Futures markets thus deliver short-selling facilities to the nondealer segment of the market through arbitrage, even when short selling per se is impossible.

This example points up another dimension to the transactions efficiency of futures markets. A nonfinancial corporation with future borrowing costs tied to the rate on Eurodollar time deposits can hedge these borrowing costs by selling short the Eurodollar contract. A straightforward alternative is to borrow funds immediately and invest the proceeds in other money market instruments until the funds are needed. Only if the futures market hedge is more efficient than this direct hedge will the futures contract be employed. The main considerations in favor of the futures market hedge are (1) it avoids cluttering the firm's balance sheet with unneeded current borrowings; (2) it leaves open the firm's bank credit lines; (3) it avoids the necessary financial expertise involved in continuously reinvesting the proceeds of the borrowing at favorable rates; (4) it does not require current balance sheet evidence of creditworthiness. These advantages represent transactions efficiencies for the futures hedge because that mechanism accomplishes the objective of offsetting price-risk exposure without requiring associated evidence of credit or special institutional relationships.

The Special Case of Index Futures. Although all financial futures offer transactions efficiencies compared with their respective cash markets, financial futures that are based on market indices have special advantages. So far the only index futures are stock market products, including Standard & Poor's 500 index, the NYSE composite index, the Value Line index, and the Major Market index. All index futures are cash settlement contracts, although the reverse is not true (to wit, the Eurodollar contract). Garbade and Silber emphasize that index products require cash settlement because the transactions costs associated with delivering the components of an index effectively prohibit physical delivery.[12] For example, 500 individual stocks make up Standard & Poor's 500 index. If physical delivery were required, then shorts would have to deliver to longs each of those 500 different securities (including fractional parts of some). The huge transactions costs incurred when assembling these securities would prevent arbitragers from forcing convergence between the cash prices of the component securities and the weighted average represented by the index. Without convergence, the hedging use of the contract would be severely hampered.

Cash settlement permits shorts to settle their obligations to longs through a cash payment determined by the market value of the index. Thus the futures contract will converge, on settlement date, to the weighted average of the prices of the securities included in the index. This arrangement creates a product in the futures market that exists in the cash market only as a market basket of various component securities. The cash settlement stock index contracts permit investors to buy and sell this market basket of securities without transacting in each of the component securities.

From this perspective, the stock index contract simply reduces the transactions costs associated with assembling the market basket of securities in the index. Alternatively, the contract can be viewed as creating a generalized "dollar value equity product" for which no corresponding cash commodity exists.[13] Although these alternative perspectives appear largely semantic, they suggest different ways of measuring the transactions economies of the stock index contracts. If the "dollar value equity approach" is taken, then one compares the cost of buying and selling a stock index contract with the cost of a similar dollar transaction in some particular equity. For example, the cost of buying and selling one Standard & Poor's 500 contract (equivalent to about $90,000 of equities) is about $50.00 ($25.00 for commissions to a discount futures broker plus $25.00 for the one tick bid-asked spread in the futures market). The cost of buying and selling $90,000 of a representative $50.00 stock is about $1,300.00.[14]

The cost of assembling a market basket of equities to replicate the weighted combination of securities in the index exceeds the estimated $1,300.00 cost. Numerous individual transactions, many of them in odd lots of stock, render a precise calculation difficult and an exact duplication of the index nearly impossible. Alternative strategies, such as buying and selling a diversified mutual fund or a subset of stocks that track the index, are somewhat cheaper. Once the time required to assemble a representative portfolio of securities is taken into account, however, the conclusion that the stock index contract creates a unique new product seems a more accurate characterization than the purely transactions-cost view.

Liquidity and the Cost of Capital. The contribution of financial futures can be summarized in the following way. The foundation is a reduction in the cost of transacting and an associated increase in market liquidity. These advantages accrue primarily to financial institutions and public traders who did not have access to the low transactions costs available to professional dealers. Moreover, the reduced transactions costs allow financial futures markets to deliver hedging and price-discovery facilities more efficiently than even the well-developed cash markets in financial instruments. In some cases the price-discovery role of financial futures is most important—as might be true of Treasury-bond futures—while in other cases the improved hedging facilities are the dominant contribution—as with the stock index contracts. In all cases the contribution of financial futures starts with reduced transactions costs.

The next step is to evaluate whether liquidity costs and transactions economies are sufficiently important in the economy to warrant the diversion of scarce resources to the financial futures industry. Although a free market approach allows the marketplace to answer questions, to provide some intuitive evidence on the importance of liquidity to the economy as a whole is useful. To do so puts the contribution of financial futures into proper perspective.

One of the most important groups of institutions in the financial sector is secondary markets in which existing securities are traded among investors. The New York Stock Exchange and the over-the-counter markets in equities, government bonds, money market instruments, corporate bonds, and municipal bonds are all examples of secondary markets. Significant amounts of technological equipment (for example, computers and electronic communications devices) are utilized in these markets. Moreover, highly skilled professional traders are employed as market makers. Thus secondary markets utilize expensive physical and human resources. The most important product of secondary markets is the liquidity inherent in the bids and offers quoted by dealers. The value of these liquidity services to the economy as a whole is measured by the returns earned by the capital and labor employed in secondary markets. Although no industry breakdown for these data exists, casual observation suggests that these resources are highly remunerated.

A more specific indication of the value of liquidity provided by secondary markets is as follows. If AT&T, IBM, or another company issued a ten- or twenty-year bond that could not be sold before maturity, the interest rate the company would have to pay would surely exceed its current cost of funds. Investors accept a lower yield on a ten- or twenty-year bond because they know they can change their mind and sell even a few days after purchasing it. This flexibility is provided by the liquidity services offered by market-making dealers in secondary markets.

A specific estimate of the value of liquidity to investors is suggested by Garbade.[15] A comparison of yields on Treasury bills and Treasury bonds with less than six months to maturity shows that bonds often yield almost ½ percent more than Treasury bills with the identical maturity. The only difference between the two securities is that Treasury bonds with only six months left to maturity have virtually no secondary market, while Treasury bills are perhaps the most liquid of all instruments. Investors apparently place a value of ½ percent on the flexibility offered by secondary markets over a six-month horizon. Quite possibly for longer-term securities the value of liquidity is even greater.

This discussion implies that the liquidity provided by financial markets clearly adds to economic welfare by reducing the cost of capital to potential real investments, with the associated benefits for capital formation.[16] Since the major contribution of financial futures is an improvement in the liquidity of financial markets, one can conclude that financial futures add to real investment and capital formation. Although this may seem a somewhat circuitous route to uncovering the ultimate economic contribution of financial futures, it is in fact no more roundabout than the economic contribution of popular secondary markets such as the New York Stock Exchange and the government bond market. More specific examples of how financial futures contribute on a microeconomic level can be illustrated by examining how financial futures are used in practice.

Financial Futures in Practice

Many of the major financial institutions use financial futures in some capacity. Commercial banks, thrifts, and other lending institutions hedge their portfolios of securities with interest rate futures. Investment bankers and other securities dealers use stock index and interest rate futures to hedge their market-making activities; and pension funds, trust companies, and mutual funds use the stock index and interest rate contracts for market-timing and hedging purposes. Rather than tediously reviewing each institution's approach, it seems more fruitful to provide some illustrations on a functional level.

Market Making. Many large commercial banks act as dealers in government bonds, municipal bonds, and mortgages. Most investment banking firms are market makers in all of these securities as well as in corporate bonds, and in over-the-counter stocks. In addition, major investment-banking firms also specialize in block trading in equities; that is, they make markets to institutional investors (such as pension funds) who trade in large blocks of stock (for example, 10,000 shares or more) listed on the New York Stock Exchange. All of these market makers quote bids and offers to investors and wind up buying and selling securities at the public's initiative. In the process of providing these liquidity services, they make extensive use of futures markets to hedge their inventory on a temporary basis.

A securities dealer will make a better market to a customer— that is, quote a narrower bid-asked spread for larger volume—if it can lay off some of the risk exposure of the inventory in the futures market. The most important characteristic of liquidity to a dealer is the ability to buy or sell immediately, without searching for the other side of the transaction. If early one morning a bank buys $500 million of long-term Treasuries and it has considerable inventory left over by 11:30 that morning, it is likely to sell Treasury-bond futures to protect itself during the 11:30–12:00 o'clock period when the Federal Reserve might intervene with open market operations. The government securities dealer cannot afford the time to search for a buyer of the specific Treasury issues. It must hedge against general price movements in Treasuries immediately. In this case the hedge might last only a short time—until the Federal Reserve's intervention period has passed.

If the dealer did not have the option of offsetting the position in the futures markets, it would have quoted a wider spread for less size to its original customer. In fact, most institutions know that the cash market in government securities becomes much less liquid after 3:00 P.M. New York time, when the Treasury-bond futures market closes in Chicago.

The equity-trading desks of investment-banking firms that are market makers in blocks of stock routinely use the stock index contracts to hedge their inventory exposure. A block desk will quote bids and offers for specific equities to large pension funds and mutual funds.

During the course of a trading day it might hold 50,000 to 100,000 shares of thirty or forty different equities. The block desk protects itself against price movements of the market as a whole by selling stock index futures if it is long equities or buying stock index futures if it is short equities. In fact, these hedges may be put on and taken off several times during a trading session as the block desk's position changes.

One of the problems inherent in market making with specific equities is the risk that a buyer or seller has information that will affect the specific price of a stock. The trade is then information based rather than liquidity motivated. A dealer will make a better market for a package of equities rather than one or two individual stocks because it is then less concerned about inside information. Such buy-or-sell progams for groups of large blocks of stock are ideally hedged in the stock index futures market.

One should note that the essence of market making severely hampers dealers from using the specific cash market as a hedging vehicle. Although one of the alternatives to hedging in the futures market is to sell out the position in the cash market, a dealer who has just bought specific equities or corporate bonds, usually cannot hedge by immediately selling out that position because the seller came to the dealer precisely to find a market maker who would inventory the securities. The only market in which hedging easily in the cash market is possible is in Treasury bonds. Recently issued Treasuries are sufficiently liquid to accommodate large-sized purchases and sales. Yet even here, after the futures market closes, the Treasury-bond market is not as liquid as it is when dealers can lay off risk in futures.

This discussion of how market makers use financial futures adds still another dimension to the liquidity contribution of financial futures. Not only are financial futures markets more liquid than the underlying cash markets, with the associated transactions economies, but financial futures also make the cash markets themselves more liquid. Thus the discussion has come almost full circle in tracing the effects of financial futures: they bring improved liquidity services to those who are not professional dealers in cash markets and simultaneously allow dealers to make more liquid cash markets. These effects stem from the transactions economies that attract a larger number of participants to the marketplace.

Portfolio Management and Timing. Pension funds, insurance companies, trust departments of banks, and mutual funds all manage large sums of money. Unlike market makers, these institutions are concerned with buying securities and earning returns over longer time horizons. In particular, they must realize a rate of return on assets under management that covers the returns promised on liabilities without exposing themselves to excessive risk.

Portfolio managers frequently use financial futures for purposes of market timing. Inflows of funds may be temporarily held in cash equivalents such as money market accounts until the appropriate package of specific equities and bonds is identified for puchase. To avoid the price uncertainty associated with the delayed purchase of securities, the portfolio manager would buy a combination of Treasury-bond futures and stock index contracts as an anticipatory hedge. When the specific stocks and bonds are actually purchased, the financial futures are sold. Market-related price movements will be offset by the long futures position.

Financial futures are also used by money managers as a temporary sale of a package of securities. Suppose the governing board of a pension fund views the next two months as undesirable for stocks. It recommends that assets invested in equities should be reduced by 20 percent as an interim measure. Rather than selling individual stocks, which may be difficult to repurchase without paying significant transactions cost (especially as a result of market maker's fears of information-based trading), the portfolio manager can neutralize market-related price movements by taking a short position in stock index futures. After the excessive price uncertainty has passed, the manager buys back the stock index contracts, with the gains or losses offsetting the price movements on the basket of equities.

In all of these cases, portfolio managers use financial futures as temporary substitutes for cash market transactions (where temporary can mean months rather than the one or two hour horizon of the market maker). An alternative description of the process is that the portfolio manager is hedging a cash market position in futures markets. From either perspective, the ultimate advantage of financial futures is that they are more transactionally efficient than the cash market. In each of these examples, the portfolio manager has the option of using the cash markets as an alternative to futures markets. Moreover, these cash market transactions frequently require the active participation of market-making dealers. Futures markets permit the portfolio manager to bypass the middleman if doing so is transactionally efficient.

Gap Management and Interest Rate Risk. Commercial banks and thrift institutions have always been confronted with the problem of managing the gap between the maturity structure of their assets and liabilities. One of the main sources of difficulty for savings and loan associations during the 1970s was that they borrowed short term and loaned funds long term. When the level of interest rates skyrocketed during the late 1970s and early 1980s, the cost of funds to savings and loans jumped while their assets showed severe capital losses. Thus a large gap between the maturity structure of an institution's assets and liabilities exposes the firm to significant risk when the level of interest rates changes.

One solution has been to develop a more flexible asset and liability structure so that these institutions can more easily match interest rate commitments on each side of their balance sheet. Matching risk exposure in this way is constrained by customer preferences, however. Borrowers from depository institutions may prefer six-month fixed-rate loans, while lenders to these institutions (the public) prefer weekly adjustments in deposit rates; or the reverse may be true. Financial futures offer depository institutions a mechanism for managing the gap between the maturity structure of their assets and liabilities that does not depend exclusively on customer preferences. If a savings and loan institution has a preponderence of three-month CDs outstanding but has committed loans with six-month maturities, it can hedge the rate it will pay when renewing its CDs by selling short CD or Eurodollar futures. If rates rise (CD prices fall) and they pay more for funds, there will be an offsetting gain on the short futures position. Although this strategy could have been replicated in the cash market by borrowing for six months rather than three, the use of financial futures permits savings and loans to satisfy their customer preferences at the same time as managing risk exposure.

Lending institutions have been especially attracted to the Eurodollar futures market, which is a cash settlement contract based on the London interbank offer rate (LIBOR). Many loans to corporations use LIBOR as a reference point for pricing. A firm will be charged LIBOR plus 1 or 2 percent, as credit ratings vary. An ideal offset to the risk exposure of the loan is the Eurodollar futures market. Although some banks have the alternative of borrowing directly in the London market through affiliates, not all domestic banks do. Moreover, a bank might not want to increase its presence in the Eurodollar market because it does not want to impair its own credit standing. By using the Eurodollar futures market to hedge its lending exposure, it effectively minimizes its risk without suffering elsewhere in its balance sheet. Thus futures permit the institution a more precise risk management tool, one that links an asset with its risk offset without additional complications.

In a broader sense, financial futures permit institutions to decentralize the task of risk management. Matching maturities on the asset and liabilities sides of the balance sheet has the advantage of a global view of the firm's risk exposure. Financial futures can be used at the micro level by individual decision makers. It is sometimes useful to allow risk adjustments at that level, with only the residual exposure passed on for corporate level adjustments.

International Risk Exposure. Multinational industrial corporations that receive and make payments in foreign currencies can hedge the risk of exchange rate variability by matching their foreign assets and liabilities directly. Over short time horizons, however, normal inflows and outflows of foreign currencies are likely to expose the firm's income to fluctuations in foreign exchange rates. Some of these risks can be offset in the dealer market in foreign exchange that is operated by major international banks. Futures contracts on foreign currencies permit multinational corporations to deal directly with one another, rather than hedging exclusively through financial middlemen.

The advantage of lower transactions costs in futures markets is offset, somewhat, by the fact that the futures market in foreign currencies is open for only about five hours a day (8:30 A.M. to 2:20 P.M. New York time), while the need for foreign currency protection emerges throughout the day. Thus, although a nonfinancial corporation could easily ignore the dealer market in bonds, making exclusive use of interest rate futures, it cannot do the same with foreign currency futures, in which the dealer market is essential for complete coverage of market risks. The Chicago Mercantile Exchange has forged a link with the futures market in Singapore precisely to provide hedging facilities around the clock. The success of this innovation will depend, in part, upon the importance of foreign currency futures to corporate hedgers.

Given the description of how financial futures are used by institutions in both the financial and nonfinancial sectors, one can reasonably conclude that each particular contract provides an important service and meets unfulfilled needs. It might be instructive, therefore, to review the success and failure of specific financial futures contracts to see whether further evidence emerges on their economic contribution.

The Success and Failure of Specific Contracts

After the success of the GNMA futures contract indicated that interest rate futures were viable instruments, numerous other specific contracts were innovated. Table 2–2 shows all of the interest rate and stock

TABLE 2–2
FINANCIAL FUTURES INNOVATIONS: 1975–1982

Contract	Exchange	Date of Innovation	Average Daily Volume	Wall Street Journal Listing	Traded in 1985
GNMA-CDR[1]	CBT	10/20/75	1995	Yes	Yes
Treasury bills (90-day)	CME	1/6/76	1610	Yes	Yes
Treasury bonds	CBT	8/22/77	7954	Yes	Yes
Commercial paper (90-day)	CBT	9/26/77	99	No	No
Treasury bills (1-year)	CME	9/11/78	63	No	No
GNMA-CD[2]	CBT	9/12/78	180	No	No
GNMA-CD[2]	ACE[3]	9/12/78	180	No	No
Commercial paper (30-day)	CBT	5/14/79	12	No	No
Treasury notes (4-6-year)	CBT	6/25/79	88	No	No
Treasury bills (90-day)	ACE[3]	6/26/79	52	No	No
Treasury notes (4-year)	CME	7/10/79	93	No	No
Treasury bills (90-day)	COMEX	10/2/79	286	No	No
GNMA-CD[2]	COMEX	11/13/79	47	No	No
Treasury bonds	ACE[3]	11/14/79	130	No	No
Treasury bonds	NYFE	8/7/80	867	Yes	No
Treasury bills (90-day)	NYFE	8/14/80	188	No	No
Treasury notes (2-year)	COMEX	12/2/80	290	No	No
CD (90-day)	NYFE	7/9/81	914	No	No
CD (90-day)	CBT	7/22/81	895	No	No
CD (90-day)	CME	7/29/81	5103	Yes	Yes
Eurodollar (3 month)	CME	12/9/81	2012	Yes	Yes
Value Line Index	KCBT	2/24/82	2683	Yes	Yes
S & P 500 Index	CME	4/21/82	24156	Yes	Yes
Treasury notes (6½–10-year)	CBT	5/3/82	4228	Yes	Yes
NYSE Composite index	NYFE	5/6/82	11656	Yes	Yes

NOTES: CBT = Chicago Board of Trade; CME = Chicago Mercantile Exchange; ACE = Amex Commodity Exchanges; COMEX = Commodity Exchange; NYFE = New York Futures Exchange; and KCBT = Kansas City Board of Trade.
1. GNMA-CDR = Collateralized Depository Receipt GNMA contract.
2. GNMA-CD = Certificate Deposit GNMA contract.
3. No longer in existence.

SOURCE: Deborah Black, "Success and Failure of Futures Contracts: Theory and Empirical Evidence," Unpublished Doctoral Dissertation, Graduate School of Business, NYU, 1985.

index contracts introduced between 1975 and 1982, including data on the date they were innovated, the average daily volume during the first three years of trading (or fractions thereof), the exchange on which the contract was innovated, whether the contract was ever listed in the *Wall Street Journal*, and whether it was still trading in 1985.[17]

Identifying a cutoff point for a successful contract is a subjective matter. Some observers advocate a volume of at least 1,000 contracts per day, others cite listing in the *Wall Street Journal*, while still others use a longevity measure, such as whether the contract is still trading three years after it is introduced. By any of these criteria, only a subgroup of the financial futures introduced have been successful. Treasury bonds, Treasury notes, and three-month Treasury bills are successful interest rate contracts on government securities, while the one-year bill, two-year note, and four-to-six-year note contracts on Treasuries failed. In contracts on private debt instruments, the successes include the CD and Eurodollar time deposit contracts, while the failures include thirty-day and ninety-day commercial paper. As far as stock index futures are concerned, all of the contracts have thus far been successful, although there may be a further shakeout as the industry develops.

One approach to explaining the pattern of success and failure focuses on individual contract terms and commodity characteristics.[18] Such an idiosyncratic analysis has considerable merit in financial futures as described above. A broader approach to explaining the viability of a contract, one that identifies a set of common ingredients for successful contracts, has considerable attractiveness, however. The key question is, do successful contracts provide transactionally efficient hedging facilities and do the unsuccessful ones not provide them?

The only study that offers a unified explanation of contract success is by Deborah Black.[19] That analysis focuses on interest rate and stock index contracts and uses volume of trading and open interest as measures of success. Not surprisingly, the empirical results show that high price volatility and a large cash market for the particular financial instrument increase the chances for success. A far more important indicator of success, however, is the reduction in risk offered by a newly innovated financial futures contract compared with the risk exposure of cross-hedging the underlying financial instrument with an already existing, close substitute, financial futures contract. According to Black's analysis, for example, the futures contract on Treasury bonds succeeded largely because the reduction in risk offered by the new bond contract to those hedging Treasury bonds was significant when compared with the residual risk exposure of cross-hedging Treasury bonds with GNMA futures. Similarly, the Treasury-note contract succeeded because it offered substantially better facilities for hedging ten-year Treasury notes compared with the risk exposure remaining from hedging Treasury notes with the bond contract. The commercial paper contract, however, failed because it did not significantly reduce risk exposure below what would be accomplished by cross-hedging commercial paper with the Treasury-bill contract.

These results provide important evidence on the economic contribution of financial futures. Only if a new contract is designed to provide transactionally efficient hedging services will it trade actively. Moreover, an important reference for comparing the efficiency of a hedge seems to be an existing alternative futures contract. These results bear considerable testimony to the transactions advantages of futures contracts in general and successful ones in particular.

Some of the results reported by Black are far from intuitively obvious. The thirty-day and ninety-day commercial paper contracts did not succeed, while contracts on two other closely related private debt instruments—CDs and Eurodollars—were successful. The facts are that the reduction in residual risk provided by the CD and Euro-dollar contracts were sufficiently large to attract substantial trading, while that for the commercial paper contracts was not. These results emphasize the danger inherent in predicting redundancy of a futures contract simply because similar alternatives are already in existence. The marketplace provides the most efficient process of natural selection; it does not permit inefficient contracts to survive for very long.

Two examples of financial futures that have withered after considerable early success emphasize the market's intolerance of ineffective contracts. The GNMA contract, the first interest rate future, averaged nearly 2,000 contracts per day during its first three years and traded an average of more than 10,000 per day during the last quarter of 1980. During the last three months of 1984 the GNMA contract traded an average of only 1,000 contracts per day. The main problem is that the GNMA contract no longer provides an effective hedge for GNMA securities. The futures contract prices off the cheapest deliverable cash GNMA, which in recent years has been high-coupon GNMAs that behave more like two-year securities than like thirty-year mortgages.[20] Thus mortgage bankers, savings and loans, and market makers in cash GNMAs have stopped hedging with the GNMA futures contract.

The CD contract has a similar history, averaging more than 5,000 contracts per day during the first half of 1982, while in the last three months of 1984 it traded about 1,000 contracts per day. Here the problem seems to be the overwhelming success of the Eurodollar contract as well as the decline in domestic CDs outstanding during 1984 and 1985. Most hedging and speculation now centers around the Eurodollar contract, rather than around CDs.

Floor traders on the Chicago Mercantile Exchange, where CDs and Eurodollars trade, followed the order flow from the CD (and Treasury-bill) pits to the Eurodollar pit. If any doubt about the importance of transactionally efficient hedging to the success of futures contracts ever existed, these examples should be more than sufficient to dispel any lingering suspicion.

Policy Issues

Despite commercial and academic testimony supporting the economic contribution of futures markets,[21] some people still maintain that futures trading is more harmful than helpful. Concern with financial futures, in particular, emerged primarily over the frenzy of innovative activity that threatened to inundate the public with allegedly ill-conceived and potentially illiquid contracts. The analogy between futures and gambling, never far below the surface, emerged in full force when cash settlement was proposed as the only feasible way to specify the stock index contracts. Finally, the fear that futures contracts would dominate the cash markets of the underlying financial instruments, thereby impairing rather than improving liquidity, is a criticism that strikes at the heart of futures markets. Although the discussion thus far should have dispelled these criticisms, a brief overview is probably wothwhile.

Contract Proliferation. One of the earliest complaints concerning the unnecessary proliferation of financial futures contracts was presented in the U.S. Treasury–Federal Reserve study on futures markets.[22] Although the discussion in the previous section clearly indicates that the marketplace is an efficient processor of new futures contracts, one of the main legislative concerns with contract proliferation stems from the costs imposed on the public by a failed contract. More particularly, unsuspecting individuals may trade a contract that is doomed to failure and then find reversing the position difficult because the market is illiquid. The cost to the exchange of a failed contract is not of public concern because that is a private profit-making decision that is properly taken into account when a new contract innovation is considered. Only the social cost imposed on others—the nonprofessional public—is a relevant cost worthy of legislative concern.

Although illiquidity is the result of a failed contract, more prudent means of protecting the nonprofessional public than stifling contract innovation exist. Account executives at brokerage firms have a fiduciary responsibility to warn public participants that a new contract might not succeed and that liquidity problems may emerge. Account executives who do not carry out this responsibility should be subjected to CFTC disciplinary proceedings and be liable for pecuniary damages. This approach addresses the social cost of a failed contract without suppressing the innovative effort that leads to transactionally efficient hedging contracts.

Another argument against unrestrained new contract innovation focuses on the fragmented order flow stemming from too many individual contracts. The results will be an excessive number of illiquid contracts that will not serve hedgers well. This approach stresses that liquidity has the characteristics of a natural monopoly, hence only one contract should be authorized on any particular financial instrument.

One cannot deny that larger order flow implies narrower bid-asked spreads with larger size quoted on each side of the market, which in turn attracts greater order flow. The problem with protecting an existing contract from innovative pressure is that determining which contract will provide the most attractive transactionally efficient hedge is impossible. The example of the Eurodollar contract's surpassing the highly liquid CD contract is most instructive in this regard.

Moreover, on a theoretical level, a growing body of literature suggests that a natural monopoly need not be protected if potential competitors are not faced with large "sunk costs" that act as a barrier to entry.[23] In particular, since exchanges can easily shift resources (floor space and local traders) from trading one contract to another, no sunk costs stifle potential competition for existing contracts. Thus, even if liquidity is a natural monopoly, this situation does not imply that licensing of exclusive rights is necessary for optimal production of liquidity services. Potential competitors will keep the existing markets honest.[24] Thus the benefits of innovative contracts are gained without impairing market liquidity if unrestrained competition in new contract design is allowed.

The Cash Settlement Controversy. One of the most important innovations in the futures industry during the past decade has been cash settlement of contractual obligations. As described previously, cash settlement makes feasible futures contracts that are priced off a basket (or weighted average) of commodities rather than a single "cheapest deliverable" commodity. Although the circumstances under which cash settlement is the best way to proceed are complex,[25] that cash settlement creates the opportunity to introduce futures products that could not otherwise exist is hardly in doubt.

Some legislators have complained that cash settlement of contractual obligations is inappropriate because it closely resembles casino gambling. In both cases wagers are made on the outcome of an event (role of the dice or price movement of the stock market), and in both cases a cash payoff (positive or negative) depends upon the outcome. This description is accurate as far as it goes, but it ignores crucial distinctions.

In the case of a futures contract (any contract), the risk exists whether or not the futures contract is introduced. Stock prices fluctuate and portfolio managers suffer losses or earn gains irrespective of their participation in stock index futures. Not so with casino gambling, in which the risk is manufactured. Futures contracts simply permit market participants to transfer existing risks among themselves; and the process uncovers people who are more willing to take on the uncertainty in exchange for anticipated gains. Thus the analogy with casino gambling is forced at best, actually perverse if one recognizes that futures trading reduces the subjective risk exposure of society, while casino gambling increases it.

The irony is that the cash settlement feature of the stock index contract, which has been maligned with the casino gambling analogy, is in fact crucial to the usefulness of the contract as a hedging device. Hedgers require comovement between cash market prices and futures prices to use futures to offset risk. The comovement is promoted by arbitragers who buy and sell in the two markets when prices are out of line. Arbitragers rely upon the ultimate convergence between the cash and futures price on the settlement date of the contract to underwrite their activities. Convergence is forced by the ability to deliver the underlying product in satisfaction of contractual obligations. But transactions costs of assembling the 500-odd securities to deliver on the Standard & Poor's 500 index, for example, would prevent arbitragers from forcing convergence on the delivery date. Only by requiring cash settlement of contractual obligations does convergence emerge. Thus cash settlement, instead of raising questions about the hedging use of the contract, turns out to be a crucial feature for satisfactory hedging.

Dominant and Satellite Markets. The relationship between cash prices and futures prices has raised the question of which market leads in price movement. The natural order of things would suggest that cash

109

prices should lead futures prices because the latter derive their value from the former. In fact, futures contracts (like options) are often called derivative securities to indicate their secondary status. The issue is often raised within the context of the potential decline in liquidity in the cash market if the futures market turns out to dominate.

Although there exists a reasonable possibility that prices in futures markets lead cash prices, this is hardly a perversion of the natural order. Rather, it simply reflects the greater transactions efficiency of futures. Market makers who quote bids and offers for securities concentrate on order flow within their own markets to gauge buying and selling interests. They also watch closely related markets to extract additional information. A market maker in CDs, for example, focuses on bids and offers for those securities but also watches the closely related Treasury-bill market for information about when to alter quotes. A market maker in relatively inactive Treasury bonds (for example, those with very low coupons) may watch the bids and offers of his own securities but surely derives far greater pricing information from the bids and offers in more actively traded, recently issued Treasury securities.

The pricing process that emerges for financial instruments with active futures markets is no different. Treasury-bond dealers get price information from bids and offers coming directly to them but concentrate at least as much on the more active futures market for a continuous reading on market conditions. The market dominating the pricing process is the one that has the largest and most continuous order flow since that is where new information first gets incorporated. Arbitrage will then ensure that the less active, satellite market is priced efficiently. Liquidity is also transferred to the satellite market through the activity of arbitragers.

Since futures markets are frequently more transactionally efficient than cash markets, they are often the dominant market. Garbade and Silber have shown that cash markets price off futures markets in the agricultural commodities, while in precious metals the relationship is more symmetric.[26] The dominant-satellite relationship between cash and futures markets for financial instruments has not yet been evaluated empirically. Conversations with market participants suggest that for foreign currencies the cash markets dominate, for debt instruments there is a symmetric relationship, whereas for the equity market there is continuous competition for leadership. These relationships depend upon the relative size and the activity in the respective markets and can change over time.[27]

When stock index futures were first introduced, most participants viewed them as satellites of the stock market. Participants took their clue about the direction of price movements for equities from the price movements of large securities like IBM, General Motors, and Exxon. With the growth in liquidity in stock index futures, that relationship has changed. As hedgers turned to the futures market to offset risk quickly and efficiently, the futures market for stock index products has become a more sensitive pricing gauge than many of the underlying equities.

The message from the dominant-satellite issue is that information emerges quickest in markets that are transactionally efficient. Futures markets contribute to the pricing process precisely because the cost of transacting there is low. Futures markets cannot, however, go off by themselves because arbitragers keep them properly aligned with their respective cash markets. This process, in fact, is precisely the price discovery role of futures markets that policymakers view as desirable.

Summary

Financial futures have become an integral component of the financial sector because they offer cost efficient transactions services to all types of financial institutions. Depository institutions use financial futures to adjust the risk exposure of their asset/liability mix, market-making securities dealers offset the risk of their inventory with financial futures, and portfolio managers hedge their income-earning assets with financial futures.

In most cases, the hedging and risk-transfer facilities offered by financial futures are available elsewhere. The cash markets for most financial instruments are well organized and highly liquid. Nevertheless, futures markets in financial instruments dominate the cash markets because homogenous contract design promotes greater liquidity than do cash markets. Even when some cash markets rival the futures markets in liquidity, such as with the Treasury-bill or Treasury-bond markets, that liquidity is usually reserved for market professionals. Financial futures bring those reduced liquidity costs to all market participants. This democratization of transactions services is a major contribution of financial futures.

Although the benefits of financial futures are felt most directly in reduced transactions costs in the financial sector, the consequences for economic welfare extend beyond that narrow focus. The increased liquidity and risk reduction facilities available to portfolio managers

111

and other investors is reflected in a reduced cost of capital to business firms. The ultimate benefit, therefore, is translated into greater capital formation for the economy as a whole.

Notes

1. See especially Commodity Futures Trading Commission, "Report of the Advisory Committee on the Economic Role of Contract Markets" (July 17, 1976); Roger Gray, "The Relationship among Three Futures Markets: An Example of the Importance of Speculation," *Food Research Institute Studies* (February 1961); Thomas Hieronymous, *The Economics of Futures Trading* (New York: Commodity Research Bureau, 1971); and Anne E. Peck, ed., *Selected Writings on Futures Markets* (Chicago: Chicago Board of Trade, 1977), and *Views from the Trade* (Chicago: Chicago Board of Trade, 1978).

2. See Board of Governors of the Federal Reserve System, Commodity Futures Trading Commission, and Securities and Exchange Commission, "A Study of the Effects on the Economy of Trading in Futures and Options," Washington, D.C. (December 1984).

3. Commodity Futures Trading Commission, "Guideline No. 1," 17 C.F.R. Part 5 (Appendix A); 1 CCH Comm. Fut. L. Rep. Paragraph 6145 (1975).

4. See, for example, Peck, ed., *Selected Writings on Futures Markets.*

5. Although all financial instruments are perfectly storable in the sense of zero physical spoilage, some are not sufficiently long-lived to satisfy the condition that they can be carried forward as inventory indefinitely. Treasury bills, for example, cannot be inventoried for more than one year because they have a maximum twelve-month maturity. Thus Treasury-bill futures could be priced as a perfectly storable commodity only within that time span.

6. See Harold Demsetz, "The Cost of Transacting," *Quarterly Journal of Economics* (February 1968); and Seha Tinic, "The Economics of Liquidity Services," *Quarterly Journal of Economics* (February 1972).

7. See Kenneth Garbade and William Silber, "Structural Organization of Secondary Markets: Clearing Frequency, Dealer Activity and Liquidity Risk," *Journal of Finance* (June 1979).

8. To construct a three-month forward contract in Treasury bills, one buys a six-month bill and sells short a three-month bill.

9. When selling short in the cash market, a government securities dealer does not have to be concerned with mark-to-market settlement. Moreover, basis risk is also avoided. *Basis* is defined as the difference between the cash market price and futures price. *Basis risk* refers to the variability of the cash price minus the futures price. High variability in the basis makes hedging difficult because the futures price cannot be relied upon to offset cash price movements.

10. The lowest offer and highest bid in the market can be uncovered instantaneously in the government bond market through the aid of broker's screens, but these are available only to government securities dealers. See

Kenneth Garbade and William Silber, "Price Dispersion in the Government Securities Market," *Journal of Political Economy* (August 1976).

11. In a short sale the dealer would have to maintain collateral at market value, but this does not entail an interest expense.

12. See Kenneth Garbade and William Silber, "Cash Settlement of Futures Contracts: An Economic Analysis," *Journal of Futures Markets*, vol. 3, no. 4. (1983).

13. Do not confuse futures contracts that have multiple delivery options with index contracts. Most futures have delivery options, for example, various coupons of government bonds can be delivered under the Treasury-bond contract or various bank CDs can be delivered under the CD contract. In these cases, the contract is priced off the cheapest deliverable cash commodity rather than a weighted average of the varieties, as would be the case in an index contract. See Kenneth Garbade and William Silber, "Futures Contracts on Commodities with Multiple Varieties: An Analysis of Premiums and Discounts," *Journal of Business* (July 1983).

14. Kling suggests the following type of calculation. A discount broker charges about thirty cents per share. Buying and selling 1,800 shares of a $50.00 stock involves the same $90,000.00 and costs $1,080.00 in commissions to the broker. In addition, if the bid-asked spread were ⅛ (.125 cents per share), this adds $225.00, for a total cost of $1,305.00. Note that the $90,000.00 value for the Standard & Poor contract is based on an index value of 180.00 and the $500.00 contract multiplier ($90,000.00 = 180 x $500.00). See Arnold Kling, "Futures Markets and Transactions Costs," Board of Governors of the Federal Reserve System, Washington, D.C. (March 1984).

15. See Kenneth Garbade, "Analyzing the Structure of Treasury Yields: Duration, Coupon, and Liquidity Effects," Bankers Trust Co. (November 1984).

16. See also Jerome Stein, "Futures Markets and Capital Formation," chapter 3 of this book.

17. The data are taken from Deborah Black, "Success and Failure of Futures Contracts: Theory and Empirical Evidence" (unpublished Ph.D. diss., Graduate School of Business, New York University, 1985). The average volume figures were calculated for the first three years of trading or until the contract stopped trading.

18. See, for example, Richard Sandor, "Innovation by an Exchange: A Case Study of the Development of the Plywood Futures Contract," *Journal of Law and Economics* (April 1973); Mark Powers, "The Effects of Contract Provisions on the Success of a Futures Contract," *Journal of Farm Economics* (November 1967); and William Silber, "Innovation, Competition and New Contract Design in Futures Markets," *Journal of Futures Markets*, vol. 1, no. 2. (1981).

19. Black, "Success and Failure of Futures Contracts."

20. High coupon GNMAs behave like two-year securities because there are rapid prepayments of principal, which shorten the duration of the security.

21. See Peck, *Selected Writings on Futures Markets* and *Views from the Trade*.

22. U.S. Treasury and the Board of Governors of the Federal Reserve System, "Treasury Futures Markets: A Study by the Staffs of the U.S. Treasury and the Federal Reserve System," Washington, D.C. (May 31, 1979).

23. See William Baumol, John Panzar, and Robert Willig, *Contestable Markets and the Theory of Industry Structure* (New York: Harcourt Brace Jovanovich, Inc., 1982).

24. The case for granting a natural monopoly license is strongest only where large sunk costs present barriers to potential competition. The best examples are local utilities such as gas and electricity.

25. See Garbade and Silber, "Cash Settlement of Futures Contracts: An Economic Analysis."

26. Kenneth Garbade and William Silber, "Price Movements and Price Discovery in Futures and Cash Markets," *Review of Economics and Statistics* (May 1983).

27. Note that the stock market itself presents an interesting example of a derivative market dominating the underlying market. Equities are nothing more than claims on the underlying firms. Price information about the value of a company is usually derived from bids and offers in the market for the firm's securities rather than from bids and offers for the company itself. The underlying market is far too illiquid to use on a continuous basis to value the firm. Of course, if the stock market's valuation differs considerably from the underlying value, this triggers an arbitrage transaction, such as the firm's buying back its shares or selling more shares to the public. In more extreme cases, transactions in the "cash market" are triggered, such as with a takeover attempt. Thus the stock market itself is an example of a derivative market that dominates pricing in the underlying market.

3
Futures Markets and Capital Formation

Jerome L. Stein

The Savings-Investment Process and Futures Markets

The simultaneous occurrence of rapid growth of trading in financial futures and increased volatility in security prices and interest rates caused concern for Congress and the Federal Reserve System. The government had had experience with the economic role of traditional commodity futures and had learned to understand it. The new and rapidly growing financial futures seemed to be different, however. Traditional commodity futures markets had been studied by academic economists for many years; and there were many studies of their economic effects.[1] Financial and stock index futures had not been analyzed theoretically by economists, so that there was no model by which their effects upon the economy could be analyzed. This lacuna induced Congress to request the Board of Governors of the Federal Reserve System, the Commodity Futures Trading Commission (CFTC), and the Securities and Exchange Commission (SEC) to study "the effects, if any, that trading in . . . [futures] has on the formation of real capital in the economy (particularly that of a long-term nature) and the structure of liquidity in the credit market; . . . the economic purposes, if any, served by the trading of such instruments."[2] This chapter addresses these questions.

I would like to thank the following for their help in understanding the institutions: Gary Seevers, Robert Mnuchin, Blair Garff, John Curtin, Nelson Abanto, Jon Corzine, and Fischer Black of Goldman-Sachs; Charles Hoyt, John Conheeny, and Carmine Grigoli of Merrill Lynch; K. Kobayashi of the Sanwa Bank; Gary Perlin of FNMA; William Nemerever and Thomas Cooper of the State Street Bank, Nils Peterson of the Harvard Management Company; David Dunford of Travelers Management Company. and Fred Arditti of GNP Company.

Akio Yasuhara of Brown University, Mark Rzepczynski of the University of Houston, and Anne Peck of the Stanford Food Research Institute are thanked for their criticisms of earlier drafts.

TABLE 3–1

SUPPLY OF AND DEMAND FOR SECURITIES (RISKY ASSETS), DURING A
SPECIFIC TIME INTERVAL

Supply of Securities	Demand for Securities
1. planned investment by firms 2. government budget deficit	3. savings less the change in the demand for money 4. change in the supply of money 5. dealers' investment in inventories of securities

The Framework of Analysis. The effects of futures markets upon the rate of capital formation can be viewed within the context of the supply of and demand for risky assets (or demand for and supply of loanable funds) during any specified period of time, as shown in table 3–1. The major users of the new futures markets are subsumed under items 1, 3, and 5. The level of security prices or rate of interest adjusts to equate the two sides of the table. The resulting cost of capital or rate of interest determines the rate of capital formation.

Item 1 is the rate of planned investment, or sale of risky assets by firms, during a time interval. This rate is positively related to the level of security prices relative to the cost of production of new capital goods. Later I explain how the use of futures markets by the Federal National Mortgage Association (FNMA) reduces the risk premium that it charges to mortgage bankers and savings and loan associations. As a result of the lower risk-premium, mortgage interest rates come down, and planned investment in housing increases.

Item 2 is the supply of risky assets generated by the government budget deficit. Futures markets have no direct effect upon this item. The sum of items 1 and 2 constitutes the supply of risky assets by firms and the government, which is a demand for loanable funds.

Item 3 is savings less the change in the demand for money. This item constitutes the savings directed toward risky assets during a time interval. A large part of the public's savings is managed by institutional investors: pension funds and insurance companies, which are subsumed under this category. In a later section I show how the use of futures markets by institutional investors improves the trade-off between expected return and risk on their investment. This improvement leads to an increase in the flow of savings directed toward risky assets. If no futures markets in Treasury securities and stock market indexes existed, the expected return for a given level of risk available to institutional investors would be lower. A greater proportion of current savings would then be directed toward holding money or near money. The lower flow demand for securities would tend to raise interest rates (that is, lower the level of security prices), which would adversely affect the rate of capital formation.

Item 4 is the change in the supply of money, which corresponds to a demand for risky assets by banks or the Federal Reserve System. Futures markets have no significant effect upon Federal Reserve behavior.

In the standard macroeconomic literature, the interest rate (or cost of capital) adjusts to equate the sum of items 1 and 2, the supply of risky assets, with that of items 3 and 4, the demand for risky assets. On average over a period of a year that view is correct. Over shorter periods of time, item 5 must also be considered.

If there were no securities dealers, then intramonth or intrayear variations in the government budget deficit or planned investment by firms would have to be absorbed by savings less the change in the demand for money. The latter is not highly responsive to changes in the nominal rate of interest. Therefore, intramonth variations in the supplies of risky assets (item 1 plus item 2) would be associated with large variations in the levels of securities prices. Such a phenomenon would increase the risks of holding equities and fixed income securities and would decrease the savings directed toward risky assets (item 3). In this manner, an increase in the variability of interest rates would raise the average level of interest rates, and capital formation would be reduced.

Dealers in fixed income securities in both the primary and secondary market, and in equities only in the secondary market, are major users of futures markets. The economic function of dealers is to provide an inventory investment in securities. Short-period variations in the excess supply of securities (item 1 plus item 2 less the sum of items 3 and 4) lead to price variations. As the price declines below the present value of the price expected to prevail later, dealers purchase the securities for temporary inventory. Conversely, as the price rises above the present value of the expected price, dealers sell the securities from temporary inventory. In this manner, dealers mitigate the magnitude of the price fluctuations. Insofar as their anticipations are correct, they are able to dispose of their inventories at higher prices or replenish them at lower prices. The greater the elasticity of demand by dealers for investment in inventories of securities, the smaller will be the price (interest rate) variation associated with short-period variations in items 1, 2, 3, and 4. Since the level of interest rates that balances the supply of and demand for securities

117

is positively related to the risks involved in holding securities, the existence of dealers tends to stimulate the rate of capital formation.

Two components of risk are involved in the dealers' purchases or sales of securities for inventory investment or disinvestment. One part is the market risk resulting from changes in the market index. For fixed income securities, it is the height of the yield curve on treasuries. For equities, it is the Standard & Poor's (S&P) 500 index. The second part is the portfolio specific risk, which concerns the prices of the particular securities purchased or sold relative to the level of the index.

Later I explain how dealers use futures markets to diversify away the market risks. As a result, they have more elastic demands for inventory. Variations in items 1, 2, 3, and 4 produce smaller variations in the levels of security prices. The riskiness of investment in securities is thereby reduced. Alternatively, the use of futures markets allows dealers to diversify away a large part of the risk associated with inventory management. This diversification leads to a reduction in the risk premium they must charge their customers via commissions and spreads. The net effect of the dealers' use of futures markets is to lower both the variance of interest rates and the cost of capital to firms. In this manner, futures markets are conducive to a higher rate of capital formation.

Planned Investment in Housing. The housing industry, through FNMA and the Government National Mortgage Association (GNMA), is a major user of futures markets; and investment in residential construction is a major part of net fixed investment. The builder finances investment in housing by selling mortgages to mortgage bankers or to savings and loan associations. In turn, the banks offer both new and old mortgages to FNMA and other investors. FNMA constitutes half of the secondary market in mortgages. If FNMA is the successful bidder, it will hold the mortgages as investments in its portfolio. FNMA finances its purchases of the mortgages by selling its own securities in the capital market where they are purchased by institutional investors.

Several elements of risk confront FNMA. At any given time, FNMA is asked to bid for large batches of mortgages offered by the mortgage banks and savings and loan institutions for forward delivery. Because of the legal documentation required to transfer the mortgages, several months must pass before the mortgages can be delivered. As a rule, FNMA is permitted to enter the capital market to sell its debentures only once a month, on a date given to it by the Treasury. The rationale for this provision is that the Treasury does not want FNMA to compete with its own borrowings or those of the other government agencies. FNMA borrowings from the capital market range between $1 billion and $1.5 billion per month. When FNMA is asked to bid on mortgages for forward delivery, it does not know at what date it will be able to enter the capital market to borrow nor at what price (interest rate) it will be able to sell its debentures. Since 1979, interest rates have undergone very large intra-year fluctuations. The uncertain date is denoted by θ, and the price of FNMA debentures at that date by $P^*(\theta)$. The asterisk denotes a stochastic variable.

Profits for FNMA depend upon two elements: (1) the spread between the sales price of FNMA debentures in the capital market, $P^*(\theta)$, and the forward bid price for mortgages denoted by $p(t)$ and (2) the fees, $gp(t)$, that FNMA receives from the sellers of the mortgages, which are 100g percent of the forward bid price. Thus the profit margin is $P^*(\theta) - (1-g) p(t)$ per dollar of face value of mortgages.

If FNMA bids too high a price, $p(t)$, for the forward purchases of mortgages, it faces the risk that the unknown sales price, $P^*(\theta)$, of its own debentures at unknown subsequent date, θ, will be below its forward bid price. Large losses would result. If FNMA bids too low a forward price for mortgages, it will be unsuccessful in obtaining the mortgages. The risk is reflected in the variance of the price, $P^*(\theta)$, of its debentures.

In the absence of any facilities for hedging, FNMA establishes its forward price bid in the following manner. It estimates the average price it will receive for its debentures at the uncertain date at which it will be able to enter the capital market. This expected price is called the expected marginal revenue. FNMA also estimates its marginal cost of purchasing the mortgages. Since FNMA is half of the secondary market, its purchases of mortgages affect the market price. Its marginal cost exceeds its average cost. If there were no risk or risk aversion, the forward price bid would be such that it would equate expected marginal revenue with marginal cost. Insofar as there is risk and risk aversion, FNMA adds a risk premium to its marginal cost; and it equates the expected marginal revenue to the sum of the marginal cost and the risk premium. The risk premium depends upon the variance of the price of a FNMA debenture and its coefficient of risk aversion.

There is a variable differential between the price of FNMA debentures and those of comparable Treasury securities. Hence the variance of the price of a FNMA debenture is the sum of the variance of the price of a Treasury security plus the variance of the price

FIGURE 3–1

THE USE OF TREASURY-BOND FUTURES BY THE FNMA TO DIVERSIFY
AWAY MARKET RISK

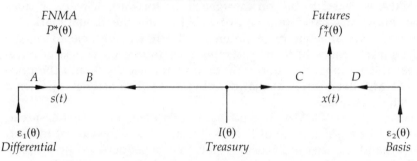

differential between them. The covariation between the price of a
Treasury security and the differential can be ignored. The pricing
formula for FNMA is the following:

> expected marginal revenue = marginal cost plus a premium,
> which depends upon the sum of the variance of the price
> of Treasury securities and the variance of the price differ-
> ential between Treasury and FNMA securities

By using the futures market in Treasury securities, FNMA can
diversify away the risk of variations in the price of Treasury securities. It does so in the following way, which is schematized in figure
3–1.

At time t, when FNMA is asked to bid forward for $s(t)$ dollars
of face value of mortgages offered by banks, FNMA can hedge its
borrowing costs by selling quantity $x(t)$ of Treasury bonds in the
futures market. The price of these futures at time t is $f_T(t)$, where T
is the maturity date of the contract. The futures price is closely related
to the expected value of the Treasury bonds at subsequent time T.
The expected price of FNMA bonds is equal to the price of Treasury
bonds less the average differential m between the price of a Treasury
security and that of a comparable FNMA security. FNMA can determine its bid for mortgages in the forward market by assuming as a
first approximation that it will sell it own debentures at the current
price of Treasury futures $f_T(t)$ less m the average price differential.
The main difference made by the use of futures markets lies in the
risk premium between the expected marginal revenue and marginal
cost.

When FNMA is allowed to enter the capital market to borrow
at time θ, it repurchases the Treasury futures that it sold earlier. By

120

using the futures market, FNMA incurs two risks instead of just one. The first concerns the price $P^*(\theta)$ of its own debentures, and the second concerns the price $f_T^*(\theta)$ at which it will repurchase it sales of futures. Risk management is based upon the positive correlation between these two risks.

A close relation in figure 3–1 (link C) exists between the cash price, $I(\theta)$, and the futures price, $f_T(\theta)$, of Treasury bonds, which results from the following arbitrage relation. One can have a Treasury bond at time T in two ways. One may either purchase a Treasury bond at earlier time θ or purchase at time θ a futures contract for Treasury bonds that matures at time T. The cost of the former is the current price $I(\theta)$ of a Treasury bond plus the short-term financing costs less the interest received on the bonds. The net financing cost, which is the difference between the two interest rates, can be positive, zero, or negative depending upon the shape of the yield curve. The cost of acquiring the bonds through the futures market is the futures price $f_T(\theta)$. Arbitrage will ensure that the percentage price differential between the futures and cash prices of Treasury bonds is equal to the net financing costs. It follows that the variation in the futures price is equal to the variation in the cash price (link C) plus the variation of the net carrying cost (link D).

By taking a short position in the futures market for Treasury bonds at the time that it takes a long position in the forward market for mortgages, FNMA can diversify away as much of the risk of variation in Treasury-bond prices as it wishes. Links B and C portray this diversification. If the level of Treasury bond prices falls at time θ when FNMA is permitted to enter the capital market, both the prices of FNMA debentures and futures prices on Treasury securities will have declined. FNMA will be selling its debentures at unfavorable prices but will be repurchasing Treasury futures at favorable prices. The gains on one transaction will tend to offset the losses on the other.

The offset does not eliminate risk completely because there is not a one-to-one relation between changes in the prices of FNMA debentures and those of Treasury-bond futures. Risks A and D remain. The first risk, A, is that the price of FNMA bonds varies relative to that of a Treasury bond. The second risk, D, is that the price of a Treasury-bond future varies relative to that of a cash Treasury bond. The major risk, which arises from changes in the height of the yield curve on Treasury bonds (variance of $I[\theta]$), can be diversified away, however. By using futures markets, FNMA substitutes the moderate risk of variations in the net carrying cost (link D) for the substantial risk of variations in the level of Treasury-bond prices.

121

As a result of the risk reduction, the risk premium that FNMA charges the mortgage bankers and savings and loan associations is substantially reduced. The price that FNMA bids forward for mortgages is such that the following relation holds:

expected marginal revenue = marginal cost plus a risk premium, which depends upon the sum of the variance of the differential between FNMA and Treasury securities and the variance of the net carrying costs

FNMA can offer banks higher prices in the forward market, because its risk premium has been substantially reduced. Competition among banks will lead to a passing on of the reduction in interest rates on mortgages from the banks to the builders. The decline in mortgage interest rates raises the rate of planned investment (table 3–1, item 1). In this manner, the use of futures markets by FNMA tends to raise the rate of capital formation.

Savings in Risky Assets. The savings that the public plans to invest in risky assets (table 3–1, item 3) interact with the desired rate of investment by firms (item 1) to determine the rate of capital formation. A large part of the savings of the public is managed by institutional investors, such as pension funds and insurance companies. The use of futures markets by institutional investors has enabled them to increase the expected return on risky assets for a given degree of risk. Since the fraction of savings directed toward risky assets, rather than to money or near money, depends upon the trade-off between expected return and risk, the use of futures markets by the institutional investors tends to raise the rate of capital formation.

Institutional investors use the futures markets in two ways to manage risk. They can dichotomize their composition of risky assets from the total risk undertaken, without selling or purchasing the underlying securities. Such dichotomy is achieved at very low transactions costs and without affecting the prices of the underlying securities.

Each fund manager has a subjective concept of expected return and risk that can be achieved with different portfolios of securities and, on this basis, chooses what is believed to be the optimum portfolio. Suppose that the fund manager is apprehensive that security prices will decline during the next month or quarter or believes that the market will be more uncertain during the next quarter. The manager would like to shift *temporarily* away from risky assets toward safe assets. The standard method to reduce risk is to sell part of the portfolio of risky assets and invest in safe assets such as Treasury bills. This approach has several deficiencies. The fund manager has carefully developed a long-term investment strategy, for example, having selected undervalued securities of new firms that are developing sophisticated technologies but that will have no positive earnings for a while. The fund manager may balance these equities with those of more established firms, to achieve an optimal mix of risky assets. If these undervalued securities had to be sold to reduce the portfolio risk during a quarter, the manager would then be reassembling the same portfolio when ready to reassume the original level of risk.

Considerable transactions costs are involved in these short-term adjustments of total risk. Direct commissions and spreads are involved in the purchases and sales of the securities. The more frequent the attempt to vary risk, the greater these transactions costs will be; and the rate of return on the portfolio will be adversely affected. In addition, the institutional investors have market power. They operate on a large scale in relation to the normal volume of trading in these securities. Moreover, the "undervalued" securities of the firms engaged in innovative processes will be thin because they are not well known. An attempt to sell securities to reduce risk quickly will cause their prices to fall and will produce capital losses for the fund. The market may even interpret such transactions as signals that the fund has new information about the value of the shares; and the market prices would then be more adversely affected.

By using the futures markets in stock market indexes, or Treasury futures in the case of a bond portfolio, the problems of high transactions costs and of power to affect the market price can be reduced considerably. When the fund manager wants to reduce the total risk on the equity portfolio quickly but temporarily, futures contracts on the S&P 500 index can be sold. In effect, the manager is selling the entire S&P 500 index at very low transactions costs, and these sales will hardly affect the price of the futures contract. No negative signals will be conveyed to the market concerning the quality of the portfolio. Transactions costs using futures are from 15 to 20 percent of those in the underlying securities. Funds can dichotomize their long-term investment strategy from the short-term variations in total risk. The former is achieved through specific securities selection. The latter is achieved through purchases or sales of futures contracts in either the S&P 500 index or in Treasury securities. The net effect is to obtain a higher expected return for a given degree of risk.

The second way that institutional investors use futures markets is to take advantage of expected rises in the level of security prices, in anticipation of cash inflows from the savers. Suppose that the fund manager expects the index of security prices to rise within the month, but the savings generated by the pension contributions will be received by the fund only at the end of the month.

If there were no futures market, the fund manager would have to borrow the funds to invest and then would have to select the securities to purchase. Borrowing is costly, and security selection is a time-consuming and difficult process. What securities should the fund manager select if he or she thinks that the overall market index will rise? If the fund manager purchased the individual S&P 500 securities quickly, their prices would be driven up.

Futures markets facilitate the ability of a fund manager to take advantage of an anticipated rise in the stock or bond market by simply purchasing futures contracts on the index (or on Treasury securities). There are no finance costs, since the manager has not borrowed to purchase the futures. No funds need be transferred before the maturity of the contract, at which time the pension contributions will have been received. Transactions costs are quite low for futures compared with those in the underlying securities. Finally, the manager does not have to decide which securities to purchase in anticipation of a rise in the index. The futures contract is on the index itself. The fund is, in effect, purchasing the stock market index without exerting any significant effect upon the prices of the underlying securities.

Through the uses of futures described above, institutional investors can raise the expected return on the portfolio for a given degree of risk. Insofar as the rate of savings directed toward risky assets depends upon the trade-off between expected return and risk (table 3–1, item 3), futures markets stimulate capital formation.

Dealers and Price Fluctuations. On the average, over the course of a year, the price of risky assets (that is, the rate of interest) equates the net supply of securities (item 1 plus item 2 in table 3–1) to the net demand (item 3 plus item 4). These four items vary considerably over short periods of time. If there were no dealers, then intrayear variations in these items would change the rate of interest until balance were achieved. Consequently, the intrayear variations in the market rates of interest would reflect the intrayear fluctuations in the supplies of or demands for risky assets. I argued above that the risk of security price fluctuations adversely affects planned investment. FNMA adds a risk premium, for example, which depends upon the price variance to its marginal cost in determining the price it will bid for mortgages. Similarly, the risk of price fluctuations reduces savings in risky assets. The net effect is that the variance of security prices is negatively related to capital formation.

The economic function of dealers is to provide a cushion between the supply of and demand for risky securities. Variations in items 1, 2, 3, and 4 lead to changes in the inventories of dealers. In turn, inventory investment or disinvestment by dealers partially offsets those variations and thereby diminishes the variance of interest rates. As a result of the reduced variance of security prices, the rate of capital formation is increased.

Dealers make markets in fixed income securities and equities in both the primary and secondary markets. They purchase securities for temporary inventory investment, or sell them for temporary inventory disinvestment, and hope to profit from the difference between their selling and buying prices, plus their commissions and spreads. They face two types of risk. The first concerns the level of relative prices of the securities purchased or sold compared with the market index. This risk involves purchasing undervalued or selling overvalued securities, relative to the market index itself. The dealer's vaunted expertise is in security selection, that is, in deciding which securities are overvalued or undervalued relative to the general level of prices. The second risk concerns the level of the market index itself.

Since 1979 the risks of doing business have increased for several reasons. First, the change in the Federal Reserve's operating procedure has permitted greater short-run variations in interest rates. Second, the magnitude of variations in items 1 through 4 has increased because of the growth in the government deficit and the growing importance of institutional investors. Third, the SEC rule concerning the registration process of new securities has changed. Formerly each new issue had to be registered with the SEC, and the process of obtaining approval was lengthy. This long procedure gave the dealer time to search for customers and determine their demand curves for the particular issues. With that information, the dealers could quote a price to the corporate treasurer for the issue. To a large extent, the dealer was acting like a broker who had bought and sold forward. The dealer had no considerable risks. Matters changed in the primary market as a result of SEC ruling 415 which established a shelf-registration process for the corporation. The corporation now registers its potential offerings over the year with the SEC in a wholesale manner. When the corporate treasurer deems the time propitious, he offers the particular issue to the dealer and demands an immediate bid. The dealer no longer has the leisure to search the demand curves of potential customers before making a bid. Moreover, the corporate treasurers have speculative supply schedules. When security prices are rising, the treasurers accelerate the sales of their issues in anticipation of subsequent price declines. Similarly, when security prices are declining, the treasurers decelerate their sales in anticipation of subsequent price rises. Thus the corporate treasurers ask the dealers for bids on primary sales of securities at times when the former think that security prices will decline.

Dealers bid a price for the securities that is equal to the present value of the expected subsequent sales price plus commissions less a risk premium. The risk premium is proportional to the position at risk times the variance of the price. Hence, the greater the price variance or risk of inventory management, the larger will be the reduction in the bid price necessary to induce the dealer to increase the temporary investment in inventories of securities. Similarly, the larger will be the rise in the dealer's ask price, which is necessary to induce the dealer to take a short position or to reduce these inventories.

Since the risks to the dealers increased in recent years, variations in the excess supply of risky assets (items 1 through 4 in table 3–1) would be absorbed by dealers only if they charged large risk-premiums. This would raise the cost of capital to firms. Moreover, the large variations in the levels of security prices would inhibit savings in risky assets.

Futures markets in government securities and stock market indexes permit dealers to diversify away the market risk associated with variations in the general level of security prices, the height of the yield curve, or the level of the stock market index. The dealer is then left with the risk concerning the relative prices of the securities purchased. Dealers specialize in assuming this risk, and they hope to profit from their superior ability to determine relative prices besides their commissions and spreads.

The dealer's use of futures markets is formally similar to that described above in connection with FNMA; and I shall use that flow chart for the exposition. Suppose that there is an excess supply of risky assets, and the dealer purchases the securities at price $p(t)$ at time t. The dealer hopes to sell these securities at subsequent time θ at price $P^*(\theta)$, which will leave him or her with a profit.

The change in the price of the portfolio of securities (net of financing costs) that has been acquired depends upon two elements. One is the change in the general level of the index of securities (net of financing costs). The variation in the price of the portfolio associated with the change in the index is the beta of the portfolio. This is link B in the flow chart. The second elment, denoted by ε_1 in the flow chart, concerns the change in the relative price of the portfolio, which is not associated with changes in the market index. If the portfolio consists of equities, for example, this element will reflect abnormally high or low earnings during the quarter. If the portfolio consists of bonds, this element will reflect only upgrading or downgrading of the quality of the bonds. These two determinants of the change in the price of the portfolio are links A and B in figure 3–1.

The dealer uses the futures market to diversify away the risk of changes in the appropriate market index, denoted by I in the flow chart. If s dollars of fixed income securities are purchased for temporary inventory, x dollars are sold in futures contracts on Treasury securities. The futures price at time θ of Treasury securities that mature at time T, denoted by $f_T(\theta)$, is linked to the cash price of Treasury securities $I(\theta)$ by the net cost of carry, link D in the flow chart. This arbitrage relation was explained above and is described by links C and D in the flow chart. It follows that variations in the prices of Treasury securities in the cash market produce variations in the prices of Treasury futures. The relation between the changes in the two prices is imperfect because of variations in the net financing costs. This second source of variation (link D) denoted by $\varepsilon_2(\theta)$, is called the basis risk.

If the stock block trader purchased a variety of equities valued at s dollars for temporary inventory, x dollars of futures contracts would be sold on the S&P 500 index or on a comparable index. The change in the average price of the securities acquired temporarily is the sum of two parts. The first part is the beta of that portfolio times the changes in the index. The second is independent of the index and represents temporary undervaluation or overvaluation.

If there were no basis risk, the dealer could hedge away all of the market risk (because of variations in the market index) by selling β dollars of futures for every dollar of securities purchased for temporary inventory. If the index changes by one dollar, the price of the portfolio will change by β dollars. The dealer has sold β dollars of futures for each dollar of temporary inventory. Insofar as there is a one-to-one relation between changes in the futures price and changes in the cash price of treasuries, the gain or loss on the futures will offset the loss or gain on the inventory, because of changes in the market index. In terms of the flow chart, by hedging ratio β of the portfolio with futures, links B and C will cancel each other, if there is no basis risk.

In reality, there is a basis risk because changes in futures prices are not perfectly correlated with changes in the cash price (net of

127

carrying costs) of the underlying instruments. By hedging, the dealer substitutes a basis risk (link *D*) for a market risk (link *B*). The risks associated with the two cases are as follows: With no futures there is an absolute price risk plus a relative price risk; with futures there is a relative price risk plus a basis risk.

The utility of using futures markets by dealers depends upon the importance of the absolute price risk of changes in the market index (link *B*) compared with the relative price risk (link *A*) on the portfolio acquired. Dealers in fixed income securities in both the primary and secondary markets use futures in Treasury securities. For high-grade fixed income securities, the interest rate differential between their yields and those on treasuries has a small variance. Practically all of the risk is market risk, concerning the height of the Treasury yield curve. This risk can be diversified away, if the dealer wishes to do so, by selling Treasury futures. The basis risk acquired is small relative to the market risk that has been diversified away. Hence the risk premium that the dealer must include in the price is considerably reduced.

Dealers in the primary equity market do not use futures for the following reason. On a single equity issue, the relative price risk is very large compared with the absolute or market price risk. This large risk occurs because the earnings of a single corporation are not closely related to the market average. Since the major risk is the relative price risk, using futures that involve basis risks does not pay.

Stock block traders in the secondary market do use futures in the S&P 500 index because they handle many different equities during the course of a day. To a large extent, they are handling a large sample of the index. The major risk to them is the absolute price risk of changes in the market index. By using futures, they can diversify away this risk and just keep the much smaller relative price risk on the securities purchased. The cost of so doing is the assumption of the smaller basis risk.

The net effect of the dealer's use of futures is to reduce the risk premium to a function of the relative price risk plus the basis risk. When an excess supply of risky assets results from variations in items 1 through 4, the dealers will be able to offer the sellers a higher price for the securities. This situation implies a lower cost of capital to the corporation because the dealers can diversify away the considerable market risk by using the futures markets. Variations in the excess supply of risky assets are now associated with smaller variations in their prices. It was shown above that the cost of capital and the variance of prices of risky assets adversely affect planned investment and savings in risky assets. Consequently, the use of futures markets by dealers is conducive to capital formation.

Dealers, Futures Markets, and the Cost of Capital

Institutional Framework: Dealer Functions and Risks. Dealers in government bonds, corporate fixed income securities, and equities are financial intermediaries between savers and investors, just as grain dealers are intermediaries between producers and consumers. Inventory management is the essence of their business because they stand ready to sell securities to customers at their ask prices and purchase from them at their bid prices. Dealers intend to offset these transactions relatively quickly, generally within five minutes, rather than acquire a long-term investment portfolio. They are often unable to even out their positions quickly without suffering large losses. Consequently, they face risks in managing their temporary portfolio of inventory. This risk management is the subject of this chapter. These professional risk bearers are transactions and customer oriented, rather than investment oriented as are institutional investors.

The investment demand by corporate treasurers to finance a dollar of capital formation (see the flow chart, figure 3–2) depends positively upon the price they receive for newly issued securities less the dealer's commissions and spreads. This is called the q ratio. The net price that dealers bid, or the quantity of securities demanded at a given price, depends negatively upon the riskiness of inventory management and the degree of competition among dealers. In turn, the degree of competition depends to a large extent upon the riskiness of inventory management. For these reasons, the ability of dealers to manage risk profoundly affects the q ratio and thereby the investment demand by firms.

Securities dealers have separate divisions for government and corporate fixed income securities, equity underwriting, and stock block trading. These divisions operate independently of each other. The profit equations and optimization calculus for all divisions or types of dealer are similar, although the institutional details and quantitative values of parameters are different. In this section I explain how futures markets in Treasury securities and stock market indexes enable dealers to (1) manage risk more effectively, (2) reduce the cost of capital to firms and raise their q ratios, and (3) provide more "depth, breadth, and resilience" to the underlying securities markets and thereby reduce the price variance of securities. The longer-run

129

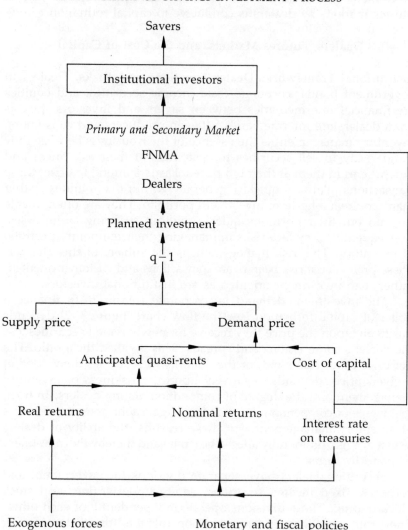

FIGURE 3–2

FLOW CHART OF SAVINGS-INVESTMENT PROCESS

Savers

Institutional investors

Primary and Secondary Market

FNMA

Dealers

Planned investment

$q-1$

Supply price

Demand price

Anticipated quasi-rents

Cost of capital

Real returns

Nominal returns

Interest rate
on treasuries

Exogenous forces

Monetary and fiscal policies

net effect is to raise the investment demand schedules of firms and the supply of savings directed to risky assets.

First I show how the risks of doing business have increased substantially since 1979 and have forced firms to use futures markets to manage risk. Second I explain how the optimal use of futures by dealers changes their demand curves for temporary inventory. The latter consists of securities purchased but not as yet sold to customers. I assume that a particular dealer takes the market price as a parameter and determines the quantity demanded or supplied. Interactions between dealers and customers then determine the market price, which reflects the q ratio for corporations.

The profit equation. The profit equation of dealers is the focal point of the analysis. Let $p(t)$ be the price and $s(t)$ be the portfolio of securities purchased $(+)$ or sold $(-)$ at time t. The dealer will sell this portfolio at price $p(t + 1)$ or, if he does not sell it, the price of his unsold inventory will be $p(t + 1)$ at time $t + 1$. The financing costs of the inventory are at rate $r(t)$, which is either the Treasury-bill or the broker loan rate from time t to $t + 1$.

The dealer has several additional sources of revenue. Commissions and bid-ask spreads contribute to his profits, and he may receive interest and dividends on the portfolio. These two sources of revenue less total operating costs can be subsumed under the term $V[s(t)]$.

Profits from these transactions derive from the change in price less financing costs $\{p(t + 1) - p(t)[1 + r(t)]\}\, s(t)$ plus interest and dividends plus revenues from commissions less total operating costs $V[s(t)]$.

When the dealer does not (N) use the futures market, profits π_N can be expressed as equation 1.

$$\pi_N(t + 1) = \{p(t + 1) - p(t)[1 + r(t)]\}\, s(t) + V[s(t)] \qquad (1)$$

Financing costs $r(t)$ depend to some extent upon the capital of the firm and the riskiness of its position.

Portfolio $s(t)$ consists of a vector of securities purchased or sold during the time period. The dealer is in business to accommodate customers by standing ready to acquire securities or to sell securities from inventory. During the course of a day, customers offer the dealers a diversity of securities. Not only are the acquired securities heterogeneous, but at times in the secondary market the selection tends to be negative. Customers may offer the stock block trader securities that they do not expect to appreciate in price. Since these customers are professional institutional investors or money managers who operate in large volume, these transactions may reflect new information about the securities not yet available to the stock block trader.

Dealers operate with very high leverage. A ratio of position at risk to capital of fifty is not uncommon for nonbank dealers.[3] Since

1979 several elements of risk, which have substantially altered the ways dealers operate, have emerged. They stem from regulatory changes, greater interest rate volatility, and an increase in the size of transactions.

Formerly a corporate treasurer would discuss with a dealer the prospects of issuing new corporate fixed income securities. A price "talkout" would ensue, whereby the dealer would conduct a roll call of institutional investors to get an indication of interest in purchasing the issue. After the relatively slow process of consulting with the distribution network of institutional investors, the dealer could quote a price, $p(t)$, that would be negatively related to the cost of capital to the corporate treasurer. A firm price could be given to the corporate treasurer, and a fixed offering price to the public could be established in a bona fide offering. The dealer would expect to profit from the commissions or spread $V[s(t)]$ in excess of any financing costs. The dealer had very little price risk because the price talkout established the price and quantity that the institutional investors were willing to accept. In effect, the dealer bought the issue forward from the corporate treasurer and sold a large part of it forward to institutional investors.

Large dealers had advantages in this set of arrangements because they have a considerable and widespread clientele distributed over the country and know what their clients' preferences for securities are. When the corporate treasurer discussed a new issue with the dealer, the latter would call the potential customers to determine the quantities demanded at various possible prices. In this manner the large dealer would sample the demand curve before he made a bid for the new corporate issue. Small dealers do not have this wide distribution network and have much less information about the state of demand.

Recent regulatory changes have fundamentally altered this process. SEC rule 415, introduced in March 1982, created a shelf registration process for new issues. Under this rule, large corporations can register the full amount of debt or equity they reasonably expect to sell over a two-year period. After the initial registration, firms can sell securities in variable amounts without further delay whenever conditions seem favorable. This technique is attractive to corporate treasurers. It offers the corporate treasurer flexibility to react quickly to market conditions; and it reduces the costs of issuing securities by saving legal, accounting, and printing expenses.

At the same time, the shelf registration rule increases the risks to the dealers. Corporate treasurers could act quickly without circulating a prospectus for a particular issue. Instead of the slow talkout process whereby the dealer had the luxury and leisure of putting together a book of the customers for the issues, the corporate treasurers can now bring the issues off the shelf quickly. The dealer is asked for an immediate firm bid, $p(t)$, for a particular issue. Some dealers have exclusive relations with particular corporations and are expected to offer the corporate treasurers the best price in the market. In other cases, if no special relation exists, the dealers bid for the issues at auctions.

Corporate treasurers tend to bring more issues off the shelf when interest rates on long-term government bonds decline, that is, the prices of government bonds rise. In table 3–2, column 1 contains the new corporate debt issued, $Y(t)$, and column 3 contains the interest rate, $i(t)$, on ten-year Treasury bonds, by month during during 1982 and 1983. Column 2 is the index of the new corporate debt issued in the month, relative to its average over the period, denoted by $IY(t)$.

The data can be viewed in several ways. The mean monthly change in the interest rate was -0.15 percent per year. One can group the data into months when the change in interest rates was greater than the mean and months when it was less than the mean and compare the value of the index $IY(t)$ of new corporate issues in the two periods:

Index of new corporate issues $IY(t)$	Periods of Interest Rate Change	
	Above mean	Below mean
Mean	81.90	125.66
Standard deviation	35.99	39.83

The mean value of the index was significantly greater ($125.66 - 81.90 = 43.76$) in periods when the interest rate changed by less than the mean (-0.15 percent per year) for the period. The pairwise t-statistic, $t = 3.79$, is significantly greater than zero at the 1 percent level.

A significant negative relation exists between the index of the value of new corporate debt issued during the month, $IY(t)$, and the change in the interest rate on ten-year Treasury bonds from the previous month, $i(t) - i(t - 1)$. When long-term government bond interest rates decline from month $t - 1$ to month t, the value of new corporate debt brought off the shelf in month t is relatively high. A regression equation of column 2 on column 4 of table 3–2 is another way to summarize the phenomenon that occurs when issues are taken off the shelf. Such an equation shows the speculative supply of securities offered by corporate treasurers during a time interval.

$$IY(t) = 93.6 - 69.15 [i(t) - i(t - 1)]; R^2 = 0.67; n = 20$$

$$t = -5.99$$

Two-thirds of the variation in the volume of new corporate debt issued in a given month relative to its mean for the period is accounted for by changes in the long-term Treasury-bond yield from the previous month. The regression coefficient is significantly different from zero at the 1 percent level. The causation proceeds from changes in the long-term government bond yield to the corporate debt issues taken off the shelf.

When government bond prices rise—that is, $i(t) - i(t - 1)$ is negative—corporate treasurers quickly bring debt issues off the shelf. They want to take advantage of the temporary rise in bond prices. Dealers are asked to quote prices for the issue immediately. There is no time to have a price talkout; and no book can be put together before bidding on an issue. Gone is the heyday of forward markets in the issuing of corporate fixed income securities.

Dealers in the primary market face two asymmetrical risks. First, corporate treasurers offer their debt as a result of the current rise in bond prices. If the treasurers thought that bond prices would rise further, they would wait longer before taking the issue off the shelf. Thus, when they offer their debt to the dealers, the corporate treasurers, all other things being equal, think that prices are more likely to decline than to rise.

Second, dealers fix an offering price to the public in a bona fide offering. This is a ceiling price. On one hand, dealers cannot raise the price to the public, even if bond prices in the market rise. On the other hand, if bond prices should fall and dealers are unable to market the issue, the offering price to the public is reduced. Dealers thus face a downside price risk but cannot benefit from a rise in the market price.

Another element of risk in both the primary and secondary markets is that interest rate volatility has increased, particularly since October 1979. Before that date, the Federal Reserve tended to stabilize the federal funds rate and, indirectly, short-term market rates of interest. As a consequence, the Federal Reserve was unable to control the growth of monetary aggregates. In October 1979 the Federal

TABLE 3–2
New Issue of Corporate Debt, Long-Term Government Bond Interest Rate, and Marketable Treasury Bonds, January 1982–September 1983

Month	New Corporate Debt Issue $Y(t)$ (millions of $)	Index $IY(t)$	Interest Rate, Ten-Year Government Bonds $i(t)$ (% per annum)	Change in Interest Rate $i(t) - i(t-1)$
1982				
January	992	24.6	14.59	—
February	1,722	42.6	14.43	−0.16
March	5,583	138.2	13.86	−0.57
April	2,266	56.1	13.87	0.01
May	5,429	134.4	13.62	−0.25
June	1,932	47.8	14.30	0.68
July	3,937	97.5	13.95	−0.35
August	7,155	177.1	13.06	−0.89
September	5,597	138.6	12.34	−0.72
October	7,287	180.4	10.91	−1.43
November	5,005	123.9	10.55	−0.36
December	3,500	86.6	10.54	−0.01
1983				
January	3,482	86.2	10.46	−0.08
February	3,582	88.7	10.72	0.26
March	4,886	121.0	10.51	−0.21
April	5,636	139.5	10.40	−0.11
May	5,836	144.5	10.38	−0.02
June	3,000	74.3	10.85	0.47
July	1,640	40.6	11.38	0.53
August	2,208	54.7	11.85	0.47
September	4,157	102.9	11.65	−0.20
Mean	4,039.6=100			−0.15

Sources: Goldman-Sachs and Co. for column 1. Economic Report of the President, 1984, for column 3. Column 2 is the ratio of the item in column 1 to its mean, times one hundred.

Reserve adopted a new operating procedure whereby the federal funds rate was allowed to fluctuate within wider limits and began to focus the conduct of monetary policy upon the growth of monetary aggregates. This new policy implied that short-term interest rates would be more volatile as a result of changes in the banks' demands for total reserves. The mean and standard deviation of monthly three-month Treasury bills in the pre- and post-1979 period reflect the greater volatility:

	Mean (percent per annum)	Standard Deviation (percent per annum)
1976	5.000	0.280
1977	5.270	0.640
1978	7.220	1.000
1980	11.613	2.876
1981	14.077	1.600
1982	10.724	2.292
1983	8.621	0.478

The increased yield or price volatility in interest rates on treasuries created more difficulty for both dealers and their customers in knowing what the price of the securities during the next period would be. Dealers are especially at risk as a result of the asymmetry of pricing of new issues.

The price risks were serious because the size of the typical transaction has increased for all dealers: stock block traders, corporate fixed income traders, and government bond dealers. Before 1976, $1 million was considered a large bond transaction in the secondary market. By 1983 dealers were thinking in terms of $10 million. A major reason for the increase in the size of dealers' transactions is that money management is now institutionalized. Because of the 1974 federal pension fund reform law and the higher inflation, pension fund assets have more than tripled since 1971. It is estimated that in 1984 approximately $1,500 billion was managed by professional money market managers, two-thirds of which was pension money. There is keen competition among money managers who are trying to outperform the market. They are much more oriented toward trading than their predecessors, who invested their money in the large corporations and had long investment horizons. As a result, purchases and sales are more volatile and are substantially larger.

The scale of the operations of government bond dealers increased as a result of the growth in the size and variability of the deficit in the national income accounts budget. From 1977:Q1 through 1979:Q4 the mean quarterly deficit seasonally adjusted at annual rates was $30.475 billion. From 1980:Q1 through 1983:Q3, the corresponding mean quarterly deficit was $107.927 billion. The public debt held by private investors grew at a rate of 14 percent per year from 1976 to 1983, when the rate of inflation was 7.2 percent per year. Hence the real public debt increased substantially during this period. The inventories of U.S. securities dealers rose by 15 percent per year from

$3.233 billion in 1979 to $9.3 billion in 1982, and their transactions increased by 13 percent per year from $13.183 billion in 1979 to $32.27 billion in 1982. There was a substantial rise in the magnitude of the real positions and transactions of government bond dealers. The net effect of these three developments was to increase the price risk on $\{p(t + 1) - p(t)[1 + r(t)]\} s(t)$ in profit equation 1 above.

Risk management: Market risk and portfolio specific risk. The portfolio of securities, $s(t)$, purchased by dealers during a day consists of heterogeneous elements. Dealers in fixed income securities manage many issues, stock block traders are constantly offered a broad spectrum of securities, and government bond dealers transact business all along the yield curve of government securities. Each day the portfolio $s(t)$ of securities purchased or sold differs. The price risk concerns the change in price net of financing costs $\{p(t + 1) - p(t)[1 + r(t)]\}$ denoted by Δp on the portfolio of securities purchased or sold during the day. At times they may anticipate a large flow of sell orders by customers. They must accommodate their customers by quoting the best price possible but must avoid building up their inventories prior to a price decline. Quite often they make mistakes and find that they cannot unwind the position with profit or limited losses, that they are holding a risky position in which the risks are concentrated on the down side.

The change in the net price $\Delta p = p(t + 1) - p(t)[1 + r(t)]$ can be divided into two independent parts. The first term, $\beta\{I(t + 1) - I(t)[1 + r(t)]\}$, denoted by $\beta\Delta I$, describes how the price of the portfolio (net of finance costs) varies with changes in the market index (net of finance costs). The market index $I(t)$ refers to a broad set of securities of which portfolio $s(t)$ is a subset. If $s(t)$ consists of a specific portfolio of corporate bonds, then $I(t)$ is the price index of corporate and Treasury bonds. If $s(t)$ consists of a specific portfolio of equities, then $I(t)$ is the S&P 500 price index. For fixed income securities, the yield would be based upon the yield curve of Treasury securities times a risk premium. Coefficient β describes the current variation in the price of the securities relative to the movement in the relevant overall market index. The change $\beta\Delta I$ is the market risk that can result from changes in monetary and fiscal policy that produce sudden and substantial rises in interest rates.

The second element of the net price change is $c_1(t + 1)$, the portfolio specific risk. It is the change in the relative price of the portfolio *not* associated with changes in the market index. If the earnings of a particular firm are significantly lower than usual, for example, then ε_1 will be negative; and its price will decline relative to its historical relation to the market index. In the case of fixed income securities, the dealer may believe that the current risk premium relative to the Treasury securities yield curve is too high and that it will decline. This means that the relative price of the bond will rise, which is a subjective ε_1 that is positive. The dealer may not in fact be better able to evaluate the relative price risk ε_1 than is the market. He hopes that a combination of the relative price change ε_1 plus commissions and spreads, $V(s)$, will lead to a profitable transaction. The ε_1 embodies the security specific risk and return. Separating the overall price risk (Δp) into its market risk ($\beta \Delta I$) and specific risk (ε_1) gives equation 2 and equation 6.

The dealer quotes a price, $p(t)$, so that the expected profit, $V[s(t)] + \{E_t p(t + 1) - p(t) [1 + r(t)]\} s(t)$ is positive. If the market index is not expected to change, $E(\Delta I) - 0$, the dealer expects to profit from $(E\varepsilon_1)s(t) + V[s(t)]$, the sum of his ability to purchase under-valued (or sell overvalued) securities plus the commissions or spreads $V[s(t)]$.

Equation 2, abbreviated as (3) is applied to transactions in fixed income securities and equities and in both the primary and secondary markets. The sources of variation, the variance of the market index (var ΔI) and the variance of relative price changes (var ε_1) differ in each case. As a result, the effectiveness of hedging is different in each case.

$$p(t + 1) - p(t)[1 + r(t)] = \beta\{I(t + 1) - I(t)[1 + r(t)]\} + \varepsilon_1(t + 1) \quad (2)$$

$$\Delta p \qquad = \beta \Delta I + \varepsilon_1 \quad (3)$$

The dealer's profit equation 1 becomes equation 4, using equation 2, and is abbreviated as (5).

$$\pi_N(t + 1) = \{\beta[I(t + 1) - I(t)(1 + r(t)] + \varepsilon_1(t + 1)\}s(t) + V[s(t)] \quad (4)$$

$$\pi_N(t + 1) = (\beta \Delta I + \varepsilon_1)s(t) + V[s(t)] \quad (5)$$

A dealer must carry inventories because they are an essential part of his business of servicing customers. At any time there are two independent risks on his inventory: the market risk measured by the variance of $\beta \Delta Is(t)$ and the independent portfolio specific risk measured by the variance of $\varepsilon_1 s(t)$. The overall risk is equation 6.

$$\text{var } \Delta p = \beta^2 \text{ var } \Delta I + \text{var } \varepsilon_1 \quad (6)$$

For a high-grade fixed income security in either the primary or the secondary market, the market risk (var ΔI) dominates the relative price risk (var ε_1) because the risk premium relative to Treasury securities is relatively constant. Therefore, the price of a high-grade corporate fixed income security varies almost proportionately with the price of a comparable Treasury issue. For lower grade corporate fixed income securities, the risk premium relative to treasuries is not relatively constant but depends upon the likelihood that full debt servicing, which varies with the fortunes of the corporation, will be made. Hence, var ε_1/var Δp is higher for low-grade than for high-grade fixed income securities.

In the equity market, there is a basic difference between the situation facing the equity underwriter (primary market) and the stock block trader (secondary market). The stock block trader acquires a net portfolio, $s(t)$, during the day, which consists of n securities. Let there be N securities in the stock index the returns of which are $\Delta p_1, \Delta p_2, \ldots, \Delta p_n, \ldots, \Delta p_N$. At any time, t, let the return on the index be $\Delta I(t)$, which is the mean of the returns on the N securities. The variance of the returns on the N securities is $\sigma^2 = E(\Delta p_i - \Delta I)^2$.

If the sample of stocks acquired by the stock block trader were a random sample of the stocks in the index, then the return on the sample (portfolio) of n securities $\Delta p = \dfrac{1}{n} \Sigma_{i=1}^{n} \Delta p_i$ would be an unbiased estimate of the return on the index.

$$E(\Delta p - \Delta I) = 0 \tag{7}$$

In this case β in equation 2 is unity and $E(\varepsilon_1)$ is zero.

The variance of the return on the portfolio of n securities is just the variance of a sample mean around the population mean.

$$E(\Delta p - \Delta I)^2 = \text{var } \varepsilon_1 = \frac{\sigma^2}{n} \left(\frac{N - n}{N - 1} \right) \tag{8}$$

The closer the composition of the portfolio is to that of the index (that is, the closer n is to N), the smaller the variance of the difference between the return on the portfolio less the return on the index will be.

A stock block trader acquires a large sample of stocks (large n) during the course of a day. An equity underwriter manages only a few issues at a time (small n). It follows from equation 8 that, if the samples were random, the variance of the return on the portfolio less the return in the index is much larger for the equity underwriter than for the stock block trader. The difference is the portfolio specific risk, var ε_1. Hence, var ε_1/var Δp is much larger for the equity underwriter than for the stock block trader.

In general, a correlation of the return on a portfolio, Δp, on the return on the index, ΔI, will yield a coefficient of determination of

R^2. This is the variance of Δp accounted for by the variance of ΔI. It follows from equation 3 that

$$\frac{\text{var } \varepsilon_1}{\text{var } \Delta p} = 1 - R^2 \qquad (9)$$

For high-grade corporate fixed income securities, the correlation of the bond price with that of the Treasury security index is very high. For a stock block trader, the correlation of the value of the stocks acquired with the S&P 500 index is high. For an equity underwriter, correlation of the price of the issue handled with the S&P 500 index is poor.

Even before the development of futures markets in government bonds and stock indexes, dealers were able to hedge the downside market risks on their temporary portfolios. Large dealers engaged in homemade hedging. Dealers created a portfolio of securities that approximated the market index, either of corporate fixed income securities or equities. The hedging portfolio was constructed to have a β of unity, although to reduce transactions costs it contained fewer securities than are in the index. This surrogate portfolio was sold or purchased as a means of hedging the market risk.

Dealers would sell part of the surrogate portfolio in anticipation of a decline in the market index. Alternatively, a government bond dealer who was or was expected to be offered a specific portfolio of treasuries by customers would try to short long-term bonds, which are the riskiest of the treasuries. He would short some of the bonds or a surrogate portfolio of bonds. At time $t + 1$ when the portfolio of securities $s(t)$ is sold at price $p(t + 1)$, the dealer repurchases the surrogate portfolio. Insofar as the change in the value of the hedging portfolio is close to the change in the value of portfolios acquired from accommodating customers, the homemade hedging has reduced the riskiness of the dealer's position resulting from movements in the market index.

This homemade hedging procedure has several problems, which account for its limited use. First, only large dealers could assemble and maintain a hedging portfolio that is a good approximation to the market index. Second, transactions costs of selling the many different securities composing the homemade hedging portfolio severely reduce the profit margin derived from the commissions, spreads, and returns $V[s(t)]$ earned on the portfolio of transactions. Suppose that $10 million of equities $p(t)s(t)$ are hedged by selling the homemade hedging portfolio. The average share price for the S&P 500 index is $41, so that 243,902 shares are involved in the homemade hedging. Under the assumption of ten cents a share commission, the round trip transactions costs would be $24,390. Such large transactions costs cut into the commissions, $V[s(t)]$, earned by the dealers. Third, for government bond dealers, the interest rate on long-term government bonds exceeds the yield on the shorter maturities that are purchased with the proceeds of the short sale. Moreover, a fee which may range as high as ½ percent must be paid to borrow securities. Short sales are often quite expensive. Fourth, insofar as a hedging portfolio of equities in the secondary market is used, selling equities is difficult in a declining market because the stock exchange restricts the ability of specialists to sell when the price is declining (the "downtick" restriction).

Dealers' Uses of Futures. Futures markets in Treasury securities and stock indexes fundamentally changed the modus operandi of dealers and facilitated risk management. The reason dealers hedge is to protect themselves against market risk while they assume the portfolio specific risks at very low transactions costs.

To hedge against the market risk, var (ΔI), on a portfolio of securities $s(t)$ purchased $(+)$ or sold $(-)$, quantity $x(t)$ units of a homogeneous futures contract are sold $(+)$ or purchased $(-)$. Futures contracts that mature at time $T \geq t + 1$ are sold at price $f_T(t)$. At time $t + 1$, when the portfolio $s(t)$ is sold at price $p(t + 1)$, the futures contracts are repurchased at price $f_T(t + 1)$. Transactions costs on the futures contracts are $T[x(t)]$. The profit equations with futures $\pi(t + 1)$ are equation 10 or 11.

$$\pi(t + 1) = \{p(t + 1) - [1 + r(t)] \, p(t)\} \, s(t) + V[s(t)] \qquad (10)$$

$$- [f_T (t + 1) - f_T (t)]x(t) - T[x(t)]$$

$$\pi = s\Delta p + V(s) - x\Delta f - T(x) \qquad (11)$$

The advantages of futures over homemade hedging are considerable. First, considerable transactions costs are saved since the homogeneous futures contract is in a large denomination. Suppose that the $10 million portfolio of equities mentioned above is hedged by selling futures contracts on the S&P 500 index. If the S&P futures index were trading (in 1983) at 140, then each futures contract would have a value of $70,000 (500 x 140). The dealer could sell 143 contracts against the $10 million portfolio. The transactions cost is $15 per futures contract. On a round trip transaction the commissions would be $4,290 ($15 x 2 x 143). This figure is only 17 percent of the commissions involved in the homemade hedging described above.

Second, there is considerable leverage in dealing with futures. For a hedger, a 3 percent margin is required; and, for a speculator in the futures contracts on the S&P 500, an 8 percent margin is required. Collateral on the initial margin can be posted in the form of Treasury bills, with no loss of interest. A dealer has no need to tie up scarce capital in a surrogate portfolio to the market index, as he does with homemade hedging.

Third, the futures market in the broad-based instrument has depth, breadth, and resiliency, which few cash markets possess. Dealers need not worry about affecting the market prices with their purchases and sales. In selling the surrogate portfolio, since some of the securities are infrequently traded or have thin markets, the dealer may be affecting the market price to his disadvantage. This market power vitiates the usefulness of homemade hedging. Insofar as futures trading in the stock index is concerned, no restrictions about selling in a declining market exist.

The structural equations. In equation 10, the dealer hedges against market risk (the ΔI term and associated variance) by selling $x(t)$ of broad-based futures contracts for $f_T(t)$ dollars per contract, which mature at subsequent time $T \geq t + 1$. At time t the prices of the portfolio $p(t + 1)$ and the futures contract $f_T(t + 1)$ that will prevail at $t + 1$ are unknown. When the portfolio of securities $s(t)$ is sold at time $t + 1$, the dealer repurchases the futures contract at price $f_T(t + 1)$.

Equation 2 or 3 states that the change in the price of the portfolio net of financing costs Δp consists of two independent parts. One is the market risk, $\beta \Delta I$, whereby the price of the portfolio changes with the price of the market index. The second part, ε_1, represents changes in the price of the portfolio relative to changes in the index: $\varepsilon_1 = \Delta p - \beta \Delta I$. This portfolio specific risk is assumed to be independent of the change in the market index.

Dealers use futures markets to eliminate market risk by utilizing two relations schematized and discussed below.

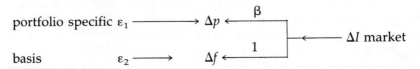

The change in the price of the portfolio Δp is related to the change in the market index ΔI as described by equation (2) or (3) above. Selling a stock index future is like selling the entire S&P 500 index with very low transactions costs and without affecting the market prices of the underlying securities. Selling a Treasury-bond future is like selling a high-grade corporate bond with a constant risk premium relative to the Treasury, with very low transactions costs and without affecting bond prices. A relation exists between the change in the price of the futures, $\Delta f_T = f_T(t + 1) - f_T(t)$, and the change in the market index, ΔI. The latter, described by equation 12, concerns the differential between the futures price, $f_T(t)$, and the underlying index, $I(t)$, on which the futures is based. This differential is approximately equal to the expected net carrying cost, $E_t r(t, T)$, from time t to maturity date T. The latter consists of the known one period net carrying cost, $r(t)$ from t to $t + 1$, plus the expected net carrying costs, $E_t r(t + 1, T)$, from $t + 1$ to maturity at T. The "no arbitrage" relation is shown by equation 12.

$$f_T(t) = I(t) [1 + E_t r(t, T)] = I(t) [1 + r(t) + E_t r(t + 1, T)] \quad (12)$$

Consider several cases of this equation. First is the conventional textbook case where, say, $I(t)$ is the cash price of a Treasury bond and $f_T(t)$ is the price of a Treasury-bond future. The cash bonds can be purchased for $I(t)$, and the net financing costs from t to T are $r(t, T)$. If financing could be arranged at time t over the interval to T, then arbitrage would ensure that the basis $f_T(t) - I(t)$ is equal to the net financing costs, $r(t, T)I(t)$, or the direct financing costs that are based upon the Treasury-bill rate or the repurchase argument (REPO) rate over the period less the interest received on the Treasury bonds.

A second case concerns the relation between the futures price of a government bond, $f_T(t)$, which matures at time T, and the index of corporate bonds, $I_c(t)$. There is a price (yield) differential denoted by $\delta(t)$ between a corporate and a Treasury bond, which reflects differential risk:

$$I(t) = I_c(t) + \delta(t)$$

Then the relation between the futures price on a government bond and a corporate bond is equation 13.

$$f_T(t) = [I_c(t) + \delta(t)] [1 + E_t r(t, T)]$$
$$= [I_c(t) + \delta(t)] [1 + r(t) + E_t r(t + 1, T)] \quad (13)$$

Both the net carrying costs $r(t, T)$ from t to maturity at T and the yield or price differential $\delta(t)$ between corporate securities and government securities vary over time.

Third, let $I(t)$ be an index (for example, S&P 500) of stock prices and $f_T(t)$ be the price at time t of a futures contract on that index, which matures at time T. At maturity, the futures price $f_T(T)$ is set equal to the index $I(T)$. The expected net financing costs $E_t r(t, T)$ from t to T are equal to the interest rate on Treasury bills less the

143

forecast dividend flows from the securities constituting the index. These dividend flows are not known with certainty at initial date t.

Professional arbitragers, dealers, and funds hold the index funds or approximations to the index. These institutions can buy either the index fund for $I(t)$ or the future for $f_T(t)$. If they buy the index fund, they expect the cost to be $I(t) [1 + Er(t, T)]$. To buy the futures costs them $f_T(t)$. In each case, at time T, their position is worth the same amount $f_T(T) = I(T)$. By arbitraging between these two alternatives, they tend to produce an approximation to equation 12.

Merrill Lynch Investment Strategy Department found that, using $r(t,T)$ as the risk-free Treasury-bill rate less the forecast dividend rates, equation 12 is a good but not a perfect description. There were arbitrage opportunities on both the near and the deferred contract. Table 3–3 indicates a frequency distribution of the magnitude of percentage deviations between the theoretical (the right side of equation 12) and the actual (the left side of equation 12) price of the S&P 500 futures. Transactions costs are approximately 0.5 percentage points. In 30 percent of the cases on the deferred contract, for example, the degree of mispricing ranged above 0.58 percent. In 10 percent of the cases, it ranged from −0.63 percent to −1.23 percent. Mispricing net of transactions costs occurs in 40 percent of the cases in the deferred contract and 30 percent in the nearby contract.

The relation between the change in the futures price $\Delta f_T = f_T(t$

TABLE 3–3

DISTRIBUTION OF PERCENTAGE MISPRICING OF STANDARD & POOR
FUTURES: DECEMBER 20, 1982, TO AUGUST 17, 1983
(percent)

Decile	Nearby Contract		Deferred Contract	
	High	Low	High	Low
1	1.73	0.65	2.60	1.33
2	0.64	0.36	1.32	0.95
3	0.35	0.16	0.88	0.58
4	0.15	0.01	0.56	0.37
5	0.01	−0.07	0.33	0.21
6	−0.09	−0.22	0.18	0.06
7	−0.23	−0.32	0.05	−0.02
8	−0.34	−0.49	−0.03	−0.21
9	−0.50	−0.80	−0.21	−0.57
10	−0.87	−1.42	−0.63	−1.23

SOURCE: Carmine J. Grigoli, *Pricing of Stock Index Futures* (Merrill Lynch Capital Markets, 1983).

+ 1) $- f_T(t)$ and the net change in the market index $\Delta I = I(t + 1)$ $- I(t) [1 + r(t)]$ is now shown. Take first differences of equations 12 and derive equation 14, abbreviated as equation 15.

$$f_T(t + 1) - f_T(t) = \{I(t + 1) - I(t) [1 + r(t)]\}$$

$$+ [I(t + 1)E_{t+1}r(t + 1, T) \qquad (14)$$

$$- I(t) E_t r(t + 1, T)]$$

$$\Delta f = \Delta I + \varepsilon_2 \qquad (15)$$

There are three components to deviation ε_2 between the change in the futures price Δf and the return on the index ΔI. First is the mispricing of the futures contract: the existence of arbitrage profits. In the early days of futures trading, this element was significant; and it enabled institutional investors to outperform the index. At present, the profits from mispricing are much smaller. Second are the effects of unexpected changes in the yield curve (the second element in equation 14) upon the more distant future. An unexpected rise in the yield curve at time $t + 1$ will raise the price of the future $f_T(t + 1)$ relative to the value of the index. When the maturity date T coincides with $t + 1$, this component will be zero. Third, where I is the index of corporate fixed income securities and f is the price of a Treasury-bond future, the variations in risk premium δ (in equation 13) are also contained in the ε_2 term.

The variance of the change in the future is equation 16, when ΔI and ε_2 are independent:

$$\text{var } \Delta f = \text{var } \Delta I + \text{var } \varepsilon_2 \qquad (16)$$

Substitute equation 15 describing the change in the futures price into profit equation 10 or 11 to obtain equation 17 for the profits of a dealer who just purchased portfolio $s(t)$. *This is the crucial equation for an understanding of dealer behavior.*

$$\pi(t + 1) = [s(t)\beta - x(t)] \Delta I + \varepsilon_1 s(t) - \varepsilon_2 x(t) + V[s(t)] - T[x(t)] \qquad (17)$$

market	portfolio	basis	deterministic
risk	specific risk	risk	

Expected profits $E\pi$ are equation 18, and the variance of profits is equation 19, when ΔI, ε_1, and ε_2, are independent.

$$E\pi = (s\beta - x)E\Delta I + sE\varepsilon_1 - xE\varepsilon_2 + V(s) - T(x) \qquad (18)$$

$$\text{var } \pi = (s\beta - x)^2\text{var } \Delta I + s^2 \text{ var } \varepsilon_1 + x^2\text{var } \varepsilon_2 \qquad (19)$$

where time subscripts are to be understood.

145

The dealer who has acquired portfolio $s(t)$, which he plans to sell to other customers as soon as possible, faces three risks. First, there is the market risk generated by ΔI, changes in the market index of securities. Dealers who purchased portfolios of corporate bonds just before the change in Federal Reserve policy in October 1979 would have suffered losses from the fall in corporate bond prices, regardless of how astutely they estimated the relative prices of the issues they purchased. Second, there is a portfolio specific risk, ε_1, which concerns the price of the portfolio relative to its historic relation to the market. The dealer's judgment involves purchasing under-priced securities and selling overpriced securities. The dealers specialize in taking this type of risk, and they hope that, combined with the commissions and spreads, $\varepsilon_1 s(t) + V[s(t)]$ will be positive. In periods of high interest rate volatility, the portfolio specific risk ε_1 is overwhelmed by the market risk in the case of high-grade corporate bonds in either the primary or secondary market or in a portfolio of many equities acquired for a short time by the stock block trader in the secondary market. This is not generally the case in the under-writing of a new stock issue. Third, when the dealer uses the futures market, he faces basis risks ε_2 concerning changes in the futures price relative to net changes in the market index. These risks are primarily due to unexpected changes in the yield curve. To facilitate the exposition, the three risks (var ΔI, var ε_1, var ε_2) are assumed to be independent. That is, the sum of the covariances are assumed to be relatively small compared to the sum of the variances. The aim of the dealer is to select the optimal temporary inventory $s(t)$ and amount of futures $x(t)$ sold ($+$) or purchased ($-$). These quantities change from day to day, if not more frequently.

Optimizing decisions. Dealers have great aversion to risk, despite the fact that they are professional risk bearers. Penalties for large losses, which may lead to bankruptcy, weigh more heavily than do rewards for large gains. Their behavior can be understood by model-ing their decisions as if they were maximizing the expectation of a concave utility function of profits from their current transactions. Equation 20 describes a general class of expected utility $EU(\pi)$ func-tions, where α is the coefficient of risk aversion of the dealer.

$$\underset{s,x}{\text{Max}}\ EU(\pi) = E\pi - \frac{\alpha}{2}\,\text{var}\ \pi \tag{20}$$

where $E\pi$ is expected profits (equation 18) and var π is the variance of profits (equation 19). The control variables are the inventory $s(t)$ and amount of futures $x(t)$.

The portfolio of transactions is held for a short time, and daily profits are associated with different portfolios. Divisions of the firm operate independently. The stock block, corporate fixed-income and government-bond divisions make split-second decisions and do not coordinate their transactions. They have no time to do so, and each dealer tries to unwind his transactions as soon as possible. Insofar as he cannot do so, he has an inventory management problem modeled by equations 18 and 19.

Two equations are derived from the maximization of expected utility (equation 20) with respect to the temporary inventory, $s(t)$, and the amount of hedging, $x(t)$. Their simultaneous determination provides the optimal values of the inventory, $s(t)$, and hedge ratio, $x(t)/s(t)$. It is instructive to examine these equations separately before considering their interaction.

The Effectiveness of Hedging by Different Types of Dealers. The optimal amount of hedging enables dealers to hedge market risks and permits them to concentrate upon trying to profit from "distortions" in the relative prices of securities. The effectiveness of hedging is negatively related to the portfolio specific risk, $\gamma_1 = $ var $\varepsilon_1/$var ΔI, and basis risk $\gamma_2 = $ var $\varepsilon_2/$var ΔI, both relative to the market risk var ΔI. When these two ratios are high, hedging is not effective. Because ratio γ_1 is high for equity underwriting, dealers in equities in the primary market do not hedge in the futures market. Because ratio γ_1 is low for dealers in high-grade corporate fixed incomes, those dealers actively use the futures market for hedging. Ratio γ_2 is high if hedging is done in distant futures; therefore, deferred futures are inferior to the nearby future as a hedging instrument.

The variance of profits is equation 19. It is convenient to consider variable y, the ratio of the variance of profits (var π) to the variance of the market index (var ΔI), which is graphed in figure 3–3.

$$y = \frac{\text{var } \pi}{\text{var } \Delta I} = (s\beta - x)^2 + s^2 \gamma_1 + x^2\gamma_2 \tag{21}$$

$$\gamma_1 \equiv \text{var } \varepsilon_1/\text{var } \Delta I = \text{portfolio specific risk/market risk} \tag{22}$$

$$\gamma_2 \equiv \text{var } \varepsilon_2/\text{var } \Delta I = \text{basis risk/ market risk} \tag{23}$$

Equation 21 is a quadratic in x, the futures position. If there were no use of futures markets such that $x = 0$, ratio y would be the vertical intercept $0N$ or equation 24.

$$y(x = 0) = (s\beta)^2 + s^2\gamma_1 \tag{24}$$

FIGURE 3–3

The Relation between Relative Risk and Hedging

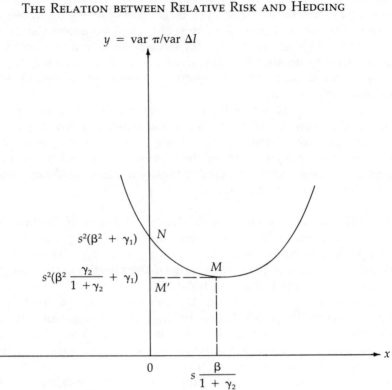

$y = \text{var } \pi / \text{var } \Delta I$

$s^2(\beta^2 + \gamma_1)$ N

$s^2\left(\beta^2 \dfrac{\gamma_2}{1 + \gamma_2} + \gamma_1\right)$ M

M'

0

$s \dfrac{\beta}{1 + \gamma_2}$

x

The value of x associated with minimal risk is $x = x_{min}$ in equation 25.

$$x_{min} = s \frac{\beta}{1 + \gamma_2} \qquad (25)$$

When the amount of hedging x equals x_{min}, then the value of y is minimal at y_{min} in equation 26. This is point M in figure 3–3.

$$y_{min} = (s\beta)^2 \frac{\gamma_2}{1 + \gamma_2} + s^2\gamma_1 \qquad (26)$$

The maximum reduction in risk resulting from hedging is to reduce y from the no-hedge point N to the minium risk point M.

The maximal percentage reduction in risk denoted MRR, ratio NM'/ON in figure 3–3 is equation 27:

$$\text{MRR} = \frac{NM'}{ON} \tag{27}$$

$$= \frac{\beta^2}{(1 + \gamma_2)(\beta^2 + \gamma_1)} \text{ maximal percentage risk reduction}$$

A special case of equation 27 is one where there is no basis risk $\gamma_2 = 0$. Then the maximal percentage reduction in risk is MRR $= \beta^2/(\beta^2 + \gamma_1)$. This can easily be related to Louis Ederington's formula.[4] When there is no basis risk then equation 15 is $\Delta f = \Delta I$ and var Δf = varΔI. Then the net change in the price of the portfolio Δp can be written as $\Delta p = \beta \Delta f + \varepsilon_1$. If the correlation between Δp and Δf is denoted by R, it follows that $R^2 = \beta^2/(\beta^2 + \gamma_1)$.[5]

Hence, equation MRR $= \beta^2/(\beta^2 + \gamma_1)$ is identical to Ederington's formula for the maximal risk reduction through hedging when there is no basis risk.

The advantage of equation 27 over Ederington's R^2 formula is that the determinants of R^2 are explicitly brought out in 27 as components of structural equations. Thereby one can understand on a theoretical level the usefulness of hedging, that is, where it will or will not be used.

The optimal futures position $x = x^*$ is equation 28. It is derived by optimizing equation 20 with respect to $x(t)$.

$$x^*(t) = \beta s(t) \frac{1}{1 + \gamma_2} - \frac{1}{\alpha} \frac{E(\Delta f_T) - T'(x)}{(1 + \gamma_2) \text{ var } \Delta I} \tag{28}$$

since var $(\Delta f_T) = (1 + \gamma_2)$ var ΔI.

Equation 28 indicates the hedging and speculative aspects of the use of futures. The first term in the equation is the optimal hedging that would be done if the futures price were not expected to change by more than the transactions costs. Then the optimal amount of hedging is equal to the amount that leads to the minimal risk $x = x_{min}$. This occurs because of equation 15 in which the coefficient of ΔI is unity. Under these conditions, fraction $\beta/(1 + \gamma_2)$ of the cash position $s(t)$ is hedged in the futures market. The greater the basis risk γ_2, the smaller will be the fraction hedged. The greater the β, the responsiveness of the price of the portfolio to changes in the market index, the greater the fraction hedged.

The second term in equation 28 is the speculative term. It is the optimal position in the futures market that would be taken if the dealer had no position in the cash market. Position $x^*(t)$ would be long (short) if the futures price were expected to rise (decline) by more than the transactions costs. The risk on a pure futures transaction, var (Δf_T), is the denominator of the second term, using equations 16 and 23, that is, var $\Delta f = (1 + \gamma_2)$ var ΔI. Thus the pure speculative element is the expected return net of transactions costs divided by the product of risk and risk aversion.

Equations 27 and 28 explain why futures are used by dealers in fixed income securities in both the primary and secondary markets and by stock block traders in the secondary market and why they are not used in equity underwriting. These equations also explain what are, and are not, fruitful uses of futures by dealers.

High-grade corporate fixed income securities bear interest rates that are linearly related to the interest rates on Treasury securities of comparable maturities. A dealer prices a corporate bond issue on the basis of the yield curve on Treasury bonds. By hedging with a Treasury-bond future, the dealer knows that the correlation between the change in the net price of the corporate bond, Δp, and the change in the price index of a Treasury bond, ΔI, is very high. The issue specific risk, var ε_1, is very small compared with the market risk, var ΔI. In equation 27, γ_1 is very small. Insofar as hedging is done in the nearby contract, the basis risk γ_2 is also very small. Hence, point M in figure 3–3 is close to the x axis, and almost all of the risk can be eliminated through hedging.

A different situation exists in the underwriting of corporate equities. The earnings of a particular corporation have a high variance, they are very difficult to predict. Earnings are affected by the quality of management of the corporation, the fortunes of the industry, and the course of the economy. The third factor would be reflected in the movements of the S&P 500 index. Hence, ε_1 reflects the first two factors. Changes in the stock price, for that reason, are poorly correlated with changes in the net price of the index. Formally, var ε_1 is high relative to var ΔI. This means that parameter $\gamma_1 = $ var $\varepsilon_1/$var ΔI is high or the regression coefficient β in equation 3 relating Δp to ΔI is close to zero. Consequently, hedging is not effective in the underwriting of equity. The futures market is not used in stock underwriting because the major risk is the issue-specific risk, var ε_1, rather than the market risk, var ΔI. Graphically, point M' is not far below point N in figure 3–3; in other words, $M'N/0N$ is quite small.

A different situation prevails in the secondary market for equities from the viewpoint of the stock block trader. The stock block trader purchases and sells many different issues during the course of a day; and $s(t)$ should be interpreted as a vector of securities. On one particular issue, the relative price risk is high compared with the market risk. When one considers the entire portfolio of purchases, one sees significant negative covariances between the relative price risks. Consequently, the major risk that a stock block trader faces is the market risk. Put another way, during the course of a day, the stock block trader may acquire a large sample (portfolio) of stocks that has a fair similarity to the market index. If in equation 8 n is close to N, the average price of the sample (portfolio) is correlated with the market index (see equation 9). By selling a futures on the S&P 500 index, the stock block trader is in effect selling the index; and he thereby avoids the market risk. His γ_1 is relatively small; therefore, distance $NM'/0N$ is large in figure 3–3.

A specific set of examples can be given. These are estimates of equation 6, var $\Delta p = \beta^2$ var $\Delta I +$ var ε_1, for portfolios consisting of n securities from the New York Stock Exchange.

Number n of securities	$R^2 = \beta^2$ var $\Delta I/$var Δp
1	0.300
2	0.462
10	0.811
20	0.896

The left column lists the number of securities and the right column is $R^2 = \beta^2$var $\Delta I/$var Δp, the proportion of total risk due to the market.[6] The maximal risk reduction to be achieved by hedging MRR is this R^2 when there is no basis risk. An equity underwriter handling one issue on a given day can avoid 30 percent of the risk by hedging in a broad-based index. A stock block trader handling twenty stocks on a given day can avoid 90 percent of the risk.

A question arises whether the stock block trader or the equity underwriter would use futures on subindexes in his risk management operations. The answer is that such futures are not very useful to the stock block trader but can be useful to someone who specializes in a subset of securities. Consider a hypothetical situation in which a stock block trader can use a futures in every single security that he purchases or sells. If he hedges each of his purchases with the corresponding future, then he is incurring very large transactions costs and, in effect, disposing of each security immediately via a sale of futures. The stock block trader operates on a sufficiently large scale that he has the ability to influence the market price. He would then be influencing the futures price. As a result, he has gained nothing by hedging rather than selling the securities immediately in the cash market. The crucial aspect of futures is the liquidity of the market: the ability of the dealers to buy and sell large quantities without affecting the price. The more specific the future, the closer it is to the cash market; and hence the futures market loses its liquidity. Moreover, transactions costs rise as they do in the home-made hedging case described previously.

During the course of a day a municipal bond dealer acquires a sample of the municipal bond index. If there were a futures contract on a municipal bond index, the dealer would be sensible to hedge the market risk on the population of municipal bonds with a futures contract on the municipal bond index. The correlation between the average price of his portfolio of municipals and the municipal bond index would be high: var ε_1/var $\Delta I = \gamma_1$ would be low. Hedging would be quite effective.

Subindexes in equities could be useful to the stock block trader but not useful to the equity underwriter for the following reason, seen mathematically in equation 8. If the stock block trader has been dealing in many equities in the industry, then he can avoid the industry specific risk by hedging in the industry subindex and still have liquidity. The equity underwriter handles few issues at a time and faces the corporation specific risk, which relates to the quality of management of the corporation. His n is quite small, so that γ_1 = var ε_1/var ΔI is high for the equity of a specific corporation.

Hedging of high-grade corporate fixed income securities is feasible because the probability of failure to service the debt is small. Hedging of an equity of a particular corporation cannot eliminate the high variance of the earnings of a particular corporation due to the quality of management: γ_1 is high. Hence, the equity underwriter is unlikely to be attracted to futures.

The advantages of futures markets for dealer risk management are as follows. There are low transactions costs because of economies of scale. Since the same futures contract is used by dealers to hedge market risk on a heterogeneous collection of securities, the market is very liquid, and no dealer can affect the market price. The hedging of market risk does not preclude the dealer from profiting from relative price distortions. There is a high correlation between the price of a futures contract on an index and the average price of a large sample of underlying securities, so that market risk can be diversified away. If a subindex futures contract is narrowly based, it does not have the first three advantages and hence is of limited use to dealers. A futures contract on the index is an inexpensive way of buying or selling a representative sample of the underlying securities without affecting market price.

The speculative component of futures transactions is $E(\Delta f)/\alpha$ var

(Δf) in equation 28. It is the expected return per unit of risk on a futures contract divided by the coefficient of risk aversion. Different dealers have different coefficients of risk aversion. Highly risk-averse dealers (those with large values of α) use futures primarily for hedging. Their sales of futures $x(t)$ are equal to the first term in equation 28. Those who are less risk averse also use futures as a speculation on price change. Their sales of futures $x(t)$ may be closer to the second term in equation 28. For these reasons, equations 27 and 28 capture the essence of dealer transactions in futures.

Futures Markets and the Cost of Capital.

The inventory investment demanded. The optimum inventory investment by the dealer during a period of time can now be derived. It is the penultimate step in deriving the cost of capital.

The optimum portfolio of securities that the dealer has on balance acquired by accommodating his customers and that he continues to hold at the end of the day is his inventory investment. It is derived from the simultaneous solution of equations 18, 19, and 20 above. Continue to consider the case where the basis risk is a negligible fraction of the market risk and neither the futures price nor the index is expected to change,[7] so that the optimal hedge ratio is β in equation 28.

$$\text{Assume } E\ (\Delta I) = 0,\ E(\varepsilon_2) = 0,\ E(\Delta f_T) = 0$$

$$\gamma_2 = \text{var } \varepsilon_2/\text{var } \Delta I \text{ is negligible}$$

Since the optimal value of x/s under the above assumptions is β, the expected profit and variance of profit are equations 29 and 30 respectively.

$$E\pi = sE(\varepsilon_1) + V(s) \tag{29}$$

$$\text{var } \pi = s^2(\text{var } \varepsilon_1 + \beta^2 \text{ var } \varepsilon_2) \tag{30}$$

The optimal cash position, s, occurs when the marginal expected profits, $dE(\pi)/ds$, are equal to the marginal risk premium, $(\alpha/2)d$ var π/ds. Then equation 31 is satisfied.

$$E(\varepsilon_1) + V'(s) = \alpha(\text{var } \varepsilon_1 + \beta^2 \text{ var } \varepsilon_2)s \tag{31}$$

The marginal expected profits from inventory investment consist of two parts. (1) The relative net price of the portfolio is expected to appreciate by $E(\varepsilon_1)$, relative to its systematic relation to the market. (2) The income earned from commissions and spreads, $V(s)$, less costs is positively related to the portfolio of transactions.

The nonspeculative profit function $V[s(t)]$ is described by equation 32 and marginal profits $V'[s(t)]$ by equation 33. The nonspeculative profit function, $V(s)$, is concave; or the marginal nonspeculative profit function, $V'(s)$, is negatively sloped, for two reasons. First, total revenue rises at a slower rate than the volume of business because the dealer competes for business by offering more favorable commissions or spreads and because the dealer's purchases and sales affect market prices. That is, the dealer faces a negatively sloped demand curve relating volume of business to both market price and to commissions and spreads. Second, marginal costs of operation are positively related to the volume of business.

$$V(s) = \left(v_0 - \frac{v_1}{2}s\right)s \tag{32}$$

$$V'(s) = v_0 - v_1 s \tag{33}$$

Term v_0 is marginal profit when $s = 0$. It reflects the state of demand for dealer services and the cost of providing them; and v_1 reflects how the spread or commission must decline to increase the volume of business and the corresponding rise in marginal cost.

Substitute (33) into (31) to derive the necessary condition for the optimal inventory.

$$E\varepsilon_1 + v_0 - v_1 s(t) = \alpha(\text{var } \varepsilon_1 + \beta^2 \text{ var } \varepsilon_2)\, s(t) \tag{34}$$

marginal expected profit = risk premium

When the optimal futures position is held the marginal expected profit $dE\pi/ds$ and the risk premium, $(\alpha/2)d \text{ var } \pi/ds$, are graphed as in figure 3–4. The term in parentheses in the risk premium is the risk per unit of inventory investment when the optimal hedge ratio β is used.

For the optimal inventory of the dealer, $s(t)$, we solve equation 34 and derive (35).

$$s(t) = \frac{E\varepsilon_1 + v_0}{v_1 + \alpha(\text{var } \varepsilon_1 + \beta^2 \text{ var } \varepsilon_2)} \tag{35}$$

when it is assumed that: $E(\Delta I) = 0$, $E(\varepsilon_2) = 0$ and $\gamma_2 = \text{var } \varepsilon_2/\text{var } \Delta I \sim 0$. The expected return on the portfolio is $E(\Delta p) = \beta E(\Delta I) + E(\varepsilon_1)$ from equation 2 or equation 3. When $E(\Delta I) = 0$, equation 35 can be written as equation 36.

$$s(t) = \frac{Ep(t + 1;t) - [1 + r(t)]p(t) + v_0}{v_1 + \alpha(\text{var } \varepsilon_1 + \beta^2 \text{ var } \varepsilon_2)} \tag{36}$$

FIGURE 3–4

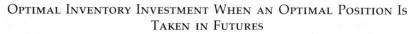

OPTIMAL INVENTORY INVESTMENT WHEN AN OPTIMAL POSITION IS
TAKEN IN FUTURES

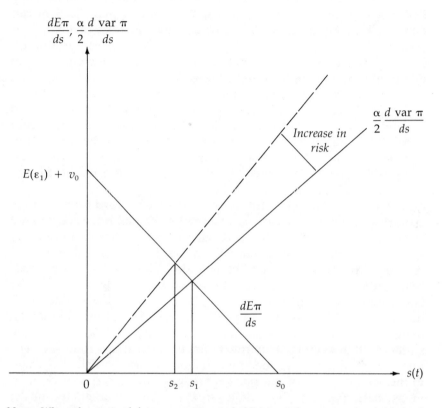

NOTE: When the optimal futures position is held (given the assumptions), optimal inventory investment $s(t)$ during the time interval is where the expected marginal profits $E\varepsilon_1 + v_0 - v_1 s(t)$ is equal to the risk premium $\alpha(\text{var } \varepsilon_1 + \beta^2 \text{ var } \varepsilon_2) s(t)$. A rise in the risk rotates the risk premium line counterclockwise. This is fundamentally different from the "separation theorem."

The dealer's inventory investment at the end of a day depends (1) positively upon the expected change in the relative price of the portfolio net of finance cost plus the marginal profit v_0, (2) negatively upon the risk when the optimal hedge ratio is used, times the coefficient of risk aversion, and (3) negatively upon the reduction in commissions and spreads required to increase business.

If there were no risk or risk aversion, then the optimal inventory investment is $[E(\varepsilon_1) + v_0]/v_1$ or s_0. With risk and risk aversion, the optimal inventory investment is s_1. As the degree of risk increases, the optimal inventory declines to s_2.

Previous writers allege that no connection between the cash position and risk exists, even when there is risk aversion.[8] They derive a separation theorem, which states that when the firm can either sell its output forward at a predetermined price or sell it later at an uncertain price, then the quantity $s(t)$ that will be "produced" is independent of risk and risk aversion. These elements simply determine the fraction of output hedged.

Equation 35 or figure 3–4 for the optimal inventory investment $s(t)$ is quite different from the separation theorem because $s(t)$ also depends upon risk and risk aversion. As risk rises, s declines from s_1 to s_2. Unlike the separation theorem, the optimal hedge ratio in equation 28 when the futures price is not expected to change, $[E(\Delta f) = 0]$, is independent of risk and risk aversion. The reason for the different results is that those who use the separation theorem are describing a forward not a futures market. In a forward market, there is no risk. What is sold forward at a predetermined price is delivered at that price, and all risk has been eliminated on those transactions. A different situation exists when the dealer hedges by selling x units of futures contracts on a broad-based index. The futures on the broad-based index do not correspond to the portfolio hedged. The dealer is not planning to deliver the broad-based index; the transaction is not forward. The risk that is eliminated by the optimal amount of hedging is the market risk (var ΔI) whereby the price of the portfolio varies with movements in the bond or stock market index. The remaining risks, as described by equation 30, are the risk of changes in the relative price of the portfolio (var ε_1) and the risk of changes in the basis (var ε_2). By hedging in the futures market, the dealer hedges away the market risk by assuming the risk of changes in the basis.

The rapidly growing futures markets are heavily used by dealers and are quite distinct from forward markets. In 1982, for example, the U.S. government securities dealers had the following positions in the cash, futures, and forward markets (in millions of dollars):

- U.S. government securities $9,328
- Futures positions

Treasury bills	− 2,508
Treasury coupons	− 2,361
Federal agency	− 224
	− 5,093

- Forward positions
  U.S. government
    securities -788
  Federal agency $-1,190$

                                     $-1,978$

When there is no futures market, the optimal inventory invest-ment $s_N(t)$ satisfies equation 37. It is derived by maximizing equation 20 with respect to s, using equations 18 and 19 and setting the futures position x equal to zero. The left side is $dE\pi/ds$ and the right side is $(\alpha/2)d$ var π/ds.

$$\beta E(\Delta I) + E(\varepsilon_1) + V'(s_N) = \alpha s_N(\beta^2 \text{var } \Delta I + \text{var } \varepsilon_1) \qquad (37)$$

When the expected return on the index net of carrying costs is zero—$E(\Delta I) = 0$—then the optimal inventory position $s_N(t)$ is equation 38. It can also be written as equation 39, which is comparable to equation 35.

$$s_N(t) = \frac{E(\varepsilon_1) + v_0}{v_1 + \alpha(\beta^2 \text{ var } \Delta I + \text{ var } \varepsilon_1)} \qquad (38)$$

$$s_N(t) = \frac{Ep(t + 1; t) - [1 + r(t)]p(t) + v_0}{v_1 + \alpha(\beta^2 \text{ var } \Delta I + \text{ var } \varepsilon_1)} \qquad (39)$$

The optimum temporary inventory, $s_N(t)$, that will be absorbed by the dealer when there are no futures markets depends upon the following factors. It depends positively upon the expected capital gain on the inventory net of financing costs, $E\Delta p = \beta E\Delta I + E\varepsilon_1$, and upon the level v_0 of commissions and spreads. It depends nega-tively upon v_1, the degree of market power that the dealer has in affecting price. The greater this market power, the smaller will be the dealer's purchases or sales per unit of time. The position depends negatively upon the product of risk aversion α and total risk β^2 var $\Delta I + $ var ε_1.

An approximation to equation 38 was examined by Burton Zwick.[9] He examined the quarterly average of dealer net positions in Treasury bills and other securities maturing during a year and dealer spreads, during the period 1962:Q1 through 1974:Q4. The regressors were (a) the actual changes in interest rates; (b) the net carrying costs, meas-ured as the quarterly average of the federal funds rate less the three-month Treasury-bill rate and (c) measures of variability in interest rates. His position variable is average inventory, whereas my $s(t)$ is the change in inventory during a short period of time. The actual change in interest rates is used as a proxy for the expected change in interest rates.

Zwick's variables (a) and (b) reflect the numerator in equation 38; and variable (c) reflects the denominator in that equation. He found the following relations. First, the average position was negatively related to the actual rise in interest rates. Second, the average net position was negatively related to net carrying costs. Third, the average net position was negatively related to the interest rate variability during the four recent quarters; but it was not related to that variability during the past twenty-four quarters. Fourth, the spreads were positively related to the measures of variability. Interest rate variability affects the average position in the short run. In the longer run, it primarily affects the spread.

A Comparison of Dealer Inventory Investment Function. The cost of capital is negatively related to the market prices of bonds or equities of the corporations. Using the above analysis of the dealer demand for inventory investment, the effects of futures markets upon the price of the portfolio, $p(t)$, or cost of capital can be explained.

The demand for inventory investment ($s \gtreqless 0$) by dealers is equation 36 when the futures market is used optimally, and equation 39 when there is no futures market. It is convenient to write these equations in inverse form and graph them in figure 3–5.

When the futures market is used optimally, the inverse inventory function is equation 40, abbreviated as (41). It is curve FF' in figure 3–5.

$$p(t) = \frac{E_t p(t+1) + v_0}{1 + r(t)} - \frac{[v_1 + \alpha(\text{var } \varepsilon_1 + \beta^2 \text{ var } \varepsilon_2)]}{1 + r(t)} s(t) \quad (40)$$

$$p(t) = A(t) - B_F s(t) \quad (41)$$

The vertical intercept of the inverse demand curve $A(t)$ is the present value of the expected price of the portfolio plus the marginal profit on the first unit acquired. This is the primary source of uncertainty. Graphically, the intercept term continually shifts up and down. The absolute value of the slope of the inventory investment demand curve $B_F(t)$ depends upon three factors. It depends upon the risk of the portfolio when the optimal hedge ratio is used. Components of this risk are the variance of the relative price, var ε_1, plus the basis risk, β^2 var ε_2. Note that (from equation 25) when the optimal hedge ratio is used, the market risk var ΔI has been diversified away. The absolute value of the slope also depends upon the coefficient α of risk aversion by dealers and on the degree of market power of a

158

FIGURE 3–5

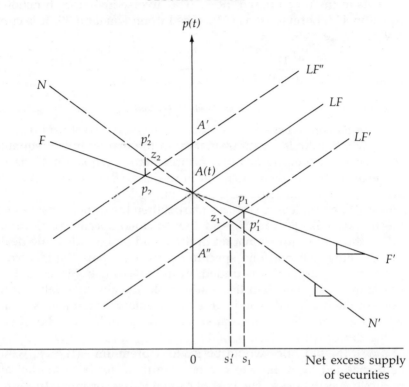

NOTE: The excess supply of securities (excess demand for loanable funds) by nondealers is curve LF, LF' or LF". The inventory investment demand by dealers is NN' when there are no futures markets and FF' when the futures markets are used optimally. Transitory variations in the LF' curve, around its mean value LF, produce smaller price variations when dealers use futures markets optimally.

dealer v_1 in affecting the price. Both $A(t)$ and $B(t)$ depend upon the particular securities acquired by the dealer.

Let s_1 of securities be offered to dealers during an interval of time. It could be a new issue of corporate fixed incomes, blocks of equity or an issue of government bonds. The aim of the dealer is to dispose of these securities to their customers as soon as possible.

The present value of the price expected to prevail at time $t + 1$ plus the marginal profit v_0 determine the intercept $A(t)$. According to figure 3–5, the dealer will bid price p_1 giving the corporate treasurer or the U.S. Treasury a cost of capital of $100 - p_1$. Risk premium

159

$A(t) - p_1$ reflects the risks of acquiring the particular portfolio plus the basis risk involved in hedging away the market risk.

Contrast this with the situation in which there are no futures markets in the broad-based index. The inverse inventory function is equation 42, abbreviated as (43), based upon equation 39. It is curve NN' in figure 3–5.

$$p(t) = \frac{E_t p(t + 1) + v_0}{1 + r(t)} - \frac{[v_1 + \alpha(\text{var } \varepsilon_1 + \beta^2 \text{ var } \Delta I)]}{1 + r(t)} s(t) \quad (42)$$

$$p(t) = A(t) - B_N s(t) \quad (43)$$

The difference between the dealer's inventory investment demand curve when there is a futures market in the market index (equation 40) and when there is no such futures market (equation 42) is not so much in the intercept $A(t)$, but in the slope B_F or B_N respectively. The slope represents the risk premium, risk aversion, and market power. When there is no futures market then the dealer must assume the market risk, β^2 var ΔI, and the portfolio specific risk, var ε_1. When there is a futures market in the broad-based index, the dealer must assume the portfolio specific risk, var ε_1, plus the basis risk, β^2 var ε_2. A market risk is traded off for a basis risk. Since the basis risk is much smaller than the market risk, the absolute value of the slope of the dealer's demand curve for inventory investment is greater when there are no futures markets. Were portfolio s_1 to be offered to the dealers (under comparable conditions during a given interval of time), the bid price would be p_1'. Risk premium $A(t) - p_1'$ would be demanded by dealers to compensate them for both market and portfolio specific risks. The cost of capital to the corporate treasurers or the government would be $100 - p_1'$.

There is also some effect of futures markets upon the intercept term $A(t)$, which is the expected price $E_t p(t + 1)$ plus marginal nonspeculative profits. When there are no futures markets, the price discovery concerning the value of high-grade corporate bonds is done through the yield curve on government bonds. The interest rate on the corporate bonds will be the interest rate on a government issue of the same maturity plus a relatively constant risk premium. Moreover, the expected interest rates on government issues at a subsequent date, that is the implicit forward rates, can be inferred from the yield curve on treasuries. In this manner, the dealer can use the yield curve on Treasury securities to price corporate issues and to learn the market estimate $E_t p(t + h)$ of the price at time $t + h$.

With futures in Treasury securities, the market obtains the same type of information concerning expected subsequent interest rates or

$E_t p(t + h)$. The main difference is that with futures, the yield curve is updated continuously and is readily available at practically no cost to all market participants. Futures permit continuous updating of $A(t)$ in a readily available form, whereas the estimate of $A(t)$ derived from the yield curve per se is not as current when there are no futures markets. Overall, however, the price discovery role of financial futures is not that significant.

The depth, breadth, and resiliency of the market. The effects of the dealers' uses of futures markets upon the macroeconomy can now be explained. Price $p(t)$ at which dealers purchase or sell securities is negatively related to "the interest rate." Suppose that the face value of a bond is one dollar and the dealer is willing to purchase it for p dollars. The discount rate is $1 - p$. If it were a zero coupon bond maturing in T years, the interest rate is $i = \dfrac{1}{T} \ln (1/p)$. Similarly, if the reproduction cost of a firm is one dollar and the dealer is willing to purchase the equity for p dollars, the q ratio is precisely p. In both cases, the rate of planned investment by firms is positively related to price p.

Consider the demand for and supply of loanable funds by nondealers, items 1 through 5 in table 3–4. The demand for loanable funds is the supply of securities offered during a time interval. The supply of loanable funds is the demand for securities during a time interval.

The excess supply of securities $y(t) \equiv I(t) + [G(t) - T(t)] + \Delta L(t) - S(t) - \Delta M(t)$, during a time interval, is negatively related to "the interest rate," or positively related to the level of security prices, $p(t)$. It is drawn as the LF (loanable funds or excess supply of securities schedule) in figure 3–5, and is equation 44 written in inverse form. Parameter $u(t)$ reflects the shifts in the LF schedule, due to variations

---

TABLE 3–4

SUPPLY OF AND DEMAND FOR SECURITIES (LOANABLE FUNDS)
DURING A SPECIFIC TIME INTERVAL

Supply of Securities	Demand for Securities
1. $I(t)$ = planned investment by firms	4. $S(t)$ = savings
2. $G(t) - T(t)$ = government expenditures less taxes = deficit	5. $\Delta M(t)$ = change in supply of money
3. $\Delta L(t)$ = change in demand for money	6. $s(t)$ = dealer investment in inventories

---

161

in income, the productivity of capital, thrift, liquidity preference, or the government deficit. A transitory rise in the government deficit, for example, shifts the excess supply of securities curve from LF to LF'. A transitory rise in the money supply increases the demand for securities and shifts the excess supply of securities curve from LF to LF".

$$p(t) = u(t) + ay(t) \qquad (44)$$

The average value of the excess supply of securities curve is LF associated with an average value of u denoted by $Eu = 0A(t)$ in figure 3–5. At this price (interest rate) $0A(t)$, the demand for and supply of loanable funds are equal, on average during the period. Dealers, on average, are neither investing or disinvesting in securities.

Dealers provide the securities marked with "depth, breadth, and resiliency." This phrase has been defined as follows:

> the market which is reflected on the order books of specialists and dealers possesses depth when there are orders, either actual orders or orders that can be readily uncovered, both above and below the market. The market has breadth when these orders are in volume and come from widely different groups. It is resilient when new orders pour promptly into the market to take advantage of sharp and unexpected fluctuations in prices.[10]

When a market has depth, breadth, and resilience, variations in portfolios offered or demanded do not lead to large price fluctuations. Figure 3–5 shows how the use of futures by dealers adds depth, breadth, and resiliency to these markets.

Let the nondealer excess supply of securities vary from curve LF' to curve LF", around its mean of LF. If there were no dealers, the price of securities (interest rate) would vary from A' to A" to produce an equality between the demand for and supply of loanable funds.

Dealers provide an inventory investment or disinvestment (see table 3–4, item 6) cushion for fluctuations in the excess supply of securities (items 1 to 5 or variable $y[t]$). Suppose that the government deficit that is being financed through securities exceeds its average value for the period and produces a transitory rise in the excess supply of securities curve to LF'. As the price declines below $A(t)$, the present value of the subsequently expected price, dealers would increase their inventories of securities.

If there were no dealers, the price would decline to A". If dealers cannot use futures markets, their inventory investment function is

162

NN'. The price would temporarily decline to z_1; and dealers' inventory investment would be s_1'. Risk premium $A(t) - z_1$ is the expected return over the financing costs.

When dealers use futures markets optimally, the inventory investment function is FF'. The transitory rise in the excess supply of securities to LF' leads to a price of p_1; and dealers' inventory investment is s_1. Risk premium $A(t) - p_1$ is the expected excess return over financing costs. The distance between the FF' and NN' curves (for example, $p_1'p_1$ or p_2p_2') is the decrease in risk premium resulting from the optimal use of futures markets.

Graphically, it is obvious that the average price $Ep = A(t)$ is not directly affected by the dealers' use of futures, or even by their existence. At this average price, the average demand for and supply of loanable funds are equal on average. The variance of the price of securities, however, is profoundly affected by the role of the dealers. If there were no dealers, the range of price variation would be from A'' to A'. If dealers could not use futures markets, the range would be from z_1 to z_2. If dealers used futures markets optimally, the range would be reduced from p_1 to p_2.

Formally table 3–4 and equations 40 to 44 imply that the expected price Ep is given by equation 45 and the variance of the price, var p, is given by equation 46.

$$Ep = A \tag{45}$$

$$\text{var } p = \frac{\text{var } u}{\left(1 + \dfrac{a}{B_i}\right)^2} \qquad i = N,F \tag{46}$$

Since slope B_F is less than slope B_N (in figure 3–5 or equations 40 and 42), the price (interest rate) variance is reduced by the dealer use of futures markets. Alternatively, the use of futures markets by dealers increases the depth, breadth, and resiliency of the market.

The percentage reduction in the slope B of the inventory investment demand of dealers can be immediately derived from equations 40 and 42.

$$\frac{B_N - B_F}{B_N} = \frac{\alpha\beta^2(\text{var } \Delta I - \text{var } \varepsilon_2)}{v_1 + \alpha(\text{var } \varepsilon_1 + \beta^2 \text{ var } \Delta I)} \tag{47}$$

A particularly simple expression for the percentage decline in the slope can be derived from equation 47 by assuming that there is no basis risk, $\varepsilon_2 = 0$, so that equation 48 describes the relation between the change in the net price Δp and futures price Δf respectively, and that coefficient v_1 is sufficiently small to be ignored.

$$\Delta p = \beta\Delta f + \varepsilon_1, \text{ since } \Delta f = \Delta I \tag{48}$$

163

Then

$$\frac{B_N - B_F}{B_N} = \beta^2 \frac{\text{var } \Delta I}{\text{var } \Delta p} \tag{49}$$

From equation 48,

$$\beta^2 \frac{\text{var } \Delta I}{\text{var } \Delta p} = \beta^2 \frac{\text{var } \Delta f}{\text{var } \Delta p} = \rho_{pf}^2 \tag{50}$$

where ρ_{pf} is the correlation between Δp and Δf. It follows that

$$\frac{B_N - B_F}{B_N} = \rho_{pf}^2 \tag{51}$$

Under the assumptions above, the percent reduction in the slope of the inventory investment function of the dealers is equal to the square of the correlation between the change in the net price of the portfolio purchased and in the change in the price of the futures contract used for hedging.

The direct or impact effect of the dealers' uses of futures markets is to increase the depth, breadth, and resiliency of the market for securities. The price variance is reduced, but there is no change in the average price.

In the remainder of this chapter, I show that futures markets also affect the nondealer excess supply of securities or net demand for loanable funds curve LF. Thereby the average price (interest rate) is affected. In particular, investment demand $I(t)$ is increased, and the savings directed toward risky assets $S(t) - \Delta L(t)$ are also increased, as a result of the development of futures markets. These longer-run effects raise the rate of capital formation.

Financial Futures and the Mortgage Market

Investment in residential housing accounted for 55 percent of net fixed capital formation in 1983. Home mortgage borrowing accounted for 37 percent of the total borrowing by the private nonfinancial sector. The total mortgage debt was 178 percent of the total marketable interest-bearing public debt (see table 3–5). For these reasons the interest rates charged by mortgage bankers and savings and loan associations for home mortgages profoundly affect the aggregate rate of capital formation.

Intermediate between the savings and loan associations and mortgage bankers, which lend directly to home buyers, and the capital market where private savings are offered are the Federal

TABLE 3–5

THE IMPORTANCE OF HOUSING IN CAPITAL FORMATION, 1983

	Value ($ billions)	Index
Net fixed investment, total	108.0	100.0
Net fixed residential, nonfarm investment	59.1	54.7
Total borrowing by private, domestic, nonfinancial sector	322.9	100.0
Home and multifamily residential mortgages	120.6	37.3
Marketable interest-bearing public debt	1,024.0	100.0
Mortgage debt outstanding	1,826.4	178.0

SOURCES: *Economic Report of the President, 1985*, tables B–15, B–70, B–79; and *Federal Reserve Bulletin* (May 1984), table 1.57.

National Mortgage Association (FNMA) and the Government National Mortgage Association (GNMA). The subject of this section is how the use of futures markets in treasuries by the FNMA has lowered the interest rates on home mortgages in relation to what they would have been if there were no facilities for hedging. Since a similar analysis applies to the effects of futures markets on the operation of the GNMA, the effects of futures markets on investment in residential housing are qualitatively similar to the effects described in this section but quantitatively larger.

The FNMA is a federally chartered, privately owned corporation. Its principal activity is the purchase of mortgages, primarily on residential properties, which are held as investments. The FNMA is the nation's largest supplier of mortgage funds. On December 31, 1983, the FNMA owned a portfolio of $75.7 billion in mortgage loans (table 3–6). Substantially all mortgage purchases are made in accordance with forward purchase commitments, which totaled $18.6 billion in 1983.

The FNMA has two sources of revenue: (1) the seller of a mortgage generally pays a fee ranging from 1 to 3 percent of the commitment on a fixed-rate mortgage; and (2) the acquired portfolio earns a rate of return. Table 3–6 indicates the average yield on the portfolio.

The FNMA acquires funds to purchase home mortgages by selling its own securities in the capital market. These obligations are treated as U.S. agency debt in the market, supervised financial institutions can invest in them without regard to legal limits imposed on investment securities. In this way the FNMA borrows in the capital market from institutions that would not otherwise invest in mort-

TABLE 3–6

SUMMARY OF FNMA OPERATIONS, 1979–1983

	1979	1980	1981	1982	1983
Net mortgage portfolio ($ billions)	49.65	55.74	59.85	69.71	75.67
Commitments issued ($ billions)	10.18	8.08	9.47	22.11	18.61
Average yield on portfolio (%)	8.74	9.20	9.82	10.69	10.70
Average cost of outstanding debt (%)	8.72	9.87	11.42	11.39	11.07
Spread: yield minus cost (%)	0.02	−0.67	−1.60	−0.70	−0.37
Net income ($ millions)	162	14	−190	−105	75

SOURCE: Federal National Mortgage Association, *Guide to FNMA Debt Securities*, March 1, 1984.

gages (see figure 3–2). Table 3–6 shows the average cost of its outstanding indebtedness. It is correct to conceive of the FNMA as a huge savings and loan association that borrows in a national and international capital market and purchases heterogeneous mortgages from local mortgage originators.

The FNMA's income is related to the mortgage fees and the difference between a weighted average yield on its portfolio and a weighted average of its borrowing costs. This spread has been negative in recent years. Although its net mortgage portfolio grew at a rate of 11 percent per annum from 1979 to 1983, its net income has fluctuated greatly, from large profits to large losses.

Savings and loan associations and mortgage bankers generate a relatively steady flow of new mortgage loans, which are offered to the FNMA. The savings and loan associations also make large sales (for example, $1 billion) of portfolios of long-term mortgage loans that were financed at low interest rates. They are trying to shorten the average duration of their portfolios. These large batches of old mortgages are offered to the FNMA at substantial discounts. Forward commitments to purchase the mortgages are usually on a three-month basis. The required documentation causes a lag between the forward commitment and the subsequent delivery. "Immediate" delivery in this market is thirty days. A distinction is made between the steady, predictable flow of new mortgages and the nonpredictable large discrete sales of seasoned mortgages by these institutions. The latter require more careful risk management than the former, for reasons discussed below.

The FNMA must obtain the approval of the Treasury for the issuance of its own obligations to finance its purchases of mortgages. The Treasury determines when the FNMA can enter the capital market once a month with its debentures. The rationale for this procedure is that the FNMA's monthly borrowing, approximately $1 billion to $1½ to billion, should not adversely affect the Treasury's ability to borrow in the capital market. The Treasury is also concerned to avoid congestion in the capital market of security sales among the several agencies. Borrowings by the Treasury or the agencies are so large that they affect market rates of interest. The FNMA can seek authority to sell public issues more frequently than one day in the month if the calendar is free, and it normally does so once or twice a year. The basic point, however, is that the FNMA is uncertain when it will be allowed to go to market and what interest rates will exist on that one day.

There is a lag between the forward commitment to purchase mortgages and the subsequent sale of FNMA securities. On October 20, 1983, for example, the FNMA was asked to bid on a pool of approximately $750 million in seasoned mortgages offered by a single thrift institution seeking to restructure its balance sheet. The sale was not part of the regular flow of mortgages offered to the FNMA. The securities would not be delivered for several months. Given that the FNMA does not know when it will be allowed to enter the capital market and what its borrowing costs will be, what bid should it make on such a batch of mortgages? Too low a bid will be unsuccessful in obtaining the mortgages. Too high a bid will be unprofitable. This phenomenon generates the need for risk management.

If a regular flow of securities were offered to the FNMA but its borrowing costs were cyclical around a given mean, the risks would be manageable. It could bid at a rate equal to its mean borrowing costs plus a markup. Movements in actual borrowing costs would average out, and the net spread between lending and borrowing rates could be expected to be profitable.

When there are discrete, lumpy batches of mortgages offered, the FNMA cannot price the batch at the mean borrowing cost plus a markup. If borrowing costs exceed the mean when the FNMA goes to market, it has no reason to believe that there will be an equally large subsequent offer that will be financed at a borrowing cost below the mean. Risk management techniques are essential to cope with the unpredictable offers of seasoned mortgages.

The Profit and Behavioral Equations When There Is No Futures Market. In this section the optimization of the FNMA when there

167

is no futures market is described. The effects on the mortgage market
of this decision are contrasted with the effects of the optimization
that results when the FNMA is able to use futures markets in treasuries.

Equation 52 describes the profits, $\pi_N(\theta)$, when there is no (N)
futures market.

$$\pi_N^*(\theta) = [P^*(\theta) - (1 - g)p(t)]s(t) \tag{52}$$

where $\pi_N^*(\theta)$ = profit at time θ when there is no (N) futures market;
$p(t)$ = forward bid price by FNMA for mortgages; $P^*(\theta)$ = sales price
at time θ of FNMA debentures of the same maturity as the mortgages;
$s(t)$ = face value of mortgages purchased at time t; $gp(t)s(t)$ = fees
charged by FNMA on the value, $p(t)s(t)$, of purchases; $EP(\theta; t)$ =
expectation, at time t, of the price of FNMA debentures marketed
at subsequent date θ; * = stochastic variable; and var P = variance
of price P of FNMA debentures.

At time $t - 1$, the FNMA agrees to purchase face value $s(t)$ of
mortgages at forward price $p(t)$ for delivery at time t. Some time
later, on a day in the month assigned to it by the Treasury, θ, the
FNMA goes to the capital market to sell its securities to finance the
purchase. Assume that the maturity of the FNMA issue corresponds
to the maturity of the mortgages purchased forward. Let the price
of an FNMA debenture at time θ be $P^*(\theta)$. Although the FNMA holds
the mortgages as investments, in effect in this case it is equivalent
to selling the mortgages for $P^*(\theta)s(t)$. Both the date of the borrowing,
θ, and the price received for the debenture, $P^*(\theta)$, are unknown at
the time the forward commitment to purchase the mortgages is made.

The FNMA will receive fees of $100g$ percent of the mortgage
from the seller. When there is no hedging, the profits are given by
equation 52. The risks are that the price, $P^*(\theta)$, of FNMA debentures
may fall below $p(t)$, the forward commitment price. All the risk is
focused on what will happen on one day of the month when the
Treasury permits the FNMA to borrow. During the period when
interest rates were stable, this risk was not great. The FNMA could
expect to profit from the fees, $gp(t)s(t)$, plus the spread, $[P^*(\theta) - p(t)]s(t)$, between the sale price of FNMA debentures and the forward
purchase price of the mortgage when the durations were similar.

The amount of mortgages that the FNMA can successfully
purchase, $s(t)$, depends on the price, $p(t)$, that it is willing to bid. It
competes against dealers and investors all over the world for the
purchase of mortgages. It must trade off volume, $s(t)$, against the
spread, $P^*(\theta) - p(t)$, between the selling price, $P^*(\theta)$, of its debentures
and the forward price, $p(t)$, offered to sellers. Equation 53 describes

the supply of mortgages to the FNMA at time t. The quantity, $s(t)$, of both the regular flow of new mortgages and the irregular, lumpy sales of seasoned mortgages depends on the forward bid price, $p(t)$, and other variables. Expository complexity is greatly reduced by writing the supply at time t as equation 53.

$$s(t) = cp(t) \tag{53}$$

The profit function is equation 54, derived by substituting equation 53 in equation 52.

$$\pi_N^*(\theta) = P^*(\theta)cp(t) - (1 - g)cp(t)^2 \tag{54}$$

Expected profits, $E\pi_N(\theta)$, are given by equation 55, and the variance of profits, var π_N, by equation 56.

$$E\pi_N(\theta) = EP(\theta; t)cp(t) - (1 - g)cp(t)^2 \tag{55}$$

$$\text{var } \pi_N = [cp(t)]^2 \text{ var } P \tag{56}$$

Risks, measured by the variance of profits, depend on the size of the forward commitment to purchase mortgages, $s(t) = cp(t)$, and the variability of the price of FNMA debentures, var P, that are used to finance the purchases.

It is hypothesized that the FNMA acts as if it attempts to maximize the expected utility of profits from transactions, $EU[\pi_N(\theta)]$, as described by equation 57.

$$\text{Max } EU[\pi_N(\theta)] = E\pi_N(\theta) - \frac{\alpha}{2} \text{ var } \pi_N(\theta) \tag{57}$$
$$p(t)$$

where α is its coefficient of risk aversion.

The FNMA's problem is to select a forward bid price, $p(t)$, for mortgages offered to maximize expected utility. It has an expectation, $EP(\theta; t)$, of what the market price of its debentures will be when it is allowed to go to market. The variance of that price, var P, is the risk it faces.

The solution of the problem is described in the equations below and is graphically presented in figure 3–6. The forward bid price, $p(t)$, is plotted along the horizontal axis. The expected price of FNMA debentures, $EP(\theta; t)$, or marginal revenue, MR, marginal cost, MC, and endogenous marginal risk premium, RP, are plotted on the vertical axis.

The net price that the FNMA expects to receive from the sale of its debt in the capital market is $EP(\theta, t)$. It is the horizontal line denoted MR, and it is the left-hand side of equation 58. The marginal cost of acquiring the mortgages from the mortgage bankers or savings

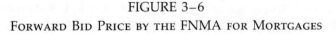

FIGURE 3–6

Forward Bid Price by the FNMA for Mortgages

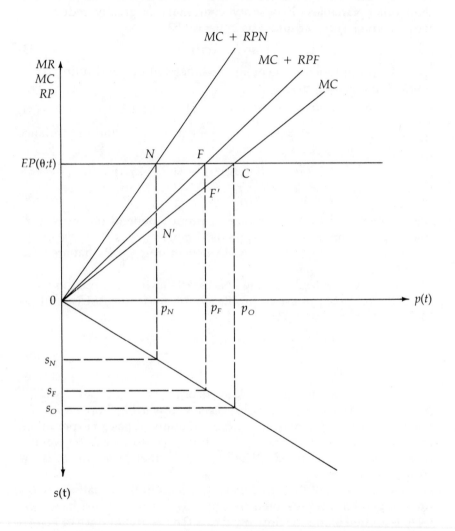

Note: The FNMA selects a forward bid price for mortgages, p, at the point where the expected price of an FNMA debenture marketed at uncertain time θ, denoted $EP(\theta;t)$, is equal to the marginal cost of purchasing the mortgages forward, MC, plus a risk premium, RP. When there are no facilities for hedging, the risk premium is RPN, the forward bid price is p_N, and the FNMA purchases s_N of mortgages forward.

When the FNMA uses the futures market optimally, the forward bid price is p_F, and s_F of mortgages are purchased forward. If there were no risk premium, the forward bid price would be p_0, and s_0 of mortgages would be purchased forward. The ratio of p_n to p_0 is $1/(1 + \delta_N)$. The ratio of p_F to p_N is $(1 + \delta_N)/(1 + \delta_F)$.

and loan institutions is the line labeled MC. If no fees were charged by the FNMA ($g = 0$), the average cost of a mortgage acquired would be p dollars per dollar of face value. Because FNMA purchases affect the market price of mortgages, the marginal cost is $2p$ dollars. When fees are taken into account, the marginal cost is $2(1 - g)p(t)$ dollars per dollar of face value of mortgages purchased. This is the first term on the right-hand side of equation 58 and the line labeled MC in figure 3–6.

The FNMA must charge an endogenous risk premium, $\alpha cp(t)$ var P, because of the risk that it faces in marketing its debentures. The risks are that it does not know when it will be permitted to enter the market to finance its securities or the price that its securities will sell for at the uncertain date. When the FNMA cannot hedge, the risk premium, RPN, is the second term on the right-hand side of equation 58. Adding the risk premium, RPN, to the marginal cost, MC, gives line $MC + RPN$, the effective marginal cost to FNMA for mortgages.

$$
\begin{aligned}
EP(\theta; t) &= 2(1 - g)p(t) + \alpha cp(t) \text{ var } P \\
MR &= \quad\;\; MC \quad\;\; + \text{ RPN}
\end{aligned}
\tag{58}
$$

The optimal bid price, $p_N(t)$, in figure 3–6 is described by equation 59. It satisfies the condition that marginal revenue is equal to marginal cost plus an endogenous risk premium.

$$
p_N(t) = \frac{EP(\theta; t)}{2(1 - g) + \alpha c \text{ var } P}
\tag{59}
$$

By bidding price p_N, the FNMA is able to acquire s_N mortgages during the time period. Thus the market interest rate on mortgages (on a discount basis) is $100 - p_N$. This rate determines the rate of residential construction, the major part of net private fixed investment.

A similar situation exists in the GNMA market. Intermediate between the builders and the institutional investors are the mortgage banks and savings and loan institutions, which make initial contact with the builders and may offer forward bid prices for the mortgages. A period of time is required before the banker assembles a pool of mortgages for conversion into GNMA certificates. Such certificates are issued by private mortgage lenders against specific pools of mortgages insured by the Federal Housing Administration (FHA) or guaranteed by the Veterans Administration (VA). The resulting GNMA certificates are highly marketable in the secondary market. The mortgage bankers and savings and loans face risks on the price at which they will be able to sell the GNMA certificates several months after they have made forward commitments to purchase mortgages from the builders. Here the mortgage banker is in a situation similar to that of the FNMA.

Another dimension of the GNMA problem is this. Some institutional investors have relatively steady cash flows. They may enter into forward commitments with the mortgage bankers to buy GNMA mortgages at fixed prices, several months before the mortgages can be assembled and delivered. In that case the mortgage banker sets a forward ask price on the GNMA certificate but does not know at what price he will be able to purchase the underlying mortgages. Ideally, he acts as a broker by quoting a bid price for forward delivery from the builder and simultaneously quoting an ask price for forward sale to the investor. If that happens, he has no uncovered position. Such a balancing is unlikely, so that the risk situation in the GNMA market is mathematically similar to that described for the FNMA.

When interest rates became more volatile, the FNMA had two ways to cope with the uncertainty. First, it could preborrow the funds at the earliest possible date after $t - 1$, when the forward purchase commitment was made. There were two difficulties with this procedure: (1) The FNMA could still come to market only once a month at a date determined by the Treasury. In the interim, bond prices could fall. (2) Preborrowing precludes the opportunity to take advantage of favorable market changes from commitment time, $t - 1$, to time t, when the mortgages are actually delivered. Preborrowing thus removes timing flexibility to avoid some interest rate uncertainty.

Second, the FNMA could engage in "homemade hedging." At the time the forward purchase commitment was made, it could sell Treasury bonds short at price $I(t)$. It would invest the funds at the Treasury bill rate but must pay interest at the Treasury bond rate to the owners of the bonds. The magnitude of this difference depends on the shape of the Treasury yield curve. At the uncertain time θ when the FNMA enters the capital market, the debentures are sold for $P^*(\theta)$, and the Treasury bonds are purchased at $I^*(\theta)$. Since the price of FNMA debentures is highly correlated with the price of Treasury bonds, homemade hedging reduces risk. This is a feasible strategy to reduce risk, but it has some deficiencies: (1) FNMA sales or purchases of large quantities of Treasury bonds in the over-the-counter market are quite noticeable to the other market participants. The identity of the seller is quickly revealed, and there is often a perceptible effect on the market price. The FNMA loses its anonymity, which it values, and has power over the market price. (2) A fee, whose magnitude depends on the availability of the coupon to borrow, is usually charged to borrow securities that are sold short. The fee may be as high as 0.5 percent of the coupon borrowed.

Risk Management with Futures Markets. A superior risk management strategy was implemented in 1982, when the FNMA began taking positions in the futures market to hedge against interest rate increases between time $t - 1$, when the forward commitment was made to purchase mortgages, and the specific time, θ, when it is allowed to enter the capital market to borrow to finance its purchases. At any time between time $t - 1$ and the uncertain time θ, the FNMA sells $x(t)$ of futures contracts on treasury bonds, treasury notes, treasury bills, certificates of deposit, or Eurodollars, depending on the maturity of the subsequent financing that it has in mind. Let the price of the future be $f_T(t)$, where T is the maturity of the contract. Assume that the FNMA sells the Treasury-bond future in the nearby maturity. When the Treasury permits the FNMA to borrow on day θ, the hedge is lifted at price $f_T^*(\theta)$. For simplicity of exposition, transactions costs on the debentures and on the futures are ignored. Profits, $\pi_F(\theta)$, are described by equation 60.

$$\pi_F^*(\theta) = [P^*(\theta) - (1 - g)p(t)]s(t) - x(t)[f_T^*(\theta) - f_T(t)] \qquad (60)$$

Two elements of risk must be taken into account. First, there is a differential, $\varepsilon_1(t)$, between the price, $I(t)$, of a Treasury bond and the price, $P(t)$, of an FNMA debenture of comparable maturity. This differential is positive but not constant. The average value of the differential is m, and its variance is var ε_1.

$$P(\theta) = I(\theta) - \varepsilon_1(\theta) \qquad (61)$$

where $P(\theta)$ = price of an FNMA debenture; $I(\theta)$ = price of a comparable Treasury security; $\varepsilon_1(\theta)$ = price differential = $I(\theta) - P(\theta)$; and $E\varepsilon_1(\theta) = m$.

The Treasury borrows at a lower rate than the FNMA, but the differential is not constant. On the basis of secondary market quotations of the comparative yields on securities, the spread between FNMA and Treasury securities on similar maturities is given in table 3–7. The variance of the spreads is apparent.

Second, the futures price at time t of a Treasury-bond contract that matures at time T, denoted $f_1(t)$, is equal to the cash price, $I(t)$, of the Treasury bond plus the net cost of carry from time t to maturity date T of the futures contract. The net cost of carry depends on the shape of the yield curve on treasuries, since the net cost of carry is the short-term rate less the bond interest rate. The net cost of carry

TABLE 3–7

DIFFERENTIAL BETWEEN FNMA AND TREASURY INTEREST RATES,
SIX MONTHS AND FIVE YEARS, AND U.S. TREASURY BOND YIELD,
1981–1983
(percent)

| | Differential | | U.S. Treasury Bond Yield, |
	Six months	Five years	Three-Year
1981	1.09	0.82	14.44
1982	0.70	0.64	12.92
1983	0.17	0.29	10.45
Mean	0.653		12.603
Standard deviation	0.462		2.014

SOURCES: Federal National Mortgage Association, *Guide to FNMA Debt Securities*, March 1, 1984, p. 11; and *Economic Report of the President, 1985*, table B–66.

from t to T can be positive, zero, or negative depending on whether the yield curve is negatively sloped, flat, or positively sloped.

Earlier, the relation between the futures price, $f_T(t)$, and the cash price, $I(t)$, of a Treasury bond was shown in equation 12, repeated here as equation 62.

$$f_T(t) = I(t)[1 + E_t r(t,T)] = I(t)[1 + r(t) + E_t r(t + 1,T)] \quad (62)$$

where $E_t r(t,T)$ is the expected net carrying costs from the present time, t, to the maturity of the futures contract at time T, and $r(t)$ is the net carrying cost from t to $t + 1$. The change in the futures price is related to the change in the cash price by equation 14, repeated here as equation 63, and abbreviated as equation 64.

$$f_T(t + 1) - f_T(t) = [I(t + 1) - I(t)(1 + r(t))] + \varepsilon_2 \quad (63)$$

$$\Delta f_T = \Delta I + \varepsilon_2 \quad (64)$$

The variance of ε_2 is the "basis risk," which arises primarily from unexpected changes in the yield curve. The latter changes the relation between the cash price, $I(t)$, and the futures price, $f_T(t)$.

Insofar as the return, ΔI, on the Treasury bond is independent of the basis risk, the variance of the change in the futures price can be written as equation 65, (which is equation 16 of Chapter Two).

$$\text{var } \Delta f_T = \text{var } \Delta I + \text{var } \varepsilon_2 \quad (65)$$

Estimates of equation 63, the relation between the change in the
174

TABLE 3–8
INDEXES OF CASH PRICE OF TREASURY BONDS AND MARCH FUTURES ON TREASURY BONDS, JANUARY 1983

Date	Cash Price, Treasury Bond $I(t)$	Future Price, Treasury Bond $f_3(t)$
3	102.51	102.43
4	101.57	101.77
5	101.49	101.32
6	100.73	101.20
7	101.67	100.99
10	100.70	100.83
11	101.44	101.28
12	101.56	101.61
13	101.53	101.49
14	101.49	101.40
17	101.25	101.36
18	100.55	100.95
19	99.54	99.71
20	99.54	99.84
21	98.56	98.52
24	97.53	97.65
25	98.45	98.23
26	97.47	97.24
27	98.39	98.02
28	97.49	97.41
31	96.57	96.75
Mean	100	100
Variance	3.1894	3.2407

SOURCE: Chicago Board of Trade, *1983 Statistical Annual* (Chicago: Board of Trade, 1984), pp. 51, 79.

futures price, $\Delta f_T = f_T(t) - f_T(t - 1)$, and the change in the cash price, $I(t) - I(t - 1)$, will convey an idea of basis risk, ε_2.

Many different Treasury bonds can be delivered against the nearby futures contract on Treasury bonds, provided that they mature at least fifteen years from the delivery day if not callable. Each coupon has a different conversion factor. To make the data comparable, $f_T(t)$ and $I(t)$ are expressed as index numbers in table 3–8. The mean value for the month is defined as 100. Column 1 is the index of the cash price of a Treasury bond during January 1983, column 2 the index of the price of the March futures contract on Treasury bonds. On a day-to-day basis the net carrying cost, $r(t)$, can be disregarded.

Over the twenty-one trading days of January 1983, the index of the March future, $f_3(t)$, and the index of the cash Treasury bond, $I(t)$, are very closely related (equation 66).

$$f_3(t) = 0.288 + 0.9971I(t) \quad R = .9785$$

$$\text{(s.e.)} \qquad\qquad (0.0339) \quad n = 21 \qquad\qquad (66)$$

The correlation between the two indexes is almost perfect: 98 percent of the variance of the March future is associated with the variance of the cash price. Moreover, a 1 percent deviation of the index of the cash price from its mean is associated with a 1 percent deviation of the March futures index from its mean.

Day-to-day changes in the index of the cash bond and the nearby March future are less closely related. This is equation 67, which corresponds to equation 63.

$$[f_3(t) - f_3(t - 1)] = -0.0903 + 0.652[I(t) - I(t - 1)]$$

$$\text{(s.e.)} \qquad\qquad\qquad\qquad (0.1787) \qquad\qquad (67)$$

$$R^2 = .66, \quad n = 20$$

Several points are worthy of note: (1) Only 66 percent of the day-to-day variation in the futures price is associated with day-to-day changes in the cash price. (2) A one-percentage-point change in the cash price is associated with less than a one-percentage-point change in the nearby futures price. The basis risk, var ε_2, can then be estimated as $1 - r^2 = 1 - 0.66 = 0.34$ of the variance of the change in the futures price, var Δf. Alternatively, the ratio

$$\gamma_2 \equiv \frac{\text{var } \varepsilon_2}{\text{var } I} = \frac{1 - r^2}{r^2} = \frac{0.34}{0.66} = 0.515$$

is the ratio of the basis risk to the risk on Treasury securities. Hedging is not a riskless operation.

The FNMA is assumed to maximize the expected utility of profits, equation 68, from the transactions. The relevant profit equation is equation 60 subject to three constraints. (1) The supply of mortgages offered during the period depends on the forward price bid by the FNMA. This is equation 53, which varies by period. (2) The price of an FNMA debenture is equal to the price of a Treasury bond of comparable maturity less a variable differential. This is equation 61. (3) Finally, the change in the nearby futures price of a Treasury bond is equal to the change in the cash price of the underlying bond less a positive or negative cost of carry, depending on the shape of the yield curve. This is equation 63 or 64. The exact specifications of these equations are made to bring out the main results simply and clearly, whereas the more complex actual relations do not change the qualitative results.

Substitute equations 53, 61, and 63 in profit equation 60 to derive the crucial equation 68 for the FNMA:

$$\pi_F^*(\theta) = x(t)I(t) - [m + (1 - g)p(t)]s(t) \qquad \text{deterministic}$$
$$+ [s(t) - x(t)]I^*(\theta) \qquad \text{diversifiable risk}$$
$$- s(t)\varepsilon_1^*(\theta)) \qquad \text{differential risk}$$
$$- x(t)\varepsilon_2^*(\theta) \qquad \text{basis risk} \quad (68)$$
$$s(t) = cp(t) \qquad \text{supply of mortgages}$$

There are four components to the profits of the FNMA when it can use the futures market. The first component is deterministic (that is, nonstochastic). This term reflects the profits of the FNMA if (1) it hedged its forward purchases completely, (2) the differential between Treasury and FNMA debentures were constant at its average value m, and (3) there were no basis risk. Insofar as hedging is not complete, $x(t)$ differs from $s(t)$.

The second term is the value of the unhedged position, $s(t) - x(t)$, times the uncertain price, $I^*(\theta)$, of the Treasury debenture at the uncertain time, θ, when the FNMA is permitted to go to market. This risk is diversifiable, since the FNMA can select its optimal unhedged position.

The third term is the risk related to $\varepsilon_1^*(\theta)$, the price difference $I(\theta) - P(\theta)$, between Treasury and FNMA debentures when the FNMA goes to market at uncertain time θ.

The fourth term is the basis risk, $\varepsilon_2^*(\theta)$, from hedging, whereby the futures price on treasuries changes by an amount different from the change in the cash price of treasuries. As discussed above, basis risk results primarily from changes in the yield curve on treasuries.

Expected profits, $E\pi_F(\theta)$, and the variance of profits, var π_F, when the FNMA can use the futures (F) market in treasuries optimally, are equations 69 and 70.

$$E\pi_F(\theta) = x(t)I(t) - [m + (1 - g)p(t)]s(t) + [s(t) - x(t)]EI(\theta;t) \quad (69)$$

$$\text{var } \pi_F = [s(t) - x(t)]^2 \text{ var } I + s(t)^2 \text{ var } \varepsilon_1 + x(t)^2 \text{ var } \varepsilon_2 \quad (70)$$
$$\text{risk} = \text{diversifiable risk} \quad + \text{ differential risk} + \text{ basis risk}$$

Equation 71 gives the ratio of the risk to the FNMA to the risk of price changes on Treasury debentures. This is practically identical with the dealer equation 21, with two changes. Here γ_1 is the risk, var ε_1, concerning the price differential between Treasury and FNMA securities, in relation to the variation in the price of Treasury securities, and the beta between $P(\theta)$ and $I(\theta)$ is unity. Therefore, equation 71 is graphed in figure 4–3.

$$\frac{\text{var } \pi_F}{\text{var } I} = [s(t) - x(t)]^2 + s(t)^2 \gamma_1 + x(t)^2 \gamma_2 \qquad (71)$$

where $\gamma_1 = \text{var } \varepsilon_1/\text{var } I = $ differential risk; and $\gamma_2 = \text{var } \varepsilon_2/\text{var } I = $ basis risk.

The FNMA simultaneously selects a forward price, $p(t)$, to bid for mortgages and a quantity, $x(t)$, of Treasury bond futures to be sold $(+)$, to maximize expected utility. Formally, the optimization is as follows:

$$\text{Max } EU(\pi_F)$$
$$p(t), x(t)$$

$$(72)$$

subject to equations 53, 69, and 70. The resulting solution for the optimal forward bid price by the FNMA is equation 73. A derivation is in the appendix.

$$p_F(t) = \frac{I(t) - m}{2(1 - g) + \alpha c(\gamma_1 + \gamma_2)\text{var } I}$$

$$= \frac{EP(\theta; t)}{2(1 - g) + \alpha c(\gamma_1 + \gamma_2)\text{var } I} \qquad (73)$$

A graphic analysis of this solution and a comparison with the situation that prevails when the FNMA cannot use the futures markets are the subject of the next section. This is the essence of the analysis.

The Effects of the Optimal Use of Futures on the Rate of Capital Formation in Housing. When the FNMA cannot hedge, the situation is described by equation 59 and curve $MC + RPN$ in figure 3–6. The risk premium, RPN, is added to the marginal cost to obtain the effective cost curve. The FNMA bids price p_N for the forward purchase of mortgages. This is the effective price of the mortgage to the seller, or $100 - p_N$ is the mortgage rate (on a discount basis) to the borrower. At this price s_N of mortgages are offered to the FNMA.

When the FNMA uses the futures market optimally, the situation is described by equation 73. This equation can be written as equation 74, which can be compared with equation 58.

$$EP(\theta; t) = 2(1 - g)p_F(t) + \alpha c(\gamma_1 + \gamma_2)\text{var } I \cdot p_F(t) \qquad (74)$$
$$MR = MC + RPF$$

The right-hand side of equation 74 is the middle curve in the figure.

The risk premium, RPF, when the futures market is used optimally depends on the risks of variations in the differential between the prices of FNMA debentures and Treasury securities, γ_1 var I, and the basis risk, γ_2 var I, concerning movements of cash and future Treasury securities. In contrast, the risk premium, RPN, when the FNMA cannot hedge depends on the variance (var P) of the price of FNMA debentures. Since the sum of the two differential risks, $(\gamma_1 + \gamma_2)$ var I, is much less than the absolute risk, var P, the risk premium with futures, RPF, is much less than RPN, the risk premium when hedging is not used. That is why curve $MC + RPF$ is below $MP + RPN$.

With futures the equilibrium point is F. The FNMA bids price p_F for the forward purchases of mortgages. The risk premium, RPF, is distance $F'F$, and the marginal cost is $p_F F'$. At forward bid price p_F the mortgage bankers and savings and loan institutions offer the FNMA quantity s_F of mortgages during the time period. The interest rate to the borrower (on a discount basis) has been reduced from $100 - p_N$ to $100 - p_F$ through the use of futures markets. Thereby the rate of capital formation in housing increases.

Quantitative estimates can be given for the reduction in the risk premium or rise in the forward bid price by the FNMA for mortgages. Compare point $p_N(t)$ in equation 59 with $p_F(t)$ in equation 73, or as shown in the figure.

Equation 59, repeated here, is the forward bid price if no hedging is possible.

$$p_N(t) = \frac{EP(\theta; t)}{2(1 - g) + \alpha c \text{ var } P}$$

If there is no risk or risk aversion (α var $P = 0$), the forward bid price is $P_0(t)$ in equation 75. In the figure it is the point where the marginal cost is equal to the marginal revenue.

$$p_0(t) = \frac{EP(\theta; t)}{2(1 - g)} \tag{75}$$

Using equation 75 in (59), the forward bid price when there are no facilities for hedging can be expressed as equation 76.

$$p_N(t) = \frac{p_0(t)}{1 + \dfrac{\alpha c \text{ var } p}{2(1 - g)}} = \frac{p_0(t)}{1 + \delta_N} \tag{76}$$

$$\delta_N = \frac{\alpha c \text{ var } P}{2(1 - g)} \tag{77}$$

179

Discount factor δ_N is applied to the no-risk bid price, $p_0(t)$, to obtain the forward bid price, $p_N(t)$, when the FNMA cannot hedge.

When the futures market is used optimally, the forward bid price, $p_F(t)$, equation 73, can be written as equation 78, using equation 75.

$$p_F(t) = \frac{p_0(t)}{1 + \dfrac{\alpha c(\gamma_1 + \gamma_2)\text{var } I}{2(1 - g)}} = \frac{p_0(t)}{1 + \delta_F} \tag{78}$$

$$\delta_F = \frac{\alpha c(\gamma_1 + \gamma_2)\text{var } I}{2(1 - g)} \tag{79}$$

Discount factor δ_F is now applied to the no-risk forward bid price, $p_0(t)$, to obtain the price that the FNMA bids forward for mortgages.

A comparison of the two discount factors provides a quantitative estimate of the effect of the use of futures by the FNMA on mortgage interest rates. Ratio δ_F/δ_N is equation 80.

$$\frac{\delta_F}{\delta_N} = \frac{\gamma_1 + \gamma_2}{1 + \gamma_2} \tag{80}$$

Quantity $\gamma_1 = \text{var } \varepsilon_1/\text{var } I$ is the variance of the differential between FNMA and Treasury prices divided by the variance of the price of treasuries. Quantity $\gamma_2 = \text{var } \varepsilon_2/\text{var } I$ is the basis risk in hedging divided by the variance of the price of treasuries.

From regression (15), $\gamma_2 = 0.515$, the basis risk component. An estimate of $\gamma_1 = \text{var } \varepsilon_1/\text{var } I = 0.053$ is derived from table 3–7. Using these estimates:

$$\frac{\delta_F}{\delta_N} = \frac{0.515 + 0.053}{1.053} = 0.539 \tag{81}$$

Hence the discount factor used by the FNMA when it can hedge on the futures market is only 54 percent of what it would use if it could not hedge.

On the basis of the previous analysis, the ratio of the price that the FNMA can bid forward for mortgages when it uses the futures market optimally, $p_F(t)$, to what it could bid if no hedging were possible is equation 82.

$$\frac{p_F(t)}{p_N(t)} = \frac{1 + \delta_N}{1 + \delta_F} \tag{82}$$

Using the estimates in equation 81, the price ratio is equation 83.

TABLE 3–9

Forward Bid Prices for Mortgages Associated with the Optimal Use of Futures Markets by FNMA

δ_N (1)	p_N/p_0 (2)	p_F/p_N (3)	p_F/p_0 (4)
0.1	0.909	1.044	0.949
0.2	0.833	1.083	0.902
0.3	0.769	1.119	0.861

NOTE: δ_N is the discount rate for risk when FNMA cannot hedge; p_N is the forward bid price when no hedging is possible; p_0 is the bid price in the forward market for $1 face value of a mortgage when there is no risk; p_F is the forward bid price when the futures market is used optimally.

$$\frac{p_F(t)}{p_N(t)} = \frac{1 + \delta_N}{1 + 0.53938\delta_N} \tag{83}$$

Table 3–9 contains estimates of this price ratio for several risk premiums, δ_N, that the FNMA might use if it could not hedge. If the risk premium, δ_N, used by the FNMA were 20 percent (row 2) when it cannot hedge, it would bid 83.3 percent of the face value of the mortgage. If it could use the futures market optimally, it could increase its bid price by 8.3 percent (column 3) to 90.2 percent of the face value of the mortgage (column 4). In this way mortgage rates to the builder are lowered, and capital formation in housing is increased.

The distinction between these two cases is extreme. Homemade hedging was used by FNMA before the development of a futures market. Hedging can be homemade by selling Treasury bonds short, or it can be done by selling Treasury-bond futures. The futures market is more liquid than the cash market. A quantity of $100 million to $200 million can be traded "more quietly" in the futures market than in the cash Treasury-bond market with little effect on the market price; and anonymity is preserved in the futures market, which is an auction market. This is less true in the over-the-counter Treasury-bond market. When the FNMA comes to market on its day of the month, it sells from $500 million to $2 billion of debentures. Because of its size, it prefers the futures market to homemade hedging. The net effect is that the forward price that the FNMA can offer to savings and loan associations is $p_F(t)$ when it hedges in the futures market, point $p_N(t)$ if it is unable to hedge (figure 3–6). With homemade hedging, the forward bid price would be between $p_N(t)$ and $p_F(t)$. In this manner hedging in general, and futures markets in particular, stimulate capital formation in residential housing.

The Uses of Financial and Stock Index Futures by Institutional Investors

An important development of the past decade is that the financial assets of the private sector are controlled by institutional investors and managed by professional money market managers. As a result of the 1974 pension fund reform law—the Employment Retirement Income Security Act (ERISA)—and inflation, pension fund assets have more than tripled since 1971.

Table 3–10 shows the annual savings by individuals that are invested in financial assets and the part invested in insurance and pension reserves. From 1973 to 1983 the fraction of savings invested in financial assets that was placed in insurance and pension reserves rose from 25.8 percent to 34.2 percent. Annual savings in insurance and pension funds grew at a rate of 13.8 percent per year during this period. Inflation of the personal consumption deflator was 7 percent per year, so that the real growth of this form of savings was also 7 percent per year.

During this ten-year period, the growth in the S&P composite index was 4 percent per year, and the average dividend-price ratio

TABLE 3–10
SAVINGS BY INDIVIDUALS AND THEIR RETURNS, 1973–1983

	1973	1983	Growth Rate (%)
Saving by individuals during the year: increases in financial assets ($ billions)	150.3	450.1	11
Saving invested in insurance and pension reserves ($ billions)	38.8	154.0	13.8
Percentage of saving in insurance and pension reserves	25.8	34.2	
S&P composite index	107.43	160.41	4
Personal consumption deflator (1972 = 100)	105.7	213.6	7
Average dividend-price ratio (%)	4.9		

SOURCE: *Economic Report of the President, 1985*, tables B–26, B–90, B–3.

was 4.8 percent. The real pretax return on equity was (8.9 − 7 = 1.9) less than 2 percent. The low pretax return and the growth of pension funds have created a keen competition among money managers to achieve maximum returns for a predetermined amount of exposure. In fulfilling the role of fiduciary or trustee, the director of the investment program is obligated to manage risk prudently.

This section describes why and how institutional investors have been using futures markets in stock market indexes and financial instruments and analyzes their optimization decisions. My conclusions can be summarized as follows: (1) Fund managers purchase or sell portfolios of securities on the basis of their expected relative price changes. (2) The principal sponsor and the fund managers purchase or sell futures on a broad-based index to benefit from or to avoid expected market changes. (3) Rapid and transitory changes in desired total risk for a trust or a fund are achieved by selling or purchasing futures, not by transactions in the underlying securities. This strategy is feasible because the sale or purchase of futures on a broad-based index is equivalent to the sale or purchase of the securities in the index but does not affect the market prices of the securities. Futures transactions have low costs and do not interfere with the difficult and arduous process of selecting securities.

Through the use of financial and stock index futures by institutional investors, the trust or fund achieves a higher expected return on transactions for a given risk. Secondary markets in equities and fixed-income securities thereby become more liquid, a dimension not captured by the portfolio models in the literature. Insofar as savings per unit of time of the private sector are affected by the liquidity of the secondary market, the new futures markets in equities and Treasury securities tend to increase savings and investment in risky assets.

Institutional Framework: The Behavioral Equations. The institutional investor is most easily understood by considering two agents: a trustee or fiduciary who is the principal sponsor of pension funds and the fund manager. The principal sponsor may manage one part of the fund himself and assign the rest to several fund managers. Each manager claims to have special expertise in selecting securities. One may have particular expertise in the securities of new corporations, another in "junk" bonds of firms in financial difficulties whose securities are believed to be undervalued by the market, another in the stocks of corporations engaged in innovation. The principal sponsor hopes to benefit from those special talents. Each fund manager selects a portfolio of securities and actively manages it in what he believes is an optimal manner. The trustee or principal sponsor distributes the assets among funds.

183

The process of institutional investment has two aspects: (1) each fund must be managed optimally; (2) the principal sponsor must manage the entire trust optimally. Each fund manager attempts to achieve an optimal combination of expected return and risk. The principal sponsor wants to achieve an optimal combination of expected return and risk for the entire trust or pension fund. The optimal risk-return point may fluctuate considerably from month to month or even week to week. My aim here is to show how these tasks are made considerably easier by the use of futures markets.

Risk Management Choices of Dynamic Adjustments. I use two examples to explain the dynamic adjustment aspects of risk management. Although the cases are symmetrical, I explain them separately and in slightly different ways. Figure 3–7 describes the risk-return possibilities facing either the fund manager or the principal sponsor. The vertical axis represents expected returns to the entire fund or trust, and the horizontal axis measures the corresponding risk, reflected by the standard deviation. Curve TT' is the subjective transformation curve of the trust or fund, which can be achieved through different combinations of portfolios. Let r be the Treasury bill rate, which is risk free in nominal terms. The subjective risk-return on the index (S&P 500 or bond index) is point I.

Suppose that a principal sponsor decides to change a fund manager whose performance at point A has been disappointing. The fund portfolio must be sold, and a new manager must be found and must acquire a portfolio. Alternatively, as pension money continues to flow into a trust, the principal sponsor must decide how to distribute it among the existing funds or whether to hire another fund manager. In either case the fund manager must decide on the optimal portfolio to acquire. What is common to both cases is that the principal sponsor either does not want to decrease risk and return exposure to the market during a given period as one fund is being liquidated for cash or wants to maintain a risk-return exposure to the market as pension funds are being accumulated during a given period.

In the first case several basic choices are possible. The principal sponsor can allocate the funds realized from the sale of the portfolio that is being liquidated to different fund managers in various proportions. He would like time to decide how to allocate the funds among managers, and each manager would like time to decide on his investment strategy. If this time is taken, the funds will be invested in highly liquid, safe, but low-yielding assets such as Treasury bills until the portfolio selection decisions are made. During this interval the principal sponsor loses exposure to the market. Graphically, if the funds are invested in Treasury bills during the interim, the fund

184

FIGURE 3–7

Expected Return and Risk of a Fund on a Portfolio

Expected return

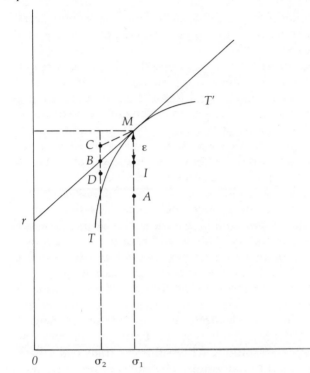

NOTE: If there were no adjustment costs, the fund could move from point M to point B. With adjustment costs, the sale described would move the fund to point D. The faster the attempt to reduce risk, the greater the distance between points D and B. By selling futures on the index but keeping portfolio M, the fund moves to point C. The difference between points C and B is due to lower transactions costs on futures. The portfolio M is expected to appreciate by ε more than the index, point I.

would be at point r while the market is subjectively expected to be at point I. This is a problem if the principal sponsor believes that the market will appreciate more than the Treasury bill rate.

If, to obtain market exposure quickly, the principal sponsor or fund manager fails to take the needed time and effort in selecting stocks, it is unlikely that the hastily chosen investment will earn the market rate of return. He believes that, with a carefully formulated investment strategy, he can achieve point M, which is better than the market performance, point I.

A symmetrical situation exists when the principal sponsor or

185

fund manager wants to reduce total risk exposure for a short time. In the situation described in the figure, the fund managers have selected what they consider to be optimal portfolios at point M. These portfolios are expected to appreciate in relation to the market, and the fund managers may have investment horizons of several years. A manager may have invested, for example, in stocks of firms engaged in innovative processes.

The principal sponsor is generally concerned with quarterly results as well as longer-term performance. Suppose he thinks that there is greater uncertainty concerning Federal Reserve policy but that it is more likely that interest rates will rise than decline in the near future. He expects the declines to be of relatively short duration, but he wants to avoid the situation that occurred in October 1979, when large portfolio losses occurred. Several strategies are available to reduce the total risk from σ_1 to σ_2 for a short period.

The principal sponsor could direct the fund managers to sell some of their risky assets or reduce their portfolios by a given percentage within a day or two and invest the proceeds in safe assets during the period of uncertainty. This would be a temporary movement from point M to point B. When the uncertainty was resolved within a few weeks or months, the principal sponsor would move back to point M, which represents a long-term investment strategy. The risk reduction strategy—moving from σ_1 to σ_2—is transitory.

This would be a costly and disruptive strategy. Each fund manager has carefully assembled a portfolio on the basis of Capital Asset Pricing Model (CAPM) reasoning, where the covariance matrix of the returns has been used to determine the optimum proportions of the securities. The portfolio includes many securities that the manager wants to keep because he believes they are grossly undervalued by the market. To be directed to sell off "risky" assets undermines his strategy. No longer would the assets be held in optimal proportions, and the fund manager would no longer be on his subjective opportunity locus between expected return and risk.

Transactions costs for the sale and subsequent repurchase of equity are considerable. If the value of the portfolio temporarily sold to reduce risk were $80 million, round-trip transactions costs would be $200,000. This is a very high price to pay to reduce risk for a short period. A formal analysis of these problems focuses on equation 84.

Let $s(t)$ be the transactions—purchases $(+)$ or sales $(-)$—per unit of time in acquiring or disposing of a portfolio. The sum of $s(t)$ is the total number of shares acquired or sold, but $s(t)$ is the rate of change of a portfolio.

In capital theory a distinction is made between the marginal efficiency of capital and the marginal efficiency of investment.[11] A similar distinction is of crucial importance in financial investment. The marginal efficiency of investment is described by equation 84. The first two terms are the marginal efficiency of capital. The third term concerns the rate at which the portfolio has been acquired or sold per unit of time; the term is a dynamic adjustment cost. Term Δp is the capital gain plus dividends in excess of the Treasury-bill rate on the transactions during the time interval.

$$\Delta p = \beta \Delta I + \varepsilon - \frac{\gamma}{2} s \tag{84}$$

That is, marginal efficiency of investment = marginal efficiency of capital − adjustment costs.

Each portfolio acquired by a fund manager has a beta (β) that describes the relation between the return during the interval t to $t + 1$ on the portfolio of risky assets in excess of the risk-free rate (Δp) and the return on the index in excess of the risk-free rate (ΔI) during the same interval. Equation 85 describes the return on the index.

$$\Delta I \equiv I(t + 1) - (1 + r - V)I(t) \tag{85}$$

where $s(t)$ = transactions per unit of time; $I(t)$ = the value of the index at time t; $V(t)$ = the dividend-price ratio on the index; and $r(t)$ = the risk-free rate.

Beta in equation 84 has no normative significance as it has in the CAPM but is simply the manager's subjective view of the relation between the market excess return, ΔI, and the excess return on this portfolio of securities, Δp.

Term ε—distance IM in figure 3–7—reflects the manager's view of unexploited market opportunities that, because of his special expertise, he can exploit profitably. One manager may acquire the securities of relatively unknown firms developing new technologies. He believes that he can successfully bet on which firms will succeed or fail, in relation to the market's evaluation. Another manager may acquire securities of firms verging on bankruptcy and believes that he can select those that will survive. In his view the market has discounted those securities at an unduly high risk premium. The claimed expertise of the fund manager consists of purchasing positive ε portfolios or those undervalued by the market. Managers have subjective distribution functions of ε based on their claimed expertise, and they induce plan sponsors to assign parts of the trust to them to manage. The first two terms, $\beta \Delta I + \varepsilon$, represent a return on the

187

portfolio. It is the marginal efficiency of capital: the return on a "stock" rather than on a "flow."

The third term in equation 84 reflects the effects of fund transactions on the market price of the portfolio. It refers to costs involved in rapid acquisitions or sales of portfolios per unit of time. It is of fundamental importance in understanding how and why fund managers and principal sponsors use the futures markets in financial instruments and stock market indexes. This element is not captured at all by the portfolio models in the literature, because of their focus on stocks, which have no time dimensions, rather than on flows per unit of time.

The immediate disposal by managers of an $80 million portfolio consisting of 2 million shares at $40 per share will tend to depress the average price per share. Travelers Investment Management estimated this effect as being between 1/8 and 1/4 of a point, an estimate confirmed by other fund managers. This means that the sale or purchase of an $80 million portfolio of stocks sold or purchased during a short interval (for example, a day) will change its value by at least $250,000 (2 million shares × 1/8) and possibly by as much as $500,000 (2 million shares × 1/4). Term $\gamma s(t)/2$ describes the change in the market price that results from transaction $s(t)$ during the time interval.

Coefficient γ has several determinants; it measures the adjustment costs and consists of the market power of a fund to affect price. First, a transaction by a fund during a given interval of time, $s(t)$, involves a heterogeneous collection of securities. Some are actively traded in broad markets, and others are traded in thin markets. The greater the fraction of the transaction consisting of sales or purchases of securities with low daily volumes, the greater the effect on the market price, and the larger will be γ. Even if all securities had the same price elasticity of demand, the larger percentage change in the volume of securities sold in thin markets would produce larger percentage price declines than for actively traded securities. Second, insofar as the fund is selling a nonrepresentative sample of securities, the number of other funds or large institutional investors interested in acquiring those securities during the time interval may be small. The price elasticity of demand over the short interval may be lower than that for a representative sample of corporations. Third, a fund transaction imparts a bias or negative signal to the market. The sale of a portfolio by a manager who is being replaced by a principal sponsor conveys a signal to the market that its ε is negative. The probability that the transaction consists of securities that are currently overvalued is high. The dealer or market may therefore absorb these securities only at a substantial reduction in price.

188

FIGURE 3–8

THE DETERMINANTS OF MARKET POWER TO AFFECT PRICE ON
TRANSACTIONS PER UNIT OF TIME

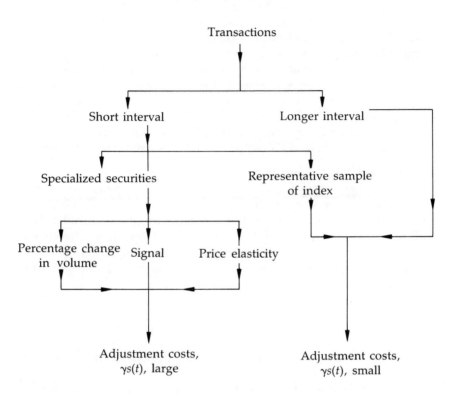

Figure 3–8 illustrates the determinants of market power: the magnitude of adjustment costs, $\gamma s(t)$, in equation 84. If the interval for a given value of transactions is lengthened, transactions per unit of time, $s(t)$, decline. The percentage change in volume per unit of time is brought to zero, and there is no effect on market price. This is the situation implicit in the CAPM and other portfolio models.

When the interval is short, for example, a day or two, transactions per unit of time are large, and the market power depends on several factors. If the transactions were in securities considered to be a representative sample of the market, there would be little effect on price. Insofar as the portfolio of securities is not a representative sample of the index of stocks, there would be an effect on market price for any or all of the reasons described above. The dynamic risk management problem facing institutional investors can be summarized in terms of figure 3–7. The faster the manager or principal sponsor wants to change the portfolio (from A to M or from M to

B), the greater will be the costs of adjustment. The marginal efficiency of investment (Δp) is reduced below the marginal efficiency of capital ($\beta \Delta I + \varepsilon$) by the costs of adjustment, which are positively related to the speed of adjustment.

Uses of Futures by Institutional Investors. Institutional investors use futures in two major ways. First, they engage in arbitrage, which permits them to earn at least the market rate of return on the index. Second, they use futures to reduce the adjustment costs of temporary changes in their portfolios. This raises the marginal efficiency of investment for any given marginal product of capital. These two factors improve the expected return-risk possibilities offered to savers and thereby increase the savings available for risky investment.

Arbitrage between futures and the index. I have made repeated use of the relation between the change in the futures price, $\Delta f_T = f_T (t + h) - f_T(t)$, of a contract that matures at time T and the change in the price of the underlying index. Let T denote the maturity date of the contract, which is time $t + h$ or later, of length h. The change in the futures price, Δf_T, can be decomposed as equation 86, abbreviated as equation 87. A discussion of this equation is the subject of this section.

$$f_T(t + h) - f_T(t) \equiv [I(t + h) - (1 + r - V)I(t)]$$
$$+ \{[(1 + r - V)I(t) - f_T(t)] \tag{86}$$
$$+ [f_T(t + h) - I(t + h)]\}$$

$$\Delta f_T \equiv \Delta I + \eta \tag{87}$$

where

$$\eta \equiv [(1 + r - V)I(t) - f_T(t)] + [f_T(t + h) - I(t + h)] \tag{88}$$

Term ΔI (in equation 85) is the first term in equation 86: the return on the index in excess of the Treasury-bill rate. The second term in equation 86 is the difference between the cost of purchasing the index of securities at time t by financing it at the Treasury-bill rate and receiving the dividends during the interval, $I(t) (1 + r - V)$, and the price, $f_T(t)$, at time t of a futures contract on the index that matures at time T. The third term is the difference at time $t + h$ between $f_T(t + h)$, the futures price of a contract that matures at time T, and the value of the index, $I(t + h)$, at time $t + h$. If time T, the maturity of the contract, coincides with time $t + h$, the third term in equation 86 is zero because at maturity the futures price is set equal to the index.

190

The second term in equation 86 represents "mispricing" of futures and offers a potential gross return to funds, for the following reason. There are two ways to invest in the S&P 500 index: (1) buy the index of stocks at time t at price $I(t)$ and receive dividends $VI(t)$; (2) invest $I(t)$ in Treasury bills yielding rate r, and purchase a futures contract on the index for $f_T(t)$. In each case the investment will be worth the same amount at maturity, $I(T) = f_T(t)$. The gross return from the direct investment in the index, R_I, and the gross return from the indirect investment by buying Treasury bills and purchasing futures, R_{FT}, are defined as follows:

$$R_I \equiv I(T) - (1 - V)I(t)$$

$$R_{FT} \equiv I(T) + rI(t) - f_T(t)$$

It is obvious that the first term in η, or the second term in equation 86, is $(R_{FT} - R_I)$, the gross return from purchasing the futures contract on the index and investing in Treasury bills less the gross return from purchasing the stock index directly. The value of η is as follows:

$$\eta = (R_{FT} - R_I) + [f_T(t + h) - I(t + h)] \tag{89}$$

If the futures contract is to be held to maturity, the only stochastic element in η is the dividend-price ratio, V, on the index. Mispricing and the possibility for quasi-arbitrage profits exist when the absolute value of η exceeds transactions costs (estimated by Merrill Lynch Capital Markets division at 0.5 percentage points).

If η is positive, it is profitable (gross of transactions costs) to short the index of stocks, invest the proceeds in Treasury bills, and purchase the futures. If η is negative, it is profitable (gross of transactions costs) to short the futures and invest in the index of stocks.

To take advantage of mispricing (when the first term in η in equation 88 is not zero), several institutional investors established performance index futures funds. In November 1982, for example, shortly after stock index futures began to be traded, the State Street Bank established a Stock Performance Index Futures Fund (SPIFF-Plus) to do the quasi-arbitrage. It describes its operations as follows:

> State Street's Stock Performance Index Futures Fund–Plus . . . provides a new alternative to conventional index funds by investing in stock index futures. Its goal is to outperform the market by taking advantage of pricing discrepancies between equities and stock index futures [a value of η that is not zero]. Overall risk will be similar to the market's risk.
>
> As such, SPIFF-Plus swaps between stocks and futures contracts, depending upon where the opportunity lies. It

191

aims to track the performance of the Standard and Poor's 500 Index in the worst possible scenario, and to exceed it by a measurable margin at best.

SPIFF-Plus cannot do worse than the Standard and Poor's 500 index. It returns R_I plus the absolute value of η when there is mispricing. When there is no mispricing, $R_I = R_{FT}$. During the early period it obtained a return 5 to 6 percent above the S&P 500 index. As a result of these quasi-arbitrage activities by funds that hold approximations to the S&P 500 index, the absolute value of η has declined. Nevertheless, funds like SPIFF-Plus still make arbitrage profits, but their quasi-arbitrage activities drive the absolute value of η toward the transactions costs.

The third term in equation 86, $f_T(t + h) - I(t + h)$, has two dimensions. Ordinarily, maturity date T does not coincide with $t + 1$, when the forward transaction is reversed. For example, a September contract may be purchased on July 11 and sold on July 18. On the latter date there is no reason why the index should equal the price of a September future. Consequently, even if there were no mispricing, there would be a variance to term η if $t + h$ is before maturity date T. The variance of η is referred to as basis risk.

Second, few arbitragers can afford to purchase all the S&P 500 stocks contained in the index. A basket of 100–200 stocks is purchased, which is a surrogate for the index. Such baskets cost from $25 million to $50 million and are good but imperfect approximations to the index.[12] Even if the futures contract were held to maturity ($T = t + h$), the futures price, $f_T(T)$, which is the price of the index, would not necessarily equal the value of the surrogate basket. Difference $f_T(T) - I(T)$, where $I(T)$ is the price of the surrogate basket, is another dimension of basis risk. Since transactions costs in futures are very low, arbitragers can afford to take this form of basis risk.

Estimates of the variance of η (equations 86 and 88) have been obtained in at least two ways. Select a futures contract, preferably the nearby one, and correlate the change in its price, $\Delta f_T \equiv f_T(t + h) - f_T(t)$, with the return on the index, $\Delta I(t) = I(t + h) - (1 + r - V)I(t)$, over interval h during a sample period. The observations are taken over the life of a contract. Let $\rho_{IF_2}^2$ be the product-moment correlation between Δf_T and ΔI. By construction ρ_{IF} is the fraction of the variance of the change in the futures price that is accounted for by the variance of the return on the index, and var η is the residual.

$$\text{var } \Delta I = \rho_{IF}^2 \text{ var } \Delta f$$

$$\text{var } \eta = (1 - \rho_{IF}^2) \text{ var } \Delta f$$

It follows that the variance of η is a multiple of the variance of ΔI.

$$\text{var } \eta = \frac{(1 - \rho_{IF}^2)}{\rho_{IF}^2} \text{ var } \Delta I \qquad (90)$$

A second method of estimating var η is to note that η is the return on a fully hedged short position in the stock index. Sell the index short at time t at price $I(t)$, and purchase a futures contract that matures at time T for price $f_T(t)$. Reverse the two transactions h periods later. During the interval the proceeds of the short sale are invested in Treasury bills, but the dividends are sacrificed. These transactions yield a return exactly described by η in equation 88. Estimated returns will depend on h.

Data are available on the means and variances of unhedged and hedged portfolios on the S&P 500 index over different interval lengths h. The variance of the unhedged S&P 500 index corresponds to var ΔI, and the variance of a fully hedged portfolio corresponds to var η. Table 3–11 presents estimates of the ratio var η/var ΔI and (using equation 90) the associated σ_{IF}^2 for different interval lengths h during the last seven months of 1982.

The table shows that, when the contract is not held to maturity, a substantial basis risk (var η) exists on a fully hedged position. Correlation ρ_{IF} is far from perfect over short intervals. Since transactions costs are low and liquidity is high in futures, arbitragers can afford to take these basis risks.

TABLE 3–11

ESTIMATES OF BASIS RISK AND COEFFICIENT OF DETERMINATION
BETWEEN CHANGE IN FUTURES PRICE AND RETURN ON S&P 500 INDEX
OVER INTERVALS DURING 1982

Interval Length (h)	var η/var ΔI	ρ_{IF}^2
1 day	0.462	0.684
2 days	0.221	0.819
3 days	0.137	0.880
1 week	0.078	0.927
2 weeks	0.068	0.937
3 weeks	0.130	0.885

SOURCE: var η/var ΔI is the square of σ_H/σ_U for a portfolio consisting of the S&P 500 that is hedged by a future on the same index, based on Stephen Figlewski, "Hedging with Stock Index Futures," Columbia University Center for the Study of Futures Markets, CSFM-62, July, 1983, table 1.

Liquidity and low transactions costs in futures. Earlier it was stated that the immediate purchase or sale of a portfolio of $80 million (consisting of 2 million shares at $40 per share) tends to affect the average price of a share by an eighth to a quarter. This was described by the $\gamma s(t)$ term in equation 84. No such market power term was included in the change in the futures price equation, (86) or (87), because funds do not have much power to affect futures prices in the index. The reasons are those sketched in figure 3–8.

First, no signals are conveyed to the market that the fund is disposing of overvalued stocks when it sells the future on the index. Such a sale cannot convey signals about relative prices of securities. Second, an $80 million sale in futures is only 1.9 percent of the daily value of S&P 500 futures traded. If a similar sale consisted of subsets of stocks, it would constitute much more than a 2 percent rise in the daily value traded in that subset. Third, the price elasticity of demand for a representative sample of stocks in the S&P 500 should be greater than the elasticity of demand for a nonrepresentative subset of those stocks. Funds may invest in portfolios that are proxies for the market index as well as specializing in different portfolios of stock. If one fund is selling a block of a particular stock and another is purchasing another block of a particular stock, it is unlikely that what one is demanding is what the other is supplying. A price change would be required to induce a fund to change its proportions of securities. If one fund is decreasing its equity investment in the index by selling futures on the index, however, it will be exactly the same future that another firm is purchasing to increase its equity investment in the index. The futures transaction on the index is equivalent to buying or selling the index of underlying securities. Consequently, both funds are trading the same homogeneous commodity: a representative sample of stocks. For this reason, no reduction in price need be offered to induce the buyer to purchase a different vector of securities than initially planned.

These three reasons explain why there is a market power term, $\gamma s(t)$, in equation 84 for the change in the price of portfolios and not in equation 86 for the change in the futures price. This is a formal way of stating that the futures market in a broad-based index is much more liquid than the market for underlying securities (or the market in narrow-based subindexes). The raison d'être of futures markets is their greater liquidity than the markets in underlying securities, as is explained below.

Transactions costs of purchases and sales in futures are approximately 15 percent of those in the underlying securities. (The following example was provided by Travelers Investment Management

Company.) Suppose that a fund purchased or sold $80 million of equity. At an average share price of $40, the transaction includes 2 million shares. At a commission rate of five cents a share (considerably lower than the average for all institutional trades), the one-way commissions amount to $100,000 (2 million shares × five cents per share).

If $80 million of the S&P 500 future were sold, the commissions would be substantially lower. With the futures selling for 160, the value of a futures contract on the S&P 500 index is $80,000 (160 × $500). To sell $80 million, 1,000 futures contracts must be sold. The one-way commission rate is $15 per contract, and the total commissions for selling $80 million in futures are $15,000 ($15 × 1,000)— 15 percent of the transactions costs in underlying securities.

The reason for this difference is the economy of scale. It may cost no more to process one futures contract for $80,000 than one block of 100 shares at $40 per share. Since bid-ask spreads are not standardized, it is difficult to know how they compare in futures transactions and those in the underlying securities. Nevertheless, the net result is that transactions costs for futures are significantly less than for the underlying securities.

Futures Facilitate Temporary Risk-Return Adjustment and Raise the Marginal Efficiency of Investment. Futures markets in the stock market index and in Treasury securities reduce the adjustment costs of temporary changes in the portfolio of institutional investors and thereby raise the marginal efficiency of investment. That is the subject of this section.

Equation 91 describes the return, $\pi(t + h)$, to the fund or trust when it can engage in futures transactions. The first three terms in equation 91—the term in brackets in equation 92—are $s\Delta p - T(s)$, the returns on the cash transactions, $s(t)$, less transactions costs, $T(s(t))$. Let $x_T(t)$ of futures that mature at time T be sold at time t. The current price is $f_T(t)$. These futures will be repurchased at a subsequent date $t + h$ at price $f_T(t + h)$. Transactions costs on the futures are $\theta(x)$. Not only is the futures market so liquid that there is no term corresponding to $\gamma s(t)$ in the cash transactions market, but transactions costs in futures, $\theta(x)$, are much lower than those in the cash instruments, $T(s)$.

$$\pi(t + h) = [\beta(I(t + h) - (1 + r - v)I(t)) + \varepsilon]s(t)$$

$$- \frac{\gamma}{2} s^2(t) - T(s(t)) \tag{91}$$

$$+ x_T(t)[f_T(t) - f_T(t + h)] - \theta(x(t))$$

195

abbreviated as:

$$\pi = [(\beta \Delta I + \varepsilon)s - \frac{\gamma}{2}s^2 - T(s)] - x\Delta f - \theta(x) \tag{92}$$

where π = return on the transactions; $x(t)$ = sales of futures, $y(t)$ = $-x(t)$ = purchases of futures; $f_T(t)$ = price at time t of futures maturing at time T; $T(s)$, $\theta(x)$ = transactions costs; and $I(t)$ = price of the index.

Equation 93 is derived by using equation 87 for the relation between the change in the futures price, Δf, and in the index, ΔI.

$$\pi = (\beta s - x)\Delta I + \varepsilon s - \frac{\gamma}{2}s^2 - \eta x - T(s) - \theta(x) \tag{93}$$

The first term, $(\beta s - x)\Delta I$, is the gross return attributable to changes in the market index. The second term, εs, is the gross return from changes in the relative price (ε) of the portfolio acquired or sold during the interval. The third term, $\gamma s^2/2$, is the change in price induced by the fund's purchases or sales of the securities during the interval. The fourth term, $-\eta x$, represents the basis risk. The last two terms are the transactions costs in dealing with the underlying securities, $T(s)$, and the futures, $\theta(x)$. Since transactions costs on purchases are the same as on sales, $T(s) = T(-s)$, and $\theta(x) = \theta(-x) = \theta(y)$.

The expected return, $E\pi$, is described by equation 94, where the expectations are taken over the stochastic variables ΔI, ε, and η. It is assumed that the expected value of η is zero, but it has a variance.

$$E\pi = (\beta s - x)E(\Delta I) + sE(\varepsilon) - \frac{\gamma}{2}s^2 - T(s) - \theta(x) \tag{94}$$

In deriving the variance of the expected return, var π, assume that the three stochastic elements are independent of one another.

$$\text{var } \pi = (\beta s - x)^2 \text{ var } \Delta I + s^2 \text{ var } \varepsilon + x^2 \text{ var } \eta \tag{95}$$

There are three sources of risk: (1) var ΔI is the variance of the return on the market index of securities; (2) var ε is the risk of relative price changes between the portfolio and the market index; (3) var η is the basis risk in equation 89.

Transition to a new portfolio. Two cases of risk management were considered at the beginning of this section. The first case concerns a principal sponsor who dismisses a fund manager whose performance puts the trust at point A in figure 3–7. A new manager is appointed who believes that he can select a portfolio, M, that will exceed the market performance at point I. I show how the use of futures markets raises the marginal efficiency of investment on the acquisition of a new portfolio.

If the new fund manager acts to reinvest the allotted funds in the market during a short time, the fund will obtain a change in the expected returns, $\partial E\pi/\partial s$, and a change in risk, $\partial \text{ var } \pi/\partial s$, on the resulting transactions, $s(t)$. Call the ratio $MRT(s)$ in equation 96, the marginal rate of transformation between risk and expected return from investment in cash securities during the time interval. It is derived from equations 94 and 95.

$$MRT(s) = \frac{\partial E\pi/\partial s}{\frac{1}{2} \partial \text{ var } \pi/\partial s} = \frac{\beta E(\Delta I) + E(\varepsilon) - \gamma s - T'(s)}{(\beta s - x) \beta \text{ var } \Delta I + s \text{ var } \varepsilon} \qquad (96)$$

Evaluated at $x = 0$ when there is no futures position, this marginal rate of transformation is equation 97. It is graphed as curve OS in figure 3–9.

$$MRT(s) = \frac{\beta E(\Delta I) + E(\varepsilon) - \gamma s - T'(s)}{s(\beta^2 \text{ var } \Delta I + \text{ var } \varepsilon)} \qquad (97)$$

The numerator is the marginal efficiency of the investment. The marginal efficiency of capital exceeds the marginal efficiency of investment for two reasons. First, the faster the portfolio is acquired, the greater are the adjustment costs, γs, where s represents the transactions during the given time interval. Second, the faster the portfolio is acquired, the lower will be $E(\varepsilon)$, its performance in relation to the index, because inadequate time is devoted to the selection of a portfolio, that is, to the formulation of an investment strategy. The fund cannot jump from point A to point M in figure 3–7. The change in expected returns from a rapid purchase program is the numerator in equation 97.

The marginal rate of transformation is different when the principal sponsor or fund manager uses the futures market. As the securities of the dismissed fund manager are sold, the principal sponsor can (1) invest the proceeds in highly liquid assets such as Treasury bills or (2) purchase futures contracts on the S&P 500 index. The new fund manager carefully devises an investment strategy.

Equation 98 describes the marginal rate of transformation, $MRT(y)$, between the change in expected return per purchases of stock index futures per unit of time (the numerator) and the change in risk per purchases of stock index futures per unit of time (the denominator).

197

It is based on equations 94 and 95. Variable $y = -x$ represents purchases of futures per unit of time.

$$MRT(y) = \frac{E(\Delta I) - \theta'}{(\beta s - x)\text{var } \Delta I - x \text{ var } \eta} = \frac{\partial E(\pi)/\partial(y)}{\frac{1}{2} \partial \text{ var } \pi/\partial(y)} \quad (98)$$

When $MRT(y)$ is evaluated at $s = 0$ when there are no purchases of cash securities, the marginal rate of transformation is given by equation 99.

$$MRT(y) = \frac{E(\Delta I) - \theta'}{y(\text{var } \Delta I + \text{var } \eta)} \quad (99)$$

which is graphed as OF in figure 3–9.

The numerator, derived from equation 94, is the change in the expected return from the purchases of futures on the index per unit of time. It is the expected return on the stock index in excess of the safe return, $E(\Delta I)$, less the transactions costs, θ'. It is assumed that there is no mispricing, so that $E(\eta) = 0$. Because of the liquidity and depth of the futures market, funds do not perceptibly affect the market price by their transactions.

With the purchase of futures, the fund can jump from point A to the market expected return in figure 3–7. The trust is totally invested in the market without the physical purchases of stocks. The essence of purchasing the futures is that the trust is in effect purchasing the entire S&P 500 index at low transactions costs and without market power. This is the meaning of the numerator. The denominator, derived from equation 95, is the change in total risk resulting from the purchases of futures per unit of time. The two components of risk are changes in the market index (var ΔI) and the risk involved if the futures are sold before maturity (see equations 86, 87, and 88). The basis risk, var η, is small in relation to the risk of changes in the market index.

Curve OF in figure 3–9 is the marginal rate of transformation between the change in expected return and the change in total risk during the interval when the funds are invested in the futures on the index. In general, as shown in equations 97 and 99, the marginal rate of transformation using futures exceeds that of using securities directly under any of the following conditions: (1) the expected appreciation of stocks hastily selected is less than the expected appreciation of the index, $\beta E(\Delta I) + E(\varepsilon) \leq E(\Delta I)$; (2) there is considerable market power when purchases are made quickly, that is, γs is large; (3) the basis risk, var η, is less than the relative price risk, var ε.

FIGURE 3–9

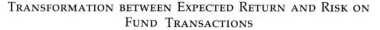

TRANSFORMATION BETWEEN EXPECTED RETURN AND RISK ON
FUND TRANSACTIONS

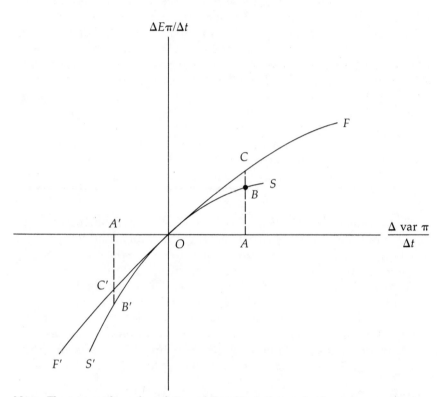

NOTE: The curves show the relation of the change in expected return over the time interval to the change in risk over the time interval. Curve SS' refers to the purchases or sales of securities, curve FF' to the purchases or sales of futures.

A comparison of the two marginal rates of transformation is most vivid if it is assumed that (1) the principal sponsor has a fund purchase s of securities or an equivalent value of futures during an interval and (2) the portfolio of securities that would be purchased has a β equal to unity. Then the left-hand and right-hand sides of equation 100 are special cases of equations 97 and 99.

$$MRT(s) = \frac{E(\Delta I) + E(\varepsilon) - T' - \gamma s}{s(\text{var } \Delta I + \text{var } \varepsilon)}$$

$$< \frac{E(\Delta I) - \theta'}{s(\text{var } \Delta I + \text{var } \eta)} = MRT(y) \quad (100)$$

The numerator of the *MRT* when stocks are purchased is less than the value when futures are purchased, because hastily conceived stock purchases are expected to perform worse than the market, $E(\varepsilon) < 0$; and the concentration of these purchases during a short interval will raise their prices, $\gamma s > 0$. In addition, the transactions costs in futures, θ', are considerably less than those involving the physical securities, T'. The denominator of the *MRT* when futures are purchased is less than that when securities are purchased, because the basis risk, var η, is substantially less than the relative price risk, var ε.

Graphically, the change in expected return for a given change in risk exposure *OA* is *AB* when the stocks are purchased rapidly during the transition period between fund managers and *AC* when futures are purchased and the stock acquisition program has been spread over a longer period of time (figure 3–9). The principal sponsor has moved the trust quickly toward point *I* from point *A* in figure 3–7.

Rapid temporary reduction of risk. The second problem of risk management discussed above concerns the rapid but temporary reduction of total risk exposure. The principal sponsor (or fund manager) wants to reduce total risk from σ_1 to σ_2 (in figure 3–7) for a short period. He is anxious to keep the portfolio described by point *M* as a long-term investment. This portfolio is expected to outperform the market: $E(\varepsilon) > 0$. I explained earlier that the attempt to move quickly to point *B* by selling a fraction of the portfolio of risky assets and then repurchasing them to return to point *M* is very costly and disruptive. Costs of adjustment are reflected in term γs in equation 84.

A more efficient strategy is available to reduce market risk quickly for a time without incurring adjustment costs, γs. The principal sponsor sells futures contracts corresponding to the risks that he wants to avoid. If he wants to reduce the risks of declines in the stock index, he sells futures contracts on the S&P 500 index. If he wants to reduce the risks of a decline in the index of long-term bonds, he sells futures contracts on Treasury bonds. These sales correspond to $x(t)$ in equations 94 and 95.

Fund managers need not be informed of these actions, and no fund portfolio is being disturbed. Managers continue to hold the desired stocks in what they believe are the optimal proportions and make no costly sales during a short interval. By increasing sales of futures, $x(t)$, the principal sponsor moves along segment *OF'* of the transformation curve in figure 3–9. Risk is reduced by *OA'* at a cost of *A'C'* in expected return, whereas the cost would have been *A'B'* if the first strategy were followed.

200

Formally, consider the case where the following conditions are satisfied: (1) Portfolio M is expected to appreciate by more than the index and has a β equal to 1. This means that $E(\Delta p) = E(\Delta I) + E(\varepsilon)$ $>E(\Delta I)$. (2) The choice is to sell securities $(-s)$ or sell an equivalent value, $x = -s$, of futures on the index. This means that $MRT(x)$ is evaluated at $s = 0$ and $x = -s$.

The two marginal rates of transformation are as follows:

$$MRT(-s) = \frac{E(\Delta I) + E(\varepsilon) + T' + \gamma s}{s(\text{var } \Delta I + \text{var } \varepsilon)} > \frac{E(\Delta I) + \theta'}{s(\text{var } \Delta I + \text{var } \eta)} = MRT(x)$$

slope: $OS' > OF'$ in figure 3–9.

The intuitive explanation is as follows. By selling portfolio M, the trust or fund loses the return on the portfolio net of the safe return, $E(\Delta I) + E(\varepsilon)$, and incurs transaction costs T' and adjustment costs of γs. This loss is the numerator of $MRT(-s)$.

By selling futures on the index, the trust loses the expected return on the index, $E(\Delta I)$, and incurs transactions costs θ'. Insofar as the portfolio, M, is expected to appreciate in relation to the index, $E(\varepsilon) > 0$, and adjustment costs are significant, $\gamma > 0$, the loss of expected return is much greater by selling the portfolio than by selling futures on the index. Moreover, transactions costs on futures are lower than on the securities, $\theta' < T'$.

The reduction in risk by selling the portfolio is s (var ΔI + var ε) and by selling an equal value of futures on the index is s (var ΔI + var η). Since the basis risk, var η, is small in relation to the risk on the index, var ΔI, the risk that is diversified away by selling the futures is similar to the risk that would be eliminated by selling an equivalent value of the portfolio.

The net result is described by comparing several points in figure 3–7. (1) If there were no adjustment costs ($\gamma = 0$), the trust or fund could move from point M to point B by selling part of portfolio M and investing the proceeds temporarily in safe assets. (2) With adjustment costs ($\gamma > 0$), the sale would move the trust or fund to point D. The faster the attempt to reduce risk, the greater the distance between points D and B. (3) By selling futures on the index but keeping portfolio M, the trust or fund moves to point C. The difference between points C and B results from the lower transactions costs on futures. Thus the advantages of using futures for temporary risk reduction are measured by distance DC: $DC = DB + BC =$ saved adjustment costs + lower transactions costs.

Savings in risky assets depend on the expected return-risk possibilities in the secondary market. By using futures in the ways described, institutional investors improve the risk-return trade-off shown in

201

figure 3–7 and thereby raise the savings invested in risky assets. I showed in the previous section how the use of futures by the FNMA raises the rate of investment in housing. These two sections together show how futures markets raise the rate of capital formation.

Appendix

Derivation of Equation 73

The optimization, when futures market are used optimally, is based on equations A-1 and A-2.

$$\frac{\partial E\pi}{\partial p} = \frac{\alpha}{2} \frac{\partial \text{ var } \pi}{\partial p} \tag{A-1}$$

$$\frac{\partial E\pi}{\partial x} = \frac{\alpha}{2} \frac{\partial \text{ var } \pi}{\partial x} \tag{A-2}$$

where $E\pi$ is equation 69, var π is equation 70, and the supply of mortgages is equation 53.

The solution of this system for the forward bid price, $p_F(t)$, is equation A-3.

$$p_F(t) = \frac{EP(\theta; t)}{\alpha c \text{ var } I\left((1 + \gamma_1) - \dfrac{1}{(1 + \gamma_2)}\right) + 2(1 - g)} \tag{A-3}$$

The denominator is approximated as (A-4).

$$\alpha c \text{ var } I\left((1 + \gamma_1) - \frac{1}{(1 + \gamma_2)}\right) + 2(1 - g)$$
$$\sim \alpha c \text{ var } I(\gamma_1 + \gamma_2) + 2(1 - g) \tag{A-4}$$

Thus the approximation of $p_F(t)$ in (A-3) is:

$$p_F(t) = \frac{EP(\theta; t)}{2(1 - g) + \alpha c(\gamma_1 + \gamma_2)\text{var } I}$$

Since

$$EP(\theta; t) = EI(\theta) - m$$

and it may be assumed that

$$EI(\theta) = I(t)$$

the expected price of an FNMA debenture may be written as:

$$EP(\theta; t) = I(t) - m$$

Equation 73 in the text is thereby derived.

Notes

1. For example, Jerome L. Stein, "Spot, Forward and Future," in Haim Levy, ed., *Research in Finance*, vol. 1 (Greenwich, Conn.: JAI Press, 1979).

2. U.S. Congress, *Futures Trading Act of 1982*, Conference Report no. 97–964, 97th Congress, 2d sess., 1982.

3. Paul Meek, *U.S. Monetary Policy and Financial Markets* (New York: Federal Reserve Bank, 1982), p. 79.

4. Louis Ederington, "The Hedging Performance of the New Futures Markets," *Journal of Finance*, vol. 34 (1979).

5. In this special case:

(a) $\Delta f = \Delta I$ so that var $\Delta f = $ var ΔI

(b) $\Delta p = \beta \Delta f + \varepsilon_1 = \beta \Delta I + \varepsilon_1$

Then:

(c) $\beta = $ cov $(\Delta p, \Delta f)/$var Δf

(d) $\gamma_1 \equiv $ var $\varepsilon_1/$var ΔI

(e) $R = \dfrac{\text{cov } (\Delta f, \Delta p)}{\sqrt{\text{var } \Delta p} \sqrt{\text{var } \Delta f}} = \beta \dfrac{\sqrt{\text{var } \Delta f}}{\sqrt{\text{var } \Delta p}} = \beta \dfrac{\sqrt{\text{var } \Delta I}}{\sqrt{\text{var } \Delta p}}$

(f) $R^2 = \beta^2$ var $\Delta f/$var Δp

From (b) above:

(g) var $\Delta p = \beta^2$ var $\Delta I + $ var $\varepsilon_1 = (\beta^2 + \gamma_1)$ var ΔI

Using (g) in (f):

(h) $R^2 = \beta^2 \dfrac{1}{\beta^2 + \gamma_1}$, which is the equation in the text.

6. Eugene Fama, *Investments*, 2d ed. (New York: Prentice-Hall, 1981), table 7–5, p. 160.

7. The general case is as follows. When the futures position is optimal, as described by equation 28, and $E(\Delta f_T) - T'(x)$ is negligible, then expected return is (a) and variance is (b).

(a) $E\pi = s\beta \dfrac{\gamma_2}{1 + \gamma_2} E(\Delta I) + sE(\varepsilon_1) - \dfrac{s\beta}{1 + \gamma_2} E(\varepsilon_2) + V(s) - T(x)$

(b) var $\pi = \left(s\beta \dfrac{\gamma_2}{1 + \gamma_2}\right)^2$ var $\Delta I + s^2$var $\varepsilon_1 + \left(\dfrac{s\beta}{1 + \gamma_2}\right)^2$ var ε_2

It follows that (c) is $dE\pi/ds$ and (d) is $\frac{1}{2} d$ var π/ds.

(c) $\dfrac{dE\pi}{ds} = \beta \dfrac{\gamma_2}{1 + \gamma_2} E(\Delta I) + E(\varepsilon_1) - \dfrac{\beta E(\varepsilon_2)}{1 + \gamma_2} + v_0 - v_1 s$

(d) $\dfrac{1}{2} \dfrac{d \text{ var } \pi}{ds} = s \left(\dfrac{\beta \gamma_2}{1 + \gamma_2}\right)^2$ var $\Delta I + s$ var $\varepsilon_1 + s \left(\dfrac{\beta}{1 + \gamma_2}\right)^2$ var ε_2

8. See Jean-Pierre Danthine, "Information, Futures Prices, and Stabilizing Speculation," *Journal of Economic Theory*, vol. 17 (1978) pp. 79–98, and Duncan Holthausen, "Hedging and the Competitive Firm under Price Uncertainty," *American Economic Review*, vol. 69 (1979), pp. 989–95.

9. Burton Zwick, "Interest Rate Variability, Government Securities Dealers, and the Stability of Financial Markets," *Journal of Monetary Economics*, vol. 5 (1979), pp. 365–72.

10. U.S. Congress, Joint Economic Committee, *A Study of the Dealer Market for Federal Government Securities,* 86th Congress, 2d sess., 1960, p. 4.

11. A. P. Lerner, *The Economics of Control* (New York: Macmillan, 1947), pp. 331–45.

12. "Is the Tail Wagging the Dog?" *Barron's*, December 10, 1984.

4

The New Option Markets

Hans R. Stoll and Robert E. Whaley

The pace of financial innovation has increased in recent years. Call option trading in sixteen individual common stocks was authorized only twelve years ago on the Chicago Board Options Exchange (CBOE). Today put options as well as call options on about 360 individual stocks are traded on five exchanges—the American Stock Exchange (AMEX), the Philadelphia Stock Exchange, the Pacific Coast Exchange, the Midwest Stock Exchange, as well as on the CBOE—and the volume of stock option trading measured by the value of underlying contracts rivals that of the New York Stock Exchange (NYSE). This period has also seen the introduction of futures contracts on financial instruments, such as government securities and other debt instruments, currencies, and stock indexes. The most recent innovation has been the creation of options on instruments other than individual common stocks: on bonds, on stock indexes, on currencies, and on commodities. These new options, introduced since 1982, are the focus of this chapter.

Because options are complex, we first provide background information. In the section "The New Option Instruments" we describe options and the new option instruments. In the following section we examine several elements in the operation of exchange option markets—the function of the clearinghouse, how profits or losses are realized, and how market making and floor trading differ between stock exchanges and futures exchanges—and briefly describe the regulation of the new options.

Policy makers have frequently expressed concern that options may not serve any economic purpose. This issue is examined from two perspectives in the section "Economic Purpose of Options." First, the uses of options as a risk management tool are examined from the perspective of private users of options. Second, the social costs and benefits of options are considered. Social costs may arise if options are merely a form of gambling, if they detract from the liquidity of underlying assets or from the capital formation process itself, or if they can be manipulated or are otherwise subject to trading abuses. We conclude that the social costs are few and that options confer social benefits by making possible more efficient sharing of risk in the economy. Insofar as option prices are linked to the price of the underlying asset, options trading can enhance the depth and liquidity of underlying asset markets by increasing investors' interest in an underlying asset and its derivative securities.

In the section "Option Pricing" we present the pricing relations linking an underlying asset, an option on that asset, a futures contract on that asset, and an option on the futures contract. Empirical evidence on the pricing process indicates that these four instruments are closely linked and that factors affecting the price of one are transmitted to the others.

The rapid expansion in the number of new option instruments has raised concerns about undue proliferation of new option instruments. We examine factors affecting the introduction, success, and failure of new options. Many new options have been introduced; many have failed. The arguments against restricting the introduction of new options are presented.

The advent of derivative financial instruments makes it possible to accomplish a given investment objective by alternative means. A long position in an underlying asset, for example, can be replicated by using a futures contract or by using put and call options. The costs of these alternative positions will be affected by the margin required. Questions relating to the appropriate margining of the new options and to margin regulation are examined in the section "Margin Requirements." The chapter ends with a section of summary and conclusions.

The New Option Instruments

In this section the general characteristics of an option on any underlying item and the payoffs to different option positions are considered. The new exchange-traded option instruments that are the focus of this study are described, and over-the-counter options are briefly examined.

What Are Options? An option conveys the right to buy or sell an underlying item at a specified price within a specified period of time. The right to buy is referred to as a call option; the right to sell is a put option. Options are generally described by the nature of the underlying item: an option on a common stock is said to be a stock option, an option on a futures contract is a futures option, and an option on a commodity is a commodity option. The specified price at which the underlying item may be bought or sold is called the exercise price or the striking price. To buy or sell the underlying item in accordance with the option contract is to exercise the option. Options traded in the United States—called American options—can be exercised at any time up to and including the expiration date. If an option can be exercised only at expiration, it is termed a European option.

The buyer of an option pays the option writer (the seller) an amount of money called the option premium. In return the buyer receives the privilege of buying—but does not incur the obligation to buy—the underlying item for the exercise price at any time up to the expiration date. If the price of the item exceeds the exercise price, the call option is said to be in the money, and the call option buyer can exercise his option, thereby earning the difference between the two prices—the exercise value. If the price of the item is below the exercise price, the call option is out of the money and will not be exercised.

An example of futures options on the Standard and Poor's (S&P) 500 stock index will help to clarify options (see table 4–1). The contract size is $500 times the index value. A buyer of a September call at a striking price of 155 paid a premium of $1,600 (3.20 × $500) for the right to buy one contract of September S&P 500 stock index futures at $77,500 (155.00 × $500) at any time before the expiration date, the third Friday in September. If the price of the September index futures, at 154.90 on July 10, increased in value, say to 160, the call buyer could exercise the call, take delivery of the futures

TABLE 4–1

PRICES OF FUTURES OPTIONS ON
THE STANDARD AND POOR'S 500 STOCK INDEX, JULY 10, 1984
(dollars)

Striking Price	Calls		Puts	
	September	December	September	December
150	6.25	n.a.	1.40	2.20
155	3.20	6.35	3.30	3.90
160	1.40	4.00	6.45	6.25
165	0.50	2.30	10.45	9.45

NOTE: n.a. = not available. S&P 500 index values: spot, 152.89; September futures, 154.90; December futures, 157.65.

contract, and sell the futures contract to earn a profit of $900 ([160.00 − 155.00 − 3.20] × $500). Alternatively, since the option value reflects its exercise value, the option itself could be sold for the same profit. Note that on July 10 the option with a striking price of 155 was slightly out of the money since the index was at 154.90. The call buyer paid a premium for the option on the expectation that sometime before September the index would reach at least 158.20 (155 + 3.20).

The buyer of a September put option paid 3.30 for the option to sell at 155. This option was slightly in the money on July 10 and thus carried a slightly larger premium than the call option. The put option would become profitable if the September index futures fell below 151.70 (155 − 3.3) before the third Friday in September. The factors explaining the option premiums for different striking prices and different maturities are described later in this chapter.

It is important to note that the call option writer faces payoffs exactly opposite those of the buyer. If the call is in the money at expiration, the option writer must deliver an item worth more than the exercise price received. In the preceding example, the option writer in effect purchases the index futures at 160 and delivers it to the option buyer at 155. The loss is offset in part by the premium of 3.30, and the total loss equals the option buyer's total profit. If the call is out of the money at expiration, the option is not exercised, and the option writer keeps the premium he collected from the buyer when the option contract was written.

The buyer and the seller of a put option contract have the same zero-sum payoffs when the option is exercised. If the item price is below the exercise price, the buyer will exercise the option and realize a net profit equal to the writer's loss. If the item price is above the exercise price, the put option is out of the money and expires worthless.

Option Positions—Profit Diagrams. In this section, the relation between the put and call option payoffs and the price of the underlying item is demonstrated graphically. The underlying item is assumed to be a futures contract, although the analysis is general in the sense that the underlying item may be any financial instrument or commodity. The options are assumed to be held to maturity, T.

To begin, it is useful to establish the profit diagrams for a futures position. An individual who enters into a long futures contract when the futures price is F agrees to pay F for the underlying item when the position is closed at time T. At time T the futures price, F_T, minus the purchase price, F, represents the profit from the long futures contract. The maximum loss from this position is F since the lowest value the futures may obtain is 0, and the maximum gain from the position is unlimited. The strategy has a zero profit when the terminal futures price equals the initial value (that is, $F_T = F$). Panel A of figure 4–1 depicts the profit diagram for a long futures position.

The profit picture for a short futures position is exactly opposite that of the long futures position because of the zero-sum nature of futures contracts. Panel B represents the short futures profit diagram. The maximum loss is unlimited, the maximum gain is F, and the break-even point is where the terminal futures price equals the initial value.

The call option profit diagrams are depicted in figure 4–2. A long call position entails a maximum loss of the option premium, C, an unlimited maximum gain, and a break-even point where the terminal futures price is equal to the exercise price of the option plus the option premium. A short call position has an unlimited loss, a maximum gain of C, and the same break-even futures price, again reflecting the zero-sum nature of such instruments.

Figure 4–3 shows the profit diagrams for long and short positions in the put option. The maximum loss of a long put position is the premium, the maximum gain is the exercise price less the premium, and the break-even terminal futures price is the exercise price less the premium. The short put position has exactly opposite payoffs.

Occasionally a long futures position is thought to be the same as a long call position. A comparison of figures 4–1 and 4–2 shows that this is clearly not the case. Although a call has the potential profits of a futures contract, it avoids the losses from a futures price decline. Thus a long futures position and a long call position are quite different.

Buying a call *and* writing a put, however, provide a long futures position. This is illustrated in figure 4–4 for the case in which the futures price equals the option's exercise price. The maximum loss from the strategy is F, which is the maximum loss from writing a put; the maximum gain from buying the call is unlimited; and the break-even terminal futures price is F. These are exactly the contingencies posed by the long futures position. The long call–short put option strategy is sometimes referred to as a synthetic long futures position. Conversely, a portfolio consisting of a short position in the call and a long position in the put provides a synthetic short position in the futures, as shown in panel B.

Certain combinations of futures and futures options provide synthetic options positions. For example, a portfolio consisting of a long position in futures and a short position in the call option on

FIGURE 4–1
PROFIT DIAGRAMS FOR NAKED FUTURES POSITIONS

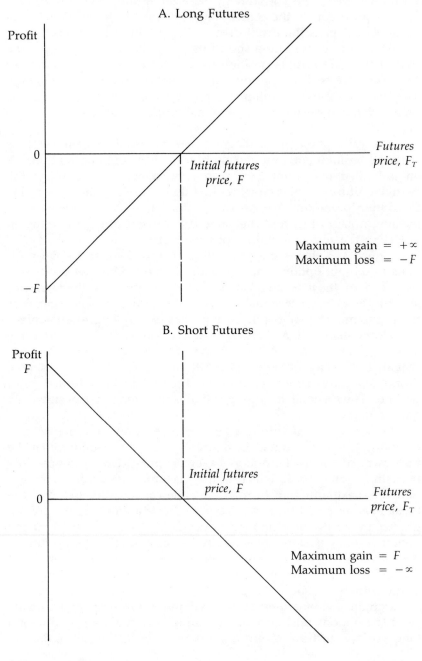

A. Long Futures

Profit

0

Futures price, F_T

Initial futures price, F

Maximum gain = $+\infty$
Maximum loss = $-F$

$-F$

B. Short Futures

Profit

F

Initial futures price, F

0

Futures price, F_T

Maximum gain = F
Maximum loss = $-\infty$

FIGURE 4–2
Profit Diagrams for Naked Call Option Positions

A. Long Call

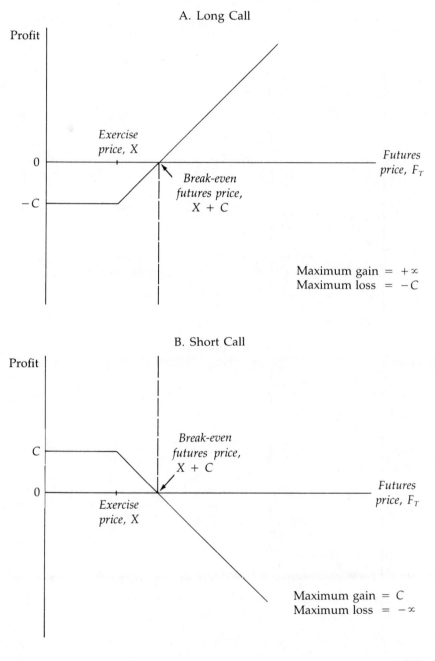

Profit

Exercise
price, X

0

Futures
price, F_T

Break-even
futures price,
X + C

−C

Maximum gain = +∞
Maximum loss = −C

B. Short Call

Profit

Break-even
futures price,
X + C

C

0

Futures
price, F_T

Exercise
price, X

Maximum gain = C
Maximum loss = −∞

FIGURE 4-3
Profit Diagrams for Naked Put Option Positions

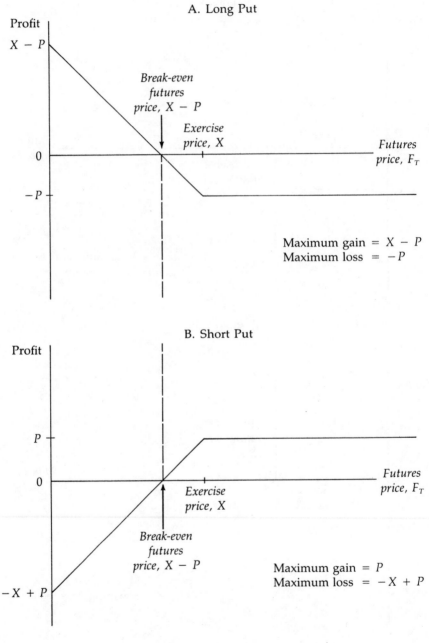

A. Long Put

Profit

$X - P$

Break-even
futures
price, $X - P$

Exercise
price, X

0

$-P$

Futures
price, F_T

Maximum gain $= X - P$
Maximum loss $= -P$

B. Short Put

Profit

P

0

Exercise
price, X

Break-even
futures
price, $X - P$

Futures
price, F_T

$-X + P$

Maximum gain $= P$
Maximum loss $= -X + P$

FIGURE 4–4

Profit Diagrams for Synthetic Futures Positions

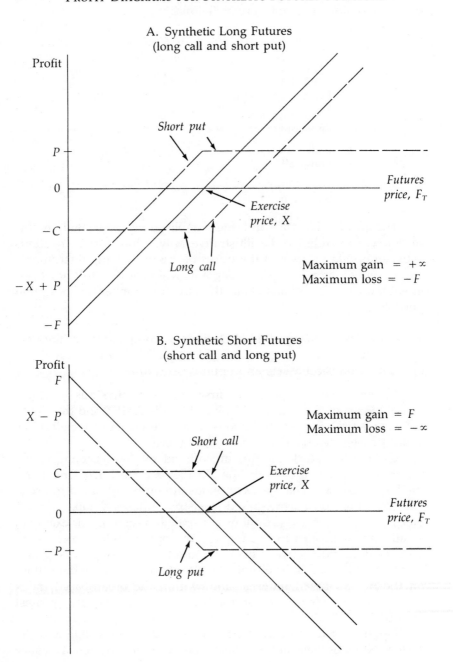

A. Synthetic Long Futures
(long call and short put)

Profit

Short put

P

0

Exercise price, X

Futures price, F_T

−C

Long call

−X + P

−F

Maximum gain = +∞
Maximum loss = −F

B. Synthetic Short Futures
(short call and long put)

Profit

F

X − P

Short call

C

Exercise price, X

Futures price, F_T

0

−P

Long put

Maximum gain = F
Maximum loss = −∞

the futures is equivalent to writing a put on the futures; that is, it is a synthetic short put position. The portfolio compositions yielding synthetic options positions are as follows:

Portfolio Composition	Synthetic Option Position
Long futures Long put	Long call
Short futures Short put	Short call
Short futures Long call	Long put
Long futures Short call	Short put

The profit diagrams and their implications presented in this section are intended to be illustrative only. More formal relations between option prices and the prices of the underlying instruments are presented later. The profit diagrams will prove useful, however, in subsequent discussions about the payoff contingencies of option portfolios.

Types of New Exchange-traded Options. A complete list of the new options instruments is given in table 4–2. They are divided into options on physical assets and options on futures.

Options on physical assets. The first options on physicals—options on debt instruments—were introduced by the AMEX and the CBOE in October 1982. Since then options written directly on stock indexes and on currencies have also been introduced.

Options on stock indexes are offered on five exchanges: the CBOE, the AMEX, the NYSE, the Philadelphia Stock Exchange, and the Pacific Coast Exchange. Six options are on broad-based indexes, and eleven are on narrow-based industrial indexes. Unlike options on common stocks, these options are settled in cash. If, for example, a call option finishes in the money, the option holder receives in cash the difference between the index and the exercise price. Options on the broad-based indexes enjoy greater trading volume than those on the narrow-based indexes, and, within the broad-based index group, the CBOE's options on the S&P 100 index have the greatest interest.

Options on debt instruments are offered on the CBOE and the AMEX. None of these options, written on U.S. government Treasury

214

obligations, has generated much interest. The T-bond and T-note option contracts require delivery of the underlying Treasury instrument if the option is exercised; the T-bill requires the delivery of a bill that has ninety days to expiration.

The Philadelphia Stock Exchange lists options on six currencies: the British pound, the Canadian dollar, the West German mark, the Japanese yen, the Swiss franc, and the French franc. If the option is exercised, the underlying currency must be delivered.

Options on futures contracts. A number of the options, as shown in table 4–2, are options on futures contracts. If a futures option is exercised, the underlying futures contract is delivered. The options may be categorized according to the nature of the item underlying the futures contract. Currently, futures options are written on stock indexes, debt instruments, currencies, and several commodities.

Under a pilot program instituted in December 1981, the Commodity Futures Trading Commission (CFTC) approved options for a limited number of futures contracts on commodities other than domestic agricultural commodities. The first of these futures options (on T-bonds, sugar, and gold) did not begin trading until October 1982. The ban on options trading in domestic agricultural commodities established in the Commodity Exchange Act of 1936 was lifted by the Futures Trading Act of 1982, and now a second option pilot program (approved in March 1984) allows for domestic agricultural options as well. Each pilot program runs for three years and is intended to allow close monitoring by the CFTC of the development of these markets and compliance with the various rules established by the CFTC. Under the first pilot program each futures exchange is allowed to propose two options. Options on stock index futures (S&P 500, NYSE composite, Value Line index), T-bond futures, German mark futures, gold futures, and sugar futures were approved under the pilot program. Under the second pilot each futures exchange is allowed to propose two agricultural options. Futures options on corn, soybeans, live hogs, live cattle, wheat, and cotton were approved under this program.

Only two of the futures options on stock indexes are currently active—options on the S&P 500 on the Chicago Mercantile Exchange (CME) and options on the NYSE composite index on the New York Futures Exchange (NYFE). Both options expire at the same time as the underlying futures contract. For the S&P 500 futures options it is the third Friday of the contract month; for futures options on the NYSE composite, it is the next to last business day of the month.

Futures options are currently traded on a long-term debt instru-

TABLE 4-2: SUMMARY OF OPTIONS ON INSTRUMENTS OTHER THAN COMMON STOCKS

Underlying Item (Exchange)	Contract Size	Expiration Months Cycle[a]	Expiration Months Number[b]	Start of Trading
Options on physical assets				
Broad stock indexes (contract size in dollars)				
S&P 100 (CBOE)	100 I[c]	Monthly	4	Mar. 11, 1983
Major market (AMEX)	100 I	Monthly	3	Apr. 29, 1983
S&P 500 (CBOE)	100 I	Quarterly	3	July 1, 1983
Market value (AMEX)	100 I	Monthly	3	Sept. 23, 1983
NYSE composite (NYSE)	100 I	M/Q	5	Sept. 23, 1983
Value line index (Philadelphia)		Monthly	3	
Narrow stock indexes (contract size in dollars)				
Computer technology (AMEX)	100 I	Monthly	3	Aug. 26, 1983
Oil and gas (AMEX)	100 I	Monthly	3	Sept. 9, 1983
S&P international oils (CBOE)	100 I	Quarterly	3	Sept. 19, 1983[d]
Computer and business equipment (CBOE)	100 I	Quarterly	3	Sept. 28, 1983[d]
Gold/silver (Philadelphia)	100 I	M/Q	5	Dec. 18, 1983
Gaming/hotel (Philadelphia)	100 I	M/Q	5	Dec. 19, 1983
Technology (Pacific)	100 I	Monthly	3	Jan. 1984
Telephone (CBOE)	100 I	Quarterly	3	Mar. 20, 1984[d]
Transportation (CBOE)	100 I	Monthly	3	Mar. 20, 1984
Transportation (AMEX)	100 I	Monthly	3	Mar. 20, 1984
Telephone (NYSE)	100 I	M/Q	5	Mar. 20, 1984
Debt instruments (contract size in dollars)				
U.S. T-bonds (various issues) (CBOE)	100,000	Quarterly	3	Oct. 22, 1982
U.S. T-notes (various issues) (AMEX)	100,000[e]	Quarterly	3	Oct. 22, 1982
U.S. T-bills (AMEX)	1,000,000[f]	Quarterly	3	Oct. 22, 1982
Foreign currencies (Philadelphia) (contract size in foreign currency)				
British pound	12,500	Quarterly	3	Dec. 10, 1982
Canadian dollar	50,000	Quarterly	3	Feb. 28, 1983
West German mark	62,500	Quarterly	3	Feb. 28, 1983
Japanese yen	6,250,000	Quarterly	3	Feb. 28, 1983
Swiss franc	62,500	Quarterly	3	Feb. 28, 1983

Instrument	Contract size	Expiration cycle	Months[b]	Date listed
French franc	125,000	Quarterly	3	
Options on futures				
Broad stock index futures (contract size in dollars)				
S&P 500 index (CME)	500 I	Quarterly	3	Jan. 28, 1983
NYSE composite index (NYFE)	500 I	Quarterly	3	Jan. 28, 1983
Value Line index (KCBT)	500 I	Quarterly	3	Mar. 4, 1983[g]
Debt instrument futures (contract size in dollars)				
U.S. T-bonds (CBT)	100,000	Quarterly	3	Oct. 1, 1982
Eurodollar (CME)	1,000,000	Quarterly	3	
Currency futures (CME) (contract size in foreign currency)				
West German mark	125,000	Quarterly	2	Jan. 24, 1984
British pound	25,000	Quarterly	2	Feb. 25, 1985
Swiss franc	125,000	Quarterly	3	Feb. 25, 1985
Commodity futures				
Sugar #11 (CSCE)	112,000 lb.	Irregular	4	Oct. 1, 1982
Gold (COMEX)	100 troy oz.	Irregular	3	Oct. 4, 1982
Live hogs (CME)	30,000 lb.	Irregular	3	Feb. 1, 1985
Live cattle (CME)	40,000 lb.	Irregular	3	Oct. 30, 1984
Corn (CBT)	5,000 bu.	Irregular	3	Feb. 27, 1985
Soybeans (CBT, MACE)	5,000 bu.	Irregular	3	
Cotton (NYCE)	50,000 lb.	Irregular	3	Oct. 30, 1984
Wheat (MACE, MGE, KCBT)	5,000 bu.	Irregular	3	Oct. 30, 1984
Silver (COMEX)	5,000 troy oz.	Irregular	3	Oct. 4, 1984
Silver (CBT)	1,000 troy oz.	Irregular	3	

NOTE: CBOE = Chicago Board Options Exchange; AMEX = American Stock Exchange; NYSE = New York Stock Exchange; Philadelphia = Philadelphia Stock Exchange; Pacific = Pacific Stock Exchange; CME = Chicago Mercantile Exchange; NYFE = New York Futures Exchange; KCBT = Kansas City Board of Trade; CBT = Chicago Board of Trade; CSCE = Coffee, Sugar, and Cocoa Exchange; COMEX = Commodity Exchange; MACE = Mid America Commodity Exchange; NYCE = New York Cotton Exchange; MGE = Minneapolis Grain Exchange.

a. Options that trade on a monthly and quarterly cycle are denoted M/Q. The nearest three months plus a six-month maturity are usually available for trading. b. Number of different expiration months trading at any time. These are the nearest months.
c. I = value of index. d. Delisted May 18, 1984. e. Contract size increased from $20,000 to $100,000 on June 20, 1983.
f. Contract size increased from $200,000 to $1 million on June 20, 1983. g. Delisted in 1983.
SOURCES: Commodity Futures Trading Commission, various exchanges, and Wall Street Journal.

ment (Treasury bonds) and on a short-term debt instrument (ninety-day Eurodollar deposits). By far the most successful of all futures options is the T-bond futures option introduced in October 1982 by the Chicago Board of Trade (CBT). This option contract expires on the first Friday preceding by at least five business days the end of the month before the futures expiration month. Options on Eurodollar futures were only recently introduced by the CME.

In January 1984 the CME introduced options on the West German mark futures. These options expire two business days before the expiration of the futures. In early 1985 options on British pound and Swiss franc futures were introduced.

Futures options in sugar and gold have been available for trading since October 1982. In late 1984 and early 1985 futures options on several domestic agricultural commodities began trading under the CFTC's second pilot program: live hogs, live cattle, corn, soybeans, cotton, and wheat. Futures options on silver have also begun trading.

Over-the-Counter Options. Although our emphasis is on exchange-traded options with active secondary markets, some discussion of over-the-counter (OTC) options, which are also growing in importance, is warranted. OTC options are contracts that are not necessarily standard in striking price or maturity and in which no active secondary market exists. OTC options on individual common stocks existed before the advent of exchange-traded stock options. This market has declined in importance, presumably because the advantage of tailoring options to the needs of a particular investor did not offset the advantages of secondary market trading. OTC options on currencies and on debt instruments appear, however, to have grown in importance with the advent of exchange-traded options in those areas, although there is no hard evidence of the amount of activity in these markets.

Two types of OTC options exist in the bond market: short-term options (limited to 150 days in maturity by regulations of the comptroller of the currency) and long-term interest rate agreements.[1] Government securities dealers, such as the major money market banks, are prepared to write short-term put and call options on particular government bonds with a striking price, maturity, and size tailored to the customer's needs. Customers with well-defined objectives, who may wish to take delivery of the underlying bond, will find OTC options preferable to exchange-traded options, particularly when the exchange-traded options market is thin.

Interest rate agreements, though not called options, serve the same function as a long-term option contract would. They protect

218

the borrower against an increase (and the lender against a decline) in interest rates beyond a certain level. Such agreements may last up to ten years. An interest rate agreement could, for example, limit the interest rate paid by a borrower on a floating-rate loan to 14 percent over the period of ten years. If the particular interest rate that is the basis for the floating-rate loan were to rise above 14 percent, the maker of the agreement would pay to the borrower the difference between 14 percent and the market rate. In effect, the borrower is buying a put option, which increases in value when interest rates rise.

Major foreign exchange traders are also prepared to write OTC currency options with terms tailored to the needs of individual customers. Such options are particularly useful for businesses engaged in international trade and planning to make delivery or take delivery of a foreign currency. A striking price, contract size, and maturity tailored to the particular needs of the business are important.

Functioning of the New Option Markets

The new option instruments are traded on fourteen exchanges. Nine are futures exchanges: CME, CBT, the Commodity Exchange (COMEX), the Coffee, Sugar, and Cocoa Exchange (CSCE), NYFE, the Kansas City Board of Trade (KCBT), the Mid America Commodity Exchange (MACE), the New York Cotton Exchange (NYCE), and the Minneapolis Grain Exchange (MGE). Four are stock exchanges: NYSE, AMEX, Philadelphia, and Pacific. One, the CBOE, trades options exclusively. There are many similarities but also important differences in the way different exchange option markets operate. In this section we examine how options trading is organized and regulated.

The Clearinghouse. Options contracts, like futures contracts, are created instruments. When option buyer and option seller meet, they create a contractual agreement obligating the seller to make delivery at the option of a buyer. The open interest is the number of such contracts outstanding. Options trading is thus quite different from trading in stocks, where a given supply of already issued securities is traded. The clearinghouse is critical to the trading of options contracts because it is their guarantor. After a contract is agreed to, the clearinghouse interposes itself between buyer and seller and, in effect, becomes the party to whom the buyer looks for delivery and to whom the seller must make delivery. Since the number of buyers always equals the numbers of sellers, the clearinghouse always has a zero net position.

TABLE 4-3

EXAMPLE OF TRADING IN OPTIONS AND ASSOCIATED CASH FLOWS

Time	Buyer	Seller	Cumulative Contract Volume	Open Interest	Option Premium	Premium Cash Flow				Margin Cash Flow			
						A	B	C	D	A	B	C	D
1	A	B	1	1	3.00	-3.00	3.00				-13.00		
2	C	A	2	1	3.10	3.10		-3.10			-0.10		
3	C	D	3	2	2.80			-2.80	2.80		0.30		-13.00
4	B	C	4	1	2.80		-2.80	2.80			12.80		
5	D	C	5	0	3.00			3.00	-3.00				13.00
Total						0.10	0.20	-0.10	-0.20	0	0	0	0

The clearinghouse and the standardization of options contracts make possible a secondary market in options. An option buyer who does not wish to exercise an option may sell a contract in the same option (that is, with the same maturity and striking price). Since the buyer is now seller of the same contract, the clearinghouse nets out the position. Of course, the buyer could always choose to exercise the option, but most options positions are offset as just described.

In over-the-counter option markets, secondary market trading is not possible, for two reasons. First, there is no clearinghouse; the option buyer must negotiate with the particular option seller with whom the contract was first arranged to undo the contract before maturity. This procedure is cumbersome and also puts the party that seeks to reverse its position at a competitive disadvantage. Second, contracts in the OTC option market are not standardized with respect to maturity month and striking price. Thus, even if a clearinghouse existed, it would be difficult to find traders on the other side willing to trade in very specific instruments. OTC options exist because the tailored contracts are sufficiently attractive to particular individuals to offset the disadvantages of not having a secondary market.

Aside from its clerical role of accounting for contracts and overseeing delivery, the clearinghouse maintains the financial integrity of the options market as guarantor of all contracts. Clearing members post margin deposits to guarantee their transactions, and most exchanges have a guarantee fund of some kind to protect clearing members and thereby customers against a failure of an individual clearing firm.[2]

Each of the futures exchanges has its own clearing organization. Options on the CBOE and the stock exchanges are issued and guaranteed by the Options Clearing Corporation (OCC). Although in principle the existence of the OCC as a common clearing corporation would make possible secondary market trading on one exchange of an option issued by another, none of the new options instruments is traded on more than one exchange.

Secondary market trading in options and the role of the clearinghouse are perhaps best illustrated with the help of a simple example. Assume, as shown in table 4–3, that at the the opening of options trading at time 1, trader A and trader B agree to trade one contract at a premium or price of $3 per unit. (The actual option premium paid will be much larger than this and will depend on the number of units per contract.) Under current arrangements the option buyer, A, pays the premium to the option seller, B. Volume at the end of time 1 is one contract, and open interest—the number of contracts outstanding—is also one. The clearinghouse becomes buyer to B and seller to A. When A decides to sell at time 2 to C, the clearinghouse becomes buyer to A and seller to C. Since A is now a buyer and seller of the same contract on the books of the clearinghouse, A's position is closed out by the clearinghouse. In effect, C replaces A as the offsetting long to B's short position (without B's knowledge). At time 2 cumulative volume has increased to two contracts, and open interest remains at one. When C buys a second contract from D at time 3, cumulative volume and open interest increase by one contract. At time 4 and time 5 offsetting positions are entered into, and open interest is reduced to zero. The typical pattern is, in fact, to close out option positions by offsetting contracts rather than by exercise.

Profits and Margin. Table 4–3 also illustrates the premium cash flow and margin cash flow associated with option trading. Current institutional arrangements require the option buyer to pay the full premium. At time 1 A pays $3 and B receives $3. The option seller must post sufficient margin to guarantee his obligation to deliver the underlying asset, an amount that is here assumed to be $13. The total cash flow for B is thus −$10.[3] At time 2 only A has offset his initial position, and A realizes a profit of $0.10. Option sellers must mark-to-market their margin deposits. Thus B must supply $0.10 to cover the losses from the increase in the option value. At time 3 B can collect profits resulting from a decrease in the option price, and D, a new seller, must post margin, which is again assumed to be $13. Traders A and C, unlike B and D, never hold a short position and are thus never required to supply margin.

That option trading is a zero-sum activity is reflected in the fact that the sum of profits of the four traders is zero. A and B gain; C and D lose. To the extent that margin is pledged in cash, there is a net loss to sellers of options in the form of forgone interest on funds pledged as margins. To the extent that such margin deposits may be made in the form of interest-earning assets such as U.S. government securities, this loss is avoided. To the extent that a broker or a clearing organization demands cash deposits, the broker or clearing organization gains at the expense of the trader.

Trading Mechanics. Anyone wishing to trade options opens an account with a brokerage firm. Options on futures contracts are traded in a commodity account, which is subject to CFTC oversight. Options written directly on financial instruments are traded in securities accounts, which are subject to Securities and Exchange Commission (SEC) oversight. Disclosure requirements, broker competency requirements, insurance of accounts, and other matters related to investors' protection differ between commodity accounts and securities accounts. These issues are beyond the scope of this chapter.[4]

In options trading, as in trading of other securities, investors can place a variety of orders. A market order instructs the broker to trade at the best price currently available. A limit order instructs the broker to buy at a price below the current market or to sell at a price above the current market price. A stop loss order is an order to sell below the market or to buy above the market. As in futures markets trading, more complex orders may be placed in options markets. Such orders usually involve spread transactions or other simultaneous transactions using more complicated option strategies.

Orders placed by customers with their account executive are transmitted through the brokerage firms to the floor of the appropriate exchange for execution. The mechanics by which such orders are executed can differ markedly among exchanges. Futures options are traded in a trading pit in an "open outcry" format in the same manner as futures contracts.[5] Options traded on stock exchanges are traded through a specialist in the same manner as common stocks on such exchanges. Options traded on the CBOE combine the features of futures markets and stock market trading mechanics.

In a specialist system market orders are usually traded at the bid or ask price quoted by the specialist, although other traders in the crowd have an opportunity to better the specialist's price. Limit orders are left with the specialist to be executed when the market price reaches the limit price. The bid or ask quotation is sometimes the specialist's own quotation and sometimes the price of the limit order. The specialist system has been criticized because, in most such systems, only one specialist makes a market in each option and investors cannot shop for better prices from other market makers. The CFTC has objected to futures contracts traded in a specialist system on the grounds that the Commodity Futures Trading Commission Act requires the commission to endeavor to take the least anticompetitive means of achieving the objectives of the act.

In a futures system there is no designated specialist. Orders are brought to a trading pit in which many traders trade directly with one another. Traders may act in a dual capacity—as principals for their own account or as brokers for the accounts of customers. Dual trading on futures markets has been criticized. Although CFTC rules prohibit commodity brokers from trading ahead of customers, price reporting statistics are not sufficiently accurate to permit customers to determine whether, in fact, they have received priority: prices are reported only for half-hour intervals or when prices change, and volume is not reported for individual transactions. The specialist on stock exchanges also trades in a dual capacity, but the volume and price of each transaction are reported. Thus a customer can more readily determine whether an order was properly executed. Futures markets do not guarantee the same degree of price and time priority as stock markets, either because two simultaneous transactions may occur in different parts of the ring at differing prices or because limit orders held by a particular broker are for some reason not exposed to all other brokers in the crowd.

Offset against these apparent disadvantages is the fact that futures markets have many competing professional traders ready to maintain the liquidity of the markets. On futures markets scalpers assume the role of the specialist and are willing to trade their own accounts to offset temporary imbalances in the order flow in much the same way as the specialist does on stock exchanges. The existence of many competing scalpers eliminates the possibility of monopoly pricing by any one of them.

The CBOE system combines elements of futures markets and stock markets. A "board" broker maintains the book of limit orders but does not trade for his own account. At the same time, many professional floor traders are prepared to trade for their own accounts to absorb temporary imbalances as scalpers in futures markets do. More than either the futures market system or the specialist system, the CBOE floor trading system constitutes a kind of trading system that many have called for in the stock market, for it combines competition among market makers with full exposure of all limit orders through the open book of the board broker.[6]

Each of the markets in which the new options instruments are traded is, however, faced with its own cost of establishing trading systems and burdened with its own history of trading procedures. One should not, therefore, be too quick to impose a system judged to be superior in the absence of a careful analysis of the costs of achieving it. An interesting feature of the new option instruments is that similar instruments are being offered by different exchanges. Investors can trade options in those markets that are judged to offer the best service. Competition among various exchanges may thus be the best means of determining the most efficient trading system.

Costs of Trading. To the options investor the costs of trading consist primarily of two components: the commission charges of the broker and the price concession that may be necessary to execute the transaction. The price concession reflects the fact that sales are made at the bid price of professional traders on the floor and purchases are made at the higher ask price of professional traders on the floor. On the average the option investor can expect to pay the bid-ask spread in a full-turn transaction. Commission charges are competitively determined and vary from broker to broker. They cover the services provided by the broker as well as charges for floor brokerage and clearing of transactions. In general, commission charges to trade a futures option contract are the same as commission charges on the underlying futures contract, but both are much less than commission charges to trade the contract amount of the underlying asset.

Regulatory Jurisdiction. Primary responsibility for regulation of trading in the new options instruments rests with the CFTC and the SEC. The SEC, created in 1934, has primarily been concerned with regulating trading in stocks and bonds issued by corporations. U.S. government securities markets are not subject to SEC jurisdiction and are not formally regulated, although the Federal Reserve and the Treasury monitor this market. Municipal bond markets have been subject to SEC regulation since 1975. Trading in options on common stocks has been regulated by the SEC since secondary market option trading began on the CBOE in 1973. Trading in OTC options, which has existed for many years and continues to exist, has not been regulated by the SEC. The CFTC, created in 1974, was given a broader regulatory mandate than its predecessor, the Commodity Exchange Authority (CEA): to oversee trading in all futures contracts, including futures on nonagricultural commodities previously unregulated by the CEA.

The development of financial futures contracts and new options instruments has generated jurisdictional conflicts between the SEC and the CFTC. Some of these conflicts were resolved by the accord of December 7, 1981, which affirmed CFTC jurisdiction over all futures trading, including futures on debt instruments (except for municipal securities), stock indexes, and currencies. Futures on stock indexes, however, were to be restricted to broad-based indexes settled in cash and not readily subject to manipulation. Specific guidelines for implementing these restrictions were put forth in early 1984 by the CFTC. The accord gave the CFTC jurisdiction over all options on futures contracts subject to CFTC jurisdiction. Options written directly on foreign currencies are also subject to CFTC jurisdiction if they are not traded on a national securities exchange subject to SEC regulation. (The currency options on the Philadelphia Stock Exchange, which is a national securities exchange, are subject to SEC jurisdiction.)

The SEC has no jurisdiction over futures contracts, but the accord establishes SEC jurisdiction over options written directly on financial instruments (on which futures and options on futures may also exist). Thus the SEC has jurisdiction over options written directly on debt securities, stock indexes, and currencies (traded on national securities exchanges). Furthermore, with respect to options on stock indexes, no restrictions on the characteristics of the index apply. Options on physical assets listed in table 4-2 are subject to SEC jurisdiction; options on futures listed there are subject to CFTC jurisdiction.

It is unlikely that the accord, which was incorporated into the Futures Trading Act of 1982, will resolve all jurisdictional disputes. In particular, the requirement that futures on stock indexes be restricted to broad-based indexes is already the subject of a suit by the Chicago Board of Trade, which challenges the procedures by which the guidelines were set and questions their arbitrariness. In addition, other futures or options instruments not covered by the accord may be developed and may test it. For example, jurisdiction over futures on individual common stocks and options on such futures is not clearly spelled out.

A more fundamental issue arises from the fact that responsibility has been allocated between the SEC and the CFTC for legal, not economic, considerations. It is already evident that very similar economic instruments (for example, options on T-bonds and options on T-bond futures) are regulated by different agencies. The issue, then, is whether similar economic products should be regulated by the same agency or whether regulatory competition has benefits akin to the benefits of competition in the private sector.[7] One objective of this study is to examine the extent to which the new options contracts are similar and to consider the implications of disparate regulation of similar products.

Economic Purpose of Options

Functions of Options. Options, like futures, are a means of dealing with uncertainty. Indeed, the growth of the new options instruments can be ascribed in part to the increased volatility of the stock market, bond market, and foreign exchange markets in the past few years. Because options have different payoffs from futures, they can be a more useful risk management tool.

In this section we examine the functions of options, as contrasted with futures, as a hedging tool and as an investment tool.[8] Options are a hedging tool insofar as they are used to reduce or eliminate an underlying business risk associated with producing and marketing a product or providing a service. Options are an investment tool insofar as they are used to modify the risk and return characteristics of an investment portfolio. In this context, as in the hedging context, options can be used to reduce risk. We restrict the term "hedging," however, to cases in which options are used to offset more fundamental business risk, rather than to tailor the risk characteristics of an investment portfolio.

Options as a hedging tool. Options are an appropriate hedging vehicle whenever an underlying business risk itself has the characteristics of an option, that is, a commitment by one party that may or may not be rejected by another.

Suppose a U.S. company makes a bid in German marks to install a computer system for a German company, and suppose the German company has the option of accepting or rejecting the bid within one month.[9] During that month the U.S. bidder faces a quantity risk and a price risk. First, the company does not know whether the bid will be accepted and thus does not know the quantity of contracts it will be working on. Second, it does not know the dollar value of the deutsche mark (D-mark) contract if the bid should be accepted. In this situation a D-mark currency option is a better hedge than a D-mark currency futures. By purchasing a put option on the D-mark, the company guarantees the price at which D-marks can be sold if the bid is accepted; if it is rejected, the put option is not exercised. Selling a D-mark futures contract provides a hedge if the bid is accepted, but if it is rejected, the futures contract could be met only by buying the futures at a later date. This would expose the U.S. company to the risk of an increase in the dollar price of the mark.

Farmers also face a combination of price and quantity risk. Before the harvest the farmer does not know the size of the crop or the price. Selling futures against the crop would hedge the farmer against a price decline if the harvest were known, but a futures hedge would expose him to risk if the harvest failed and prices increased. The farmer would take a loss in covering the futures contract, which would not be offset by a corresponding gain on the actual commodity, because of the failure of the harvest. Buying a put option on the underlying commodity provides a more effective hedge against price and quantity risk than selling futures. If prices fall, the put is exercised (or liquidated at a profit). If prices rise, the put option expires worthless, and the farmer can realize the revenues from his crop whatever the size of the harvest. The cost of this one-sided protection for the farmer is the put option premium.

Lending commitments at fixed interest rates also have the characteristics of an option and can therefore be more effectively hedged in options markets than in futures markets. Suppose a bank makes a mortgage loan commitment of $1 million at 14 percent to finance a project the terms of which are not yet fully complete. Such a commitment might be outstanding for a month or two. If interest rates rise, the loan commitment will be "taken down," and the bank, if unhedged, will suffer the costs of borrowing funds at a higher rate. If interest rates fall or the project is unsuccessful, the commitment will not be taken down. By buying a put option on a T-bond, the bank can protect itself against an increase in interest rates; for if interest rates rise (and bond prices fall), the profit on the put will tend to offset the loss on the loan commitment. If interest rates fall, the put will not be exercised. Interest rate futures would be less effective. Selling interest rate futures would yield a gain if interest rates were to rise, but a loss would occur if interest rates fell. A put option prevents that loss.

Stock index options and options on individual stocks can provide useful hedges to investment bankers who make commitments to buy at a fixed price the shares of a company for resale in a public offering. Suppose an underwriter makes a commitment to purchase at a price of $18 per share 100,000 shares currently selling at $20 per share. The commitment is outstanding while the public offering is being prepared and the regulatory requirements are being met. The underwriter seeks protection against a price decline below $18 but is not concerned about a price increase, in which case the stock will be sold in the public offering. The purchase of a put option provides the necessary protection.

Ideally, a put option on the specific stock should be purchased, but if options in the stock do not exist, the purchase of a put option on a stock index can provide partial protection against a price decline in the individual stock since price movements in individuals stocks and in the market as a whole are generally positively correlated. The hedge ratio—the ratio of the puts purchased to the size of the offering—can be adjusted to reflect the systematic relation between the price of the stock and the index. If a $1 change in the index is usually accompanied by a $2 change in the stock price, for example, options on $3.6 million worth of the index should be purchased to hedge the commitment to purchase $1.8 million worth of shares. Because price changes in the index and the individual stock may not, in fact, be in a one-to-two ratio, a considerable amount of basis risk may continue to exist, but that is true of any cross hedge.

The examples presented illustrate that options not only provide insurance against price risk that is conditional on an event (receiving the bid, having a successful harvest, making the loan, making the stock offering) but also avoid any penalty if the event does not occur (the bid is rejected, the harvest is poor, the loan is not taken down, or the stock issue is not sold). It is in this sense that options provide protection against both price and quantity risk and are, therefore, a better hedging tool than futures contracts in some cases. The insurance provided by an option is, of course, not free since a premium must be paid to purchase the option. In futures contracts risks to buyers and sellers are symmetric, and no premium changes hands. The purchaser of an option must therefore consider whether the risk that is being avoided warrants the premium that must be paid.

It is not accidental that our illustrations of options hedging have involved the purchase of put options. In most cases hedges are used to provide protection against price declines on existing positions. Hedging with the purchase of call options, however, can also be useful in locking in the price of an input. A U.S. importer may wish to lock in the price of deutsche marks needed to purchase a good being imported from Germany. A lending institution that makes a commitment to pay a fixed interest rate would find it desirable to buy call options on debt instruments and would thereby protect itself against a decline in the interest rates at which the funds it receives can be reinvested.

The usefulness of options as a hedging tool, like that of futures, depends on the degree to which the price behavior of the option mimics that of the underlying commitment. If the association between the behavior of the option and the underlying commitment is not perfect, basis risk exists. The existence of over-the-counter options can be explained by the desire of certain hedgers to avoid this basis risk and to purchase an option that is more directly tailored to the specific needs of the hedger. OTC markets in bond options have grown in recent years. By providing greater flexibility in option maturity, striking price, and the underlying bond against which the option is written, OTC bond options can be a more useful hedging instrument than exchange-traded options. Similar reasons explain the existence of OTC currency options. The growth in OTC bond and currency options has coincided with the growth in exchange-traded bond options and exchange-traded currency options. These markets are complementary for two reasons. First, both buyers and writers of OTC options can use the prices of exchange-traded options as pricing guides in their negotiations. Second, writers of OTC options can hedge their positions in the exchange-traded option markets (though imperfectly).

Options as an investment tool. The new options can also serve an important function as an investment tool for investors or financial institutions responsible for managing investment portfolios. Options provide a means of increasing or limiting risk in a manner consistent with investors' expectations and attitudes toward risk. They can also facilitate changes in portfolio composition or reduce the costs of achieving certain positions. It is beyond the scope of this chapter to consider the full range of option strategies available to investors. These are discussed in detail in a variety of books, articles, and investment literature. Our purpose here is more limited: to provide some examples and some understanding of the investment uses of options.

The principal benefit of options as an investment tool is that they allow the investor to generate nonlinear profits as a function of changes in the price of the underlying asset, which cannot readily be done by trading the underlying asset or futures on the underlying asset alone. Payoffs to the underlying asset or to futures contracts on the underlying asset are linear in the asset's price, as shown in figure 4–1. Options permit losses to be limited (at the cost of the premium) or limit gains (in return for a premium). Combinations of options can limit the range over which profits are earned or losses incurred. Thus a long position in an underlying asset or a futures contract on that asset exposes the investor to losses if the asset price falls. The purchase of a naked call option produces the same upside potential as ownership of the underlying asset but avoids potential losses (as shown in figure 4–2). Similarly, short positions in the underlying asset or the futures contract expose the investor to losses if the underlying asset price rises; the purchase of a naked put protects the investor against a rise in the asset price while generating profits if the price falls (see figure 4–3).

Investors holding a portfolio of assets, such as stocks and bonds, can use options to modify the payoffs to the underlying assets so as to produce nonlinear payoffs that restrict or expand risk. Consider a portfolio of bonds. The purchase of puts on T-bond futures would provide protection against a fall in bond prices without eliminating the potential profit from a rise in the price of the bonds in the portfolio. This strategy, which creates a synthetic call position in the underlying bonds, would be sensible if the portfolio manager expected a temporary decline in bond prices. (The degree of protection would depend on the degree of correlation between the price movements of T-bond futures—on which the option is written—and the price movements of the bonds in the portfolio.) The portfolio manager could, of course, sell the bonds, but this can be difficult or costly.

An alternative strategy is to write call options against the bond portfolio to earn premium income. This strategy eliminates the possiblity of a gain from an increase in bond prices and would be appropriate if the investor believed that bond prices would be relatively stable over the near future. In effect, writing call options against a position in the underlying asset is like writing naked puts, since the investor stands to lose from price declines and makes no profit from price increases.

The availability of options on a variety of underlying assets permits the investor to purchase protection for various components that may influence the performance of a portfolio. The manager of a portfolio of common stocks, for example, may wish to protect that portfolio against a general decline in the stock market without giving up the benefit of a market increase. This objective can be met by purchasing put options on a broad-based index. Purchasing put options on individual stocks is also possible but might be time consuming and costly, and options on many stocks are not available. Furthermore, the manager may believe that the stocks in the portfolio will outperform the market as a whole. If puts on the index are purchased, the potential gain if the individual stocks decline less than the index is not eliminated.

Alternatively, the investment manager may be concerned about the adverse effects on a portfolio of common stocks of an increase in interest rates but willing to accept the risk of other factors that might cause stock prices to decline (for example, lower corporate earnings). Purchasing put options on debt instruments would provide protection against this risk. Selling interest rate futures could provide some of the same protection, but at the risk of loss if bond prices should rise.

These simple examples illustrate two fundamental motives for using options. On one hand, investors anticipating increased volatility in the price of the underlying asset will wish to buy protection for an existing position (buy puts against the long position, calls against the short position) or, alternatively, to purchase naked options. On the other hand, investors anticipating decreased volatility in the price of the underlying asset will wish to sell protection and earn premium income. That is, they will be willing to write naked calls or puts or to write calls against a long position (a synthetic put) or puts against a short position (a synthetic call).

More complicated option positions than those just illustrated are available. Some of these entail spreading put or call options with different exercise prices or different maturities. A money spread, for example, entails the purchase of an option at one exercise price and the sale of an option on the same underlying asset at a different exercise price. The purchase of a call option on the S&P 500 index at a striking price of 150 and the sale of a call option on that index at a striking price of 160 is a bullish money spread. The spread makes money if the index rises but eliminates any gain above 160; it also eliminates any losses below 150. The correspondng bear money spread would entail the sale of a call option at 150 and the purchase of a call option at 160. This spread makes money if the price of the underlying index falls but limits profits at 150 and losses beyond 160. A time spread entails the purchase or sale of an option of one maturity and the sale or purchase of an option on the same underlying asset at a different maturity.

Other complicated options positions combine puts and calls on the same underlying asset. A long straddle, for example, entails the purchase of a put and a call with the same exercise price. Such a position makes money if the price of the underlying asset either increases or decreases greatly and loses money if the underlying asset price remains the same. A strangle and a guts involve the same option positions as the straddle and thus have similar payoff contingencies. The only difference between the strategies is that in a strangle the exercise price of the put is less than that of the call and in a guts the exercise price of the put is greater than that of the call.

Options can be useful in managing changes in the composition of an investment portfolio. At times the purchase or sale of an underlying asset may be costly or difficult, perhaps because of illiquidity in that market. The purchase of a call option on the underlying asset or a closely related asset can lock in a price while the underlying asset is being purchased. Similarly, the purchase of a put option can lock in the sale price of an asset while the disposition of the underlying asset is being arranged. In a similar way, options can be helpful to market makers in particular securities by giving them greater flexibility to modify or hedge particular portfolio positions imposed on them by public transactions. The availability of options can reduce the risks assumed by the market maker and can therefore improve the depth of markets and reduce the costs of providing the services of market making.

Social Benefits and Costs of Options. *Social benefits.* The benefits to society of options trading are similar to the benefits of other financial markets, such as the bond market, the stock market, and futures markets. First, options are a means of allocating risk. Second, trading in options provides price information that is useful in allocating resources in the economy. Third, the new options markets may lower the transaction costs of trading in the financial markets below the costs of trading existing financial instruments.

An important social benefit of options is their usefulness in shifting risk from one individual to another, both business risk and investment or portfolio risk. Options can make it possible to buy protection against certain business risks (price and quantity risk) and thereby allow a business to concentrate more fully on those areas of activity at which it is most expert, thus facilitating specialization and efficiency in productive activities. Options also provide greater flexibility in structuring the risk-return composition of a portfolio and permit investors to pass off certain risks to other investors more willing to bear them. Although there is no direct connection to productive activity in this case, options thus increase the utility of investors.

Some trading in options markets, as in other financial markets, arises not because individuals have a desire to shift risk but because they have different information and disagree about the correct price of the option. This kind of informational trading may also be termed speculative trading. Society benefits from speculative trading because the analysis and search for information on which it is based cause the prices of options to correspond more closely to their correct value. Prices that are "correct" in this sense ensure that prices are fair, allocate risk correctly, and give proper signals for productive activity in the economy.

The way in which disagreement produces options trading can be illustrated by the following example. Consider an underlying asset selling at $50. If both the option writer and the option buyer agree that there is a 50 percent chance of the asset's going to $60 and a 50 percent chance of its staying at $50, they will both agree that the actuarial value of an option with a $50 exercise price is $5. If the writer is averse to risk, he will demand slightly more than $5; if the buyer is averse to risk, he will only be willing to pay less than $5. As a result, no trade will take place even in the absence of transaction costs. A trade will take place if the writer and buyer disagree by sufficient amounts about the actuarial value of the option. If the buyer believes that the actuarial value is $6 and the writer believes that it is $4, a trade will take place. Assume that that trade is at $5. Permitting the writer and the buyer to trade at $5 makes both better off because it raises the *expected* income of each by $1. Of course, after the fact, neither may profit, or one may profit and the other lose.

From the point of view of society, informational trading in options is beneficial because it is likely to increase the interest and the number of judgments bearing on the underlying asset's price. Since option prices are related to the price of the underlying asset by an arbitrage relationship, factors affecting option prices tend to be conveyed to the price of the underlying instrument; conversely, factors affecting the price of the underlying instrument tend to be conveyed to option prices. Thus, to the extent that option trading in a given asset increases the total interest in that asset (asset plus option interest) and the total number of judgments about the asset's value, the asset price will be more broadly based and less susceptible to a few judgments.

A related benefit to society is that an option market encourages specialization of research and analysis, which leads to greater efficiency in the production of information if the securities analysis industry is like other industries. Since option values depend in an important way on the projected volatility of the underlying instrument, an option market creates an incentive to investigate and to project correctly future uncertainty. A superior analyst could, for example, profit by writing calls on assets believed to be less volatile than implied by the current price of those calls and buying calls on assets believed to be more volatile than implied by their current price. The analyst's trading strategy will be based on an analysis of the risk of each underlying asset, which depends on an understanding of the fundamentals affecting the asset's value as well as general economic and regulatory factors that may affect value. The result of such analysis will cause option prices more accurately to reflect projected uncertainty about an underlying asset's value. This kind of information is also reflected in the price of the underlying asset, but the option price in relation to the price of the asset depends critically on the market's judgment about the future volatility of the asset's price.

Because price changes in options are directly related to price changes in the underlying asset, options are sometimes called redundant assets. This view implies that options provide no social benefits, because any portfolio position achievable with options can be achieved by appropriate trading of the underlying asset. The existence and social benefits of certain options depend, then, on the savings in transaction costs that they provide. The down-side protection that the purchase of a put option provides could also be provided by instructing the broker to sell the underlying asset at the striking price of the put; that is, to give the broker a stop-loss order where the stop price is the same as the exercise price of the put.

The stop-loss order, however, has several drawbacks in comparison with the purchase of a put. First, the transaction costs of trading the underlying asset—the commission and the bid-ask spread—are greater than the cost of trading the option. Second, the stop-loss order may be executed at a price somewhat below the stop price since a stop order becomes a market order when the market reaches the stop price. Third, the stop order will be executed if the price of the underlying asset reaches the stop price, whereas the put option need not be exercised and can continue to provide protection even if it is not exercised. The put option thus gives the investor the opportunity to stay fully invested. If the underlying asset is sold, the reinvestment of the proceeds generates additional transaction costs. Put and call options can thus provide social benefits by saving transaction costs or otherwise making it easier to accomplish certain investment objectives. The growth of options in common stocks and the advent of the new options instruments imply that the objectives of options cannot be provided at the same transaction costs by trading in the underlying asset.

Social costs. Options trading in the United States has had a checkered history and has at times been prohibited on a variety of grounds. Options on common stocks and commodities were traded in the 1920s and 1930s before option markets were formally regulated. The Commodity Exchange Act of 1936 banned trading in options on all domestic agricultural commodities regulated by that act. The ban reflected a congressional concern that options trading would destabilize commodity prices.[10] The SEC, though not banning stock options outright, urged securities exchanges to prohibit members from trading securities in which they also traded options. Such regulations were passed, with the result that options were for many years not traded on national securities exchanges. Today those national securities exchanges on which stock options are traded (AMEX, Philadelphia, Pacific) do not permit specialists to make markets simultaneously in options and in the underlying stocks.[11]

Objections to options markets are of three kinds. First, the benefits are questioned on the grounds that options trading is a form of gambling that does not, as argued in the preceding section, contribute to price formation and the allocation of resources. Second, the benefits of option trading are not disputed in principle, but their existence in practice is questioned; there is concern that options markets operate to the disadvantage of unsophisticated investors. Third, options are said to have certain adverse external effects even if they operate efficiently and fairly.

Some critics argue that options trading is a form of gambling that does not contribute usefully to the allocation of resources in the economy, although it may provide enjoyment for some participants.

235

In this view options trading is a bucket shop—a series of side bets—with respect to the underlying assets and the functioning of the underlying economy. Futures markets and the stock market are at times also viewed in this light.

As argued in the preceding section, however, even if options trading is purely speculative—based on disagreements among traders—it has social benefits. A useful distinction between speculation and gambling is that gambling entails the assumption of created risks (for example, roulette, poker) and speculation the assumption of natural risks (for example, droughts, uncertainty of aggregate output, and interest rates). In this sense trading in the new options instruments is speculation, not gambling, because it involves the assumption of underlying risks in the economy that generate price volatility in bonds, stock indexes, and commodities. The arguments in favor of options markets are, to a large extent, the arguments in favor of speculation, and the arguments against options markets are the arguments against speculation. The arguments against are that speculators cause prices to deviate from true underlying values. The arguments in favor are that speculators cause prices to move toward underlying values because doing so is profitable. Options have benefits that go beyond the benefits of speculation since they have hedging uses directly related to productive activities in the economy.

A second concern about options arises not out of any belief that options have no social value but out of the belief that options trading can be abused to benefit professionals at the expense of unsophisticated traders. A study by Mehl of trading in agricultural options examines some of these issues, and a special study of options markets by the SEC in 1978 considered trading abuses in options on common stocks.[12] Three types of trading abuses were identified by the SEC study.

The first of these is *artificial trading,* in which professional traders report fictitious trades or enter into prearranged transactions among themselves: transactions between two individuals that they know will be reversed at the same price. Artificial trading may arise to create the impression of volume or to register an option price that conforms more closely to the price of the underlying instrument. Artificial trading is undesirable insofar as it creates the impression of liquidity where none exists and thereby attracts public orders that will be poorly executed. This kind of abuse is most likely to occur when several markets are trading in competitive instruments and thus create a special incentive to inflate volume figures.

A second abuse is the *capping* or *pegging* of the price of the underlying asset with respect to which an option is written. A writer of call options would like to cap the price of the underlying asset at or below the exercise price to avoid having to deliver the asset at a loss and to profit by any decline in the price of the call option. Capping would be accomplished by selling the asset itself. Similarly, the writer of a put option would like to peg the price of the underlying asset at or above the exercise price to avoid purchase of the asset at a loss and to profit by any decline of the price of the put. This would be accomplished by buying the asset. Thus the ability to establish an unjustified price of the underlying asset—to manipulate the price—is critical to capping and pegging. The ability to manipulate the underlying asset's price need not by itself be profitable, however, since profits on the option position could, in principle, more than offset losses in the asset.

The depth of the underlying market and the presence of other traders that could profit from an unjustified price limit manipulation. The sale of an underlying asset to cap the price would do little to lower the price given the presence of other knowledgeable traders that would provide depth to the market. In this case a manipulator puts himself in a very risky position: short the underlying asset and short call options on it. An increase in the price of the asset caused, for example, by the arrival of new information would generate substantial losses. An important defense against manipulation is thus the presence of a large number of traders with ready access to the market. The new options instruments tend to be written on underlying assets for which the markets are broader and deeper than the markets for many of the individual stocks in which options are also written. They are therefore less subject to manipulation than many assets already trading.

The issue of the manipulation of the prices of financial instruments must be viewed in perspective.[13] Manipulation is, in principle, possible in any market; but it is also very difficult because (1) manipulating prices through heavy buying or selling tends to produce an opposite movement in prices when a position is reversed and (2) a manipulated price is an unjustified price that creates profit opportunities for other traders. Manipulation based on trading activity alone therefore tends to be held in check by competing traders. The existence of options trading increases the number of traders interested in determining the correct price of the underlying asset. Through arbitrage links between the option and the asset, the liquidity of the asset is increased and the manipulation made more difficult.

The role of government regulation in limiting manipulation should also be viewed in perspective. Although legal prohibition of manipulative practices is important, particularly insofar as those practices are fraudulent,[14] regulatory oversight is not adequate to detect many unjustified price movements resulting from trading activity alone. Many of those movements are smaller than the transaction costs of nonprofessional traders. Important regulatory objectives should be to see that sufficient competing investors, each with an interest in detecting unjustified price movements, are present and to ensure that transaction costs are as low as possible. Competing investors cannot be effective if transaction costs are high and trading in a security is restricted to a few professional traders. Public policy should therefore be aimed at a market structure that minimizes commission rates, bid-ask spreads, and other costs of trading and reduces communication costs. Moreover, exchanges have an incentive to eliminate manipulation since a market in which manipulation is possible does not attract traders.

A third abuse that has recently received considerable publicity is *front running*.[15] Front running is trading an option in anticipation of a large transaction in the underlying asset. A trader who knows that a large block of stock will be sold that will depress the price of the stock can purchase a put option or write a call option. When the price falls, these options' positions become profitable. Front running thus involves inside market information concerning pending transactions. Trading on market information is, of course, a common practice with or without options. Indeed, most professional traders are in search of such information, and most block traders are therefore secretive about their efforts. Options are not critical to front running since a stock can be sold short in anticipation of a large block sale to accomplish the same objective.

From the perspective of society, the harmful effects of front running are not clear. On the contrary, front running is desirable insofar as it causes securities prices to reflect the information arriving in the market more quickly. The sale of call options on 20,000 shares of stock will convey information not dissimilar to the sale of the 20,000 shares themselves, and it will depress call option prices. The information conveyed by the sale of the call options and the reduced call option price will in turn tend to depress the price of the underlying stock before the actual sale of the stock. From the perspective of market efficiency, this is desirable. The redistribution of income implied by successful front running (from the block seller to the option seller) may, however, be considered unfair. Furthermore, a market in which front running is possible is likely to discourage traders.

A third objection to option markets arises from a concern about adverse external effects on existing markets in the underlying and related instruments or on other risk-taking activities. Options might shift trading interest from the underlying instruments to the options market and thereby reduce liquidity in the underlying markets. Or options might attract risk-taking capital from other areas of economic activity, such as the new issues market for small firms or the venture capital market.

These issues have been investigated with respect to options trading in common stocks.[16] These investigations and the experience with such trading suggest that it has not had adverse external effects of the kind described. First, options do not involve the shifting of capital. Although premiums are paid in options markets, there is no reason to believe that such premiums are systematically shifted away from investment in underlying assets. Options are primarily a means of shifting risk, not of shifting capital.

Second, although options trading can, in principle, reduce the volume of trading in underlying instruments, evidence and recent experience indicate that it has not done so. The liquidity of trading in individual common stocks has been maintained in the presence of options in those stocks. Even if the volume of trading in the underlying instrument were reduced, liquidity—in the sense that large transactions can be accomplished without affecting the price— need not be adversely affected if the amount of potential volume is great. To the extent that options increase the total interest in a security, potential volume is increased. Furthermore, the existence of options permits risk shifting that can reduce the risk of taking large positions in the underlying asset and thereby increase liquidity. A contradictory objection to options trading sometimes voiced is that it increases congestion of markets when options positions are closed out or various hedge positions are offset.[17] But such activity increases volume and should be desirable from the perspective of increasing liquidity.

According to Robbins et al., the concern that options trading detracts capital from new issues is unwarranted.[18] Indeed, options do not shift capital. They may provide a useful service in broadening the range of high-risk investments available to investors. This is desirable because there is considerable academic evidence that excessive buying of new issues sometimes forces their prices to unwarranted levels.

Option Pricing

We have argued that options markets can enhance the depth and liquidity of underlying asset markets by increasing the number of

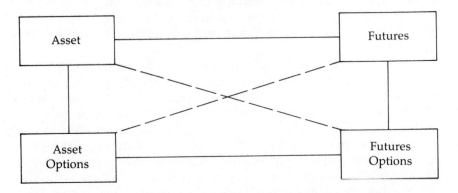

FIGURE 4–5
INTERMARKET PRICING RELATIONS

judgments bearing on the value of the underlying asset. For this argument to hold, option prices must be closely linked to underlying asset prices so that new information and other factors causing prices to change can be quickly conveyed between option and asset markets. In this section we present the pricing relations linking the underlying asset, the futures, the asset option, and the futures option and summarize the empirical evidence on the tightness of these links.

The pricing relations linking the four markets, depicted by the solid lines in figure 4–5, are maintained by two kinds of trading strategies. The first is a costless arbitrage strategy that leads to the put-call parity relation linking puts, calls, and the underlying item. The second involves hedging the option against the underlying instrument and leads to explicit valuation equations for options in terms of underlying asset prices and certain other factors.

To make statements about the pricing of options, it is useful to introduce certain notation:

S = price of the underlying asset

F = price of the futures contract written on the underlying asset

X = exercise price or striking price of the option

T = time to expiration of the option

r = (continuously compounded) riskless rate of interest

b = (continuously compounded) constant cost of carrying the underlying asset

$c(S,T,X,)$, $p(S,T,X)$ = price of European call or put option where the asset price is S, the time to expiration is T, and the exercise price is X

$C(S,T,X)$, $P(S,T,X)$ = price of the corresponding American call or put option

Prices of options on futures contracts are denoted by using F instead of S as the first argument within parentheses.

Certain option pricing results are more easily understood if the relation between the futures price and the underlying asset price is developed. For this reason we present the cost-of-carry model linking the futures price and the asset price at the outset. This is followed by discussions of the links between asset prices and asset option prices, between futures prices and futures option prices, and between asset option prices and futures option prices.

Cost-of-Carry Model. The relation between the futures price and the price of the underlying physical asset is referred to as the cost-of-carry model. To understand this relation, consider two strategies for acquiring one unit of the physical asset on a future date T. Under the first strategy, purchase $e^{(b - r)T}$ units of the asset at a cost S per unit, and hold the position until time T. The difference between b, the total cost of carrying the asset, and r, the opportunity cost of tying up funds in inventory $(b - r)$, is the component of carry costs reflecting out-of-pocket storage costs, such as warehouse rent, insurance, and spoilage. In this formulation, $b - r$ is the rate at which inventory would have to be sold off to cover the storage costs and leave one unit of the asset at time T. Under the second strategy, take a long position in the futures contract and purchase Fe^{-rT} riskless bonds.[19] At time T the proceeds from the futures position, $S_T - F$, are combined with the bond proceeds, F, to buy one unit of the asset at price S_T. This alternative provides the same inventory at T, but for a cost of Fe^{-rT} dollars. Since both strategies have the same terminal values, their initial costs must be equal, that is,

$$Se^{(b - r)T} = Fe^{-rT}$$

which implies

$$F = Se^{bT} \tag{1}$$

Equation 1 is the relation between the futures price and the underlying asset price in "full carry" market. (The horizontal link across the top of figure 4–5.)[20]

The components of the carry cost, b, depend on the nature of the underlying commodity. For an agricultural commodity such as wheat, the carrying cost includes interest plus storage costs, such as rent, insurance, and spoilage. For the assets underlying the new financial futures contracts, the only carrying cost is interest. Holding a T-bill, for example, involves only the opportunity cost of the funds used to buy it. Occasionally a financial asset underlying the futures contract pays a yield that offsets the interest cost, which results in $b < r$. The holder of a stock portfolio, such as the S&P 500 stock index, receives dividends that offset the interest cost of funds used to finance the investment. Similarly, holding a T-bond yields coupon interest, and holding a foreign currency yields the foreign interest rate.

Figures 4–6 illustrates the typical cost-of-carry relation as the futures contract approaches expiration. At any time before the expiration of the futures contract, the futures price is greater than the underlying asset price, assuming the total cost of carrying the asset is positive (that is, $b > 0$); at expiration the futures price is equal to the asset price. Both these results are used later in this section.

Linkage between the Prices of the Asset and the Asset Option. The pricing links between the asset and the asset option, depicted by the leftmost vertical line in figure 4–5 are now developed. We consider the put-call parity relation, the valuation of asset options in relation to the asset, and empirical evidence on the price links.

FIGURE 4–6

FULL CARRY COST BETWEEN FUTURES AND ASSET PRICES

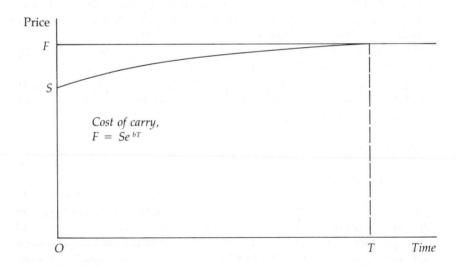

Cost of carry,
$F = Se^{bT}$

Put-call parity in asset options. Put-call parity is an arbitrage relation derived from the fact that payoffs from a position in the underlying asset can be replicated by a position in puts, calls, and riskless bonds.[21] The profit diagrams in figure 4–4 show, for example, that it is possible to generate a long position in the underlying asset by buying a call and selling a put. When alternative positions yield the same payoffs, their prices must equal; otherwise arbitragers could profit risklessly by selling the overvalued asset or portfolio and buying the undervalued asset or portfolio.

The precise nature of the put-call parity relation depends on whether the options are European (that is, can be exercised only at expiration) or American (can be exercised at any time up to and including expiration). The primary focus of this chapter is on American options since they are the only type traded in the United States; however, it is useful to develop put-call parity for the simpler European option and then extend the result to American options. In this way the mechanics of the costless arbitrage transactions can be better understood.

Put-call parity for European options on physical assets may be derived by considering a portfolio created by (1) buying $e^{(b-r)T}$ units of the asset at a cost of $Se^{(b-r)T}$; (2) buying a put option at a cost of $p(S,T,X)$; (3) selling a call option with the same exercise price as the put for proceeds, $c(S,T,X)$; and (4) borrowing Xe^{-rT}. At the expiration of the options, the value of this portfolio is equal to zero because the asset position will have deteriorated (or increased) in value to S, the long put–short call position will have the value $X - S$,[22] and repayment of the borrowing will require a cash flow of $-X$. In efficient capital markets the initial value of the portfolio must also be equal to zero, or

$$c(S,T,X) - p(S,T,X) = Se^{(b-r)T} - Xe^{-rT} \tag{2}$$

It is interesting to note that when the current asset price is equal to the exercise price of the options (that is, $S = X$), the difference between the call and the put price is

$$c(S,T,X) - p(S,T,X) = S(e^{bT} - 1)e^{-rT}$$

the present value of the cost of carrying the underlying asset to the expiration of the options.

If put-call parity is violated, a trading strategy can be used to earn an arbitrage profit. Consider, for example, options written on the S&P 100 stock index. Suppose the current index price is 100 and the call and put options with an exercise price of 100 and three months to expiration are priced at 2.50 and 1.50, respectively. If the riskless rate of interest is 12 percent annually and the dividend yield on the S&P 100 is 6 percent annually, put-call parity is violated because

$$2.50 - 1.50 < 100e^{-.06(.25)} - 100e^{-.12(.25)} = 1.47$$

The appropriate strategy to implement here is a conversion: buy a call, sell a put, sell the stock portfolio, and invest the proceeds at the riskless rate of interest. Such a strategy will ensure a riskless profit of $1.47 - 1.00 = 0.47$. Arbitragers taking advantage of such profit opportunities ensure that relation 2 holds.

The put-call parity relations for American options written on physical assets, developed by Stoll and Whaley,[23] are

$$S - X \le C(S,T,X) - P(S,T,X) \le Se^{(b-r)T} - Xe^{-rT}, \qquad \text{if } b \ge r \quad (3)$$

and

$$Se^{(b-r)T} - X \le C(S,T,X) - P(S,T,X) \le S - Xe^{-rT}, \qquad \text{if } b < r \quad (4)$$

Here the equality of the European option relation has been replaced by two inequalities because the American options may be exercised early and therefore have early exercise premiums built into their market prices.[24] The conversion and reverse conversion trading strategies used to derive relations 3 and 4 are the same as those used to derive the European put-call parity relation, except that the amounts invested in the physical asset and the riskless bonds change, depending on the nature of the asset-option price configuration.[25]

Asset option valuation. The asset option and the underlying asset are also linked because options are valued in relation to the underlying asset value. The development of asset option valuation equations requires an assumption about the nature of the underlying asset's price distribution, and the most common assumption is that the distribution is log normal. Under this assumption and the assumption that a riskless hedge may be formed between the option and the underlying asset, Black and Scholes derive the valuation equation for a European call option written on a non-dividend-paying common stock.[26] The fact that the stock does not pay dividends makes the carry cost of holding the stock equal to the riskless rate of interest ($b = r$). Asay notes that the Black-Scholes model is easily extendable to the case in which the underlying instrument is any physical asset with a continuous cost of carry b, not necessarily equal to the interest rate, r.[27] The valuation equation for a European call option written on an asset is

$$c(S,T,X) = e^{-rT}[e^{bT}SN(d_1) - XN(d_2)] \qquad (5)$$

where $d_1 = [\ln(S/X) + (b+0.5\sigma^2)T]/\sigma\sqrt{T}$; $d_2 = d_1 - \sigma\sqrt{T}$; σ is the standard deviation of the asset's rate of return; and $N(.)$ is a cumulative standard normal density function with upper integral limit d.

Although the formula appears technically complex, its meaning is fairly straightforward. At expiration the call option is worth zero if it is out of the money ($S_T \leqslant X$), and it is worth the asset price less the exercise price, $S_T - X$, if it is in the money ($S_T > X$). The expected terminal call price is therefore equal to the expected difference between the asset price and the exercise price, conditional upon the option terminating in the money times the probability that the option will expire in the money. Equation 5 merely quantifies this value. The term $Se^{bT}N(d_1)$ is the expected terminal asset price conditional upon the option finishing in the money times the probability that the option will finish in the money, while $XN(d_2)$ is the cost of exercising the option times the probability that the option will be exercised at expiration. The discount factor, e^{-rT}, merely brings the expected terminal value of the option back to the present.

The European call option valuation equation specifies the call as a function of six variables: the asset price (S), the exercise price (X), the time to expiration (T), the cost of carry (b), the riskless rate of interest (r), and the standard deviation of the underlying asset's returns (σ). The call price increases with the asset price, the time to expiration, the cost of carry, the riskless rate of interest, and the standard deviation of the asset's return and decreases with the exercise price of the option. Changes in the asset price will, by equation 5, be reflected in the option price; similarly, changes in the option price will be reflected in the asset price.

The European put option valuation equation may be derived by substituting the European call formula, 5, into the put-call parity relation, 2. The resulting equation is

$$p(S,T,X) = e^{-rT}[XN(-d_2) - e^{bT}SN(-d_1)]$$

where all notation is as it was defined for the call.

The American option valuation equations are too cumbersome to be presented here; however, it is useful to recall that the difference between American and European option prices results from the fact that American options have an early exercise privilege. The value of this privilege varies with the characteristics of the option. Below are some simulated European and American option values intended to illustrate how valuable the early exercise privilege may be.

Stock Price S	European Call c(S,T,X)	American Call C(S,T,X)	European Put p(S,T,X)	American Put P(S,T,X)
80	0.05	0.05	19.16	19.99
90	0.77	0.77	10.08	10.37
100	4.15	4.15	3.66	3.71
110	11.14	11.14	0.85	0.86
120	20.22	20.22	0.13	0.13

The values are based on the following parameters: $X = 100$, $b = 0.02$, $r = 0.10$, $\sigma = 0.20$, and $T = 0.25$. Such values might be reasonable for three-month options written on the S&P 100, where the index pays a dividend yield of 8 percent annually. For calls the European and American valuations are identical in this example, but a difference arises for puts. As one would expect, an American put is more valuable than a European put because of its early exercise feature.

Empirical evidence on the price links between assets and asset options. In efficient markets securities prices reflect underlying values. Asset options are linked to the value of the underlying asset by the put-call parity relation such as equation 2 and by valuation equations such as 5. Empirical tests of option market efficiency are tests of the degree to which these links are observed in actual markets—the degree to which options reflect underlying value as described by equations like 2 or 5. Some empirical results for stock options as well as the available evidence on the new options are summarized here.

The earliest test of put-call parity by Stoll examined weekly prices of over-the-counter options written on twenty-five stocks during the period January 1966 through December 1967.[28] Stoll did not examine the profitability of the trading strategy directly but performed various tests to verify the structure of the European put-call parity relation. His conclusion was that put and call option prices were linked to each other and to the underlying stock price by the put-call parity relation.

Klemkosky and Resnick examined the American put-call parity relation using transaction data for CBOE stock options during the period July 1977 through June 1978.[29] They determine violations of put-call parity and set up appropriate arbitrage positions to attempt to profit from the violation. A total of 606 positions were constructed during the period. Only 27 percent were profitable after a $20 transaction cost was imposed, and only 7 percent were profitable after a $60 transaction cost was imposed. They concluded that the CBOE is an efficient market and that the put-call parity pricing links are well supported within the bounds of transaction costs.

Chin investigated the put-call parity relation for American asset options, using weekly option prices for the West German mark options trading on the Philadelphia Stock Exchange during the period October 1982 through December 1984.[30] He found that only 2 of the 207 arbitrage positions were profitable before transaction costs and that none were profitable after reasonable transaction costs were imposed. He concluded that the West German mark options are efficiently priced, at least with respect to finding costless arbitrage opportunities.

The second category of market efficiency tests involves using an option valuation equation like 5 to identify mispriced options. Under-priced options are assumed to be bought and overpriced options sold in an attempt to investigate whether abnormal profits may be earned. If they can, mispriced options must have existed, and the market is deemed to be inefficient.

The first systematic test of option market efficiency using an option valuation model was by Black and Scholes.[31] The data used in their examination were call option prices for OTC options written on 545 common stocks during the period 1966 through 1969. The model used was the Black-Scholes European call option pricing equation. They found that significantly positive excess returns could be earned by trading on the basis of their model but, once reasonable transaction costs were imposed, the profits disappeared.

Whaley investigated the efficiency of the CBOE, using the American call option pricing equation.[32] On the basis of weekly call option data for the period 1975 through February 1978, Whaley's trading strategy generated a 2.46 percent weekly return. Using the Phillips and Smith estimates of transaction costs for CBOE options, Whaley found that after transaction costs trading profits were eliminated.[33] He concluded that CBOE market efficiency is well supported.

Shastri and Tandon examined the efficiency of the Philadelphia Stock Exchange's foreign currency options market, using transaction data for the period February 1983 through August 1984.[34] The pricing model used was the American asset option valuation equation, where the cost of carrying the currency is the domestic interest rate less the foreign interest rate. No profitable deviations from the pricing model (after transaction costs) were found.

In summary, the empirical tests of put-call parity and asset option valuation indicate that the over-the-counter, CBOE, and Philadelphia

247

option markets are efficient and that option prices and asset prices are closely linked. Not even member firms that have low transaction costs can benefit by engaging in arbitrage activities based on put-call parity or a valuation model. The information impounded in option prices appears to be quickly and efficiently impounded in asset prices, and vice versa.

Linkage between the Prices of the Futures and the Futures Options. This subsection is devoted to a description of the pricing links between the futures and the futures option markets (those depicted by the rightmost vertical line in figure 4–5). The discussion is divided into three parts—put-call parity, option valuation, and empirical evidence.

Put-call parity in futures options. The put-call parity relation for European futures options is

$$c(F,T,X) - p(F,T,X) = e^{-rT}(F - X) \qquad (6)$$

To derive this relation, consider a portfolio consisting of a long position in the futures contract, a long position in the put option, a short position in the call option, and a long position of $(F - X)e^{-rT}$ riskless bonds. The terminal value of this portfolio is equal to zero because the futures contract will have a value $F_T - X$ and the long put–short call position will have a value $X - F_T$. As a result the initial net investment cost must also be equal to zero; otherwise costless arbitrage profits could be earned. If the net investment is equal to zero, then equation 6 must hold.

Note the similarity between the put-call parity for European futures options (equation 6) and the put-call parity for European asset options (equation 2). If the futures price, F, from the cost-of-carry relation (1) is substituted for Se^{bT} on the right-hand side of (2), the right-hand side of (6) is obtained. The intuition here is that the futures price in (6) impounds the cost of carrying the underlying asset, which appears explicitly in (2).

Put-call parity for American futures options, derived by Stoll and Whaley,[35] is

$$Fe^{-rT} - X \leq C(F,T,X) - P(F,T,X) \leq F - Xe^{-rT}$$

Again the inequalities result from the early exercise premiums of the American options. Conversion and reverse conversion trading strategies in an efficiently operating capital market ensure that the relationship holds.

Futures option valuation. Under the assumption that futures prices are log-normally distributed, Black derived the valuation equation for a European call option written on a futures contract.[36] The valuation equation is

$$c(F,T,X) = e^{-rT}[FN(d_1) - XN(d_2)] \tag{7}$$

where $d_1 = [\ln(F/X) + 0.5\sigma^2 T]/\sigma\sqrt{T}$ and $d_2 = d_1 - \sigma\sqrt{T}$. All other notation has been previously defined.

Again the formula has intuitive appeal. The term $FN(d_1)$ is the expected terminal futures price conditional on the call option finishing in the money times the probability that the option will finish in the money, and $XN(d_2)$ is the cost of exercising the option times the probability that the option will be exercised. In other words, the current value of the call is simply the present value of the amount that is expected when the call option expires.

The European put option written on a futures contract has the value

$$p(F,T,X) = e^{-rT}[XN(-d_2) - FN(-d_1)]$$

where all notation is as it was defined for the call.

The American call option formulas are too cumbersome to be presented here, but a numerical example may prove illuminating.

Stock Price S	European Call $c(S,T,X)$	American Call $C(S,T,X)$	European Put $p(S,T,X)$	American Put $P(S,T,X)$
80.40	0.05	0.05	19.16	19.59
90.45	0.77	0.77	10.08	10.18
100.50	4.15	4.17	3.66	3.68
110.55	11.14	11.25	0.85	0.85
120.60	20.22	20.62	0.13	0.13

The values are based on the following parameters: $X = 100$, $b = 0.02$, $r = 0.10$, $\sigma = 0.20$, and $T = 0.25$—the same as those used to price the asset options. As before, the American put is more valuable than the European put, because of its early exercise feature. But now the American call on a futures contract is more valuable than the corresponding European call, something not observed for asset options. This result is due to the daily settlement feature of futures contracts, which makes cash available when in-the-money futures options are exercised.

Empirical evidence. Since futures option markets are a relatively recent development, little empirical research on the pricing links such as (6) or (7) has been carried out, although some unpublished research on these links is under way.

Chin investigated the efficiency of the West German mark futures option market at the Chicago Mercantile Exchange, using weekly price observations for the period January 1984 through February 1985.[37] Of the 532 arbitrage positions he constructed, only 13 were profitable before transaction costs. After transaction costs only 11 remained, roughly 2 percent of the sample. On the basis of this result, Chin concluded that the put-call parity price linkage is supported for the West German option.

Whaley used the American futures option valuation equations to identify mispriced S&P 500 futures options during the period January 1983 through December 1983.[38] He demonstrated that the option pricing model is able to generate significant abnormal profits before transaction costs and, for out-of-the-money put options, after transaction costs. His evidence provides weak support of inefficiencies in this market.

Using the same methods, Stoll and Whaley examined the efficiency of the T-bond futures option market at the Chicago Board of Trade during the period October 1982 through December 1983. Before transaction costs trading profits did appear; after reasonable costs were imposed, however, the average profit was not significantly different from zero.

In summary, the results of the tests of futures option market efficiency are not as strong as they are for asset option market efficiency since one market—the S&P 500 futures option market— appeared to exhibit certain pricing inefficiencies. As market participants gain experience, however, one would expect these inefficiencies to disappear. Overall, the preliminary evidence of these studies indicates that arbitrage forces are active in establishing and maintaining the put-call parity pricing link as well as the valuation link.

Asset Option–Futures Option Pricing Relations. When the futures, futures options, and asset options expire at the same time, T, and have the same exercise price, the prices of European asset and futures options are equal (the horizontal line at the bottom of figure 4–5), that is,

$$c(F,T,X) = c(S,T,X)$$

and

$$p(F,T,X) = p(S,T,X)$$

The reasons for these equalities are that (1) the options are European and hence cannot be exercised before their expiration; and (2) the value of the futures contract is equal to the value of the underlying asset when the contract expires. Since the payoff contingencies are the same as those posed by the asset options, they must have the same value.

The American options trading in the United States, however, do not share the same values. The American call option on a futures contract is worth at least as much as the American call option on the asset.

$$C(F,T,X) \geqq C(S,T,X) \qquad (8)$$

The American put option on a physical asset is worth at least as much as the American put option on the futures contract.

$$P(S,T,X) \geqq P(F,T,X) \qquad (9)$$

These results arise because, before expiration, the futures price exceeds the asset price. Therefore, the American call written on the futures contract has a higher value than the American call written on the asset, other factors remaining the same. Conversely, the American put option on the asset has a higher value than the American put option on the futures contract because the lower the value of the underlying instrument, the higher the value of the right to sell the underlying asset at the exercise price.

One asset on which both asset options and futures options are traded is the West German mark. The asset options trade on the Philadelphia Stock Exchange and the futures options on the Chicago Mercantile Exchange. Since the two options expire within a couple of days of each other, conditions (8) and (9) should hold in an approximate sense for these options. Chin investigated these relations, using weekly data for the period January 1984 through February 1985.[39] Before transaction costs the call options violated (8) in 286 of 393 cases, and put options violated (9) in only 14 of 209 cases. After transaction costs, the number of violations were 21 and 3 for calls and puts, respectively. He concluded that the German mark option markets were efficient and the links, (8) and (9), reasonably tight once transaction costs were accounted for.

Summary and Conclusion. In this section, the pricing relations linking an underlying asset, futures on the asset, options on the asset, and options on the futures have been developed and empirically examined. The empirical evidence supports the hypothesis that these pricing links are reasonably tight—generally within the bounds of transaction costs. Because the markets appear to be closely linked, the evidence indirectly supports the hypothesis that the option markets provide greater depth and liquidity in the underlying instrument's market and vice versa.

Success and Failure of the New Option Instruments

In this section the factors underlying the introduction, success, and failure of financial innovations are discussed, and some limited evidence on recent experience in the new options instruments is presented. We also consider policy issues related to the need for regulatory oversight of the introduction of new options instruments and the issue of contract proliferation.

Preconditions for Exchange-traded Options. The success of the new options instruments requires that certain preconditions that would apply equally well to other financial innovations, such as the new futures contracts, be met.

Uncertainty. Trading in options, like trading in futures, depends on the existence of uncertainty about the future value of the underlying instrument. Indeed, the basis for trading options is disagreement about the degree of uncertainty or the allocation of uncertainty among different market participants. Currency options, for example, would not exist if exchange rates were fixed. Similarly, options in agricultural commodities would not arise if government price support programs limited price variability.

Standardization. Exchange-traded options require standardized contracts, for without standardization secondary markets do not arise. An important role of exchanges and clearinghouses is to legitimate and guarantee standardized contracts so as to minimize the credit risk of dealing with a particular individual. In the view of Telser and Higinbotham, the creation of a standard contract that facilitates "trade among strangers" is the key reason for trading in futures contracts.[40] In their view futures contracts provide an alternative, lower-cost means of trading the underlying asset.

Liquidity. Like futures contracts, exchange-traded options cannot succeed without sufficient interest on the part of users to ensure a liquid market. A liquid market is one in which a reasonable number of contracts can be traded without affecting the price. Liquidity thus requires sufficient competing investors, with no single investor having an overwhelming influence on the price either of the option or of the underlying asset. Liquid markets not only facilitate day-to-day trading but also guard against the possibility that the price may be manipulated or that a short squeeze or corner may be engineered.

Deliverability. In the past deliverability was considered essential to futures and options contracts.[41] Many of the new options and futures contracts do not call for delivery but instead call for cash settlement. Under cash settlement the individual exercising the option receives the difference between the exercise price and the current price of the underlying asset in cash instead of receiving the asset itself. Cash settlement is desirable because it eliminates delivery problems associated with acquiring the asset to make delivery. Cash settlement is problematic if the price of the asset is difficult to determine.[42]

Sophisticated financial markets. The new option instruments demand a considerable degree of sophistication on the part of financial institutions, market professionals, individual investors, and other market participants because options instruments are complex and the factors determining options prices are more complicated and less familiar than those determining the prices of other financial instruments. The successful experience with options on common stocks and the growth of the financial services industry have undoubtedly helped to set the stage for the new option instruments.

Options versus Futures. The preconditions for options apply equally well to futures contracts. What explains why futures markets arise for some underlying assets, options markets for others, and both options and futures markets for still others? In a recent paper Jaffee suggests that

> futures markets will arise first for those commodities with particularly imperfect spot markets (for example, with respect to facilities for margin purchases and short sales), whereas option markets will first appear for those commodities that have relatively well functioning spot markets, but which require additional facilities for risk sharing and hedging.[43]

He cites as evidence for this suggestion the development of stock index futures before options on stock indexes, because of spot market problems of trading stock indexes, and the development of options on individual stocks rather than on futures because of the efficient spot markets for trading but not risk sharing of individual stocks.

This view is consistent with the Telser-Higinbotham justification of futures markets as an alternative means of trading the underlying asset. Options provide an additional benefit—a means of sharing risk—that futures do not provide. Thus it would not be surprising to find both futures and options in underlying assets that have trading imperfections, which would include most commodities but also stock indexes and bonds. Stock indexes are not readily tradable, although mutual funds might approximate them. Most mutual funds are not traded in secondary markets, cannot be purchased on margin, and cannot readily be sold short. Similarly, many bonds are not traded actively in smaller amounts. One might thus expect both futures markets and option markets to arise in these markets. Since individual stocks are actively traded in an efficient market, however, an option market would seem to suffice, and futures on individual stocks would not be expected to arise.

Elements of Contract Design. A critical factor in the success or failure of the new options instruments is contract design. Optimal design in options, as in futures, necessitates that precise specification and standardization of the contract be balanced against its liquidity requirements. Precise specification can lead to a clearly but narrowly defined contract that is extremely useful to a few traders but of limited interest to the majority of traders. Such a contract may fail because of a lack of liquidity. A more broadly defined contract of some use to many market participants may succeed even though it is not ideal from the perspective of any participant.

Number of contract series. Any option on an underlying asset is a series of option contracts varying in expiration month and exercise price. The choice of these is an important element in contract design.

Too many expiration months detract from liquidity in any one month. Too few expiration months force certain traders to trade options of a maturity not suited to their needs. Thus the number of months chosen is restricted by the need to maintain liquidity in each of the months. The new options instruments rarely trade in more than three expiration months, and volume in the more distant months tends to be less than volume in the nearer months. As shown in table 4–2, most options written directly on stock indexes have a monthly cycle, that is, have contracts that expire in each of the next three months. Expiration months of options on futures tend to be determined by the futures maturity cycle, although trading is usually limited to the three nearest months.

Interest in options tends to be greatest when the striking price is at the price of the underlying asset. Consider a call option. If the striking price is too low, the option is in the money and begins to trade more like the underlying instrument and less like an option.

If the striking price to too high, the option is out of the money and has reduced price sensitivity. Exchanges therefore introduce option series the striking prices of which bracket the current market price of the underlying asset. Whenever the underlying asset price changes by a predetermined amount, a new option series is introduced. In the futures options on the S&P 500 stock index, for example, a new option series is introduced whenever the underlying index changes by five or more. In the futures options on T-bonds, new options are introduced whenever the underlying futures price changes by two or more.

The underlying asset. A key factor in the success of new options is the nature of the underlying item against which the option is written and the delivery terms associated with that item.

The strong similarities between an option on the physical asset and an option on the futures on the asset have been noted. Options on futures appear to have some practical advantages, however. First, many physicals make income payments or cause holding costs to be incurred that make pricing the option on the physical more complicated than pricing the option on a futures. In bonds, for example, accrued interest must be taken account of. In stock indexes dividend payments must be taken account of. Agricultural commodities incur storage costs that affect the price of the cash commodity. Options on futures are simpler because futures contracts make no payments and incur no costs of this kind. The futures price is based on the expectation of the price of the underlying asset after the period over which payments are made or costs incurred. In other words, futures contracts take account of income payments or storage costs so that options on futures need not.

Second, futures options simplify exercise of the option since the futures contract itself is delivered. Exercising an option on the physical may call either for delivery of the physical itself or for cash settlement. Delivery of the futures contract is frequently simpler, particularly since futures exchanges have tested methods for making such deliveries.

Third, futures contracts are themselves traded in exchange markets and thereby provide price information useful in pricing options. Prices are not so readily available for certain underlying assets. Prices for most debt instruments, which trade in over-the-counter markets, are difficult to determine. Prices of stock indexes are calculated from the prices of individual stocks at certain intervals and with some delay.

Another factor determining the success of an option, whether

255

written on the futures or directly on the physical, is the choice of underlying asset. A variety of debt instruments could serve as the underlying asset for a debt option. Similarly, a variety of stock indexes could serve as the underlying asset for a stock index option. Clearly, the recognition of and level of activity in the particular underlying asset are important. But beyond these a number of more complicated issues arise.

Several choices of debt instruments are possible: an index of debt instruments, a specific existing debt instrument, or a specific, yet-to-be-issued debt instrument. A debt index, like a stock index, would be a weighted combination, or a portfolio, of certain debt instruments. No options on debt indexes are now traded.

Options on specific government securities with broad markets are traded on the CBOE and the AMEX (options on T-bonds and on T-notes). These options are written on specific debt instruments existing at the time the option is originated, and they call for delivery of that instrument. Over the life of the option, the maturity of the underlying debt instrument declines, and this can affect the pricing of the option (beyond the complications associated with accounting for accrued interest).

Options on T-bond futures (on the CBT) are less complicated since they call for delivery of the futures contract if exercised. Options on T-bills (on the AMEX) are written on a yet-to-be-issued thirteen-week T-bill. If exercised, the option calls for delivery, on the Thursday of the week following the exercise, of a T-bill having thirteen weeks to maturity (which is generally the bill to be auctioned in the next week). Thus the instrument to be delivered is fixed in its characteristics (that is, maturity) but is not outstanding at the time the option is written. Arbitrage between the option and the underlying item is thus more complex and requires the use of the nearby T-bill.

Other factors in contract design. Several other factors are relevant in contract design. These include contract size, allowable price variation, position and exercise limits, trading hours, and margins. Of these, margins have received the most attention, in part because of the disparities in margin regulation of futures products and stock products. This issue is analyzed in greater detail later.

Competitive Factors. Another important element in the success or failure of particular options is the degree of competition among exchanges offering the same or similar options. As is evident in table 4–2, direct competition among two or more exchanges exists in options written on similar underlying assets. Physical options on stock indexes are offered by the CBOE, the NYSE, the AMEX, the Philadelphia

Stock Exchange, and the Pacific Coast Exchange; and physical options on Treasury securities are offered by the CBOE and the AMEX. Futures options on stock indexes are offered by the CME and the NYFE, and futures options on Treasury securities are offered by the CBT.

Given identically designed options instruments, two competitive factors are relevant to the success or failure of a particular exchange's contract. These are (1) which exchange is first to market and (2) which exchange has the superior reputation.

First to market. Evidence suggests that trading in financial instruments is a natural monopoly, all other things being equal. In a natural monopoly the average cost of producing a product or service declines with the volume. A natural monopoly in the trading of a security arises because trading goes where trading is. Investors desire liquidity and will trade at the exchange that has existing volume. Thus the exchange that is first to market and generates initial volume is more likely to attract additional volume than an exchange that introduces a contract at a later date.[44]

The rush by exchanges to introduce new financial instruments and their concern about regulatory delay reflects their recognition of the importance of being first to market. To the extent that the exchanges are successful in bringing similar products to market at approximately the same time, the advantage of being first to market is eliminated. Success and failure then depend on other factors, such as contract design.

Exchange competence. The success of a contract also depends on the public's view of the exchange's competence. This depends on the exchange's experience, financial integrity, and trading efficiency. Experience depends, among other things, on the number of years that an exchange has successfully offered contracts similar to the one being introduced. The financial integrity of an exchange is based on mechanisms that ensure the integrity of its members and on evidence of financial strength. Trading efficiency is derived from trading mechanisms that minimize the cost to investors of trading the instrument. Some exchanges use specialist-based trading systems; others use futures trading systems. The success of contracts depends in part on the efficiency of the trading system.[45]

Government Policy. Government regulatory policy has influenced the pace of financial innovation both broadly, by affecting the general economic conditions conducive to financial innovation, and narrowly, by affecting the success of particular new instruments.

Broad government policy. Broad government policy has affected the pace of financial innovation in at least two ways. First, the deregulation of financial markets, including such regulatory changes as lifting interest rate ceilings that apply to banks, lessening barriers to competition among financial institutions of all types, and deregulating the stock market, have reduced the profit margins of financial institutions and intensified the competition for customers. This situation, along with increased uncertainty in the economy and the increased sophistication of investors, has generated a demand for new financial instruments on the part of retail customers and a need on the part of many financial institutions for new tools for managing risk.

Second, government tax policy has influenced the development of new financial instruments. The taxation of futures contracts, in particular, has received significant attention in recent years. Trading in certain futures contracts was stimulated by their use as a means of postponing or avoiding taxes. For example, by setting up a spread— a long position in one contract month and a short position in another— traders created for themselves an option to realize the leg of the spread that generated a loss that could be used to reduce taxes. The tax treatment of futures contracts was modified by the Economic Recovery Tax Act of 1981 to require taxation of gains and losses whether realized or not. Such gains and losses on commodity futures positions are taxed at a maximum rate of 32 percent under current law (60 percent of any gain or loss is long term, taxed at a maximum of 20 percent; 40 percent is short-term gain, taxed at a maximum rate of 50 percent). The 1984 tax bill accords options on instruments other than individual stocks or narrow-based stock indexes the same tax treatment as futures contracts.

A significant number of complications and unresolved issues remain with respect to the taxation of options and futures. These are beyond the scope of this chapter. Suffice it to say that the growth of trading in particular options instruments will be influenced by their tax treatment. To the extent, for example, that a position using options permits an investor to replicate a position in an underlying instrument at a lower tax obligation, trading in such options will be stimulated. Hamada and Scholes discuss some instances of tax arbitrage that can benefit certain kinds of investors.[46]

Specific regulatory policy. Specific regulatory policies of the SEC and the CFTC affect the success of new option instruments. Options on futures can be purchased only in a commodity account from an account executive qualified to trade commodities, and options on physicals are purchased in a securities account from account executives qualified in options. Since securities accounts outnumber commodity accounts, options on futures contracts are at a marketing disadvantage with respect to options on physicals. Individual investors may be reluctant to set up a commodity account and may choose simply to trade those options eligible for trading in a securities account.

A number of other regulatory disparities can affect the success of options on futures vis-à-vis options on physicals.[47] Disclosure requirements and surveillance procedures, for example, differ between futures and physicals. Margin regulations also differ. In particular, the cost of margining securities products appears to be higher than the cost of margining futures products. This issue is discussed in greater detail later in this chapter.

Evidence. Evidence on the relative success of the various new options instruments is presented in table 4–4, in which option contracts are ranked by open interest on July 26, 1984, within four major categories—options on stock indexes, on debt instruments, on currencies, and on commodity futures. Corresponding volume data for the week ending July 27, 1984, are also presented. (Ranking contracts by volume instead of open interest would have produced nearly the same ranking.) Several conclusions emerge from this evidence, although a more complete history and a more careful analysis will be required to reach definitive conclusions.

• The broad stock indexes have been extremely successful as a group. The top five options accounted for put and call contracts on over $13 billion of the underlying assets on July 26, 1984.
• The narrow stock indexes have generated much less interest. The five most successful narrow-based indexes had a total open interest of about $250 million, less than 2 percent of the total open interest of the top five broad stock indexes. Several contracts have been delisted.
• The competitive success of different contracts is not yet wholly clear. The options on the S&P 100 (CBOE) are by far the most active of the broad index options, followed by the CME futures options on the S&P 500. Some factors contributing to the success of this contract are that it was nearly first to market (second to the S&P 500 futures options), that it was introduced by an exchange with experience in option trading, and that it benefits from the existence of futures on the same underlying index, something that is helpful in pricing the option.[48] The greater success of the CBOE S&P 100 option than of the CME S&P 500 futures options may also be due to the larger

TABLE 4–4

Dollar Open Interest and Dollar Volume of Trading for Options Ranked by Dollar Value of Open Interest on July 26, 1984

Underlying Instrument (Exchange)	Open Interest ($ million)	Volume Week Ending July 27, 1984 ($ million)
Options on stock indexes and stock index futures		
S&P 100 (CBOE)	10,097	16,290
S&P 500 futures (CME)	1,820	854
NYSE composite (NYSE)	1,018	497
Major market (AMEX)	646	230
NYSE composite futures (NYFE)	250	148
Computer technology (AMEX)	116	161
Oil and gas (AMEX)	69	17
Market value (AMEX)	62	52
Gold/silver (Philadelphia)	55	25
Transportation (AMEX)	7	13
S&P 500 (CBOE)	3	0.5
Gaming/hotel (Philadelphia)	a	a
Technology (Pacific)	a	a
Transportation (CBOE)	a	a
Value Line index (KCBT)	Delisted	
S&P international oils (CBOE)	Delisted	
Computer and business equipment (CBOE)	Delisted	
Telephone (CBOE)	Delisted	
Options on debt instruments and debt instrument futures		
T-bond futures (CBT)	28,276	19,669
T-bonds (CBOE)	2,443	645
T-bills (AMEX)	1,840	951
T-notes (AMEX)	a	a
Options on currencies and currency futures		
British pound (Philadelphia)		
Canadian dollar (Philadelphia)		
West German mark (Philadelphia)	2,024[b]	902[b]
Japanese yen (Philadelphia)		
Swiss franc (Philadelphia)		
West German mark futures (CME)	1,625	927
Options on commodity futures		
Gold (COMEX)	2,107	953
Sugar	18	182

NOTES: Dollar open interest is the sum of put open interest and call open interest times the dollar value of the contract. Dollar volume is the put and call contract volume times the contract value. For abbreviations of exchange names, see table 4–2.

a. Data not available in the *Wall Street Journal*. Presumed to be small.

b. Only the total number of contracts in all Philadelphia currencies was available. Dollar figures based on a dollar contract size of $22,000 in each currency. Dollar contract size ranged from approximately $17,500 for the British pound to approximately $38,500 for the Canadian dollar.

SOURCE: *Wall Street Journal*.

number of investors trading CBOE stock options in securities accounts and the lack of familiarity of futures market traders with the stock market. Some of the other broad index options appear to be sufficiently profitable to continue their operation. The option on the NYSE composite index benefits from the strength of the NYSE as an institution and the existence of a futures on the same index. The failure of the option written directly on the S&P 500 is somewhat surprising in view of the success of the option on the S&P 100 and the fact that the S&P 500 is much more widely known. The failure of the option on the Value Line futures index on the KCBT reflects the low volume of the underlying futures, the secondary status of the exchange, and the problematical characteristics of the Value Line index.[49]

• Among the debt options only the option on the T-bond futures is a clear success. Unlike the most active stock index options, this is an option on a futures contract, which has a number of benefits (pricing information is readily available; arbitrage and delivery are simpler). Options written directly on debt instruments do not appear to have generated much demand.

• Options on currencies and on currency futures, though not generating the level of activity of some of the options on stock indexes, appear to be successful. The relative advantages of options on futures (the German mark on the CME) and options directly on the currency (the Philadelphia currency options) have yet to be fully tested.

• Only two options on commodity futures had traded at the time these data were compiled. The gold options had had some success, but the sugar options had attracted very little interest.

Competition, Regulation, and the Option Approval Process. The pace at which new futures and options contracts are being introduced to the financial markets has confused the public and overwhelmed even expert market observers. Cries for a more orderly introduction of new instruments have arisen from various sources, including legislators, regulators, and the industry. The costs and benefits of moderating the pace of financial innovation are considered here.

A characteristic of an innovating industry is a state of confusion in the early stages of development as many firms rush to be first to market. Frequently an incomprehensible array of products, not all of which function properly and some of which are poorly designed, are brought onto the market. Consumers are confused, and prices are highly variable. These characteristics describe the introduction not only of new financial instruments but also of new products in other industries, such as the personal computer industry in the 1980s or the automobile industry in the 1920s. A shakeout phase and a period of confusion are typical of new industries. Usually competitive forces are left to determine which producers and which products survive.

Our analysis of success and failure has already shown that this competitive process is rationalizing the market for new options instruments. Relatively few contracts are outstandingly successful. Many have been failures, including most of the narrow stock indexes and options written directly on Treasury securities. In fact, there may be little need for regulatory oversight of the innovation process since the competitive process appears to be a relatively quick and effective means of disciplining exchanges.

Financial instruments do differ from other products, however, in that certain external effects may be associated with the introduction of similar competing financial products by different exchanges. As Silber has noted, competition among exchanges in the same instrument fragments trading and reduces the liquidity in each market.[50] This is undesirable since the efficiency of a market is related to its volume of trading. No exchange introducing a new product will take account of this external effect, although exchanges acting as a group or acting through regulators might well agree to share markets in some way so as to avoid fragmentation. An argument, therefore, for regulation of the innovation process and contract review is that they are needed to guard against fragmentation of markets.

There are two counterarguments to this position, as Silber has also noted.[51] First, fragmentation of financial markets is less serious than it may at first appear since an arbitrage mechanism connects the various markets. Market professionals have memberships on a variety of exchanges and are in a position to arbitrage price discrepancies. As long as prices in one market are kept from deviating from prices in another, various physically separate markets behave, from the perspective of pricing, as if they were one market. The ease of such arbitrage, of course, depends on the transaction costs and communication costs associated with accomplishing it, and regulators should be concerned that no artificial barriers are imposed on arbitrage. A second counterargument is that limiting fragmentation by limiting the introduction of competing instruments limits competition and favors one exchange over another. Restricting competition also limits the innovation process.

The CFTC options pilot program limits the pace of financial innovation, and the desirability of restricting the number of options that each exchange may trade may be questioned. Regulatory oversight may be desirable from the perspective of customer protection and maintenance of the integrity of financial markets, so that regulators may gain experience with new products and so that financial markets may assimilate new products in an orderly fashion.[52] The pilot program can be broadened, however, to allow the introduction of more products while still permitting the CFTC to maintain the necessary oversight and gain the necessary experience. This broadening of allowable products is particularly justified if additional products of a similar kind are to be offered for which regulatory analysis has already been performed.

Margin Requirements

The advent of related financial instruments under the jurisdiction of different regulatory agencies raises issues of regulatory disparity. One of the most important of these is the issue of margin requirements. Under the Securities Act of 1934, the SEC has the authority to oversee exchange rules including margin rules, and the Federal Reserve has the authority to set initial margins on equities and other "securities." The Federal Reserve has for a long time regulated margins on equity securities but did not establish margins on securities options until 1977, when it issued margin requirements that mirrored industry practice. Margins on futures contracts and on options on futures contracts are set by individual futures exchanges and have not been subject to the jurisdiction of the CFTC or the Federal Reserve. In this section we review the rationale for regulatory authority over margins as applied to options, the factors relevant to setting margins on options contracts, and alternative margin systems for options. Some of these same topics are discussed in recent papers by Figlewski and by Phillips and Tosini.[53]

Margins on Stocks versus Margins on Futures versus Margins on Options. Margins on options and futures should be distinguished from margins on common stocks. The margin on a common stock constitutes the percentage of the total purchase price paid by the investor. The remainder is borrowed. Currently, the initial margin on common stocks, set by the Federal Reserve, is 50 percent, and the maintenance margin, set by the individual exchange, is 30 percent. Margins on common stocks control the amount of credit that various lenders may extend for the purchase of stocks. The desire to control the extension of credit was a reason for establishing margin requirements on stocks.

Margins on futures contracts constitute a guarantee of performance of a contractual obligation. When a futures contract is entered into, no credit is extended, no asset changes hands, and no payment

263

is made by the buyer to the seller. Only if delivery is made is full payment (part of which could be borrowed) required. Both the buyer and the seller of a futures contract deposit margin, which may frequently be in the form of interest-earning assets rather than cash. Positions in futures contracts are marked to market daily as the futures price changes. Investors are required to make up any losses or to withdraw any profits. These payments from losers to gainers, called "variation margin," must be in cash.

Options have some features of common stocks and some features of futures contracts. As in common stocks, a payment is made when the option contract is entered into. The buyer of an option pays a premium for an insurance service rendered by the seller of an option. The buyer of a call option, for example, has a right to purchase the underlying asset at a known exercise price and is insured against any losses if the underlying asset price falls below the exercise price. Although no asset changes hands when an option contract is entered into, payment for the "insurance service" is made, and money changes hands. Under current margin procedures for futures options as well as securities options, the buyer of a put or call pays 100 percent of the premium. Suggestions have been made, however, that premiums on futures options be marginable. Sellers of options have contractual obligations, and margins on sellers are performance guarantees in the same way as margins on futures contracts. The clearinghouse that guarantees the performance of the seller must be assured that the seller can carry out his obligation, and it requires margin at least as great as the current market value of the seller's obligation. In the subsequent discussion, margins are viewed as a performance guarantee, not as a method for regulating credit.

Current Margins on Options. Appendix A lists customer margin requirements on naked long or short positions in put and call option contracts representative of margin requirements established by the different futures exchanges and stock exchanges.[54] In all cases— whether individual common stocks or futures contracts—the buyer of options (the long) pays 100 percent of the premium.

Substantial differences arise in the margining of the seller's position (the short position). Options on common stocks and narrow-based indexes have margins based on the cost of acquiring the underlying instrument for delivery, whereas margins on other options are premium based. The writer of a call option on an individual stock is required to post 30 percent of the value of the stock—the stock exchange's maintenance margin on long stock positions. This is the minimum margin required as collateral on a loan to purchase common stocks, and it is in this sense that margins on stock options are security based. As Figlewski has pointed out, this can lead to substantial overmargining.[55]

Margins on other options are premium based in the sense that the investor is required to post as margin the premium plus a "cushion." A premium-based margining system assumes that the option seller's obligations may be met by covering his short position, not necessarily by delivering the underlying asset. As long as the seller posts sufficient funds to cover the short position, which would require the outlay of the current premium, the obligation is met. Premium-based systems thus require the premium to be marked to market and a cushion to protect the broker during the period in which the margin call is made.

Rationale for Margin Regulation. The rationale for officially regulating margin requirements is conditioned by their purpose. Margin regulations may be viewed as protection for the customer or as protection for the financial system.[56]

Protection for customers. The rationale for margin as a protection for customers hinges on the idea that investors must be protected from excessive speculation. Setting margin requirements sufficiently high makes speculation costly and thereby reduces it. This rationale played an important role in the 1930s legislation that gave the Federal Reserve authority to set initial margins on common stocks.

The efficacy of margin requirements in limiting speculative excesses in the stock market is subject to considerable dispute. First, there is evidence that securities markets are efficient in the sense that prices reflect underlying values. Indeed, excessive margin requirements may limit the supply of risk capital that maintains market efficiency and contributes to market liquidity. Second, empirical evidence on margin requirements in the stock market suggests that margin requirements have little effect on stock prices.[57] Margin requirements may be ineffective because the bulk of investors behave in the same way regardless of the margin requirements or because margin requirements may be evaded by using other assets as collateral for borrowing.

The dispute arises because proponents of margin regulation question the efficiency of the stock market and the limited effect ascribed to margin regulations. Furthermore, their concern is with respect to small, unsophisticated investors who are drawn unknowingly into a playing arena with which they are unfamiliar. Margin requirements are needed to protect these unsophisticated investors from committing excessive capital to the stock market or the futures markets. At issue then is what Figlewski calls "investor sovereignty"—whether individual investors will be allowed to make their own mistakes or will be inhibited in their investment decisions by margin requirements set for them by a regulatory authority.[58]

Protection for the financial system. A second rationale for margins is the protection of the financial system. Brokers, dealers, and other financial institutions are linked with one another and with their customers by a variety of financial obligations. Loss of confidence in a particular broker can produce a run on that broker and place strains on the entire financial system. Margin requirements are thus necessary to protect the financial integrity of individual brokers and thereby the entire financial system.

This rationale for regulating margins has been questioned, however. It is in the interest of each brokerage firm to protect itself against bankruptcy and to ensure that its customers can meet their obligations. Furthermore, it is in the interest of exchanges to ensure the financial integrity of their members, since the desirability of trading on an exchange depends in part on its financial strength. Exchanges establish minimum margin requirements for their members and customers of their members whether or not such requirements are mandated by regulatory authorities. Moreover, exchanges typically maintain a guarantee fund to support any member firms that are in danger of failing.

Only when regulatory authorities provide insurance, as through the Securities Investor Protection Corporation (SIPC) in the securities industry, is the rationale for the regulatory establishment of margins clearer. For then the ultimate guarantor of firms is the government, and the government must protect its guarantee fund in the same way that any exchange would wish to protect itself. This rationale for margin setting applies to options on common stocks and on indexes purchased in securities accounts eligible for SIPC protection. It does not apply to futures contracts or options on futures, which are not eligible for SIPC protection. This rationale does not necessarily imply that government margin on options in securities accounts insured by SIPC would be different from margins on options in futures accounts not insured by SIPC but guaranteed by an exchange. Nor does it imply that margins are necessarily the optimal method of protecting the government insurance fund. Other methods, such as reserves, segregation of funds, and capital requirements, may be more effective.

Factors Affecting the Appropriate Margins on Options and Futures.
Setting margins on options and futures, whether from the perspective of a regulator, an exchange, or an individual firm, is a complex
process. The optimal margin depends on characteristics of the customer,
characteristics of the security, characteristics of the market, and characteristics of the transaction.

Characteristics of the customer. Margins are a guarantee that the
customer will adhere to the contract. The need for such a guarantee,
therefore, depends on the customer's ability and willingness to honor
the contract. Among other things, these depend on the customer's
honesty and integrity and on total wealth. An individual who is
known to the broker and who has substantial wealth invested in a
well-diversified portfolio would generally be able to post lower margin
than a new customer with uncertain wealth. In practice, minimum
margins set by exchanges or regulatory bodies cannot take account
of investors' characteristics.

Characteristics of the item. Margin is intended to protect the broker
during the period required to collect funds or issue a margin call.
Margin on individual options or futures contracts should provide
sufficient protection against short-term price volatility over the period
required to collect additional funds from the customers. Highly volatile options or futures contracts would therefore require greater margin
than stable futures contracts or options. Since volatility changes over
time, margins should also be changed.

Characteristics of the market. Optimal margins depend on the characteristics of the market. A market with price limits, for example,
may inhibit excessive price moves and give time to reconsider and
collect additional margin. In such a market the financial integrity of
brokers and dealers may be ensured with lower margin requirements.
Margins are also required to protect brokers and dealers during the
period in which settlement of transactions is completed. In the stock
options market, for example, the settlement period is five business
days. In principle, customers' deposits and margin requirements
ought to be greater in this market than in a market in which settlement takes only one day. Other characteristics of a market, such as
its liquidity, which affects the speed with which a customer's position
can be liquidated, should also influence the margin.[59]

Characteristics of the transaction. Most options and futures contract
transactions are not conducted in isolation. Investors hold other assets.
To the extent that the option's or futures contract's price movements

267

are less than perfectly positively correlated with the price movements of the remainder of an investor's portfolio, the risk to the investor and to his broker is reduced, and hence the margin requirement should be lowered. Exchanges recognize the importance of considering the purpose of a transaction by setting different margin requirements for spreads or hedges than for naked positions in options or futures.

Current margin systems seem to generate the greatest inconsistencies in their attempt to take account of the characteristics of the transaction, that is, the extent to which a particular transaction is a spread or hedge that actually reduces risk. Current practice uses a pairing procedure to adjust margins in an option position when positions in related options or in the underlying item are held by the investor. The margin for the seller of a call, for example, is reduced or eliminated if the seller buys a call or holds the underlying instrument. Some examples of margin requirements on spread positions involving options and futures are contained in appendix B.

Margining systems that use a pairing procedure are, however, cumbersome and frequently inaccurate. An investor with a large number of options positions would, under this procedure, be required to pair various options in some optimal manner to determine the margin obligation. As Figlewski points out, algorithms to do this can give substantially different results.[60] Furthermore, many pairings are not permitted for margin purposes, with the result that margins are too high. Although margin adjustments are made for vertical spreads in options (long call, short call or long put, short put), only one-for-one pairings of a long and short option are considered. A short position in an at-the-money option cannot be paired against a long position in two out-of-the-money options.

A second difficulty of current margin systems is that option payoffs are nonlinear with respect to the price of an underlying item with which an option may be paired, a condition that is not always properly reflected in the margin system. A deep in-the-money call, for example, will have absolute price changes much like the underlying item, while an out-of-the-money call will experience price changes much smaller than those of the underlying item. Current margining systems do not properly take account of the different volatilities of these two kinds of options or of the risk reduction possible by pairing the options with the underlying item. This problem has given rise to proposals for "delta" margining systems, which take explicit account of the volatility of options in relation to underlying items.

The delta of an option is the price change in the option associated with a one-dollar price change of the underlying item. Thus a short position in two call options each with a delta of $-\frac{1}{2}$ paired with a long position in the underlying item is not a very risky position, since a one-dollar decline in the value of the call options position will tend to be offset by a one-dollar increase in the value of the long position in the underlying item—the delta of the total position is zero. Under a delta margining system, margin for such a position would be much less, for example, than for the position long one in-the-money call with delta of $\frac{3}{4}$ and short one out-of-the-money call with delta of $-\frac{1}{4}$. This position has an overall delta of $\frac{1}{2}(\frac{3}{4} - \frac{1}{4})$, which would require margin approximately one-half that required for the underlying item.

Optimal Margins. The purpose of any margining system is to ensure that investors have sufficient equity to meet their obligations, even in the presence of unexpected events that would lower the value of their equity. Equity is the market value of all the investor's assets (including long options) less the market value of all the liabilities. Thus "margin" and "equity" are synonymous. The purpose of a margin requirement is to ensure a current equity, V_O, such that

$$\text{Prob}(\tilde{V}_t > 0 | V_O) \geqq \alpha^* \qquad (10)$$

where $\tilde{V}_t$ = the uncertain future value of the investor's equity in t days, where t is the number of days required to issue a margin call and collect funds or sell assets, V_O = current market value of the investor's equity, and α^* = a critical probability. In words, the equation says that the investor's equity must remain positive with a probability that exceeds a critical level. Condition 10 can, of course, be modified to require equity to exceed any number greater than zero with the same critical probability. Whether this condition will be met depends on the variability of investors' portfolios and the time period t. The variability of the portfolio depends on its composition. For example, a portfolio of fully paid for T-bills can easily meet the condition. A portfolio of one T-bill and fifty futures contracts may not meet the condition. If not, either more T-bills must be supplied, or the number of futures contracts must be reduced.

Assuming $\tilde{V}_t$ is normally distributed, condition 10 is equivalent to

$$V_O - k\sigma(\tilde{V}_t) \geqq 0$$

where k = number of standard deviations below V_O that corresponds to α^*.[61] The minimum equity, or margin, required is thus given as

$$V_O^* = k\sigma(\tilde{V}_t) \qquad (11)$$

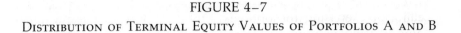

FIGURE 4–7

DISTRIBUTION OF TERMINAL EQUITY VALUES OF PORTFOLIOS A AND B

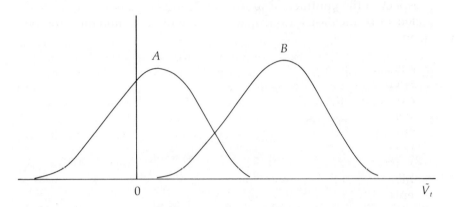

In figure 4–7, the distribution of $\bar{V}_t$ given by portfolio A is under-margined since the probability of values below zero exceeds an acceptable level. The distribution of portfolio B is sufficiently margined since there is virtually no probability that the equity value will fall below zero.

The approach outlined here for setting margins can be applied to various portfolios, as is done in appendix C. Appendix C shows that when financial instruments are considered in isolation, the total margin is considerably greater than when the margin on the portfolio as a whole is calculated, because the diversification of the portfolio reduces risk and therefore reduces the required margin. The margin requirements from this perspective are quite different from those that would be calculated in a security-by-security margining system. Failure to consider the entire portfolio of the investor introduces the same margins on a particular transaction for investors with widely different risk positions. Under the current regulatory structure, which requires separate customer accounts for commodities instruments and stock instruments, a margining system of this kind is difficult to implement in practice. In addition, when investors choose to maintain a variety of separate accounts, it is virtually impossible and inappropriate. It is feasible, however, to consider each investor's account as the portfolio that is to be margined in this manner.

Margining the Option Premium. Unlike a futures contract, a call or put option has a positive market value when purchased. The premium paid is the initial value of the option; if the price of the underlying asset moves in a favorable direction, the market value of the option increases. Such increases in value can be realized, however, only by selling or exercising the option. A futures contract, has no initial value. It has value only if the futures price changes favorably with respect to the contractual futures price initially agreed to. Profits on such price increases are realized daily without liquidating the position.

These features of options result in certain asymmetries first noted by Asay.[62] Increases in option values require additional collateral to be deposited by option sellers but do not permit withdrawal of profits by option buyers. Thus someone with a synthetic long position in the futures contract (buy call, write put) hedged against a short futures position would, if prices increased, be required to make cash payments to cover losses on the short futures position but would not have cash profits on the synthetic long position. This feature inhibits arbitrage between options and futures. Current arrangements also provide an incentive for early exercise of in-the-money options, because interest may be earned on the exercisable proceeds of the option. This early exercise feature complicates option pricing as well as arbitrage between options and futures.

In response to suggestions by futures exchanges, the CFTC has proposed a futures-style margining system for options.[63] Under such an arrangement the buyer of an option would agree to pay the option premium when the option is exercised. The performance of this agreement would be guaranteed by appropriate performance margins, as in the case of futures. The seller of the option would likewise post performance margin (greater than that of the buyer since the seller's obligation is greater). If the market price of the option declined, the buyer would pay the losses in cash to the clearinghouse, and the seller would collect profits from the clearinghouse.

This proposal is somewhat different from a situation that would allow borrowing against the value of the option, as in a stock-style margining system. In effect, a futures-style margining system redefines the option contract to call for payment of the premium at a future date, whereas a stock-style margining system would retain the existing definition of an option contract but would simply allow an option to serve as collateral for borrowing. The CFTC has favored a futures-style margining system because such a system is more compatible with existing procedures on futures exchanges.

The benefits of a futures-style margining system for options on futures contracts arise from the elimination of asymmetries in cash flows between options and futures. Arbitrage would be better facilitated, and option pricing would be simplified. Opposition to such a system arises from a desire to protect customers and the financial system. Since options premiums constitute only a fraction of the value of the underlying asset, margining of the premium appears to be a pyramiding of financial obligations. There is concern that customers do not fully understand the risks of posting only a fraction of the premium and that the stability of the financial system might also be impaired. Apparently for this reason, the CFTC proposal calls for customers to pay 100 percent of the premium and would allow only exchange members the freedom to use a futures-style margining system.

This distinction between public customers and exchange members is unfortunate. It is not evident that public customers are necessarily less sophisticated than members. Most important, however, this distinction introduces a number of difficulties. One of these is a practical one of setting up computer margining systems that differentiate between members and nonmembers. Second is that such a system appears to generate free cash for members at the expense of public customers. If the public pays 100 percent of the option premium in cash and a member need only pay a performance guarantee, members receive cash deposits from customers. Furthermore, the pricing of options from the perspective of customers is different from the pricing of options from the perspective of members. Clearly, this is unacceptable. A futures-style margining system should apply equally to members and nonmembers. Concerns about protection of customers can be met by requiring a sufficiently large performance guarantee. This is not burdensome, even if the guarantee is 100 percent of the option premium, as long as the margin pledged is in the form of interest-earning assets. The key benefit of a futures-style margining system is that cash is not paid at the outset. The adoption of such a margining system would put options and futures on the same footing and simplify pricing relations between them.

How Costly Are Margin Requirements? We have viewed margin as the investor's equity and optimal margins as the amount of equity sufficiently large in relation to liabilities that positive equity would remain even in the face of large, unexpected price changes. No requirement was established that optimal margin be supplied in any particular form such as cash, only that margin be sufficiently large, in light of all the potential price changes of the assets and liabilities in an investor's portfolio, to guard against his bankruptcy. Margin requirements are costly if an investor is compelled to hold equity in a particular form, such as cash. Cash margin requirements force the investor to forgo the interest earnings on the cash. One of the characteristics of existing stock-margining systems is that they sometimes impose costs of this kind on the investor. The margining cost of selling an individual stock short is substantial and has been an impetus for trading in options and in stock index futures.

Futures contracts margin can usually be pledged in the form of U.S. Treasury securities. Even though this appears to be restrictive, investors can usually modify the rest of their portfolio to account for this fact and still achieve an optimal overall portfolio.

Brokers naturally have an interest in requiring cash margin deposits from their customers. But this is difficult in a competitive system because customers choose brokers that allow margin to be pledged in the form of interest-earning assets or that pay interest on margin deposits. Only the brokerage industry as a whole could effectively impose cash margin requirements, especially if regulatory authorities mandated such deposits.

Thus an important issue for regulatory authorities, beyond the issue of setting mandatory margins, is the form in which these margins may be pledged. If they may be pledged as interest-bearing assets, the cost of a mandatory margin system is small, and the arguments against regulating margins are less forceful. Issues of regulatory disparity in the setting of margins for stock products and futures products are also muted. But if margin must be pledged in the form of cash, the cost is high, and arguments against mandating such margins are strengthened. Issues of regulatory disparity also become more forceful and must be dealt with in a "fair" way.

Regulating Margins. In determining whether, and to what degree, margins on various financial instruments, including options, should be set by regulatory authorities, several factors must be considered.

- the need for customer protection and maintenance of the integrity of the financial system
- whether government authorities insure brokers
- the extent to which, under a nonregulated margining system, brokers would have an incentive to protect the integrity of the financial system
- the complexity of margining systems
- the cost of margins

In our view brokerage firms and exchanges have strong incentives to set appropriate margins that protect the integrity of the financial system and thereby protect customers. Indeed, this is one of the ways in which exchanges compete. When governmental authorities insure customers' deposits at brokerage firms, that incentive is mitigated to some degree, and an argument for governmental oversight of the financial integrity of individual brokerage firms is justified. Only securities accounts are now insured by the SIPC, and margin regulations are thus more readily justified for stock products than for futures products. But even for stock products other forms of maintaining the integrity of brokerage firms exist, particularly net capital requirements, segregation requirements, and reserve requirements.

The process of setting margins is highly complex, particularly for the new options instruments and for futures products. Appropriate margins depend on characteristics of the customer, characteristics of the security being margined, characteristics of the market, and characteristics of the portfolio of the investor and of the particular transaction (whether speculative or hedged). These complexities, as well as the fact that appropriate margins change over time, would make the setting of detailed margin requirements a regulatory nightmare. It appears to be appropriate, however, for regulatory authorities to oversee the establishment of general margining systems, without specifying detailed margin requirements. Such oversight would also ensure that margining systems did not benefit brokerage firms at the expense of their customers (for example, by imposing cash margin requirements). In our view the recent recommendation of the Federal Reserve that specific federal margin regulations be repealed and the authority to set margins be assigned to various self-regulatory organizations, under general government oversight, is sensible.[64]

Summary and Conclusions

Options on instruments other than common stocks are the most recent of a series of financial innovations introduced by futures exchanges and stock exchanges. Options on U.S. government debt instruments began trading in October 1982; since then options on stock indexes, options on currencies, and options on particular commodities have begun to trade. These new option markets are the focus of this chapter.

The chapter begins with an introduction to options and to the new option instruments: describing the new options and distinguishing among options on physicals, options on futures, and over-the-counter options. The procedures for trading the new option instruments are explained. Options on all exchanges are issued and guaranteed by a clearinghouse, much as futures contracts are originated, but the trading mechanisms vary. Options on futures exchanges are traded like futures contracts, and options on stock exchanges are traded like common stocks. The advantage of a futures market is the high degree of competition on the floor, but a disadvantage is the lack of continuous price reporting and fully effective time and price priority rules. The advantage of a stock exchange trading system is the existence of effective price reporting and rules for time and price priorities, but a disadvantage is the lack of competition among traders on the floor.

The new options are regulated both by the SEC and by the CFTC. The CFTC has regulatory jurisdiction over options on futures contracts, and the SEC has regulatory jurisdiction over options written directly on debt instruments, stock indexes, and currencies.

We then discuss the economic benefits of options in some detail. Options are a unique hedging tool because they provide hedges that are not available with the use of futures contracts. Options are also a useful investment tool because they provide a means of increasing or limiting the risk of a portfolio that is not available with the use of other financial instruments. The social benefits of options arise from their ability to allocate risk more efficiently than other financial instruments and from their role in increasing the interest and the number of judgments bearing on the price of the underlying asset. Social concern about options arises from the belief that they are merely a form of gambling and have no fundamental economic purpose. Other sources of concern are that options trading can be abused to benefit professional traders at the expense of unsophisticated traders and that certain undesirable external effects on the underlying asset arise from the existence of options trading. These criticisms of options trading merit attention, but they are not, in our view, sufficiently forceful to warrant limiting the new options markets. The new instruments have important economic uses, and they do not adversely affect the markets in the existing instruments.

The link among option prices, futures prices, and the underlying asset prices are discussed. We show how the price of an option is related to the price of the underlying asset and to prices of related options. The put-call parity relation that links put and call options to each other and to the underlying item is developed, and the distinction between put-call parity for options on physicals and options on futures is drawn. Valuation equations for options on physicals and on futures show how the value of an option depends on the volatility of the underlying instrument and certain other factors. Arbitrage links the prices of related financial instruments and causes price changes in one market or one instrument to be transmitted to other markets or instruments.

Empirical evidence on the efficiency of the new options markets— or the "tightness" of price links—is summarized. The T-bond futures options market appears to be efficient after transaction costs are accounted for. The S&P futures options market exhibits some inefficiencies, but these appear to be related to the lower trading volume in that market and the fact that observed prices may not be prices at which arbitrage transactions can take place.

We next examine the roles of contract design, interexchange competition, and government policy in influencing the success or failure of the new options instruments. The market mechanism appears to discipline undue contract proliferation effectively. Evidence on open interest and volume indicates that many of the new option contracts have not been successful. Only certain options on broad stock indexes and the T-bond futures options have been clearly successful. Regulatory limit on the introduction of new financial instruments may be counterproductive insofar as they limit competition among exchanges, favor one exchange over another, and limit financial innovation itself.

Finally we examine margin requirements. An important regulatory disparity arises from the fact that margins on equities and other securities are set by the Federal Reserve and the SEC whereas margins on futures contracts and options on futures contracts are set by individual futures exchanges and are not subject to governmental regulation. The desirability of regulating margin requirements has been much discussed. On the one hand, brokers and exchanges have incentives to set margins that protect brokers and thereby customers and the financial system against the failure of any brokerage firm. Furthermore, the setting of margins is inherently complex, particularly with respect to positions in options and futures, and does not lend itself readily to detailed regulation. On the other hand, when government agencies insure customer deposits, some government involvement in the setting of margins is justified. The cost of margin requirements to the investor is not high if margin may be pledged in the form of interest-earning assets. In that case, governmental setting of margin requirements, even if somewhat arbitrary, does not impose a great burden on individual investors. Recent proposals to permit the margining of the option premium have merit, but the recent CFTC proposal to draw a distinction between brokers and customers has some unfortunate consequences.

Economists have long recognized the benefits of trading in contingent claims.[65] A contingent claim is a contract that gives the individual a payoff contingent on a particular outcome for some underlying event or asset. The existence of markets in contingent claims permits individuals to plan their investment and consumption for future periods more effectively. Although markets are not complete in the sense of allowing individuals to plan for any contingency, the advent of the new options markets and the introduction of options on particular commodities broaden markets in a way that allows individuals to deal more effectively with economic uncertainty.

Appendix A

Margin Requirements on Naked Options

1. *Options on common stocks*
   Long put or call: 100 percent
   Short put or call: 30 percent of value of underlying stock plus in-the-money amount or minus out-of-the-money amount; minimum of $250 per contract

2. *Options on narrow-based stock indexes*
   Same as options on common stocks

3. *Options on broad stock indexes*
   Long put or call: 100 percent
   Short put or call: premium plus 10 percent of index value less out-of-the-money amount; minimum is premium plus 2 percent of index value

4. *Options on (broad) stock index futures* (S&P 500 futures on the CME)
   Long put or call: 100 percent
   Short put or call: premium plus futures margin less one-half amount option is out of the money; minimum is premium plus $1,000

5. *Options on debt instruments* (T-bonds, T-notes, T-bills)
   Long put or call: 100 percent
   Short put or call: premium plus $M less out-of-the-money amount; minimum premium plus $M'; M and M' vary according to underlyng debt instrument

6. *Options on debt futures contracts* (T-bonds on the CBT)
   Long put or call: 100 percent
   Short put or call: same as option in stock index futures

7. *Options on foreign currency*
    Long put or call: 100 percent
    Short put or call: 130 percent of premium plus $750 less out-of-the-money amount

8. *Options on foreign currency futures* (D-mark on the CME)
    Long put or call: 100 percent
    Short put or call: same as options in stock index futures except that minimum margin is premium plus $400

Appendix B

Margin Requirements on Option Spread Positions

Margining of positions involving related options and futures is complex. This appendix contains Chicago Board of Trade margin regulation with respect to options on T-bond futures, which are representative of the margining of complex positions involving options on futures.

431.05 Margin on Options—Under the provisions of Rule 431.00, the Board hereby fixes the following minimum margins for option transactions (minimum margin requirements which go into effect when trading limits are increased are in parentheses):

A. U.S. Treasury Bond Options

1.	Long put or long call	Premium must be paid in full. See Regulation 2805.01.
2.	Short call or short put	Premium (marked-to-market) plus the greater of (a) the futures margin minus one half the amount (if any) that the option is out-of-the-money or (b) initial $750 ($1125), maintenance or hedging $600 ($900).
3.	(a) Long future and short call or	Premium (marked-to-market) plus the maximum of the (a) futures margin minus one half the amount that the option is in the money or (b) initial $750 ($1125), mainte-

(b) Short future and short put   nance or hedging $600 ($900).

4. Short call and short put (straddle)   Market value of both option premiums (marked to market) plus, the underlying futures margin.

5. Vertical Spreads— (one long call and one short call or one long put and one short put, with the same expiration date.)

  (a) Long call (put) option strike price is less (greater) than or equal to the short call (put) option strike price.   Long option premium is paid in full. No margin is required for short option premium.

  (b) Long call (put) option strike price is greater (less) than the short call (put) option strike price.   Long option is paid in full. Margin is equal to the difference between strike prices, not to exceed the margin requirements for the naked short option.

6. Horizontal Spreads— (one long call and one short call or one short put and one long put, with different expiration dates.)

  (a) Long call (put) option strike price is less (greater) than or equal to the short call (put) option strike price.   Long option premium is paid in full. Margin equals $200 per contract for option positions involving months which are 12 months or more apart plus the amount, if any, that the short option premium exceeds the long option premium plus, if the long option expires before the short option, initial $750 ($1000), maintenance or hedging $500 ($750).

(b) Long call (put) option strike price is greater (less) than the short call (put) option strike price.

Long option premium is paid in full. Margin equals the amount by which the short option premium exceeds the long option premium plus the minimum of the difference between the strike prices, or, per contract, the underlying futures margin.

7. (a) Long call—short future

or

(b) Long put—long future

Long option premium is paid in full. Margin equals the underlying futures margin minus any amount by which the market value of the option premium exceeds the appropriate futures spread margin.

8. (a) Long call—short future—short put (reverse conversion) or

(b) Long put—long future—short call (conversion) assumes same expiration month for all three positions, and same strike prices for two option positions

Long option premium is paid in full. Margin equals amount by which short option premium exceeds long option premium.

9. Box Spread—(Long call vs. short put with the same exercise price coupled with a short call vs. long put with the same exercise price. All options in the same expiration month.)

(a) Credit Box—Long call/short put of higher strike price than short call/ long put. (Total

Long option premiums paid in full. Margin is the difference in strike prices.

short option
premiums exceed
total long option
premiums.)

(b) Debit Box—Long
call/short put
option at lower
strike price than
short call/long put
option. (Total long
option premiums
exceed total short
option premiums.)

Long option premiums paid
in full. No further margin
required.

10. Butterfly Spread—
One vertical bull
spread (put or call)
combined with one
vertical bear spread
(put or call). The
spread shares one
common strike price
which is between the
two other strike
prices. All options
expire on the same
date.

(a) Debit Spread—
Total long premi-
ums exceed total
short premiums
when position is
established.
Middle strike price
is exactly halfway
between outer
strike prices.

Long option premiums paid
in full. No further margin
required.

(b) Credit Spread—
Short option
premiums exceed
long option
premiums at time
position is estab-
lished. Middle
strike price not
halfway between
outer strikes.

Long premiums paid in full.
Margin equals largest difference between two adjacent
strikes, not to exceed the
futures margin plus the
amount (marked-to-market)
by which the short option
premiums exceed long
option premiums.

Appendix C

Margining Portfolios versus Margining Individual Securities

The minimum margin of an investor is given by

$$V_0^* = k\sigma(\tilde{V}_t) \tag{C-1}$$

This is equation 11 in the text. We now consider some examples of particular simple portfolios and the appropriate margin for each.

Consider first a two-asset portfolio consisting of b units of riskless securities with face value of $1 paying R_{ft} interest and z_1 units of a futures contract, the current futures price of which is F_{10}. The uncertain future value of this portfolio is

$$\tilde{V}_t = b(1 + R_{ft}) + z_1(\tilde{F}_{1t} - F_{10}) \tag{C-2}$$

where $\tilde{F}_{1t}$ = the uncertain futures price at time t. The current value of the portfolio is

$$V_0 = b$$

The futures contracts do not enter into this current value because the current value of a futures contract is zero, since profits and losses are marked to market daily. The standard deviation of (C-2) is $\sigma(\tilde{V}_t)$ = $z_1\sigma(\tilde{F}_{1t})$. For purposes of illustration assume the futures contract is for one bushel, $k = 3$, $t = 14$ days, $\sigma(F_{1t}) = .20$, and $z_1 = 5,000$ bushels. Then the minimum margin, given by (C-1), is $V_0^* = \$3,000$. This implies that the current value of equity, which in this case is just the T-bill, must be at least $3,000. If, as is assumed here, the investor may pledge his portfolio rather than cash, there is no cost of margin because the investor earns a return of R_{ft}. Margining systems that require cash to be posted are costly because the investor loses the earnings on his posted funds.

Consider now another portfolio identical with the preceding one except that a short position in a futures contract in the same commodity with a different maturity is also held. The uncertain future value of this portfolio is

$$\tilde{V}_t = b(1 + R_{ft}) + z_1(\tilde{F}_{1t} - F_{10}) + z_2(\tilde{F}_{2t} - F_{20}) \tag{C-3}$$

where $z_2 < 0$ = number of units of futures contracts held in a short position (a negative value indicates a short position); and $\tilde{F}_{2t}$ = the uncertain futures price at t of the second futures contract. The current value of the portfolio is $V_O = b$.

The variance of (C-3) is

$$\sigma^2(\tilde{V}_t) = z_1^2\sigma^2(\tilde{F}_{1t}) + z_2^2\sigma^2(\tilde{F}_{2t}) + 2z_1z_2\rho_{12}\sigma(\tilde{F}_1)\sigma(\tilde{F}_2)$$

where ρ = correlation between F_1 and F_2. Since (C-3) is a spread position, the variance will generally be less than the variance of (C-2) as long as the correlation of price changes in the two futures contracts is not too small. Assume that $\rho = .9$, $\sigma(F_1) = \sigma(F_2) = .2$, $z_1 = 5{,}000$, and $z_2 = -5{,}000$. Then $\sigma(\tilde{F}_t) = 447.2$, and, assuming $k = 3$, $V_O^* = \$1{,}342$.

Thus, when account is taken of the correlation of the two futures positions, the required margin is $1,342. If margins were calculated separately on each position, margin of $6,000 would have been required. Futures markets and options markets do account for various spread and hedge positions that reduce the portfolio risk in the manner just shown, but they do not take account of all combinations in the way that would be accomplished if the investor's portfolio were the thing being margined.

In the case of options, the difficulty of taking account of a large number of offsetting options positions can result in overmargining, even when a premium-based margining system is used. Consider now, as a third example, a portfolio consisting of a riskless security and several options written on the same underlying asset, say a futures index. The options positions are long a call and short two other call options of different exercise prices or different maturity. The uncertain future value of this portfolio is

$$\tilde{V}_t = b(1 + R_{ft}) + n_1\tilde{C}_{1t} + n_2\tilde{C}_{2t} + n_3\tilde{C}_{3t}$$

and the current value of the portfolio is

$$V_O = b + n_1C_{10} + n_2C_{20} + n_3C_{30}$$

where n_i = number of options held long or short. A short position is indicated by a negative value. We assume $n_1 > 0$, $n_2 < 0$, and $n_3 < 0$. C_{iO} = current market value of the option premium.

The change in the call premium can be related to the change in the value of the underlying asset as follows:

$$(\tilde{C}_{it} - C_{iO}) = h_i(\tilde{F}_t - F_O) + \tilde{e}_{it}$$

or

$$\tilde{C}_{it} = C_{iO} + h_i(\tilde{F}_t - F_O) + \tilde{e}_{it}$$

where F_O is the present price of the futures index, which is the instrument underlying the option, and $\tilde{F}_t$ is the uncertain future value of the underlying index. The coefficient, h_i, is the "delta" value of option i over the period t. It represents the amount of change in the option premium for a \$1 change in the futures index. Since this relation is not exact, a residual term, $\tilde{e}_{it}$, is necessary.

The uncertain future value of this portfolio can now be written as

$$\tilde{V}_t = b(1 + R_{ft}) + \sum n_i C_{iO} + \left(\sum n_i h_i\right)(\tilde{F}_t - F_O) + \sum n_i \tilde{e}_{it} \quad \text{(C-4)}$$

The variance of (C-4) is

$$\sigma^2(\tilde{V}_t) = \left(\sum n_i h_i\right)^2 \sigma^2(\tilde{F}_t) + \sigma^2\left(\sum n_i \tilde{e}_{it}\right)$$

We assume the following values for the three options:

Options	n	C	h
1	100	30	.7
2	− 100	8	.5
3	− 100	2	.2

In addition, we assume $\sigma^2(\tilde{F}_t) = (1.15)^2$ and $\sigma^2(\sum n_i \tilde{e}_{it}) = (30)^2$. Given these values, $\sigma(\tilde{V}_t) = 30$, which is the standard deviation of the portfolio arising from the imperfect association of the option prices and index prices. Because $\sum n_i h_i = 0$, the index volatility has no bearing. The three option prices move in offsetting directions. In effect, they have a "systematic" risk of zero because their delta values sum to zero.

Assuming $k = 3$, the minimum margin is $V_O^* = \$90$. The current value of the portfolio is

$$V_O^* = b + 30 - 8 - 2 = b + 20 \quad \text{(C-5)}$$

This implies $b = 70$ as the minimum amount of cash or T-bills that must be pledged. This amount is quite different from what would be required if each option were considered in isolation or, indeed, if margin were calculated using the present pairing system. In effect, the margin calculated in equation C-5 is based on a delta margining system of the type also recommended by Figlewski.[66] Such a system recognizes that margins on the same underlying instrument have the same underlying source of variability. Thus offsetting positions in such instruments provide a hedge and reduce the risk of the portfolio.

If one accepts the premise of this section that the optimal margin is the amount of equity an investor must possess to assure the broker that the investor's obligations can be met in the face of adverse price changes over some period of time, then what is to be margined is not a particular security but the portfolio of the investor taken as a whole.

Notes

1. For a discussion of over-the-counter debt options, see Laurie S. Goodman, "An Introduction to Options on Debt Instruments," Citibank Capital Markets Group, Working Paper (May 1984).

2. For a more detailed discussion of the guarantor role of clearing organizations, see Franklin R. Edwards, "The Clearing Association in Futures Markets: Guarantor and Regulator," in Ronald Anderson, ed., *The Industrial Organization of Futures Markets: Structure and Conduct* (Lexington, Mass.: D.C. Heath, Lexington Books, 1984).

3. The topic of appropriate margin is discussed in greater detail later in this chapter.

4. These issues are discussed in greater detail in Philip Johnson's chapter on federal regulation of futures and securities markets in this volume; and Daniel Fischel and Sanford Grossman, "Customer Protection in Futures and Securities Markets," *Journal of Futures Markets*, vol. 4 (Fall 1984), pp. 273–96.

5. For a discussion of futures markets floor trading procedures, see Seymour Smidt, "Trading Floor Practices on Futures and Securities Exchanges: Economics, Regulation, and Policy Issues," in Anne E. Peck, ed., *Futures Markets: Regulatory Issues* (Washington, D.C.: American Enterprise Institute, 1985).

6. Much has been written about a national securities market system in which market makers could compete but for which there would be a single consolidated limit order book. See, for example, Junius Peake, "The National Market System," *Financial Analysts Journal*, vol. 34 (July–August 1978); Ernest Bloch and Robert A. Schwartz, eds. *Impending Changes for Securities Markets: What Role for the Exchanges?* (Greenwich, Conn.: JAI Press, 1979); and Smidt, "Trading Floor Practices."

7. For a view that regulatory competition is desirable, see Edward J. Kane, "Regulatory Structure in Futures Markets: Jurisdictional Competition between the SEC, the CFTC, and Other Agencies," *Journal of Futures Markets*, vol. 4 (Fall 1984), pp. 367–84.

8. See also Eugene Moriarty, Susan Phillips, and Paula Tosini, "A Comparison of Options and Futures in the Management of Portfolio Risk," *Financial Analysts Journal* (January–February 1981), pp. 61–67.

9. The hedging uses of currency options in this kind of situation are also examined in Ian Giddy, "The Foreign Exchange Option as a Hedging Tool," *Midland Corporate Finance Journal*, vol. 1 (Fall 1983) (Reprinted in Donald Lessard, ed., *International Financial Management* [New York: John Wiley, 1985]) ; and George Feiger and Bertrand Jacquillat, "Currency Option Bonds, Puts

285

and Calls on Spot Exchange, and the Hedging of Contingent Foreign Earnings," *Journal of Finance*, vol. 35 (December 1979), pp. 1129–39.

10. More recently, in 1978, trading in unregulated "London options" was banned because of fraudulent sales practices that included bucket shops, high-pressure sales, and "Ponzi" schemes.

11. For a discussion of this issue, see U.S. Securities and Exchange Commission, *Report of the Special Study of the Options Markets* (for House Committee on Interstate and Foreign Commerce, 96th Congress, 2d session, December 22, 1978), pp. 870ff.

12. Ibid.; and Paul Mehl, *Trading in Privileges on the Chicago Board of Trade*, U.S. Department of Agriculture, Circular no. 323 (December 1934).

13. For an excellent legal and economic discussion of manipulation in futures markets, see Linda Edwards and Franklin Edwards, "A Legal and Economic Analysis of Manipulation in Futures Markets," *Journal of Futures Markets*, vol. 4 (Fall 1984), pp. 333–66.

14. Implicit in this claim is a distinction between manipulation based solely on trading activity and manipulation based on misstatements of fact, inside information, and fraudulent publicity. The former is difficult to detect and sometimes difficult to condemn: is a block trader a manipulator? The latter are clearer cases of manipulation.

15. See, for example, "Puts and Calls: Some Options Trading Raises New Questions on Markets' Fairness," *Wall Street Journal*, July 11, 1984.

16. See, for example, Chicago Board Options Exchange, "Chicago Board Options Exchange: The First Three Months" (April 26, 1973, to July 31, 1973); Sidney Robbins, Robert Stobaugh, Francis Sterling, and Thomas Howe, "The Impact of Exchange-traded Options on the Market for New Issues on Common Stock of Small Companies," *Financial Review* (Winter 1979), pp. 1–22; and Robert R. Nathan Associates, "Public Policy Aspects of a Futures-Type Market in Options on Securities" (Report prepared for the Chicago Board of Trade, November 1969).

17. See, for example, Mehl, *Trading in Privileges*.

18. Robbins et al., "Impact of Exchange-traded Options."

19. For a discussion of the specific nature that this futures position must take, see Hans R. Stoll and Robert E. Whaley, "New Options Instruments: Arbitrageable Linkages and Valuation" (Paper prepared for Money, Banking, and Insurance Symposium, University of Karlsruhe, West Germany, December 1984).

20. Most nonagricultural commodities, such as financial assets and precious metals, are always in a "full carry" market. Agricultural commodity prices, however, are frequently inverted before a new harvest. We can accommodate this fact simply by letting b be negative. More critical is our assumption of constant b, which is not likely to be satisfied in an inverted market, where changing expectations of the coming harvest cause frequent unanticipated changes in the relation of spot and futures prices (and thus the value of b).

21. Put-call parity was first derived for non-dividend-paying stocks by Hans R. Stoll, "The Relationship between Put and Call Option Prices," *Journal of Finance*, vol. 24 (1969), pp. 802–24.

22. To see this, note that if $X > S$, the value of the put is $X - S$, and the value of the short call is 0. Alternatively, if $X < S$, the value of the put is 0, but the value of the short call is $X - S$. Thus, regardless of the final asset price, the value of the long put–short call position is $X - S$. Figure 4–4 shows this position after premium income or premium payments.

23. Stoll and Whaley, "New Options Instruments."

24. Where the underlying asset is a non-dividend-paying stock, the cost of carry is the interest rate, and the put-call parity for American stock options is

$$S - X \leqq C(S,T,X) - P(S,T,X) \leqq S - Xe^{-rT}$$

25. The exact portfolio compositions necessary to derive the put-call parity relations 3 and 4 are provided in Stoll and Whaley, "New Options Instruments.

26. Fischer Black and Myron Scholes, "The Pricing of Options and Corporate Liabilities," *Journal of Political Economy*, vol. 81 (1973), pp. 637–59.

27. Michael R. Asay, "A Note on the Design of Commodity Option Contracts," *Journal of Futures Markets*, vol. 2 (1982), pp. 1–7. See also James Hoag, "The Valuation of Commodity Options," in Menachem Brenner, ed., *Option Pricing: Theory and Applications* (Lexington, Mass.: Lexington Books, 1983) for a discussion of the valuation of commodity options.

28. Stoll, "Relationship between Put and Call Prices."

29. Robert C. Klemkosky and Bruce G. Resnick, "Put-Call Parity and Market Efficiency," *Journal of Finance*, vol. 34 (December 1979), pp. 1141–56.

30. K. Chin, "Foreign Currency Options: Tests of Rational Pricing Restrictions," Working Paper, University of Alberta (April 1985).

31. Fischer Black and Myron Scholes, "The Valuation of Option Contracts and a Test of Market Efficiency," *Journal of Finance*, vol. 27 (1972), pp. 399–418.

32. Robert E. Whaley, "Valuation of American Call Options on Dividend-paying Stocks: Empirical Tests," *Journal of Financial Economics*, vol. 10 (1982), pp. 29–58.

33. Susan M. Phillips and Clifford W. Smith, Jr., "Trading Costs for Listed Options," *Journal of Financial Economics*, vol. 8 (1980), pp. 179–201.

34. Kuldeep Shastri and Kishore Tandon, "Valuation of American Options on Foreign Currency," Working Paper no. 579, University of Pittsburgh, School of Business (February 1985).

35. Stoll and Whaley, "New Options Instruments."

36. Fischer Black, "The Pricing of Commodity Contracts," *Journal of Financial Economics*, vol. 3 (1976), pp. 167–79.

37. Chin, "Foreign Currency Options."

38. Robert E. Whaley, "Valuation of American Futures Options: Theory and Empirical Tests," Working Paper 84–101, Vanderbilt University, Owen Graduate School of Management (April 1984).

39. Chin, "Foreign Currency Options."

40. Lester Telser and Harlow Higinbotham, "Organized Futures Markets:

Costs and Benefits," *Journal of Political Economy*, vol. 85 (October 1977), pp. 969–1000.

41. Deliverability also usually meant storability. Futures markets do exist, however, in nonstorable commodities, such as fresh eggs.

42. For a detailed discussion of these issues, see Allan B. Paul, in "The Role of Cash Settlement in Futures Contract Specifications," in Peck, *Futures Markets: Regulatory Issues*.

43. Dwight M. Jaffee, "The Impact of Financial Futures and Options on Capital Formation," *Journal of Futures Markets*, vol. 4 (Fall 1984), p. 430.

44. See Smidt, "Trading Floor Practices."

45. The AMEX and the Philadelphia Stock Exchange plan to start commodity units to trade futures and options. Their product is distinguished from that of futures exchanges primarily by the trading mechanism—a board broker (as on the CBOE)—and a prohibition against dual trading. See "American and Philadelphia Exchanges Are About to Start Up Commodity Units," *Wall Street Journal*, April 18, 1985.

46. Robert S. Hamada and Myron S. Scholes, "Taxes and Corporate Financial Management," Center for Research in Security Prices, Working Paper no. 123 (March 1984).

47. For discussion of regulatory disparity, see, for example, Thomas A. Russo, "The SEC and CFTC in the Post Accord Era: Continued Autonomy or a Shotgun Marriage?" (Cadwalader, Wickersham and Taft, undated); Douglas Scarff, "The Securities and Commodities Markets: A Case Study in Product Convergence and Regulatory Disparity," in Yakov Amihud, Thomas Ho, and Robert Schwartz, eds., *Market Making and the Changing Structure of the Securities Industry* (Lexington, Mass.: D.C. Heath, Lexington Books, 1985); and Johnson, chap. 5 of this volume.

48. The futures contract on the S&P 100 index was not, however, introduced until July 14, 1983.

49. The cross-sectional geometric averaging of stock prices to compute the Value Line index reduces the covariability of price changes in the index with price changes in a stock portfolio. The options on the Value Line futures index will therefore be less effective for hedging and portfolio management.

50. William Silber, "Innovation, Competition, and New Contract Design in Futures Markets," *Journal of Futures Markets*, vol. 1 (Summer 1981), pp. 123–55.

51. Ibid.

52. An argument along these lines is provided by Gary L. Seevers, "Comments on Innovation, Competition, and New Contract Design in Futures Markets," *Journal of Futures Markets*, vol. 1 (Summer 1981), pp. 157–59.

53. Stephen Figlewski, "Margins and Market Integrity: Margin Setting for Stock Index Futures and Options," *Journal of Futures Markets*, vol. 4 (Fall 1984), pp. 385–416. Susan M. Phillips and Paula A. Tosini, "A Comparison of Margin Requirements for Options and Futures," *Financial Analysts Journal* (November–December 1982), pp. 54–58. See also Board of Governors of the Federal Reserve System, *A Review and Evaluation of Federal Margin Regulations*, Staff Study (December 1984).

54. In futures markets, margin requirements are also established by the clearinghouse for clearing members. Clearing members establish margins for futures commission merchants (FCMs), who establish customer margins. The customer margins established by an exchange are the minimum margins required of customers. For a more complete discussion of futures margining practice, see Edwards, "Clearing Association in Futures Markets"; and William Tomek, "Margins on Futures Contracts: Their Economic Roles and Regulation," in Peck, *Futures Markets: Regulatory Issues.*

55. Figlewski, "Margins and Market Integrity."

56. We are not concerned with the credit control rationale applicable in stock and bond markets.

57. See Kenneth Garbade, "Federal Reserve Margin Requirements: A Regulatory Initiative to Inhibit Speculative Bubbles," in Paul Wachtel, ed., *Crises in the Economic and Financial Structure* (Lexington, Mass.: Lexington Books, 1982).

58. Figlewski, "Margins and Market Integrity."

59. Margins established by the clearinghouse for its members or by clearing members for FCMs also depend on the existence and nature of other regulations for ensuring the financial integrity of firms. These include the existence of requirements to regulate customers' margin deposits and other funds, the existence of required reserve accounts, and the existence of capital requirements.

60. Figlewski, "Margins and Market Integrity."

61. The distribution of the terminal portfolio value is assumed to be normal; if it is not, modifications must be made in the analysis.

62. Asay, "Design of Commodity Option Contracts."

63. For further details, see U.S. Commodity Futures Trading Commission, "Notice of Proposed Rule Making—Commodity Options; Margins," *Federal Register,* vol. 49 (March 9, 1984); and R. Chandrasekar, "The Case for 'Futures-Style' Options," *Financial Exchange* (Fourth Quarter 1983).

64. See letters dated January 11, 1985, from Paul A. Volcker to Senator Jesse Helms, chairman of the Committee on Agriculture, Nutrition, and Forestry, accompanying submission of Federal Reserve Board, *Federal Margin Regulation.*

65. For a recent discussion, see Kenneth J. Arrow, "Futures Markets: Some Theoretical Perspectives," *Journal of Futures Markets,* vol. 1 (Summer 1981), pp. 107–15.

66. Figlewski, "Margins and Market Integrity."

5

Federal Regulation in Securities and Futures Markets

Philip McBride Johnson

The Evolution of Competitive Tensions

Centralized securities markets in the United States are commonly traced to the formation of the New York Stock Exchange in 1792. They serve primarily as an adjunct to the process of raising capital for enterprises through the public sale of new equity or debt securities. While the initial accumulation of this new capital generally takes place elsewhere, the exchanges aid that process by providing a secondary market in which the securities can later be resold and traded.[1] Transactions in these securities define their current value, and investors seek to realize gain through price appreciation as well as through distributions of dividends or interest.

The modern American futures market came later, around 1860 at the Chicago Board of Trade (CBT). Futures contracts reflect the parties' agreement to complete the sale of a product at a later time but for the price set when the commitment is first made. In this way, those who deal commercially in that product can "pre-price" the item and thus help to insulate themselves from adverse value changes that may occur during the intervening period. Use of the futures markets for this purpose is known as *hedging*. Those who assume the price risk shed by hedgers are motivated by much the same profit objective as most securities investors but have come to be called speculators.[2]

For many decades, the securities exchanges and the futures markets operated quite independently of each other. Little if any interaction took place between them, and as a result there was no compelling need for cooperation nor occasion for confrontation. This separation remained when, in the 1920s and 1930s, Congress designed the basic regulatory systems for each industry.[3] The resulting federal requirements were similar in many key respects, such as in prohibiting fraud and market manipulation, but there were significant differences as well. Those distinctions, however, remained largely safe from invidious comparison so long as the markets followed different paths.

This is not to suggest that commodities and securities were comfortably separated even then. Although the futures regulator was content to restrict its activities to hard commodities like wheat, vegetable oils, and cattle, the scope of the federal securities laws was stretched far beyond stocks and bonds; and, on several occasions, those laws were applied to sales of interests in commodities (though not futures contracts).[4] For example, certain types of investments were ruled to be securities even though they involved farm produce,[5] coins,[6] salt,[7] and whiskey.[8] Similarly, a security was found to exist for certain investments in dairy cattle,[9] brood mares,[10] chinchillas,[11] and even earthworms.[12] Most of these expansive applications of securities laws and regulations, however, involved activities occurring off the central exchanges.

During the past decade, the crowding became more acute as the organized securities exchanges and futures markets began introducing new products that have drawn them closer together. From the securities industry have come standardized, exchange-traded options said to offer hedging services, like futures contracts. The futures markets have begun trading futures contracts related to the value of equity and debt securities. These developments have created a perception that the two industries, at least in the arena of new products, are growing more similar and more directly competitive.

The overlap of products in the two industries can be illustrated by listing, below, some of the instruments sponsored today by the securities and futures markets that closely approximate each other. Typically, the same underlying item is involved in both instances, but the traded instrument differs somewhat:

Futures Markets

- Futures on Treasury bonds
- Options on Treasury-bond futures
- Futures on Government National Mortgage Association (GNMA) certificates
- Futures on Standard & Poor's (S&P) stock indexes
- Options on S&P futures
- Futures on foreign currencies
- Options on currency futures

Securities Exchanges

- Options directly on Treasury-bonds
- Options directly on GNMA certificates
- Options directly on S&P stock indexes
- Options directly on foreign currencies

A clash between the securities and futures industries has also become more likely because the newer products introduced by the securities markets look and trade far more like futures contracts than conventional stocks and bonds. Funds used to acquire standardized securities options, for example, do not contribute capital to an enterprise, nor do the owners of those options become either shareholders or creditors of an organization.

Trading in these options also has a distinctly futures-style flavor: (1) the exchange itself creates the options; (2) trading is allowed only on the originating exchange (that is, no private or over-the-counter dealings); (3) obligations are guaranteed by the market's own clearinghouse; (4) all options are marked to market daily;[13] (5) limits exist on how many options an investor may own; (6) options are sufficiently standardized so one can use a single, uniform disclosure statement; and (7) on the largest of these new markets, members are permitted to compete with each other on the exchange floor for pending transactions, using an auction system of open outcry, whereas the traditional securities markets continue to conduct business through exclusive specialists for each investment.

Trepidation over potential competition between these products has been a major catalyst for recent suggestions that the regulatory structures in both industries should be harmonized. In some quarters it is assumed (though not yet empirically verified) that regulatory differences could bias the investing public in favor of one industry's products over the other.[14] As a result, proposals have been made to the Securities and Exchange Commission (SEC), the Commodity Futures Trading Commission (CFTC), and the Congress that greater uniformity among the two regulatory programs should be required, at least where potentially competing products are involved.

The purpose of this paper is to examine in a general way the forces, attitudes, and interests behind the regulatory programs fashioned over many decades by the SEC and the CFTC (or its predecessor).[15] This analysis will not venture an opinion on which of the two regulatory schemes is the better in the aggregate. Whether one system is superior to another depends largely on what one thinks a regulatory scheme should achieve. Differing views whether regulation should absolutely control, emerge only in times of crisis, or be little more than advisory dictate one's assessment of whether or not particular regulatory programs are working. Similarly, the priorities and objectives established by the CFTC and the SEC (and by their respective congressional overseers) have differed over the years. Assessing whether a particular regulatory regime is effective depends heavily on what was intended to be achieved. In this paper, few stones will be thrown for these reasons.

The Nature of Regulation Generally

Regulation is typically a reaction to some negative experience. Regulation is seldom suggested when a particular activity is trouble free (except perhaps when monopolies are awarded). The form that regulation takes is governed largely by the nature and intensity of the adverse reaction. Especially harsh regulation often signals a vengeful response designed as much to punish as to reform and, in some instances, with little interest in whether the regulatory program ultimately destroys its target. Regulation may reflect a messianic attitude that the activity can be improved if only it is forced in a new direction. Here the regulator's aim is to prove that a better system can be created and, for this reason, has a stake in the ultimate survival of the target but in revised form. Finally, the aim of regulation may be purely anticompetitive, that is, the creation of barriers that protect certain private interests at the expense of others. Clearly, a single purpose of regulation cannot easily be identified under these circumstances.

The same is true of investor protection. By definition, investors are risk takers. Determining what these risk takers need protection from must be carried out in this context. The present paper assumes that investor protection is not meant to insulate investors from the consequences of free economic forces, or from their own poor judgment, but rather from abuses perpetrated by other persons. On one hand, some activities within society are so intrinsically dangerous to public health and safety that they are flatly prohibited by law, such as murder, rape, robbery, and arson. The criminal justice system is commonly enlisted to enforce those proscriptions through arrest, prosecution, and punishment. On the other hand, a vast number of activities are acknowledged to be socially beneficial unless pursued in an abusive or injurious manner. Regulation is the legal tool designed to harness and guide these valued resources for the betterment of society.

The objectives embodied in prohibitory laws enjoy broad public consensus and support. A policeman witnessing an assault, for example, can be highly confident that the offender's capture will please the community. Regulation, however, is often too remote from the pressing concerns of the general population and too highly specialized in its focus to generate a reliable public consensus on whether, when, or how particular forms of activity should be regulated.[16] As a result, a regulatory agency must proceed with considerably less certainty that what it does will be greeted by the general public as either necessary or wise.

Left largely adrift from public consensus, an independent federal regulator normally hears only from its creator—Congress—and from the small segment of society that has a special interest in its policies. Because the general public is often unaware of or indifferent toward a particular matter, these two forces can exercise considerable influence over the shape of regulatory policy and, equally important, with little fear of backlash from the legislators' constituencies or the industry's customers. By the same token, of course, this insulation from public sentiment makes it difficult for either Congress or private interests to generate popular clamor for their views on regulatory questions.

The influence of Congress over the regulatory process occurs on at least two levels. First, regulatory policy is affected by congressional attitudes toward the exercise of governmental power generally. A regulator is a power center by reason of its authority to control particular activities and, as such, serves as a convenient focal point for the debate over whether too much or too little governmental power exists in American society. When an agency takes action, advocates of an aggressive government presence in the private sector will examine the regulator's conduct to determine whether or not it is too meek, while their opponents will ask whether or not it is excessive.

Second, Congress sometimes examines specific regulatory policies on their merits. With rare exceptions, a legislator cannot obtain guidance on these frequently esoteric issues by polling constituents or conducting public surveys, as might be possible and useful on issues of broader public import. Bluntly put, the vast majority of voters could not care less. Thus decisions are based largely on input from the combatants in the drama and from a handful of colleagues in Congress who are considered to be knowledgeable, in general if not specifically, in the work of the regulator. While the outcome might be characterized as public policy, it is arrived at through a process in which popular sentiment plays, at best, a minor role.

The other principal source of influence on regulatory policy is the limited segment of society that is either affected by the agency's actions or has a specific interest in its work. The regulated industry is obviously affected and, therefore, plays an active—and largely defensive—role in the process. Another category consists of special-issue groups interested in the agency's performance as it may advance or retard their broader political or social goals. Of course, users of the regulated industry's products or services, too, will participate when they perceive that their interests are involved. Once again, however, no general sounding of public opinion can normally be taken.

Similarly, the public image and the reputation of a regulatory agency often take form without meaningful participation by the general public. Most citizens (including many members of Congress) are too remote from the agency's work to assess its performance. Instead, they rely heavily on the opinions of those who deal directly with the regulator: a few members of Congress, other governmental units, the industry, and special-issue groups.

An agency held in high esteem is both a stronger ally and a more formidable opponent than a regulator in disrepute. Accordingly, the agency can expect to be portrayed favorably by those who stand to benefit from the official position or decision taken by that regulator. When a regulator stands in the way of an objective, however, efforts are sometimes made to tarnish the agency's image, including (a) when the outcome of a contested regulatory issue pits the reputation of the agency against that of the adversaries;[17] (b) when another governmental unit seeks to justify a raid on the agency's jurisdiction by portraying itself as better; and (c) when one congressional committee wishes to seize from another committee the role of principal agency overseer and, to that end, claims that problems at the agency necessitate the shift in congressional assignments. The image thus created, which is seldom meant to persist beyond the particular skirmish, may nevertheless penetrate the public memory and remain there for years.

Regulation rarely writes on a clean slate. It is often imposed upon activity with a long history and an established structure. Fundamental change is seldom the objective of regulation since, if it were truly necessary, the problem could be better addressed through prohibitory laws that would clear the way for an entirely new design. Moreover, a complete overhaul of the existing structure could interfere unnecessarily with the activity itself, which as noted earlier is of acknowledged social value when conducted properly. Instead, regulation seeks to adapt itself to the structure already in place.

As a result, no two regulatory programs are exactly alike. Those differences do not, in themselves, warrant or support the conclusion that one regulatory scheme is better than another. Nor does an agency's desire to develop regulatory policy that harmonizes with constructive industry customs justify a conclusion that it has been captured.

To summarize, regulation often lacks a broad public following; and, in fact, the general population may be too removed from the process to provide useful guidance either to Congress or to the agency. Instead, the formulation of regulatory policy, the resolution of contested issues, and the development of the agency's image may depend upon the interaction of the regulator with Congress and other interested parties that have various motivations and objectives. With some notable exceptions, there is little danger of voter backlash or public outcry regardless of how specific issues are decided. Thus arises a climate in which power plays and competitive maneuvers can assume the cloak of public policy.

The Natural Limits of Regulation

Regulation is not a panacea. It has certain value in moderating the excesses that can afflict legitimate commercial activity, especially under severe competitive stress. The fear of failure (however measured) can sometimes impel businesspeople to compromise the quality of their goods or services or the integrity of their actions. Regulation can control those propensities by setting fairly uniform standards that act as a competitive equalizer.

One should note, however, that the underlying premise of regulation is that businesspeople seek to survive and to succeed. This motivation necessitates regulation. Perhaps more important, this motivation makes regulation work.

The underpinning of all regulation is the premise that commercial enterprises want to remain in business. The entire regulatory scheme is designed to exploit that desire, to use it as a weapon for compliance. At the heart of most regulatory programs is a form of licensing, also known as registration, certification, designation, or approval. Licensing becomes the thin thread by which each business enterprise hangs. It is the authority to do business, to reap the economic fruits of the businessperson's investment of human and financial capital. Conversely, loss of the license means immediate expulsion from the industry, with devastating economic consequences in many cases.

The objectives of regulation, therefore, are achieved through the threat of being put out of business. Legitimate commercial enterprises will not incur this risk. If an infraction occurs, the venture will quickly correct the problem. Some have been known to expel top management, radically to restructure their entire operations, and to pay huge fines to fend off a revocation of their licenses.

Not all enterprises seek to perpetuate themselves, however. Some, in fact, plan for a very short life. They make the minimum investment necessary to conduct business and design ways to conceal and protect their profits. To be shut down is not only expected; it is virtually painless. Examples would include holiday merchandise scams and investment "boiler rooms."[18] The *modus operandi*, here, is hit-and-run.

Regulation is helpless in the face of these operators. Since they have no expectation of remaining in business beyond the immediate sting, they will ignore any licensing requirements that are imposed. Similarly, these charlatans will not file regulatory reports, permit inspections of their operations, respond to subpoenas, or do any of the other things that regulation expects from ongoing enterprises. Criminal law enforcement is the only meaningful deterrent.

Even so, Congress often has difficulty coming to grips with the essential difference between business regulation and crime fighting. Frequently, it will blur the two by directing a regulatory agency to undertake the doomed task of regulating criminals. An instance of this phenomenon is the recent effort within Congress to assign to the CFTC the duty of dealing with commodity boiler rooms.[19]

One might suggest that a regulatory presence is good, even though the targets are unresponsive, because it provides an easy way to close a suspect operation. Although a particular venture may be guilty of horrendous fraud (or worse), for example, closing its doors on the technicality that the firm was unlicensed is easier than establishing the main charges. Thus regulation can be a convenient way to stop a criminal operation at minimum expense. This argument, however, overlooks the severity of the criminal activity, which cannot be adequately addressed through regulatory sanctions. Although the culprit's current operation may be closed, his record remains clean except for a seemingly minor violation of a civil statute—failing to obtain a license. One might properly question whether this result is genuinely in the public interest, especially in light of the lower prosecution rate for con artists who have been stopped through these less exacting means.

One might argue that involving a regulatory agency is good because, at a minimum, it adds another pair of eyes to help detect criminal activity. Under this theory, the regulator may be impotent to deal effectively with the problem but can at least sound a warning for criminal law enforcement agencies to heed. This position has superficial appeal, but the public will not accept the idea that a regulator should simply act as a sentry; the results that it expects from regulators are far greater than that.

From childhood on, we have come to equate good criminal law enforcement with pursuit, apprehension, and conviction of criminals, usually after the fact. The bank has already been robbed, the victim has already been shot, or the mark has already been fleeced. We are not taught to expect criminal agencies as a routine to prevent those events. The public, however, has precisely that expectation when regulation is involved. The popular view is that misconduct simply should not occur in a well-regulated industry, and, if it does, something is wrong with the regulator. After-the-fact punishment does little to mute the public criticism; the misconduct ought not to have happened in the first place. Whereas no one asked "How did the government let this happen?" after the Charles Manson murders, that question is the first raised when a regulatory program fails to achieve perfect results.

Perhaps this elevated expectation among the public would be warranted if the agencies were left to regulate the regulatable. These agencies, however, are frequently called upon to use regulatory tools against hardened criminals who choose to ignore them. The result is inevitable failure by the agency. Yet the public reaction is unlikely to differ from that under orthodox circumstances. Just as Congress sometimes overlooks the limitations of regulation by assigning impossible criminal justice functions to civil agencies, the public cannot easily distinguish whether the agency is doing genuine regulation, and thus deserves to be condemned for missteps; whether it is substituting for criminal law enforcement agencies, for which it should be forgiven the inevitable failures that occur; or whether it occupies some netherworld in which it is a sentry for federal and state criminal prosecutors. To date, at least, the public has applied only the strictest standard in judging regulatory agencies: if an offense is allowed to occur, the regulator has failed.

As long as that public sentiment persists, suggestions that regulatory agencies can perform criminal justice roles without harm to themselves are fanciful. On the contrary, public confidence is quickly eroded, even to the point at which routine regulatory functions (performed well) are questioned. For these reasons, one can only hope that Congress, and well-meaning officials within the agencies themselves, will gain a deeper appreciation for the limitations of regulation and, in the process, for the damage done to an agency whenever it undertakes to do the impossible.

The Origins of Regulation

The function of this paper is not to recount the history of regulation in the securities and futures markets. To describe in general terms the public attitude toward the two industries, since both past and present federal regulation have been influenced by it, is useful, however.

Futures regulation surfaced in an atmosphere of chronic distrust and suspicion toward those markets, hardened by decades of campaigns to outlaw futures trading entirely.[20] Securities regulation, however, emerged during a time of public shock when the stock markets, a symbol of American wealth and power, were implicated in the economic crash of the 1930s. In simple terms, the futures markets were perceived as inherently suspect, even if they offered some valuable benefits as well (an attitude not too dissimilar from the public's ambivalence toward nuclear energy today), while the securities exchanges were viewed as having merely strayed from what is unquestionably a noble path.

For the first 100 years, futures markets traded primarily in agricultural products. Today, farm futures account for a smaller—but still substantial—portion of trading. Life is frequently hard for farmers, who plant their crops with the perennial (and somewhat inconsistent) hope of a bountiful harvest and strong prices. Drought, overproduction, pestilence, and other forces often intervene to frustrate those hopes. Producers can be relatively fatalistic about the vagaries of nature and even the laws of supply and demand. They find it difficult to accept the idea that futures markets should play a part in pricing their crops, however.

Throughout the Farm Belt, a suspicion of futures trading has persisted, especially among farmers who believe that their incomes are being dictated by people in urban centers who have no real connection with agriculture and who seek profits in hours or days rather than over the growing cycle by which farmers measure their own results. The general sentiment of the farm community toward the futures markets was summed up in 1921 by a senator from Illinois:

> For years previous to the present crisis in the agricultural industry the men frequently referred to by orators as the "backbone of the Nation" have averaged barely more than a decent living by working their wives and children as well as themselves, and have realized no return for their capital. The real job we have on our hands is to find out how farming can be made as safely profitable as any other American

occupation. . . . The one vital industry on which the Nation's welfare and prosperity depend, must have its chance to live and prosper if the rest of us expect to, and if it is to have this chance, the grain gambler must go.[21]

At the other end of the spectrum, but equally suspicious of futures markets, is the consuming public. Their anxiety was fueled historically because nothing less than food was at stake, and unbridled speculation might raise the cost of groceries for those who could ill afford it. With the advent of financial futures in the 1970s, some of the same concerns were voiced about the impact of futures speculation on the cost of home mortgages or other money needs. Thus, even though producers like high prices and consumers prefer low prices, they sometimes share a common distrust of the futures markets.

The poor image of the futures industry has been exacerbated to some degree because profit opportunities are as available during catastrophes as in times of triumph. A natural disaster, an assassination, or even a war can send the futures markets into a frenzy while the general public looks on in stunned disbelief. The vision of trading floors crowded with profit seekers while the nation grieves is not a scene likely to endear futures markets to the public. This problem is perhaps even worse today because these images can be conveyed instantly and vividly by national television to tens of millions of Americans.

Although the securities markets suffer criticism and distrust from time to time, they have enjoyed deeper public confidence than the futures industry for several reasons. The public associates the stock market with economic vitality. A strong stock market is commonly equated with a strong nation. Even persons who do not invest in securities may feel some concern for their own well-being when the stock market suffers a sustained bearish period.

The stock market and the public also rejoice and mourn together. The restrictions that exist on short sales of securities[22] cause most investors to gain only when the economic news is good and to lose when the public as a whole is suffering. Thus securities traders are rarely viewed as either the cause of economic distress or as beneficiaries of that condition.

Moreover, the securities industry's known connection with capital formation encourages the public to view it as a money source to fuel economic growth, create new jobs, and provide a better life. Roughly 42 million Americans own at least one security[23] and often rely on those investments to help meet important needs, such as educating the children or planning for retirement.

In part, the image gap between the futures and securities markets has been due to the public's difficulty in understanding how it is benefited by futures trading. The fundamental purposes of the futures market—to hedge against price risks and to discover prices—must often be taught in the classroom, on the lecture circuit, or in the academic journals. Those purposes are seldom grasped as easily or as quickly as the role of stock exchanges in the economy. A comparison of testimony by the CFTC and the SEC before congressional committees, for example, demonstrates that the CFTC must frequently explain what futures are and how the economy benefits from them, whereas the SEC is rarely called upon to justify the securities exchanges.

Because the general process of raising capital to stimulate the economy is viewed as valuable and proper, and the securities markets are an accepted part of that system, the SEC is not called upon to prove—security by security—that each particular offering will benefit society in some specific way. Thus, for example, the SEC will treat as equal the common stock of a cancer research center, a casino, and a cigarette manufacturer. Securities regulation allows potential investors to make their own value judgments whether a particular stock deserves to receive their capital and, in aid of that, focuses principally on ensuring that all material information is disclosed by the issuer.

But each new futures contract must be individually justified as a vehicle to shift commercial price risk or to provide valuable price discovery.[24] No amount of disclosure to potential traders will save a futures contract that lacks that economic purpose. Each new futures product is subject to intense screening by the CFTC, which may reject the instrument unless satisfied that it meets this test. Unlike the SEC, therefore, the CFTC can prevent new products from entering the futures market, even though investor interest is keen and full disclosure is made, if the product's economic benefit—hedging or pricing—has not been persuasively documented. This obligation to prove a specific benefit to society from each new futures contract is a further manifestation of public wariness toward these instruments and their markets.

Bases for Regulatory Comparison

As noted earlier, the securities markets and the futures industry operated in relative harmony so long as the former dealt in traditional stocks and bonds and the latter traded tangible commodities like soybeans, cattle, or silver. The securities exchanges offered the public an opportunity to become owners or creditors of an enterprise, to share in its hoped-for success, and, in the meantime, to hold a bankable asset (the security). Futures markets offered none of these benefits. Although a futures contract allowed the trader to participate in commodity price changes, it did not convey title to that commodity and was not treated as an asset in its own right. The futures contract was, instead, an agreement that, in most instances, resulted in an eventual cash payment between the parties based upon price changes rather than in the conveyance of property.

Accordingly, securities regulation has been concerned with protection of the public as existing or would-be owners of securities. Of particular interest is the atmosphere in which these assets are offered and sold, since securities have no intrinsic value and are priced instead on the known or projected success of the venture itself. For this reason, the SEC insists upon full disclosure, usually in the form of a lengthy prospectus, regarding the enterprise's business, management, earnings history, if any, and other material attributes. In addition, the purchase terms are regulated. Since borrowed funds can be used to purchase securities, efforts are made to ensure that imprudent credit risks are not taken. For this purpose, lending limits (margin requirements) are imposed when securities are bought.[25]

Futures regulation, however, deals principally with uncompleted promises, not assets, and with the value of generic items rather than single enterprises. A futures contract to buy corn, for example, does not convey title to corn. Similarly, the value of corn is determined by myriad factors, such as weather, demand, and quality, rather than by the business acumen or success of any entrepeneur. Thus a prospectus about the nation's largest corn merchant would not normally impart much useful information about the value of corn itself.

A prospectus about corn specifically might be more relevant, but most of that information is already widely available from many sources. What is not generally known are the risks associated with trading; and, for that reason, disclosure of those risks is required.[26] These risks include the possibility of losing far more than the original futures deposit, for instance, as well as the occasional difficulty of leaving the market when prices reach their daily limit and trading ceases.

Futures regulation, moreover, is not concerned about overextension of credit. After all, a futures contract is not a purchase, on credit or otherwise. On the contrary, the objective of futures margin is to ensure that traders always have on deposit more than their current indebtedness.[27] The risk exists, however, that a party's promise to purchase or sell later will not be honored and, as protection against that contingency, both sides of the contract must deposit funds in the nature of earnest money or a performance bond. These deposits, although called margins, are not associated in any way with lending or borrowing and, therefore, have not been federally set like securities margins.

I do not suggest that there is general agreement that margin controls are solely a credit-regulating device. A staff study by the Federal Reserve Board sets forth the idea that margins may also create troublesome leverage whereby persons with modest capital can have an undue influence on prices for the underlying item or may overextend themselves at the peril of themselves and those around them (for example, their brokers).[28] Thus other arguments for government margin controls include the avoidance of excessive price fluctuations and the minimization of financial collapses that may flow from leveraging a modest amount of capital to control large positions in the securities or futures market. While this paper does not undertake to assess the merit of those claims, one can observe that the efficacy of a Federal Reserve Board role in the regulatory process comes into doubt once credit monitoring ceases to be a rationale, that is, saving investors from themselves and each other is a curious role for a central bank.

Whereas the distinctions between futures contracts and conventional stocks or bonds are quite sharp, they are not when the new exchange-traded securities options are compared with futures. Here exist several similarities that might be cited as reason for greater regulatory harmony. To some degree, the process of modifying regulatory policy is already underway; and, in general, the trend has been toward the futures model. The controversy focuses on those areas where the harmonization effort has faltered or been opposed.

The rationale for comparable regulation between futures and centralized, standardized securities options is that the latter instruments resemble futures contracts far more than they do the traditional products of the securities industry. Neither futures nor securities options represent an ownership interest in the underlying item or a relation with a going enterprise (for example, as stockholder or creditor). Both involve commitments to later action, either absolutely or conditionally. Neither involves an extension of credit since no true purchase has yet occurred, and the deposits required serve the same performance-bond purpose. In both instances, the instruments are creatures of the host exchange and may be bought and sold only there.

That regulatory policy ever diverged in the case of futures and exchange-traded securities options is attributable more to timing than to conscious public-policy choice. The innovator of the latter products was the CBT, the world's largest futures market. Originally the CBT had considered forming a new family of futures contracts in equity stocks. The regulator of the futures markets at that time, the Department of Agriculture, however, did not have jurisdiction over such an instrument because its authority was then limited to futures on specified agricultural products. Moreover, the securities industry was better acquainted with securities options because of the longstanding existence of a small over-the-counter "puts and calls" market. Since options could approximate the desired instrument, and a regulator was already in place (the SEC), the CBT determined in 1973 to form a new securities exchange, the Chicago Board Options Exchange (CBOE).

Shortly after those decisions were made, a new futures regulator — the CFTC — was created by Congress with sweeping jurisdiction over every type of futures contract. Had these amendments been made to the Commodity Exchange Act only a few months earlier, the CBT itself might have offered securities futures instead, on the same trading floor and under the same scheme of regulation as other futures contracts.[29]

Initially, the SEC imposed on the CBOE many of the trappings of conventional securities regulation. Although CBOE options were exchange created, the SEC insisted that there must be an issuer, as in the case of traditional securities, and that a prospectus must be provided to investors in these standardized options. To accommodate these demands, the clearinghouse of the CBOE (now the Options Clearing Corporation) would serve as issuer and would generate the required prospectus. Even though transactions in options did not involve borrowings or credit, the SEC and the Federal Reserve Board imposed securities-type margin limitations on these new instruments. Finally, certain customer-protection requirements tailored to conventional securities, such as the constraints upon investment recommendations known popularly as suitability rules, were imposed.

Certain accommodations, however, have been made by the SEC because of the special nature of exchange-traded securities options. As noted earlier, for example, the SEC allowed the CBOE to operate an auction-style trading system resembling far more the CBT than the conventional stock exchanges. Also, the SEC has gradually shifted from use of a lengthy prospectus for options to a far shorter, futures-style disclosure statement.[30] Changes are also underway to adjust option margins to reflect more accurately their true purpose as safeguards against default rather than as controls on credit extension.[31]

Regulation as a Barrier to Entry

The remainder of this chapter will touch briefly on certain regulatory features affecting the securities and futures industries that might be cited as creating either a competitive advantage or a competitive disadvantage. In general, the regulatory requirements pertain to attributes that ease entry into a given market or, conversely, attributes that impede or discourage participation. Differences in the level of margins imposed on exchange-traded securities options and futures products are the subject of another chapter in this series.[32]

Neither futures regulation nor securities regulation appears to have had much discernible effect (positive or negative) on the size of the trading population. Despite what is regarded by many as a stringent program, securities regulation has nevertheless admitted roughly 42 million people into the equity securities markets. The population of futures traders is believed to be far smaller — fewer than 500,000 — even though it is asserted in securities circles that futures regulation is less onerous than SEC requirements. The population of securities option traders is also relatively small (roughly the same as for futures), despite operating under an SEC program quite similar to the scheme that has admitted 42 million outright stockholders.

Thus the statistics offer little support for the proposition that business patronage has been skewed by different CFTC/SEC policies. Instead, regulatory policy appears to have been less a factor than other considerations, such as the complexity of futures and option instruments, price volatility accentuated by leverage, and the special attention required because of the limited life of the products. These disincentives, of course, would exist in the total absence of formal regulation.

If, as the statistics seem to confirm, futures contracts under CFTC regulation pose no competitive threat to the securities industry's bread-and-butter products (equity and debt instruments), then the clash if any must be between futures and their own offspring, standardized securities options. Here the trading populations appear to be closer in number and in composition. Accordingly, to compare in a general way those regulatory features of CFTC and SEC policy that might have competitive implications within that narrow field of contest can be useful.

Suitability Rules. Regulatory requirements may include effective barriers to market entry by particular potential traders. Among the perceived impediments in the securities industry are the exchanges' account-opening and suitability rules, although, as explained below, they are neither particularly restrictive nor privately enforceable.

Perhaps the best known suitability rule for securities trading appears in Article III, section 2 of the Rules of Fair Practice of the National Association of Securities Dealers, Inc. (NASD). This form of know-your-customer rule has a fairly limited reach, however, because it applies only when the broker-dealer is making investment recommendations. No such duty is imposed when the broker opens accounts or fills orders for investors who trade without recommendations from the broker:

> In recommending to a customer the purchase, sale or exchange of any security, a member [of NASD] shall have reasonable grounds for believing that the recommendation is suitable for such customer upon the basis of the facts, if any, disclosed by such customer as to his other securities holdings and as to his financial situation and needs.

A formulation with no stated nexus to investment recommendations, however, appears in Rule 405 of the New York Stock Exchange (NYSE). Rather, the NYSE calls upon its members to use "due diligence" in relation to customers' accounts:

> Every member organization is required through a general partner, a principal executive officer or a person or persons designated under the provisions of Rule 342 (b) (1) to
> (1) Use due diligence to learn the essential facts relative to every customer, every order, every cash or margin account accepted or carried by such organization.

The emphasis of NYSE Rule 405 is on account supervision by major officials within each member organization. The provision offers no insight into what essential facts should be ascertained about each customer or what duties the member firm assumes in the handling of that account (for example, whether recommendations should be confined to conservative investments or may include securities of higher risk) after those essential facts are elicited.

In connection with trading in securities options, the NYSE provides more specific guidance in its Rule 721. According to that rule, each new customer options account must be approved by designated personnel within the member organization. While the phrase "due diligence to learn the essential facts" appears in Rule 721 as well, specific reference is made to the customer's "investment objectives and financial situation." In supplemental materials, the NYSE explains that the minimum information collected about each options customer should include investment objective (for example, principal safety, growth, or speculation); employment status; estimated annual income; estimated net worth; marital status; number of dependents; age; and investment experience. These data are collected so that the member firm may decide whether to accept the customer's option account and apparently, in light of the emphasis on financial capability, so that the firm can protect itself against the risk that customers losses might have to be absorbed by the organization.

The NYSE, however, has also adopted a suitability rule in the case of options customers. NYSE Rule 723, like the NASD provision, applies only to investment recommendations:

> No member organization or member, allied member or employee of such member organization shall recommend to a customer an opening transaction in any option contract unless the person making the recommendation has a reasonable basis for believing, at the time of making the recommendation, that the customer has such knowledge and experience in financial matters that he can reasonably be expected to be capable of evaluating the risks of the recommended transaction, and is financially able to bear the risks of the recommended position in the option contract.

The CBOE, the largest of the securities options markets, has both an account-opening rule (CBOE Rule 9.7) and a suitability standard (CBOE Rule 9.9) substantially the same as those of the NYSE.

The SEC itself does not have regulations covering these matters (except Rule 15b10-3, governing a handful of broker-dealers) but relies instead on private self-regulatory rules. Although the exchanges and the NASD have an obligation to the SEC to enforce those requirements, that the standards are privately set has interfered with efforts by injured investors to recover damages for violations against them.[33] Thus whether or not securities suitability rules offer the degree of investor protection commonly attributed to them remains unclear.

In the case of futures trading, the exchanges do not generally have rules regarding collection of essential facts for new accounts or for determining the suitability of trading recommendations. This is true even in those instances in which a futures market is affiliated with a securities exchange, such as at the New York Futures Exchange subsidiary of NYSE.

The absence of a suitability rule for futures trading is offset to some degree by policies within the brokerage community that seek to weed out those potential customers who may be unable financially to weather the severe storms of the futures markets and who, as a result, may default on substantial financial obligations that the brokerage firms themselves must then satisfy. Evidence exists, for example, that several brokerage houses handling retail customer business in the futures markets set substantially higher account-opening requirements for their futures clients than for either securities or stock-option customers.[34] More specifically, the annual income and net worth requirements are more stringent. To the extent that this practice is widespread in the brokerage community, and the rate of customer default is relatively low, the need for formal suitability requirements imposed upon the industry by either government or self-regulatory bodies may simply not be as acute as in securities trading where entry is easier and, with limited exceptions,[35] the brokerage community faces less risk of financial default by customers.

For commodity options trading, however, the CFTC has acted directly and affirmatively. It has announced that the disclosure duties of brokers include an obligation to acquaint themselves sufficiently with the personal circumstances of each options customer to ensure that all material facts are conveyed:

> The risk disclosure statement is only one element of the informational duty of the FCM [futures commission merchant] to its option customers. The Commission further expects FCMs to make every reasonable effort to see that all option customers and prospective option customers are informed as to the risks involved in option trading. Thus, the FCM must acquaint itself sufficiently with the personal circumstances of each option customer to determine what further facts, explanations and disclosures are needed in order for that particular option customer to make an informed decision whether to trade options. This requirement of inquiry into the option customer's personal circumstances is more stringent than in futures transactions.[36]

In fact, the duty of inquiry and disclosure created by the CFTC could be viewed as more stringent than securities suitability rules. Whereas the latter apply only to customers who receive investment recommendations, the CFTC requirement protects all commodity options customers. Because the duty is federally created, commodity traders may have less difficulty recovering damages for violations than their securities colleagues have experienced under private suitability rules.[37] The CFTC continued:

> While this requirement is not a "suitability" rule as such rules have been composed in the securities industry, before the opening of an option account the FCM has a duty to acquaint itself with the personal circumstances of an option customer. The procedures to be followed by the prudent FCM in ascertaining those personal circumstances may require

an FCM to make an inquiry into an option customer's financial situation as well as an option customer's market sophistication for purposes of determining to what extent risk disclosure above and beyond the disclosure statement itself might be advisable. The Commission believes, however, that the extent of the inquiry should be left to the prudent judgment of the FCM.[38]

Insider Trading Prohibitions. While some regulatory requirements may seek to control market entry or investment selection, others may limit or prohibit trading under certain circumstances, such as when a corporate insider seeks to buy or sell securities before material information becomes public.

In recent months, the SEC has focused intense effort on the detection and prosecution of insider-trading offenses under the federal securities laws.[39] This effort has given rise to questions of whether or not futures regulation, which rarely attends to the concept of insider trading, is adequate. Here the concern has not arisen solely in the context of competing securities/futures products but has surfaced also in connection with more traditional commodity instruments.

To compare the regulation of securities and futures markets for purposes of insider trading, one must first recognize several pertinent differences between securities and futures markets, especially in the pricing of these products and the fundamental purposes of the markets. These differences affect one's attitude toward the fairness of permitting persons with special knowledge to enter the market when other participants are less well informed.

The pricing of securities is highly judgmental. Although many different formulas have been proposed to assess the true worth of a particular security, none has been universally accepted. Nor is there an external reference point to consult since investors alone determine the prices of specific issues. IBM common stock, for example, is worth what investors say, period. Its price need not bear any intended relation to the amount that a shareholder would receive if the company were liquidated, or the annual yield on the security, or any other objective measure.

Under these circumstances, possession of information that may cause investors to react, even for a brief time, is viewed as an enormous advantage. It is understandable, therefore, that investors consider unfair any system except one that gives them equal access to what they consider to be material information. In particular, they object to the use of confidential data by corporate managers or other company insiders to enrich themselves in the market at the perceived expense of other investors. The concern is not that the market price will become aberrational because of the special knowledge of a few investors (on the contrary, the price may be truer) but rather that outsiders will not be able to play. As in gaming, whether the winning combination is cherries or oranges does not matter so long as the machine is not rigged.

The futures markets have an investor (speculator) element, too; but speculators are not the sole (or most important) users. Moreover, most futures contracts involve commodities that are actively bought and sold in independent commercial channels,[40] so that an external pricing reference point exists by which to judge whether the futures contract is being valued consistently with commercial transactions.

The presence in the futures markets of business hedgers, and the existence of separate pricing points for most commodities, give rise to a somewhat different environment to which futures regulation must be responsive. Both of these features necessitate, for example, greater attention to the accuracy of futures pricing and the responsiveness of the futures markets to economic developments. If investors or speculators could cause futures prices to deviate irrationally from commercial reality, hedging would be severely impaired. Or if the futures markets are unable to respond immediately to economic stimuli because of regulatory restraints or otherwise, while commercial transactions are adapting to those changed circumstances, futures prices would likewise lose their hedging utility. In other words, that the futures markets are reliable hedging and pricing tools is more important than that they ensure equality among investors or speculators.

Securities insider-trading principles are fairly narrow in scope. They do not prohibit the possession of nonpublic information, nor the use of those facts to trade, under most circumstances. The securities laws recognize that some investors will be better informed than others and that equal knowledge among all investors is not the objective. Rather, the aim of insider-trading prohibitions is to prevent limited classes of persons—company officials, for example—from using confidential information given them in trust to enrich themselves (or their compatriots) by trading in the company's stock. The practice is considered especially abusive because, for the corporate insider to gain, trading must occur with existing or prospective stockholders to whom the insider already owes a fiduciary duty. Thus an insider who buys stock on undisclosed good news about the company effectively cheats the selling stockholder, while an insider who sells stock without disclosing bad news about the company has deceived the new stockholder. Although fraud would not be charged if the transaction had occurred between strangers, the insider has a special duty to protect the interests of the stockholders and, by overreaching them in this fashion, is legally culpable.[41]

To find an exact parallel to illegal insider trading in the futures markets is difficult. One trader seldom enjoys a fiduciary relation with other traders in the market, which is an essential prerequisite to a securities offense. Moreover, since a futures contract is rarely affected by the happenings within a single enterprise, but responds mainly to macroeconomic developments, the equivalent of inside information is often lacking.[42] Finally, even if a trader is a company manager or other insider of a particular enterprise, trading does not occur in that company's securities but in exchange-created futures contracts. Thus even the normal nexus between the investor's occupation and the traded instrument is lacking.

Although under certain hypothetical circumstances something akin to securities insider trading might occur in the futures markets,[43] apparently as a general matter the type of practice prohibited by the federal securities laws is not commonly found in those markets. This circumstance has not, however, dissuaded some legislators from attempting to curtail futures trading by persons with special knowledge, even though it would result in restrictions far beyond securities insider-trading principles. Indeed, some critics of the futures markets have urged that a concept of equal knowledge among traders be imposed, a result that the courts have roundly rejected in the context of securities regulation.[44]

A recent manifestation of this attitude is section 23(b) of the Commodity Exchange Act, added in 1982 at the behest of a member of Congress who was persuaded that officials within certain cattle enterprises could predict with 100 percent accuracy when the cattle futures market would experience a downturn. The alleged inside information was knowledge of when those enterprises would sell short in the futures market. Assuming that such a system actually existed, those company officials could trade cattle futures in advance of the price decline and ensure themselves a profit.

This is an example of unequal information but not of insider trading in the legal sense. First, the cattle firms' executives had no fiduciary relation with other participants in the futures market. Second, they did not trade any interest in their own organization but rather an instrument created by a third party (the exchange) that applied to cattle in general. The shareholders or owners of the cattle firms were not injured in their investment (company stock) even if the officials made heavy futures profits. This conduct, therefore, would not be illegal under the federal securities laws even if securities were involved. Accordingly, the attempt to restrict trading under these circumstances, if successful, would create an entirely new offense with no counterpart in the securities markets.

Disclosure Duties. Another possible impediment to market entry, although the investors have the choice of whether or not to let regulations keep them from the market, is the use by regulators of extensive disclosure requirements that often detail the investment and emphasize the negatives. Disclosure of material facts is a linchpin of federal securities regulation. The intrinsic merit of an investment— at least in social terms—receives far less attention from the SEC than whether the warts, bruises, and scars of the offering are fully displayed to potential investors. This emphasis on conveyance of facts is manifested not only by the lengthy prospectuses that must generally accompany an offering of equity securities but also by proxy statements, annual reports, and periodic filings with the SEC that are open to public inspection.

To a degree, arduous and lengthy disclosure is unavoidable in the securities context, once disclosure is adopted as public policy. Acquiring an interest in a business enterprise is quite different from purchasing a commodity. Each company is unique, and investors look toward its future health and well-being, including the performance of its management over time. At least as important as understanding the products or services offered by the company is the opportunity to assess the abilities of the firm's leaders to succeed in the marketplace, often under severe competitive pressures. Obviously, conveying this information to prospective investors or existing shareholders requires tailor-made disclosure documents. Thus a prospectus must be drafted for each of the thousands of companies that are publicly owned.

The futures markets, however, deal in a finite number of generic commodities. Whether trading is to occur in corn, gold, or Treasury bills, the objective is to gain from changes in the value of that product, which is a function of supply/demand forces rather than the management skills of any particular corn processor, metals refiner, or government securities dealer.[45] The economic data that influence those prices are already largely in the public domain, as in USDA statistics, international precious metals reports, or Treasury Department bulletins. Whereas special disclosures might be necessary to acquaint a securities investor with the schooling, business background, and past successes of a company's management, most essential facts about commodities are obtainable from various public sources.

Accordingly, futures regulation does not require a prospectus

313

for individual commodities. Futures regulation does demand, however, that the risks of futures trading be disclosed to prospective traders.[46]

Regarding the options markets for securities and commodities, the SEC requires a prospectus-type document to be delivered to each new options trader. That document as adopted in the early 1970s was a lengthly booklet exceeding sixty pages and bore a remarkable resemblance to the typical securities prospectus;[47] recently, however, the SEC has authorized a much shorter document focusing—as in futures—on the risk of participating in the securities options markets.[48]

While the SEC has shortened the required prospectus for securities options, the CFTC has adopted rules expanding the degree of disclosure necessary for commodity options as compared with futures disclosure.[49] In addition, a duty exists, beyond furnishing the disclosure document, for the futures commission merchant to disclose such other facts to a customer as may be needed to make an informed decision whether to trade commodity options.[50] These developments have brought the SEC and the CFTC closer together with respect to disclosure duties in the options area and offer some hope that regulatory policies of the agencies addressing similar products can be harmonized in this fashion through cooperation.

The convergence of SEC and CFTC disclosure policy with respect to options products may reflect a growing recognition that options fall somewhere between traditional securities and futures contracts concerning investor information. Unlike common stocks or corporate debt issues, laborious, particularized disclosure is not needed because the trading vehicle is a single instrument having uniform terms and fungible features irrespective of what security or commodity underpins the options. Unlike futures, however, options have no built-in disincentive to trading by unsuitable persons, such as the potential for crushing losses, repetitive margin calls, or even delivery of the product itself. Because options, when bought, limit the maximum loss that can be sustained, people who would shun futures might be attracted to options. Indeed, the investing public might find options more similar to equity stocks in which, as with options, losses are limited to the purchase price paid. Thus the nature of the options customer may account at least in part for the fact that SEC/CFTC disclosure policy has joined somewhere between their respective requirements for equities and futures.

In the final analysis, of course, the value of disclosure depends largely on the investor's willingness to pay attention to it. Months, or even years, can be spent by regulators devising the perfect disclosure statement, leaving no risk or uncertainty unmentioned, only to find that investors lack the interest or endurance to read it. Here quality can be more important than quantity, and the decisions by the SEC and the CFTC to provide more selective disclosure for exchange-created instruments should result in increased readership. Even so, some customers will continue to disregard risk disclosure documents. Recognizing that fact, the CFTC—but not the SEC— requires that the disclosure statement be received by each customer before the first trade can be made and, as protection for the broker against later pleas of ignorance by those who choose to disregard it, mandates that the document must be signed by the customer as having been received and read.[51]

Broker Insolvency. The bankruptcy of a securities broker-dealer or a futures commission merchant can pose a major threat to customer funds. Fears among potential investors that their accounts might be jeopardized if their broker becomes insolvent could influence their choice of whether to trade securities or commodities, especially if the safeguards against that risk are not equally effective. In this regard, the SEC and the CFTC have taken different precautions but with good success for each.

The CFTC requires that customer funds must be totally segregated from the assets of the futures commission merchant.[52] Barring unlawful conduct, therefore, the financial collapse of the organization usually leaves all customer funds safe and insulated.[53] As a result, customer losses from 1938 until 1985 were limited to roughly $7 million, or about $160,000 per year.[54]

Total segregation is not required by the SEC of funds connected with securities transactions. Instead an organized insurance program has been developed under the auspices of the Securities Investor Protection Corporation (SIPC) and funded from revenues of securities broker-dealers.[55] As with other insurance programs, SIPC thereby spreads the cost of losses over the entire investor population. From this pool, SIPC has paid out over $109 million since its formation in 1971, or roughly $10 million per year.[56]

The purpose of segregation in futures regulation is to prevent losses to customers and thus to avoid a need for reimbursement, by insurance or otherwise. Losses, if any, are not recouped but are contained. The SIPC program, in contrast, is a remedial mechanism consisting of a pool of funds created and maintained ultimately at the expense of the investing public. Customer losses from futures insolvencies each year have been only a small fraction of the annualized pay-out from SIPC; and, indeed, those losses to commodity

315

customers appear to be less than even the routine administrative expenses incurred by SIPC during each of the past dozen years, before payment of any losses as such.

There is no indication that CFTC-type requirements will be imposed upon the securities community in the foreseeable future or that SIPC will be replaced. Conversely, the CFTC has previously rejected the idea of forming a SIPC-style insurance program in light of the relative success and low investor cost of the segregation policy.[57] The net result is that market participants in both securities and futures are better protected than in the absence of those agencies' programs.

Marketing Controls. Both futures and securities regulation take an intense interest in the quality of sales practices, including the accuracy of promotional materials as well as the integrity and competence of the sales force dealing with the public. Prohibitions against fraud and misrepresentation, while they exist in both fields,[58] are not deemed to be sufficient protection for investors. Restrictions are frequently imposed on advertising.[59] In addition, sales personnel must typically be schooled and tested before contacting existing or potential customers.[60] Such a chill has been placed on securities promotion that brokers rarely employ more than sterile "tombstone" ads to announce a new offering. Although advertising is somewhat less restrained in the futures industry, the fairness of promotional literature is often judged far more by the number of risks (however improbable) disclosed than by how thoroughly the product's virtues are identified.

The precautions taken for the public's sake when investments are involved stand in sharp contrast to how most forms of commerce—some involving greater risks and costs—are treated. A typical securities investment made by a nonprofessional (the class principally protected) is only a fraction of the cost of a new luxury automobile or a home and yet is vastly more circumscribed from a marketing perspective. Why investing has been given this treatment, while most other commercial events have not, cannot be definitively answered here, although some observations are possible.

First, investing uses money as both the means and the end of the exercise. Investing has no residual benefits, such as shelter or convenience, that can help in most purchase situations to justify an otherwise uneconomic decision. A losing investment stands stark and alone, which may account for the humorless and often suspicious reaction of the disappointed investor and, in turn, the existence of extraordinary sales restrictions. Second, most of the funds used for investing are at the discretionary end of the family budget and, therefore, are equally available to buy a summer cottage, a second car, or another luxury item. Because of the importance to the economy of raising public capital, even a hint of impropriety in the investment markets could result in the diversion of discretionary funds into other areas. Finally, if one subscribes to the view that investment markets defy prediction and that, as a result, brokers would do best to say as little as possible, the existence of stringent limits on marketing activity may help to insulate the community from the eventual wrath of bad losers.

With respect to potentially competing products, namely, certain securities options and futures products, the options markets[61] and futures exchanges[62] act as reviewers of promotional literature for the various options products offered by each. This review is not specifically mandated by SEC regulations, whereas the CFTC has directed the commodity options markets to undertake this function.[63] The advertising and promotional literature for futures contracts (as contrasted with either securities options or commodity options), however, is not required by the CFTC to be specially reviewed, although the CFTC's antifraud rule applies and, presumably, so do the commodity exchanges' own rules against misrepresentation and deceit.[64]

The securities options markets require sales personnel to be tested.[65] While not mandated by the CFTC, the larger commodity exchanges require similar testing.[66] In addition, the 1982 amendments to the Commodity Exchange Act directed each registered futures association (such as the National Futures Association) to establish training standards and proficiency testing for sales personnel.[67]

Proper sales controls necessitate a system of effective supervision within the brokerage houses and such are mandated under both securities and futures regulation. In the securities markets, the supervisory structure is quite detailed,[68] while for futures and commodity options a CFTC-required duty exists to supervise diligently all marketing;[69] and, in addition, the commodity options exchanges must enforce and monitor those supervisory functions.[70]

A significant point of departure between securities and futures regulation relates to the charging of performance-related fees by investment managers, such as securities investment advisers or commodity-trading advisers. Several securities self-regulatory organizations prohibit the charging of performance fees under most circumstances.[71] The CFTC, however, has not restricted use of such fees provided that they are disclosed and any potential conflicts of interest arising from that method of compensation are revealed.[72] The CFTC has expressed the view that performance-based fees may be salutory in that they reward the manager for the venture's success and reduce the risk of excessive trading (churning) or other abuses attendant to compensating the manager on the basis of volume.[73]

Market Integrity. Both securities and futures regulation prohibit manipulation of market prices.[74] Under the Commodity Exchange Act, manipulation is referred to many times and is perhaps the principal offense under the statute.

Manipulation in the futures markets has been defined through a series of judicial decisions,[75] rather than in statutory language. It consists basically of using the ability to affect market prices to create artificial prices intentionally. Since all futures contracts (with minor exceptions) can be created and liquidated only on a designated contract market, a manipulation is generally an event affecting market-wide pricing to the potential detriment of speculators and hedgers alike. For this reason much effort is devoted to its prevention.

In securities regulation, a somewhat similar policy exists but with some notable variations. First, although activity in the futures market to shore up a contract against downward price pressure is as unlawful as affirmative efforts to inflate or retard prices,[76] the securities laws permit in a limited way the stabilization of securities prices, especially for new issues.[77] Another distinction of practical importance is that securities can be acquired through private transactions as well as through market operations, and prices may not be the same. To illustrate, a company may agree to repurchase the shares of a major stockholder at a substantial premium to fend off a hostile takeover or proxy fight by that person. This practice, called greenmail because of the profits extracted from the company to avoid a contest, can take place privately and without directly affecting the price of the stock quoted in the open public market. Such a tactic, if it were attempted in the futures context, could not be conducted privately because all futures trading (with minor exceptions) must occur on a designated contract market and all orders must be open to public participation. Thus sales made at a much higher greenmail price would necessarily affect public prices generally and would likely provoke a manipulation inquiry. Finally, the principal antimanipulation provision of the federal securities laws applies only when a person seeks to bring about a price change for the purpose of inducing others to purchase or sell that security.[78] In futures markets, a manipulation occurs even in the absence of such a purpose, as, for example, when futures prices are changed intentionally to affect the sale price of the underlying commodity.

Conclusion

The securities and futures markets of the United States are among the most heavily regulated institutions in the world. Therefore, that a debate should arise over which is regulated better must seem odd to many people. The controversy can be traced in large part to a relatively new phenomenon: competition between the two industries in which any distinction—including regulatory variations—causes concern among the combatants, fearful that any edge enjoyed by the other will determine the ultimate outcome.

Most complaints about regulatory disparity and lack of a level playing field have come from the securities industry. This fact is somewhat ironic considering that perhaps 100 securities customers exist for each futures trader and that the competition has consisted mainly of efforts by the securities industry to emulate futures-type products. Even so, this new rivalry has encouraged comparisons between the regulatory programs of the SEC and the CFTC, a sort of beauty contest that neither agency wins decisively. The most that can be concluded, apparently, is that both regulatory schemes work adequately.

The broader message, however, pertains to the manipulation of public policy to achieve competitive goals. Regulation is especially vulnerable to this use because it is generally too esoteric for the public to monitor effectively. As a result, regulatory policy can be little more than the outcome of a largely self-interested exercise involving, from time to time, combat between the agency and the industry, two competing industries, single-issue pressure groups, or even rival congressional committees. Accordingly, the real issue is not whether the SEC or the CFTC is the better regulator but how to protect both of them from being used to achieve the ambitions of others.

Notes

1. Securities may also be traded over the counter through brokerage intermediaries or in private dealings between investors.

A variant of the traditional exchange also exists with the computer-assisted National Market System operated by the National Association of Securities Dealers, Inc. (NASD), and certain other automated execution programs such as Instinet.

Trading in securities puts and calls (options), once conducted by private negotiation, is now largely centralized. The largest such market is the Chicago

Board Options Exchange (CBOE), which specializes exclusively in these products. Others include the American, Philadelphia, and Pacific Stock Exchanges.

2. Virtually all futures trading takes place on the floors of the exchanges, and all transactions must occur under an exchange's rules. Over-the-counter transactions and private dealings in futures are prohibited by law. See section 4(a) of the Commodity Exchange Act, as amended [7 U.S.C. § 6(a)].

3. The futures markets are regulated under the Commodity Exchange Act [7 U.S.C. §§ 1 et seq.], which was originally enacted in 1922.

The first major federal securities statutes were the Securities Act of 1933 [15 U.S.C. §§ 77a et seq.], which principally governs the original issuance of securities; and the Securities Exchange Act of 1934 [15 U.S.C. §§ 78a et seq.], which primarily governs exchange operations.

4. See, for example, McCurnin v. Kohlmeyer & Co., 347 F.Supp. 573 (E.D. La. 1972), aff'd, 477 F.2d 113 (5th Cir. 1973).

5. Riegel v. Haberstro, 30 A.2d 645 (Pa. Sup. Ct. 1943); Securities and Exchange Commission v. Howey, 328 U.S. 293 (1946); Securities and Exchange Commission v. Tung Corp. of America, 32 F.Supp. 371 (N.D. Ill. 1940).

6. Securities and Exchange Commission v. Comstock Coin Co., [1964–1966 Transfer Binder] CCH Fed. Sec. L. Rep. ¶91,414 (D. Nev. 1964).

7. Securities and Exchange Commission v. International Scanning Devices, Inc., [1977–1978 Transfer Binder] CCH Fed. Sec. L. Rep. ¶96,147 (W.D.N.Y. 1977).

8. Securities and Exchange Commission v. Haffenden-Rimar International, Inc., [1973–1974 Transfer Binder] CCH Fed. Sec. L. Rep. ¶94,577 (4th Cir. 1974).

9. American Dairy Leasing Corp. [1971–1972 Transfer Binder] CCH Fed. Sec. L. Rep. ¶78,584 (SEC 1971).

10. Kentucky Blood Horse, Ltd., [1973 Transfer Binder] CCH Fed. Sec. L. Rep. ¶79,430 (SEC 1973).

11. Continental Marketing Corp. v. Securities and Exchange Commission, 387 F.2d 466 (10th Cir. 1967).

12. Smith v. Gross, 604 F.2d 639 (9th Cir. 1979).

13. Marking to market is a procedure, common in futures trading, under which the value of the product is recalculated each day, and profit is credited or losses are debited to the holder's account. In the clearinghouse, funds are either received or paid between clearing firms on a daily basis depending upon the net gain or loss experienced by positions carried by those firms.

14. While the rationale for this fear is seldom clearly articulated, the focus of concern is probably not customer protection issues. On one hand, for investors to find more attractive a market in which their interests are least safeguarded would be irrational. On the other hand, regulatory policies that have a significant impact on investor costs—to enter, maintain, or liquidate a position—could influence choice among otherwise similar products. One might expect, however, that investors will not lower their costs to the point where they feel in peril of being defrauded or otherwise exploited. Thus, if investors express a preference, it may reflect an assessment that the costs

associated with one regulatory scheme are reasonable for the protections needed, while the costs of the other regime are excessive.

15. Before 1974, the futures markets were regulated by the secretary of agriculture through a USDA bureau, the Commodity Exchange Authority.

16. Some regulatory issues, of course, do attract broader public attention. Two examples are environmental and nuclear energy policies. As a rule, however, such is not the case. Both the CFTC and the SEC fall within the general rule except on rare occasions.

17. Because of the complexity of particular regulatory disputes, or even a lack of interest in the issues among third-party arbiters (for example, Congress), the willingness to support one of the warring viewpoints can be profoundly affected by the parties' images or reputations.

18. The phrase "boiler room" is used generally to depict a variety of high-pressure sales operations, usually making random contacts by telephone with potential customers and promising or inferring great profits in a short time and urging immediate payment.

19. See, for example, U.S. Congress, Senate, Permanent Subcommittee on Investigations of the Committee on Governmental Affairs, *Report on Commodity Investment Fraud* (Senate Report no. 97–495), 97th Congress, 2d session, July 13, 1982.

20. See Senate Report no. 93–1131, 93d Congress, 2d session, reprinted in *U.S. Code Congressional and Administrative News* (1974), pp. 5843, 5853–55.

21. 61 Congressional Record 4768 (1921) (remarks of Senator Capper). A more positive view of futures markets has emerged in recent years, at least within the leadership of agricultural trade associations and among agribusiness companies that operate between the original producer and the ultimate consumer. See, for example, U.S. Congress, House of Representatives, Subcommittee on Conservation, Credit, and Rural Development of the Committee on Agriculture, *Hearings on H.R. 5447*, 97th Congress, 2d session, February 24, 1982, pp. 374, 452; Senate, Subcommittee on Agricultural Research and General Legislation of the Committee on Agriculture, Nutrition, and Forestry, *Hearings on S. 2109*, 97th Congress, 2d session, March 2, 1982, p. 490.

22. See SEC Rule 10a-1 [17 C.F.R. § 240.10a-1], which generally prohibits short sales of securities except at or above the previous transaction price.

23. New York Stock Exchange, Tenth Annual Survey of Shareownership (1983).

24. See section 5(g) of the Act, 7 U.S.C. § 7(g); and CFTC Guideline No. 1, 17 C.F.R. Part 5 (Appendix A); 1 CCH Comm. Fut. L. Rep. ¶ 6145.

25. The principal regulations restricting credit on securities purchases are Regulation T (brokers and dealers) [12 C.F.R. Part 220]; Regulation G (other lenders) [12 C.F.R. Part 207]; and Regulation X (borrowers) [12 C.F.R. Part 224]. The Federal Reserve Board (FRB) exercises this authority pursuant to section 7 of the Securities Exchange Act [15 U.S.C. § 78g], which states that restrictions are imposed "for the purpose of preventing the excessive use of credit for the purchase or carrying of securities."

26. See CFTC Regs. §§ 1.55 (futures) and 33.7 (options) [17 C.F.R. §§ 1.55, 33.7].

27. To elaborate, a futures trader neither owes nor is owed anything (except transaction costs) at the moment the position is first acquired. Even so, a deposit (margin) must be made. If losses are incurred subsequently, not only must they be paid promptly but the margin must also be restored, again creating excess funds in the account.

28. Federal Reserve System, Board of Governors, *A Review and Evaluation of Federal Margin Regulation* (Washington, D.C.: FRB Staff, 1984).

29. Section 2(a) (1) of the Commodity Exchange Act [7 U.S.C. § 2] was amended to extend the CFTC's jurisdiction beyond the enumerated farm products to "all other goods and articles [except onions], and all services, rights, and interests in which contracts for future delivery are presently or in the future dealt in." This language was broad enough to subsume securities under futures contracts, and, in fact, the CFTC undertook to regulate several such products, such as futures on GNMA certificates; Treasury bonds, bills and notes; and stock indexes. (No exchange applied to the CFTC to trade futures on individual equity securities.) Not until January 1983, when section 2(a) (1) was again amended, was the CFTC's authority to approve and regulate futures or options on individual equity securities withdrawn by Congress. See section 101 of the Futures Trading Act of 1982 [7 U.S.C.§ 2, as amended].

30. See *Prospectus of the Options Clearing Corporation—Put and Call Options* (September 23, 1983).

31. Proposed amendments to Regulation T. CCH Sec. L. Rep. (current) ¶ 83, 735 (February 6, 1985); See also FRB, *A Review and Evaluation of Federal Margin Regulations*, pp. 16–17, 65–84, 114–31.

32. For a discussion of margins, see William G. Tomek, "Margins on Futures Contracts: Their Economic Roles and Regulation," in Anne E. Peck, ed., *Futures Markets: Regulatory Issues* (Washington, D.C.: American Enterprise Institute, 1984).

33. See, for example, Landy v. Federal Deposit Insurance Corp., 1973 CCH Fed. Sec. Dec. ¶ 94, 094 (3d Cir. 1973) (NYSE Rule 405); Jablon v. Dean Witter & Co., 614 F. 2d 677 (9th Cir. 1980) (NASD suitability rule); Klitzman v. Bache Halsey Stuart Shields, Inc., 499 F. Supp. 255 (S.D.N.Y. 1980) (NASD rules); Rizika v. Merrill Lynch, Pierce, Fenner & Smith, Inc., 1981 CCH Fed. Sec. Dec. ¶ 97,934 (D. Md. 1981) (NASD rules).

34. See, for example, U.S. Congress, House of Representatives, Subcommittee on Telecommunications, Consumer Protection, and Finance and Subcommittee on Oversight and Investigations of the Committee on Energy and Commerce, *Hearings on H.R. 5447 (Part 1)*, 97th Congress, 2d session, April 23, 1982, p. 78.

35. In most securities transactions and in the buying of securities options, the customer makes full payment, and the brokerage firm is not at risk. Exceptions include purchases of securities on margin from a broker (with the risk that the balance will not be paid, but this risk is collateralized by the securities themselves and is thus minimized) and the writing of securities

options (in which the writer is at the full risk of adverse changes in market prices).

36. [1980–1982 Transfer Binder] CCH Comm. Fut. L. Rep. ¶ 21,263, at pp. 25, 295.

37. See section 22 of the Commodity Exchange Act [7 U.S.C. § 25], creating certain express private rights to single damages for conduct in violation of the act.

38. [1980–1982 Transfer Binder] CCH Comm. Fut. L. Rep. ¶ 21,263, at pp. 25, 295.

39. Insider trading is deemed to constitute fraud under § 10(b) of the Securities Exchange Act [15 U.S.C. § 78] and SEC Rule 10b-5 [17 C.F.R. § 240.10b-5].

40. The independence is not total, of course, since many commercial deals are priced with an eye on, or even based upon, futures market quotations. Even so, an opportunity exists, unlike in securities trading, to compare prices being paid by noninvestors for the same product.

41. See, for example, Chiarella v. United States, 445 U.S. 222 (1980); Dirks v. Securities and Exchange Commission, 51 U.S.L.W. 5123 (1983).

42. Compare Freeman v. Decio, 584 F. 2d 186 (7th Cir. 1978), in which knowledge of rising lumber prices was held not to be insider information.

43. For instance, the necessary ingredients of illegal insider trading might exist if an official of the Treasury Department, knowing confidentially that the next Treasury-bill auction would be substantially larger than normal, took a position in the Treasury-bill futures or options market to profit. The official could be viewed as an insider with a fiduciary duty to potential Treasury-bill purchasers and would be trading on the value of his department's securities.

44. See Dirks v. Securities and Exchange Commission, p. 5126, and Chiarella v. United States, p. 233. The author commented on this matter in an article: "Act Seeks to Halt Futures Trading on 'Nonpublic' Data," in the *Legal Times of Washington* (September 26, 1983), pp. 12ff.

45. Instances in which management skill is relevant in futures markets include managed account programs and commodity pools because business acumen is being purchased. In those instances, CFTC regulations call for substantially more disclosure concerning the business background and performance record of the principals involved. See 17 C.F.R. §§ 4.21 and 4.31.

46. 17 C.F.R. § 1.55.

47. For example, *Prospectus of the Options Clearing Corporation* (October 29, 1979).

48. *Prospectus of the Options Clearing Corporation—Put and Call Options.*

49. 17 C.F.R. §§ 32.5 and 33.7.

50. 46 Federal Register 54500, [1980–1982 Transfer Binder] CCH. Comm. Fut. L. Rep. ¶ 21,263, at pp. 25, 295.

51. 17 C.F.R. §§1.55 and 33.7.

52. 7 U.S.C. § 6d(2); 17 C.F.R. §§ 1.20–1.29.

53. A possible exception to this conclusion is the collapse in March 1985

323

of a futures commission merchant following the failure of three customers to satisfy a margin call for roughly $26 million. At that time excess funds belonging to certain customers were evidently applied to reduce the deficit in the combined customer segregated account at the clearinghouse. Since those events have not yet run their full course, whether or not customers will ultimately sustain financial loss remains to be seen. The precedent of applying the excess funds of some customers to meet shortfalls of other customers, rather than retaining the former intact, has been set, however.

54. See House, *Hearings on H.R. 5447 (Part 1)*.

55. 15 U.S.C. §§ 78aaa et seq.; 17 C.F.R. §§ 300.100 et seq.

56. See House, *Hearings on H. R. 5447 (Part 1)*.

57. See section 417 of the Commodity Futures Trading Commission Act of 1974. P.L. 93–463; and [1975–1977 Transfer Binder] CCH Comm. Fut. L. Rep. ¶20,235 (November 1, 1976).

58. See, for example, 7 U.S.C. §§ 4b and 15 U.S.C. § 78j(b).

59. See, for example, NYSE Rule 472; COMEX Rule 5.02(c); CBT Rule 287.00.

60. See, for example, NYSE Rule 345; CBT Rule 480.06; CBOE Rule 9.3; National Futures Association Bylaw 305.

61. See, for example, CBOE Rule 9.21.

62. See, for example, CBT Rule 490.06.

63. 17 C.F.R. § 33.4(b) (8).

64. See, for example, COMEX Rule 5.02(c); CBT Rule 287 ("No member shall publish any advertisement of other than strictly legitimate business character."); CME Rule 442 (advertising, market letters, and similar information "shall observe truth and good taste"). Furthermore, the CFTC has promulgated a rule designed specifically to regulate the accuracy of advertising by commodity pool operators and commodity trading advisers. 17 C.F.R. § 4.41.

65. See, for example, NYSE Rule 345; CBT Rule 480.06; CBOE Rule 9.3.

66. Ibid.

67. 7 U.S.C. §§ 21(p)–(q); NFA Bylaw 305.

68. See, for example, NYSE Rules 342–344; CBOE Rule 9.8.

69. 17 C.F.R. § 166.3.

70. 17 C.F.R. § 33.4(b) (5).

71. 15 U.S.C. § 80b-5.

72. See, for example, 17 C.F.R. §§ 4.21(a) (7), 4.31(a) (4).

73. U.S. Congress, House of Representatives, Subcommittee on Telecommunications, Consumer Protection, and Finance and Subcommittee on Oversight and Investigations of the Committee on Energy and Commerce, *Hearings on H.R. 5447 (Part 2)*, 97th Congress, 2d session, June 7, 1982, p. 337.

74. See, for example, § 9 of the Securities Exchange Act, 15 U.S.C. § 78; and § 9(b) of the Commodity Exchange Act, 7 U.S.C. § 13(b).

75. See, for example, Great Western Food Distributors, Inc. v. Brannan, 201 F. 2d 476 (7th Cir. 1953); Cargill, Inc. v. Hardin, 452 F.2d 1152 (8th Cir. 1971); Volkart Bros., Inc. v. Freeman, 311 F.2d 52 (5th Cir. 1962); and In re

Indiana Farm Bureau Cooperative Ass'n Inc., [1982–1984 Transfer Binder] CCH Comm. Fut. L. Rep. ¶21,796 (CFTC 1982).

76. See, for example, In re Vincent W. Kosuga, 19 A.D. 603 (1960); In re David G. Henner, 30 A.D. 1151 (1971); and Great Western Food Distributors, Inc. v. Brannan.

77. See Securities Exchange Act § 9(a) (6) and SEC Reg. §240.10b-7; 17 C.F.R. §240.10b-7.

78. See SEC Release No. 34–3056, 11 Federal Register 10967 (October 27, 1941); and Securities and Exchange Commission v. Bennett, 62 F. Supp. 609 (S.D.N.Y. 1945).

Contributors

Project on the Economics and Regulation of Futures Markets

*DENNIS W. DRAPER is an associate professor of finance in the Graduate School of Business, University of Southern California, Los Angeles.

*MICHAEL A. HUDSON is an assistant professor of agricultural economics in the Department of Agricultural Economics, University of Illinois at Urbana-Champaign.

PHILIP MCBRIDE JOHNSON is a partner in the law firm of Skadden, Arps, Slate, Meagher & Flom in New York, and former chairman of the Commodities Futures Trading Commission.

*ALLEN B. PAUL is a former senior economist with the Economic Research Service, U.S. Department of Agriculture, Washington, D.C.

ANNE E. PECK is an associate professor in the Food Research Institute at Stanford University, Stanford, California, and a resident fellow at the American Enterprise Institute while serving as director of the project on the Economics and Regulation of Futures Markets.

*WAYNE D. PURCELL is a professor of agricultural economics in the Department of Agricultural Economics, Virginia Polytechnic Institute and State University, Blacksburg, Virginia.

*CHARLES M. SEEGER is a partner in the law firm of Neill, Mullenholz, Shaw and Seeger, Washington, D.C.

WILLIAM L. SILBER is a professor of economics and finance in the Graduate School of Business, New York University, New York, New York.

---

*Chapters by these contributors appear in the companion volume, *Futures Markets: Regulatory Issues.*

*SEYMOUR SMIDT is the Nicholas H. Noyes Professor of Economics and Finance in the Graduate School of Management, Cornell University, Ithaca, New York.

JEROME L. STEIN is the Eastman Professor of Political Economy in the Department of Economics, Brown University, Providence, Rhode Island.

HANS R. STOLL is the Anne Marie and Thomas B. Walker, Jr., Professor of Finance in the Owen Graduate School of Management, Vanderbilt University, Nashville, Tennessee.

*WILLIAM G. TOMEK is a professor of agricultural economics in the New York State School of Agriculture and Life Sciences, Cornell University, Ithaca, New York.

ROBERT E. WHALEY is an associate professor of finance in the Department of Finance and Management Science, University of Alberta, Edmonton, Canada.

Project on the Economics and Regulation of Futures Markets

Advisory Committee

Research Advisory Committee

See also the companion volume:

Futures Markets:
Regulatory Issues

376 pp. / 1985 / $24.95

SELECTED AEI PUBLICATIONS

A Treatise on Markets: Spot, Futures, and Options. Joseph M. Burns (145 pp., $5.25).

The Political Economy of Deregulation: Interest Groups in the Regulatory Process. Roger G. Noll and Bruce M. Owen, eds. (164 pp., paper $7.95, cloth $15.95).

Incentives vs. Controls in Health Policy: Broadening the Debate, Jack A. Meyer, ed. (156 pp., paper $7.95, cloth $15.95)

Parties, Interest Groups, and Campaign Finance Laws. Michael J. Malbin, ed. (384 pp., paper $8.25, cloth $15.25)

Reducing Risks to Life: Measurement of the Benefits. Martin J. Bailey (66 pp., $4.25)

Occupational Licensure and Regulation. Simon Rottenberg (354 pp., paper $8.25, cloth $16.25)

Deregulation of Natural Gas. Edward J. Mitchell, ed. (163 pp., paper $7.95, cloth $15.95)

Regulation, The AEI Journal on Government and Society, published bimonthly (one year, $24; two years, $44; single copy, $5.00)

Regulating Consumer Product Safety. W. Kip Viscusi (116 pp., paper $5.95, cloth $14.95)

The Regulation of Pharmaceuticals: Balancing the Benefits and Risks. Henry G. Grabowski and John M. Vernon (74 pp., $4.95)

• *Mail orders for publications to:* AMERICAN ENTERPRISE INSTITUTE, 1150 Seventeenth Street, N.W., Washington, D.C. 20036 • *For postage and handling, add 10 percent of total; minimum charge $2, maximum $10 (no charge on prepaid orders)* • *For information on orders, or to expedite service, call toll free* 800-424-2873 *(in Washington, D.C., 202-862-5869)* • *Prices subject to change without notice.* • *Payable in U.S. currency through U.S. banks only*

AEI ASSOCIATES PROGRAM

The American Enterprise Institute invites your participation in the competition of ideas through its AEI Associates Program. This program has two objectives: (1) to extend public familiarity with contemporary issues; and (2) to increase research on these issues and disseminate the results to policy makers, the academic community, journalists, and others who help shape public policies. The areas studied by AEI include Economic Policy, Education Policy, Energy Policy, Fiscal Policy, Government Regulation, Health Policy, International Programs, Legal Policy, National Defense Studies, Political and Social Processes, and Religion, Philosophy, and Public Policy. For the $49 annual fee, Associates receive

- a subscription to *Memorandum,* the newsletter on all AEI activities
- the AEI publications catalog and all supplements
- a 30 percent discount on all AEI books
- a 40 percent discount for certain seminars on key issues
- subscriptions to any two of the following publications: *Public Opinion,* a bimonthly magazine exploring trends and implications of public opinion on social and public policy questions; *Regulation,* a bimonthly journal examining all aspects of government regulation of society; and *AEI Economist,* a monthly newsletter analyzing current economic issues and evaluating future trends (or for all three publications, send an additional $12).

Call 202/862-7170 or write: AMERICAN ENTERPRISE INSTITUTE
1150 Seventeenth Street, N.W., Suite 301, Washington, D.C. 20036